After a century of exponential growth, the international oil industry suddenly slowed down in the 1970s, faltered during the 1980s, and by the early nineties was only just about back to its 1979 level. That discontinuity in its dominance of world energy became clear after 'the Opec decade' from 1973 onwards had gained an intoxicating but temporary surge of riches for oil-exporting countries.

In a descriptive analysis of current influences upon the world oil trade, this book explores the reasons behind that slowdown – which are *not* all attributable to Opec or its nationalisation of international major oil companies. It assesses the growth and decay of Opec monopoly power in the crude oil market, as the latest demonstration of a paradoxical but persistent imbalance in this international business: its tendency to maximise the production of high-cost rather than low-cost oil.

The author draws upon nearly thirty years of experience as a consultant to oil companies and governments on all sides of this trade. His book is objective and forward-looking: it is not a history.

Oil trade:
politics and prospects

# CAMBRIDGE STUDIES IN ENERGY AND THE ENVIRONMENT

EDITORS

Chris Hope   *Judge Institute of Management Studies, University of Cambridge*
Jim Skea   *Science Policy Research Unit, University of Sussex*

We live in a time when people are more able than ever to affect the environment, and when the pace of technological change and scientific discovery continues to increase. Vital questions must continually be asked about the allocation of resources under these conditions. This series aims to provide readers interested in public policies on energy and the environment with the latest scholarship in the field. The books will address the scientific, economic and political issues which are central to our understanding of energy use and its environmental impact.

*Other titles in the series:*

Energy efficiency and human activity: past trends, future prospects
*Lee Schipper and Stephen Meyers*

Energy policy analysis and modelling
*Mohan Munasinghe and Peter Meier*

# Oil trade: politics and prospects

J. E. HARTSHORN

CAMBRIDGE
UNIVERSITY PRESS

CAMBRIDGE UNIVERSITY PRESS
Cambridge, New York, Melbourne, Madrid, Cape Town, Singapore,
São Paulo, Delhi, Dubai, Tokyo, Mexico City

Cambridge University Press
The Edinburgh Building, Cambridge CB2 8RU, UK

Published in the United States of America by Cambridge University Press, New York

www.cambridge.org
Information on this title: www.cambridge.org/9780521147453

First published 1993
First paperback printing 2010

*A catalogue record for this publication is available from the British Library*

*Library of Congress Cataloguing in Publication data*

Hartshorn, J. E.
Oil trade: politics and prospects / by J. E. Hartshorn.
　　　p.　　cm. – (Cambridge Studies in Energy and the Environment)
Includes bibliographical references (p.　) and index.
ISBN 0 521 33143 9 (hardback)
1. Petroleum industry and trade.　2. Crude oil – Production costs.
3. Organization of Petroleum Exporting Countries.　I. Title.　II. Series.
HD9560.5.H32　1993
338.2′7282–dc20　92–18233　CIP

ISBN 978-0-521-33143-2 Hardback
ISBN 978-0-521-14745-3 Paperback

*To Judy and Jemima*

No one really knows the cost of Middle East oil; but it is reasonably certain it is so low that the extent to which the expanding free world demand is met from this region will be governed by policy and not by either scarcity or comparative cost.

de Chazeau and Kahn,
*Integration and Competition in the Petroleum Industry*
(Yale University Press, 1959)

# Contents

| | | |
|---|---|---|
| *List of figures* | *page* | x |
| *List of tables* | | xii |
| *List of tabular boxes* | | xii |
| *Preface* | | xiii |
| *List of abbreviations* | | xv |

| | | |
|---|---|---|
| 1 | Pause or plateau? | 1 |
| 2 | A discontinuity in trade | 31 |
| 3 | Cost: concepts and comparisons | 50 |
| 4 | Ambitions of autarky? | 76 |
| 5 | Still the prime mover | 93 |
| 6 | An industry restructured | 114 |
| 7 | Governments in the oil business | 138 |
| 8 | The Opec performance | 169 |
| 9 | A confusion of prices | 195 |
| 10 | Perspectives of supply | 225 |
| 11 | A contrast of expectations | 252 |
| 12 | A sustainable paradox? | 272 |

| | |
|---|---|
| *Appendix 1* What are oil reserves? | 288 |
| *Appendix 2* A note on energy and oil statistics | 292 |
| *Bibliography* | 294 |
| *Index* | 299 |

# Figures

1.1 World crude oil production, 1913–1990        *page* 3
1.2 World consumption of primary energy and liquid fuels, 1910–1990    4
1.3 World primary fuel consumption, 1955–1989    5
1.4 Crude oil production and projections, former Soviet Union and United States, 1960–2010    15
2.1 World oil consumption and interregional trade, 1938–1990    33
2.2 Oil reserves (1990), consumption and capacity (1989), and output (1990), by region    42
3.1 Ranges of development cost for world oil production capacity, early 1990s    69
3.2 Middle East proportion of world interregional oil trade, 1955–1990    74
4.1 Changes in degree of self-sufficiency in energy supply, 1973 vs 1987    86
4.2 Largest deficit countries, energy and oil, 1973 and 1989    88
5.1 Refining capacity and oil demand, WOCA, 1950–1990    105
6.1 Oil market structure, 1972, 1979 and 1989: (a) transfers of ownership and (b) major companies' refinery runs and product sales    116
6.2 Dominant oil market structure: (a) 1972, (b) late 1980s    122
7.1 Opec: GNP and oil revenues, 1960–1989    142
8.1 Oil production: world, WOCA, Opec and Gulf Opec, 1960–1990    172
8.2 Opec's capacity expansion problems, early 1990s    173
8.3 Crude oil prices and Opec's oil export revenues, in real terms,1960–1990    176
9.1 Crude oil prices, 1861–1990    204
9.2 Price variability, 1861–1990    205

10.1  US crude oil production: as forecast in 1956 and actual    226
10.2  (a) S-curves of cumulative discoveries, cumulative production, and proved oil reserves. (b) Cumulative oil discoveries in US, 1880–1989. (c) Cumulative world oil discoveries, 1880–1989    230
10.3  Potential new oil discoveries, by region    239
10.4  Oil production over time    245
10.5  Long-term oil production scenario    249
10.6  Hydrocarbon opportunities with current technology at various levels of crude oil price    250
11.1  Oil price expectations, 1981–1991    254
11.2  Ranges of oil demand projections to year 2020    255
11.3  (a) Projections of world oil consumption in 2005 by IEA, Opec and US Department of Energy. (b) Economic growth assumptions underlying projections    261
11.4  OECD carbon emissions expected to 2005    269
11.5  Carbon hopes versus expectations    270
12.1  Prospects for non-Opec oil production    273
12.2  A sketch of world oil supply curves, actual and potential    283

# Tables

2.1 Consumption and trade: energy and oil, 1970–1989    *page*    32
2.2 Known reserves of fossil fuels, 1990    34
2.3 Regional consumption: energy and oil, 1965–1989    36
2.4 Oil: largest producers and consumers, 1989    38
2.5 Commercial energy consumption among rich and poor, 1965 and 1989    40
2.6 Oil reserves to production ratios, 1979 and 1990    46
3.1 Decline rates in existing production, and the gross additions required for net additions to capacity    64
3.2 Comparative oil production costs, 1988–1991    67
4.1 Regional self-sufficiency: oil and energy, 1965–1989    81
4.2 Oil production outside Opec, 1965–1990    83
5.1 OECD: total oil consumption and transport use, 1960–1989    96
5.2 Total energy and oil supply, and transport use, 1989    96
5.3 Patterns of oil consumption, 1989, main products by regions    107
5.4 Carbon content of the different fossil fuels    111
6.1 Downstream ventures abroad of Opec governments, 1990–1991    135
7.1 Value of Opec petroleum exports and current account balances, 1963–1989    146
11.1 Expectations for the nineties    260
App.1 Possible world petroleum occurrences as at end-1987    290

## Tabular boxes

2A Where oil is found    44
3A Exploration    53
3B Production    55
9A Oil pricing    198

# Preface

During and after the Suez affair in 1956, as an economic journalist, I became interested in the international oil business, and in 1962 I wrote a book about oil companies and governments. In the late 1980s, Richard Eden asked me to do the same again for Cambridge Studies in Energy and the Environment. This book is the result. The first one looked at 'the kaleidoscopic international circumstances of an industry in course of change'. Those circumstances have been transformed, though not out of recognition. They remain no less kaleidoscopic.

In the thirty years between, moving out of journalism, I have had reason to study the business more closely, as a consultant on many facets of oil companies' relations with governments of all kinds, advising one side or the other. That career drew me more deeply into some of the relationships involved. But one's role as a consultant continued to be outside the oil industry looking in, as distinct from the practical experience within it of company and government oilmen, many of whom became friends. So my judgement of this business has remained detached, for whatever that is worth.

Rather to my surprise, initially, closer contact with the industry did *not* bring me much more 'inside' information than a journalist could readily obtain; simply, more time to watch what went on. (This is a business remarkably well served by an expert daily and periodical press, upon which everyone in it depends.) The occasional confidences of clients remain outside the scope of this book. But those too, I hope, contributed to such understanding as I gained of what we all saw.

I am indebted primarily to three people who read this book in manuscript (one of them a second time, after the hiatus of the second Gulf war), and gave me painstaking and salutary comments, page by page: John Jennings, John Gault and David Heal. Other friends and former colleagues read parts of the MS and discussed some of the questions in it with me: Morris Adelman (continuing a long argument over the years),

Frank Parra, Edith Penrose, Sylvan Robinson and Joe Roeber. None of them agrees with most of what is said here.

I am sorry not to have had the chance to show this book to the person who more than anyone else provoked me into closer acquaintance with what she so often called 'this fascinating business': Wanda Jablonski, who died early in 1992. The files of *Petroleum Intelligence Weekly*, which she founded in 1961, with those of Ian Seymour's and the late Fuad Itayim's *Middle East Economic Survey*, together form an indispensable database, current as well as historical, for all students of the international oil trade.

In this text, the $ sign always means US dollars, and the word 'billion' means a thousand million. Quantities of oil are expressed mostly in terms of barrels per day (b/d; MBD for millions of barrels per day), but occasionally in tonnes per year, usually for refined products priced wholesale in tonnage or for comparison with the 'oil equivalent' of other forms of energy. (For detailed conversion factors, also in process of change internationally, see Appendix 2.) In the simple rule of thumb of the trade, a barrel of crude oil a day equals 50 tonnes a year.

# Abbreviations

| | |
|---|---|
| API | American Petroleum Institute |
| CGES | Centre for Global Energy Studies, London |
| CIF | cost, insurance and freight (delivered price) |
| EIA | Energy Information Administration, US Department of Energy |
| FOB | free on board (export value or price) |
| IEA | International Energy Agency |
| IPE | International Petroleum Exchange |
| LNG | liquefied natural gas |
| LPG | liquefied petroleum gases (produced in refining crude oil) |
| *MEES* | *Middle East Economic Survey* |
| NGL | natural gas liquids (separated in natural gas production) |
| NCW | non-Communist world |
| OAPEC | Organisation of Arab Petroleum Exporting Countries |
| *OGJ* | *Oil & Gas Journal* |
| OGSP | official government selling price |
| OIES | Oxford Institute for Energy Studies |
| Opec | Organisation of Petroleum Exporting Countries |
| *PIW* | *Petroleum Intelligence Weekly* |
| USGS | United States Geological Survey |
| WOCA | world outside Communist areas |
| WOCANA | world outside Communist areas and North America |

# CHAPTER 1

# Pause or plateau?

During the last quarter of the twentieth century international oil ceased to be a growth industry. After more than a hundred years of expansion far faster than both energy in general and the rest of the world economy, it slowed down abruptly in the 1970s. In the eighties, with a short sharp decline followed by a halting recovery, it achieved no net growth at all. By 1992, it was only just about back to its level of 1979.

That may have been no more than a pause. The growth resumed after 1985 may be continuing, albeit uncertainly. By some physical measures, oil is still the world's biggest business. But it is in its third decade of *relative* decline compared with most other forms of energy. There is a distinct possibility that during the nineties this business will not grow much further. This reopens a recurrent question. Will its soaring historical trajectory soon level off onto a shallow dome or plateau over the next two or three decades, until 'conventional oil' – the qualities of crude oil that the industry has found it economic to produce so far – slides into gradual decline? (Even then, the world would in no sense be 'running out of oil'. But it would already be moving on increasingly to other forms of petroleum that are more costly to produce, move or convert into the oil products that we are accustomed to use.)

In timing, at any rate, this slowdown was not inevitable. For many years past, there have been long-term predictions that this industry would pass its peak around the end of the century. But few ever suggested that such a transition would have set in as early as the eighties. Also, most of what has happened can as readily be explained by short-term political and economic changes in the industry during the last two decades, culminating in two wars. Some of those changes, too, were predictable; but again, not in timing. They followed from moves made by the main actors in the current world oil performance – which is now not only political and economic, but as often as not theatrical. None of

1

these actors wants the industry to level off. However, this may be the best that they can manage.

The Gulf war of 1990–1 refocused world attention upon one aspect of a political problem that underlies the slowdown in world oil. It revived some hopes of reaching a durable Middle East peace within this century. At the time this book was completed, that looked neither impossible nor likely – in spite of the potentially overwhelming influence of the world's sole remaining superpower. But even if it can be achieved, it would resolve only half of the main geopolitical problem that besets the world oil business.

Any regional peace that proved lasting *might* eventually make consumers elsewhere fully confident in depending on oil imported from the Gulf for most of the extra energy they want. But it would not remove the sharp disparity in supply costs between oil in that region and most other energy produced anywhere else. Would energy producers elsewhere – or their governments – be content to accept the 'logical' economic consequences of that comparative advantage? Historically, they never have. Given any other option, probably few ever will.

The 1990–1 war was not simply an 'oil war', as some protested at the time. (Still less 'a war for cheap oil'. None of the governments involved, inside or outside the Gulf, displayed any interest in keeping oil cheap.) Iraq's 1990–1 war, like its previous aggression in 1980–8, *was* about who owns the world's largest reserves of conventional oil, and who will control their future development. But both wars may have helped make that ownership issue, eventually, less important. They may turn out only to have helped delay the development of the Gulf's prodigious reserves even further beyond what might have been economically logical – and thus to have eroded their ultimate value.

### The sudden slowdown

From the raw statistics, the slowdown in oil's historical growth trend appears to have begun in the early seventies. The deceleration was rapid, concentrated into little more than five years. It ended more than a century of exponential growth, in the last quarter of which oil's expansion rate had even been increasing (Figure 1.1). The industry's long-run growth rate from 1913 to 1948 had been around 6.5 per cent annually, doubling world production every twelve years. (In oil, statistics of production are the longest on record, and until recently were the least unreliable.)[1] But in the next twenty-five years oil production rose nearly

---

[1] Historically, two independent economic interests were usually involved in any oil production: the actual producer, and the owner of title to the subsoil – in North America a private surface landlord

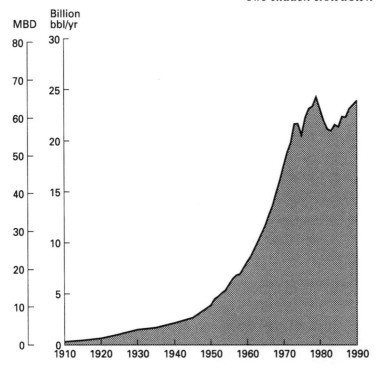

Figure 1.1. World crude oil production, 1913–1990. (*Sources:* BP, Oil Economists' Handbook.)

sixfold, by over 7.5 per cent annually. In that heady postwar generation, moreover, the volume of oil moving through international trade rose more than tenfold.

During the seventies oil's soaring increase was checked, slowed and finally halted. Production in 1979 was only 12 per cent higher than in 1973; trade only 3 per cent higher than in 1976. Then, temporarily, both fell. By 1985, world oil production was 12 per cent lower than in 1979; in the non-Communist world, it was 17 per cent lower. International trade in oil fell by nearly a third. A price collapse in 1986 and another fall during 1988 again turned demand, production and later trade slightly upwards. By 1991–2 demand and production had just about

but in most other countries a local or national government. The producer had to pay the subsoil owner a 'royalty' on every barrel 'won and saved'. So both needed to be sure exactly how much oil was produced for sale. That made production statistics verifiable. Of late, however, perhaps 70 per cent of world oil production has been completely in the hands of state-owned oil companies. In those countries, the government owns the companies as well as the subsoil rights. No such separation of interests is present. Whether or not production statistics are manipulated, nobody is in a position to check them independently. Sometimes no regular production statistics are published at all.

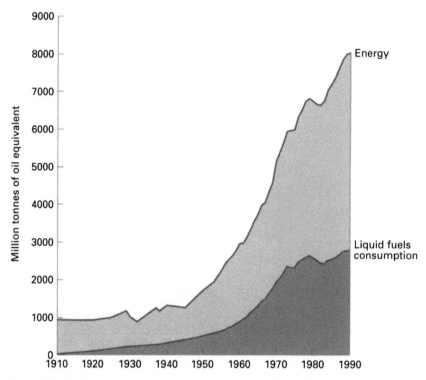

Figure 1.2. World consumption of primary energy and liquid fuels (oil plus natural gas liquids), 1910–1990.
(*Sources:* United Nations, BP.)

recovered. Oil trade had not, and may not pass its 1979 level before the mid-nineties.

In Figure 1.2 those oil growth rates are compared with demand for energy in general. Long-run growth rates of the world's total energy consumption and of the 'gross world product', over the first half of this century, were probably both of the order of 3–3.5 per cent annually. In the twenty-five postwar years those rates accelerated too, approaching 5 per cent annually. Both slowed down in the seventies. Also, the two growth rates began to diverge: world economic output rose by just under 4 per cent annually; energy consumption by only about 3 per cent. In the early eighties this 'decoupling' of economic growth from energy demand widened for a time; but the two may now again be converging. The world economy, in spite of recessions at the beginning and end of the eighties, grew on the average by about 3.5 per cent annually through that decade. Energy consumption rose at not much more than half that

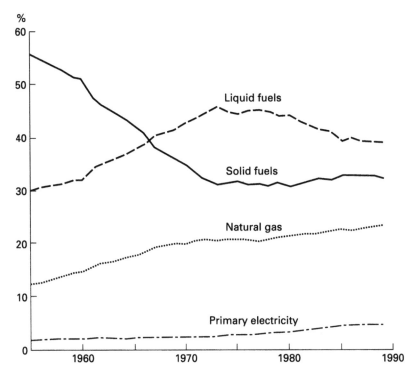

Figure 1.3. World primary fuel consumption: changing shares, 1955–1989. (*Source:* David Heal, 'Efficiency or self-sufficiency'.)

rate. But total energy demand no more than faltered before resuming fairly steady growth; oil fell more significantly, and did not turn firmly upwards until 1986. Oil's share of world energy consumption, therefore, is today much lower than in the mid-seventies (Figure 1.3).

When the slowdown in world oil began, hardly anybody saw it as a point of inflection in an established long-term trend. That was not surprising. Such changes in growth curves are seldom recognised immediately. Also, this slowdown began at about the same time as, and was immediately associated with, a concentration of political turbulence that radically altered the control, the ownership and eventually the structure of international trade in crude oil. That turbulence, set off by a startling though ultimately ineffectual embargo imposed by the most important oil-exporting countries, radically altered economic relationships between the industrialised countries and some of those others that it had been fashionable since World War II to characterise with patronising economic labels, as first the 'undeveloped' and later the 'developing' countries.

The countries among these that were involved in oil exporting developed money wealth – at least – more rapidly than anyone in the industrialised countries had ever quite expected. The way they did so put paid, in passing, to some of the comfortable economic assumptions that the Western industrialised countries had been nurturing – one in particular, the myth of the omnicompetence of multinationally integrated corporations. In that confrontation between several of the world's most powerful companies and a slightly larger number of much less sophisticated governments asserting their sovereignty, it did not turn out to be sovereignty that was at bay. However, some of the most important of these oil-exporting governments gained little from that confrontation but money. As was brutally demonstrated in 1990–1, the power that the oil wealth brought such governments was essentially defenceless, internally or externally.

The effects of those political and structural changes in the seventies were certainly profound. They weakened, though they did not wreck, the industry's economic performance. During the eighties, though the political turbulence in oil-exporting countries continued and crystallised into internecine war, some of its economic effects seemed likely to prove transitory. But at the beginning of the nineties, those hopes were dashed by renewed war – which did not remain internecine. The second Gulf war demonstrated how much more effective an oil embargo imposed by importing governments could be than anything exporting governments could try. That rapidly hardened into superpower military protection in the most critical region of world oil supply. Since then, the course of this industry's development, once again, has depended less on supply and demand 'fundamentals' than on government policies at both ends of the business.

Longer-term factors, however, were also at work in oil's sudden slowdown. In the longest-established oil-producing regions, advance signs of a levelling off were discernible even before the seventies began. Coincidentally or not, the short-term geopolitical changes involved in the current slowdown could now be converging with a longer-term trajectory of world oil, passing its peak around the end of this century, that had been forecast for many years past by eminent geophysicists and geologists. The eventual peak followed by decline that those earth scientists have in mind, however, would not be a matter of policy; nor would it be transitory. They regard it as irreversible.

Another set of influences that is already affecting the oil business and might help level it out is also long-term, though only recently perceived.

This is our social desire to reduce damage to the global environment from energy production and consumption. It has already affected certain oil development and transport, notably in Alaska. But much the most important of its influences may be upon demand for all fossil fuels.

Apart from the air pollution that is already obvious in all cities, scientists believe the 'greenhouse effect' of increasing concentrations of carbon dioxide and certain other gases in the upper atmosphere may cause increases in earth surface temperatures. The complex of processes involved in such 'global warming' is not yet sufficiently understood to allow confident prediction. Feedbacks within the world's ecosystem may at least partly offset the harm it threatens; our societies may prove able to adapt economically to warmer and drier climates. But the potential danger over time is already recognised as fearsome. Moreover, we need to begin adapting to this presumed greenhouse effect even before we can be sure it is really occurring. Waiting to be sure how much it really matters, or counting wholly upon market responses to compensate if it does, could be too late. Undoubtedly the best short-term adaptation we can engage in – useful in itself even if global warming turns out to be less of a threat than is currently perceived – will be to use fossil fuels more efficiently. That again may help level out demand for oil. In any case, it adds to the uncertainties of planning oil supply for the first decade of next century – which, allowing for time-lags, has to be the purpose of this industry's investment decisions during the nineties.

In sketching the international oil trade at the beginning of the nineties – possibly approaching its economic peak, and still brutally convulsed with politics – one has therefore also to reckon with the earth scientists' longer-term predictions, and with environmental externalities that may impose new constraints upon oil and other fossil fuels.

This preamble sketches the economic and political predicament, and some of the uncertainties, of the diverse groups of decision-makers now influencing world oil. The book seeks to outline the present state of the trade, following its transition from a more stable but outmoded pattern of operations. It is offered as a descriptive analysis of current circumstances with a forward orientation, not as a history. It draws on the past only to illustrate changes still in train.

It begins with the fundamental patterns of oil trade, meeting demand with supply (Chapter 2), and comparative costs arising from geology, geography, technology and timing (Chapter 3); takes note of geopolitical ambitions for autarky in energy (Chapter 4); and examines the durability of oil demand, for specialised products and as one general fuel among others (Chapter 5).

Then it outlines the transformed structure of the world oil business
(Chapter 6); and the new, still uncertain role of exporting governments as direct participants in the oil business (Chapter 7).

It describes the continuing attempts of exporting governments,
through the Organisation of the Petroleum Exporting Countries
(Opec), to 'administer' crude oil prices by informal and formal
cartel procedures (Chapter 8); and the new short-term markets in
which nowadays, Opec notwithstanding, oil prices are in practice
'discovered' (Chapter 9).

On the supply side, it turns to the longer-term potential of world oil
reserves as the geologists appraise these and foresee possible trajectories of future production; and lists the cost ladder of conventional
oil and the alternatives that are becoming available (Chapter 10).

In conclusion, it summarises sharply contrasting expectations about
end-century prospects for oil demand and prices, across a politically melting world of rapidly rising population outside the
former blocs of economic power, with all regions now beset by
new, tightening environmental constraints and regulation (Chapter
11); and considers both the patterns of regional supply that might
'logically' be developed from now on to meet this oil demand, and
those that probably will be (Chapter 12).

### Maturity without stability

People within the international oil trade had quite enough unprecedented things happening for a decade from the early seventies
onwards to worry about, or welcome (or both), without thinking about
longer-term trends. In rapid succession, oil 'shocks' and 'crises' provided plenty of plausible proximate reasons to explain what was happening in the short run. Moreover, the shocks and crises were manifes-
ted initially as sharp price increases. Those temporarily enriched almost
everybody producing oil – and most other energy – everywhere.

The slowdown in physical growth, therefore, was compensated and
perhaps masked by surges in revenue. Measured in money value, the
industry's performance did not weaken, but went on growing for a
decade after 1973. Radical underlying changes in control over prices,
industry ownership and market structure were associated with only a
few fluctuations in output and some pauses in the development of
capacity. The short-term pauses soon began to accumulate. But the
transition was hardly looked on as a longer-term change in the industry's physical performance until the early eighties. Then, at last, prices
began to fall, as well as demand. That registered more sharply. A little

later, it suddenly became fashionable for oil company executives to talk about 'a mature industry' in process of 'normalisation'.[2]

To call something mature, however, may suggest that it is also becoming calm and stable. By the mid-1980s, nothing like that had happened to the oil industry. It had become, and remains, unstable and precarious.

The industry's current instability reflects an imbalance between ample capacity to supply, backed by abundant reserves, and a level of demand that is still inadequate to absorb all the oil on offer, because going prices have never fallen enough to clear the market. Theoretically, such a market imbalance might sound unsustainable beyond the very short term. But political influences on the oil industry and vested interests in energy industries everywhere have been powerful enough to sustain this particular imbalance, much of the time, for nearly two decades. They may remain sufficient to do so.

At the prices at which oil was being offered in the world market at the beginning of the nineties, demand was perhaps 10 per cent less than the supply potentially available from existing capacity. Even after its response to a price collapse in 1986 and recurrent weakness ever since, world consumption was little higher than in 1979. Yet world capacity to produce oil is still being increased, and probably will continue to be for some years into the nineties.

A central paradox of this recently perceived 'maturity' of the world industry, moreover, is that much of the new productive capacity installed in the last two decades and still being developed is higher in cost than most of the capacity still being underutilised. Most of the oil production in the world that was temporarily 'shut in' during the eighties is far lower in operating cost than a large proportion of the production that continues elsewhere. Capacity in the regions where current costs are low, moreover, can probably still be expanded with much lower capital investment than the new capacity being developed elsewhere. Yet total capacity in the regions of low cost was only about half utilised during much of the 1980s, and was indeed significantly run down. How far it will be replaced and expanded during the nineties remains politically debatable.

Such a situation, to classical economists, would no doubt have

[2] The US Geological Survey, later, defined maturity in a petroleum industry as being 'unable to maintain production within the limits of historical prices...When prices, over the range of historical experience, limit entry of the industry into frontier or high-cost areas or prevent sufficient drilling to maintain production, the industry is mature.' (C. D. Masters *et al.*, 'Resource constraints in petroleum production potential', *Science*, 12 July 1991, p. 149.)

Industrialists define maturity with less rigour. For them, it may mean simply, but crucially over time, finding it harder to recruit the best graduates as management trainees.

implied collusion of producers to restrain supply, in 'conspiracy against the public'. Modern 'new classical' economists, following recent intellectual fashion, might be inclined to blame it more upon 'government interference' with the trade. Both are undoubtedly present. But both concepts have perhaps more meaning within single national economies than in international trade. Also, purely economic criteria are inadequate to analyse anything as politicised as the world oil trade.

As it happens, the suppliers now in open collusion and sometimes contriving as a cartel to maintain the price of crude oil at a level far above incremental cost – a price that moderates demand, and has at times weakened world macro-economic performance too – are indeed governments. These are the twelve member governments of Opec. They own and directly control national oil industries – on which *their* own national publics largely depend. If their collusion can fairly be called conspiracy, it is intended to be *on behalf of* those national publics, against a remote and ill-defined range of foreign consumers. (Even when successful, would it in practice benefit all their national publics in the long or even the medium run? Nobody is sufficiently informed to judge.)

The member governments of the cartel, however, are not wholly responsible for the paradoxical current condition of the international oil trade; nor alone in sustaining it. They do indeed seek to limit the total supply on offer, by agreement to produce less themselves – and at times fulfil their agreements. But they never had any desire to hold down low-cost supply and keep all the higher-cost capacity in the world operating fully. The low-cost capacity happens to be all that they own and have tried, some of the time, to regulate.

### Moral tales about Opec

In the oil business and even outside it, the seventies were soon aptly nicknamed 'the Opec decade'. From 1973 to 1986, the somewhat melodramatic sequence of political and structural changes in the world oil performance that the decade brought about pre-empted the attention of most analysts, as well as the general public. Opec, as one principal troupe of performers, played on in repertory during the eighties, doubling as villains or heroes depending on where in the world audience you happened to be sitting (and even, occasionally, as clowns). Many analysts of this industry attributed what was happening to oil during the period wholly or almost wholly to Opec behaviour. Much of the interpretation and criticism of this melodrama seemed for a time to become politically and even emotionally charged; this was so from various standpoints, at academic as well as popular levels. A temptation soon developed to rationalise all that was occurring as a kind of moral tale told in terms of oversimplified political economy. Like many parables, this could be interpreted in more ways than one.

One interpretation of the moral tale is familiar to all citizens of industrialised oil-importing countries:

'A cartel of oil-exporting governments repeatedly raised taxes on the companies that had discovered and developed their oil for them. Then, unilaterally abrogating long-term contracts, they seized control of the world trade and forced prices up to unreasonable levels, twice within six years. This generated huge transfers of wealth from oil-importing nations, both rich and poor, to oil-exporting nations. To start with, the exporters could not spend all of their surplus revenues, which were effectively withdrawn from all oil-importing countries' spending on other goods and services. That dislocated the world economy, simultaneously causing recession and stoking runaway inflation in the oil-importing countries. Naturally, oil demand, being elastic to price, fell in response to the increases imposed by the cartel, as consumers switched to competitive fuels. Similarly elastic, the supply of those other fuels and of oil by producers outside the cartel was stimulated by the price increases. The consequent reduction in trade was concentrated upon the over-priced exports of the cartel. In spite of monopolistic restraints on production for export, prices soon collapsed ...'

Perhaps Western economic moralists would like to continue their parable:

'The cartel has now virtually collapsed too, with its prices obliged to follow those set in open markets. And as these prices return to a competitive level, oil demand and the industry may now become free to resume the virtuous rapid growth that was so rudely interrupted by Opec.'

Analysts on the oil exporters' side of the trade always interpreted the morals of the same tale quite differently:

'For twenty-five years after the war, an oligopoly of international companies backed by their foreign governments controlled oil development and production in most oil-exporting countries. These companies, in collusion, held crude prices and government revenues per barrel far below what consumers abroad were ready to pay them for oil products. Their government backers shared the difference, by imposing high income and excise taxes in importing countries. Both benefited at the expense of the host nations whose basic, irreplaceable natural resources they were exploiting, forcing the host governments to form Opec in order to defend their national revenues. At the beginning of the seventies import demand for crude rose rapidly, and open market prices rose beyond the artificial tax reference prices set by these companies. After months of fruitless negotiation the Opec governments were forced to begin determining prices themselves. In 1973–4 and again in 1978–9 market prices soared: Opec simply followed, and sought to stabilise, the market. Ever since, oil companies and their parent governments have been developing high-cost non-Opec oil production and manipulating stock levels in an attempt to undermine Opec. In defence, Opec has restricted its own production and sought to maintain price stability – for the benefit of everybody, including consumers. Now, gradually, the exaggerated level of non-Opec production is sliding into decline, demonstrating the need for the Organisation's prudent price administration. Opec should soon be back in the saddle.'

All the happenings in that ambiguous moral tale about Opec, up to the price collapse of 1986 and the upturn of demand and trade since, did indeed take place, though not all in quite the storytale order. Its dramatic sequence of economic challenge and response served quite effectively to rationalise and illustrate much of what happened to international oil in the seventies and has since. The two price upsurges after Opec governments took over official price determination were clearly prime moves in this sequence of change – whether or not one regards the Organisation as a collective and effective prime mover. Objectively, nevertheless, that rationalisation looks to have fitted only where it touched; and both sets of slanted moral arguments missed a lot of what was happening.

On the demand side, the actual course of events fitted the Opec parable of economic cause and effect fairly well, albeit loosely. The oil price upsurge of 1973–4 did contribute somewhat to increasing inflation elsewhere. It dealt a powerful body-blow to Western business confidence (not in the oil industry alone). It probably also contributed to recession then; more certainly, the second upsurge in 1979 contributed to recession in the early eighties, though inflation was contained in that second period. The economic response of oil demand elasticity to price did belatedly manifest itself. Demand ceased to grow; fell briefly, bringing a collapse into price instability; then began its slow, halting recovery. But the first demand response to higher prices took much longer to show itself than many economists had counted upon. Precisely how it eventually worked, also, has remained somewhat opaque to analysis in hindsight.[3] This has also demonstrated the difficulties, given the current

---

[3] The prices dramatically raised in 1973 and 1979 were for crude oil. But demand for oil is for refined products, at prices that also cover transport, refining, marketing and distribution – and, in many countries, high percentages of excise tax. Hence the final consumer prices to which demand responds

state of the art, of quantifying and predicting further demand responses to price change, up or down; and in particular the time-lags involved.

However, certain general changes in energy demand in the seventies, affecting oil, had little or nothing to do with responses to oil prices raised by the Opec governments, or to fears of oil's political potential for instability. One was a similar shift in trend for electricity in most industrialised countries, suddenly decelerating from rapid exponential growth. This had shown itself slightly *before* the oil trend broke. This is the only other form of energy, or way of supplying energy, that had steadily matched or surpassed the growth rates of oil over the past century. Electric utility engineers used to have a rule of thumb that infuriated many other observers because it was quite arbitrary, but worked better than painstaking market analysis. Demand for electricity, they said, doubled every ten years; the growth rate was dependable, 7 per cent or more annually. This rule of thumb had worked quite triumphantly in electricity supply for about ninety years, from the industry's beginnings up to the end of the 1960s. Then, suddenly, the electricity demand curve broke, fluctuated and then turned into much flatter growth, in the OECD economies. From 1970 to 1984, the growth rate averaged less than 3.5 per cent annually; in the early eighties, it was not much over 2 per cent, and recovered to no more than 4 per cent by the end of the decade. That shift in trend had little to do with oil – except to help slow down demand for it as a power station fuel – and nothing to do with Opec.

The change in trend for electricity may have had more to do with a broader development that appears to have been affecting demand for all energy during the last two decades This is a secular, continuing shift in world industrial and technological patterns. In the most advanced economies, 'energy co-efficients' and 'energy ratios', which measure relationships between economic growth and energy demand,[4] have tended to decline over time, to well below one-for-one growth. The decline of 'smokestack industries' in the main OECD economies during the seventies and eighties continued a long-established shift of emphasis in these most developed economies towards commercial and financial service activities, and away from manufactures. The shift may have been accelerated somewhat by oil price increases in the 1970s. But it was in no

often change significantly less than what the world sees as 'the Opec price of oil', and always with significant time-lags.

[4] The *energy co-efficient* is the percentage growth in a nation's energy demand divided by the percentage growth in its GDP. This measure, derived from an earlier observed relationship between energy demand and industrial production, can produce statistical anomalies. The *energy ratio*, generally defined as the amount of standard energy, say tonnes of oil equivalent, used per dollar of GDP (also standardised in constant dollars of some given year) measures the same thing but is statistically less ambiguous (and more fashionable).

sense caused by them. (In the less developed countries, mostly still only seeking to industrialise, the energy co-efficients are often well above unity and the energy ratios much higher than in the richer countries approaching a post-industrial era. Decline in energy-intensive heavy industries within OECD has been partly offset by their growth in newly industrialised developing countries. But even so, total world production in these heavy industries stagnated in the 1970s and 1980s.)

A technological shift from electromechanical towards 'weak-current' electronic engineering, during the last decade in particular, is also, no doubt, affecting growth rates in demand for electricity in more ways than one. It has mechanised service activities and office work every-where, and may have increased their energy intensity. The balance, plus or minus, between extra electronic input and greater white-collar productivity is not easy to assess. Electronics, in its refinement of communications and control, is certainly increasing the technical potential for energy saving throughout many industrial processes. These too are substantial developments affecting long-term world energy demand, and within it oil demand, that have been almost entirely independent of Opec cartel performance.

*Not according to parable*

It was on the supply side, however, that the Opec parables fitted least adequately. Developments in world oil production have hardly corres-ponded at all with its neat sequence of cause and effect. The two largest changes in world supply during the 1970s and 1980s occurred in the world's two largest oil industries, which are both outside Opec. Pro-duction in the US peaked in 1970, levelled off at a slightly lower volume for two decades, and is now in decline. Production in the USSR con-tinued to grow, but at a slower rate. In the seventies, the then Soviet oil industry grew at only about half the rate of the sixties. In the eighties, it too managed little further growth, and may also have passed its peak (Figure 1.4). During this decade, following the collapse of central economic planning, the USSR's recent levels of petroleum output will be technically difficult to regain, and perhaps economically impracticable.

Those two industries, it is worth noting, had in aggregate accounted for about 40 per cent of the growth of total world oil production in the postwar decades. They had expanded then at sharply different rates, and with completely different economic motivations. But their pro-duction, if considered together, had still been increasing by more than 5 per cent annually up to the beginning of the seventies. Their subsequent

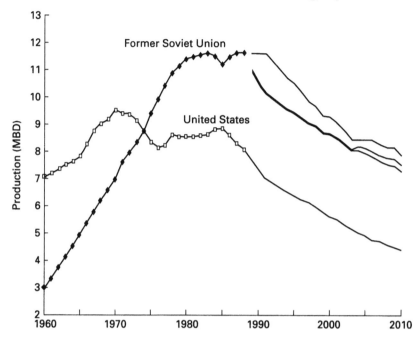

Figure 1.4. Crude oil production and projections, former Soviet Union and United States, 1960–2010. (*Source:* Masters *et al.*, 'Resource constraints'.)

deceleration occurred before, and quite independently of, the 'Opec revolution' from 1973 onwards. (The end of near self-sufficiency in the US, and the country's need to depend more on imports, was indeed a prerequisite for Opec's assertion of market power.) That revolution in oil prices might also have been hoped to stimulate substantial extra output in both the US and the Soviet industries, by making it possible for both to develop higher-cost production. There is not much direct evidence that it did, though in the early eighties it probably kept a fringe of the highest-cost US output in being longer than might have happened otherwise. (Soviet oil production costs were already rising independently, across its whole industry.)

Some additional petroleum supply has indeed been generated by the increases in price. A number of developing countries, in particular, have generated local production of oil (and gas) to substitute for expensive imports. But by far the largest additions to non-Opec oil supply during the Opec decade were in the North Sea, Alaska, Siberia and the new oil provinces of Mexico. Those were in no sense responses of supply elasticity to Opec's price increases. The initial investment decisions that began to bring all of them about had been made before 1973.[5]

Oil companies' investment in production capacity was in any case rising rapidly from the late sixties onwards – more of it indeed *within* Opec countries than outside them. It was companies that took all such decisions then, along with the decisions to expand tanker and refining capacity. They tended to extrapolate the sheer momentum of demand growth up to that time, which their practical planners had plausible reasons to assume would be maintained. (For two decades, the industry's forecasts had almost always turned out to have been too low. In 1969–70, the pace of expansion in total oil demand did falter, across the non-Communist world as well as in the US. But *import* demand went on rising fast, as US domestic production levelled off and spare capacity there disappeared.)

Opec influence was indeed rising somewhat before the seventies. Its level of 'government take', the income tax and royalties that made up Opec oil revenues in those years before participation and nationalisation, jerked upwards significantly in 1970–1, and was indexed, albeit tenuously, to inflation for the next couple of years. Opec's demonstrable strength in negotiating with the beleaguered companies suggested that this government take could steadily be ratcheted upwards. Once government participation was conceded in 1972, new layers of government gain were inserted, and passed on into the prices that importing countries paid. It became worth while for concessionaire companies with expectations of steadily higher 'tax-paid costs' to carry somewhat larger operating stocks. Moreover, a few operators from outside the integrated business were attracted to speculate. For the first time since the war, oil prices thus began to reflect some linkage to general inflation: the crude price stopped falling in real terms. Opec pressure to raise taxes was indeed one of the factors contributing to a widespread feeling by late 1972 that at last the world oil market was really tightening; but it was only one of several factors.

Outside oil, the development of other fuel industries since the mid-seventies has certainly been affected by the sharp rises in oil prices. But the competitive responses have hardly been decisive in the development of any other energy industry.

Substitution of other fuels for oil when its prices rose would have been expected to show up most significantly in electricity generation and

---

[5] All of these giant fields had been discovered by 1971. Decisions to develop them were made in the light of expectations about oil prices – *and* development costs – at that time. Many of the cost expectations turned out to have been wildly wrong. Fortunately for those developers, so did the price expectations.

in energy-intensive heavy industries. These often have flexible combustion plant, and are prepared to switch fairly rapidly to 'the cheapest Btu' of primary energy whenever relative prices change. But the most significant shifts in their consumption are usually incremental, in the choices made between fuels for use in new plant. The Opec decade turned out to be a period of much slower than expected growth for electricity; and a good deal of nuclear capacity was being newly commissioned to take up much of the growth that there was. It was also a decade of actual decline for some energy-intensive manufacturing industries. So less new energy-intensive capacity was commissioned than in previous decades; and these industries' incremental choices did not add up to as much fuel switching as might have been expected.

In the US, price competition as well as governmental policy after the mid-seventies certainly favoured the choice of coal in the incremental development of fossil fuel generating capacity for electric power. But slower growth in electricity demand, and subsequently environmental concerns about pollution from coal-burning, limited the extra recourse to coal then; and more recently the electricity supply industry has been turning increasingly to gas. Few other industrialised countries enjoy the self-sufficiency in low-cost coal production of the US.[6] For most of them, using more coal to reduce dependence on oil would logically have meant importing the extra coal. Large-scale extra capacity to produce and export open-cast steam coal has indeed been developed since the mid-seventies, in South Africa, Australia and Colombia. Undoubtedly, Opec's increases in price accelerated those developments. But in Western Europe at least, the shift to these diversified sources of energy imports was still hampered by protective policies towards long-established and economically moribund deep-mined coal industries.

The world's two largest producers and consumers of natural gas, as of oil, are again the former Soviet Union and the US. (At the beginning of the Opec decade, the US was ahead in both. But the USSR became the largest gas producer in 1983 and the largest consumer in 1985.) World oil price levels have to be considered constantly by the managers of both these enormous gas industries. But oil prices are only one consideration among many. Each is governed primarily by its own internal circumstances, problems and possibilities – which in the US as well as in the USSR are political as well as economic. To suggest that Opec pressures upon the price of oil strongly influenced the development of either of those countries' gas industries during the seventies and eighties would be quite unrealistic.

---

[6] China and the former Soviet Union rank second and third among the world's producers of coal, and in reserves.

During those decades, natural gas supply in Europe and Japan also increased rapidly. However, so it had in the sixties. Undoubtedly the competitive opportunities for gas in these industrialised markets were enhanced by increases in oil prices. But the growth of these markets for gas was driven initially by declines in local supply for certain developed gas markets; by new large increments of gas supply becoming available elsewhere; and by the technical development of long-distance transport systems for gas. These allowed natural gas to be exported in large volumes to top up markets that were becoming short of local gas, and to reach fuel markets that had been too remote before, such as Japan.

Some of the distant gas reserves that could thus be developed for export were in Opec countries. For a time, gas export prices were linked to the crude oil prices that Opec sometimes managed to manipulate. Since the eighties, also, some developing countries are becoming able to utilise gas reserves locally that might have remained uneconomic if the costs of oil imports had never risen. But this acceleration of gas development in markets outside the USSR and the US during the past two decades was not driven primarily by increases in world oil prices. Most of it would probably have happened anyway.

The most rapid development of any 'primary' energy[7] from the mid-seventies onwards (from a very low initial base) was, temporarily, in electricity generation from nuclear fission. That in its turn would be easy to attribute to the increase in oil prices. In France, and to a lesser extent in Japan and Germany, that was specifically the motive – mainly as a political rather than an economic response. However, almost all the nuclear capacity commissioned during the seventies and early eighties had been decided upon before the Opec decade began. The investment worldwide in nuclear electricity generating capacity that had been decided on during the decade *before* 1973 exceeded the capacity decided upon in the decade after the first 'oil shock'. During the eighties, a great deal of nuclear capacity decided upon in the late sixties came into commission; some is still being completed. But not much more has been newly ordered; some projects have been abandoned, and others probably will be.

In nearly all countries, the decisions about nuclear generation made to date have been primarily political. The politics involved have not

---

[7] Strictly, electricity is 'secondary' energy, generated by transforming some form of primary energy into power. Uranium is the primary fuel transformed into electricity by nuclear generation; and much of the input into the world's nuclear plant is indeed imported. But the amounts involved are relatively small, and world supplies are ample. Also, the most essential input to nuclear development is technological know-how, mainly available in advanced industrial economies. So import dependence on uranium has never yet become politically worrying; and nuclear electricity can be regarded as 'primary energy supply' where it is generated.

always been related solely to reducing oil import dependence on Opec. Often, they have also represented government support for heavy engineering industries in the countries concerned. Also, the accounting applied to measure nuclear 'success' or 'failure' has often been somewhat politically creative. (Nuclear accounting, in any case, needs to be creative. Some of the problems posed by extremely capital-intensive technology that might require as much investment to close down as to put up – but maybe a century later – almost baffle conventional techniques of investment appraisal. But the accounting double-think in which some state power utilities have been encouraged by their political masters to indulge has further blurred and compounded those inherent complexities.)

Only in the United States were the decisions mainly commercial, made by private power utilities and subject to standard accounting procedures. There the success record was not impressive technically or commercially. After the mid-seventies, not one more nuclear plant was ordered by American utilities. At the end of the eighties, a British government nearly as committed ideologically to nuclear electricity as to privatisation of state-owned utilities found that the two were incompatible. It was forced to keep its sizeable but expensive nuclear capacity nationalised because the City advised that private investors were not prepared to buy these stations. Even then, the government required the utilities that it did privatise, which burn fossil fuels, to buy costly power from and thus in part effectively to subsidise its nationalised rump of uneconomic nuclear stations.

Thus one can hardly identify much of the recent non-Opec development of oil and other energy production as a supply response to cartel pricing of oil. Right up to the mid-eighties, only a small proportion of the additional energy production capacity that had come into operation since 1973 could be firmly identified as having been decided on even after, let alone because of, the Opec price upsurge.

## The other price supporters

Various governments outside Opec share some responsibility for – and appear at least as anxious to maintain – a world price level for crude oil well above the costs at which abundant extra supply could readily be developed and brought to market. These include the governments of several of the richer industrialised countries. A few of these, including Britain, Canada, Norway, and the Netherlands, are significant net exporters of petroleum. On balance, for a time, they have probably gained from high prices (though in macro-economic terms this is sometimes debated). A few of the world's poorer countries too, including China, have developed enough local energy production, at high cost, to achieve energy self-sufficiency. These now, at least temporarily, may prefer world oil prices to remain high. And the former USSR, still the world's largest oil and gas producer, has to export petroleum for its only dependable earnings of foreign exchange. So its attitude towards Opec, under Communism and since, has remained one of very benevolent neutrality, with occasional gestures of open co-operation.

Japan, Germany, France and most other industrialised countries are heavily dependent on importing the oil they use. Of the twenty-four OECD countries, eighteen import more than 50 per cent of their supplies. Though the US reduced its net imports after 1979, it remained the largest single importer, and by 1990 was again importing about 45 per cent of its supplies. Most of the developing countries outside Opec, too, have based their recent economic growth almost entirely on imported oil. Economically, all these countries should on balance gain from lower prices. Japan and Germany, with little energy supply of their own and very limited stakes in petroleum production abroad, have no chance of avoiding import dependence, and are confident of sufficient manufacturing prowess to go on affording dependence on (diversified) energy imports. But politically, US attitudes towards international crude oil pricing have always remained ambivalent, reflecting its mixture of interests.[8]

German and Japanese attitudes towards international oil pricing may derive partly from the fact that after two world wars both countries were largely shut out of any significant economic interest in the world's most important oil-exporting area. The US government had backed the entry of American companies into Middle East oil after the first of those wars, and it had greatly strengthened the companies' and its own economic interests, in a region becoming vastly more important, after the second. The governments of two of the other then victorious powers had retained vestigial colonial claims to political influence there. More importantly, 'international' companies, some initially sponsored and all always politically backed by their Western parent governments, then retained control over oil production and development throughout the region. In developing low-cost oil there, those companies did not choose to drive higher-cost oil production elsewhere out of business. They owned a large proportion of it. (Moreover, cost patterns in oil make it hard for new cheap oil to supplant costlier existing production. As those

---

[8] So have its attitudes towards pricing petroleum in its domestic market. US governments have achieved quite impressive effective improvements in automobile miles per gallon by regulation. But they still maintain lower excise duties on gasoline than the rest of OECD.

companies had learned painfully during the thirties, new discoveries developed competitively at low cost can render all oil production unprofitable for a time, without putting much of it right out of business.)

During the 1950s, it was those international companies, with the backing of their parent governments, that set the policies governing Middle East oil development, though not without difficulties. They were able to nullify an initial takeover of part of the region's low-cost production by one host government in the region, Iran. Twenty years later, however, such control was taken over by all host governments throughout the Middle East. That heightened the unease that most industrialised importing governments were already feeling about dependence upon supplies from the Middle East, much as they had benefited from the exponential growth of exports from there during the postwar decades.

During the early postwar decades, the US had first informally and later formally limited oil imports to protect its own huge domestic oil-producing industry. This was comparatively high in technical costs, and even higher in the cost of investment to offset decline. From the late seventies onwards, not even the development of Alaska could do more than stabilise US output for about a decade. Of late, even at the prices that Opec had jacked upwards, it has moved into decline. So the US is facing, once again, a growing import dependence during the nineties. Historically, US governments always strongly backed American companies' positions in Middle East concessions. They have continued to encourage the companies' profitable dealings there in the post-concessionary aftermath. But most US governments have also regarded the Middle East as politically dangerous, and likely to remain so.

Surreptitiously, therefore, while producing ritual complaints every time that Opec has sought as a cartel to raise or support world oil prices, every US government has generally been very content to see prices maintained at a level that keeps high-cost energy production commercially viable in other regions, which are more firmly within Western control or can be considered politically safer. At critical times, its governments have hardly bothered to be surreptitious. Dr Henry Kissinger's response to Opec pricing in 1973–4 was to found the International Energy Agency as a counter-cartel of oil-importing countries. He did not want this to restrain further price increases. He wanted it to agree on a 'floor price', at about 75 per cent of the levels that Opec had set, below which prices should not be allowed to fall back again. (Characteristically, the notion was too clever, and sank without trace.)

More practically, President Bush had considerable direct experience of the US domestic oil industry before he entered politics. His most notable contribution ever to that industry, and arguably his most effective single political act while Vice-President in the Reagan era, was in April 1986, when on a visit to Riyadh he besought the Saudi Arabian government to abandon its then policy of boosting exports of its low-cost oil almost regardless of price. (It soon did.) As President, his action in the Gulf in 1990–1 was a remarkably rapid response to aggression. He did not flinch from asserting US military control there. But at the same time he announced an energy policy intended to increase domestic American oil production, in spite of its inevitably high comparative cost. Although in unchallengeable strategic control of Gulf oil, he showed once again the continuing unease of all US governments about depending more and more for their country's supply upon the region from which low-cost oil is mostly available.

Even before it asserted its military protection over the southern Gulf in 1990–1, US political influence in the region was widespread and pervasive. But until then, this influence had always been potentially self-frustrating. It may remain so, even as the world's sole superpower, no longer challenged. Politically, the US is now more firmly than ever locked into supporting two client states in the region with deeply conflicting interests. Its support of Israel, its strongest military ally there, and protection of Saudi Arabia, as the world's long-run marginal oil supplier, have remained hard to knit into any convincing 'peace process' between Israel and all Arab states. It is often prepared to assert a powerful military presence in support of one Middle East faction or another (though seldom for very long). But it can never be sure of backing 'the right ones'. Indeed, for Western interests in the Middle East there may never be any *permanently* right ones to back.

Various different groupings of governments, therefore, share much of the responsibility for keeping the oil price uncompetitively high. But they are supported by an enthusiastic consensus, effectively an international political constituency, of higher-cost producers of oil and other energy, with their entourage of suppliers of technology, services and finance. Those other producers can serve world markets with very comfortable profits, if only the world oil price remains high enough. The oil producers among them gain higher profits from their own production than from paying the prices that the cartel governments ask for much lower-cost oil. For the present, these other producers benefit much more from high prices than Opec does. *Their* volumes and total revenues have never collapsed. So long as Opec keeps some of the cheapest potential supply shut in, the rest can produce a great deal of oil that in strictly economic terms could not compete in a really free market. This was most cold-bloodedly analysed in August 1990 by the chairman of British Petroleum at that time. Reacting to the price effects of Iraq's invasion of Kuwait, Mr Robert Horton told his share-holders, 'Each dollar a barrel on the price of crude feeds through to $200 million of after-tax profits for BP in a full year.' (On that occasion, as it happened, the extra dollars a barrel did not feed through for more than a few months.)

### Prices beyond control?

In principle, admittedly, it has not been getting any easier of late for this consensus of vested interests in energy to keep prices high. Structurally, at least, world oil markets have been getting much freer and more transparent. From 1979 onwards, far less of the world's crude supply than before has been moving through oil companies' vertically integra-ted channels, or even under firm long-term sales contracts. (That con-centration of world trade had been in existence much longer than Opec.) More trade than before now moves through open markets dealing in single cargoes and short-term contracts; and the influence of these markets far outweighs their shares of trade by volume. In 1979, panic reactions by traders in these markets contributed to the second price upsurge. But by the mid-1980s, as their expertise and coverage broadened, these markets had become the main price indicators for the whole world oil trade. That heightened day-to-day price instability, and encouraged the organisation of forward and futures markets to hedge price risks. Such markets are by definition highly transparent. Moreover, they draw upon the expectations and expertise of a wider financial community, accustomed to handling risk in other commodity markets and newly prepared to trade in oil or speculate on oil prices.

The prices arising in these open markets for crude oil might in principle appear impossible for any cartel or even consensus of integra-ted producers to control. (Those arising in the longer-established spot markets for refined oil products certainly are.) They are more rapidly and precisely reported than the prices set in longer-term deals, and far more people are prepared to buy and sell in such 'paper markets' than engage in the actual 'physical' world oil trade. Thus these markets may be moving towards 'efficiency' in the stock or commodity market sense – i.e. accurately reflecting the balance of current 'rational expectations' about prices.

Customarily, these markets display shrewd short-term reactions to hectic uncertainty. The finance houses nicknamed 'Wall Street refiners' draw upon wide expertise in 'risk management' elsewhere to handle just such volatility. Some of the professionals trading within these open markets for oil disclaim any particular concern with the fundamentals of the business, except as these affect short-term movements in market prices. Their expertise, they claim, is neutral: they should be able to make as much money out of correct judgement in a falling market as in a rising one. (Some of them admit, however, to preferring movement one way or the other. Dependable price stability might leave futures traders unemployed.)

This new transparency in trading did help to reduce crude prices significantly in the early eighties, and made it easier for a shift in Saudi policy to collapse prices in 1986. It has kept them highly flexible ever since. However, it has not yet served to clear the world oil market as in theory *competitive* open markets 'should', or to bring world oil prices down close to the long-run incremental cost of supplying extra oil. Demonstrably, transparent pricing in these open markets has not removed a sizeable overhang of spare production capacity from which oil could be supplied quickly and profitably at say half current price levels.[9] (Stock market efficiency has nothing necessarily to do with copybook competition in the businesses about which rational investors form their expectations.)

### Overestimating Opec?

Not all the elements that moderated oil demand and supply in the seventies, therefore, fit explanations that put all the responsibility onto Opec as a cartel.

Among the few academic economists who had devoted much attention to international oil before 1973, some of the most experienced continue to blame the cartel. Others have argued that during the sixties, additions to oil reserves from new discoveries had failed to match production, so that 'normal' market forces could explain most of the price increases during the seventies that were attributed to Opec.[10] Analysts close to Opec[11] recalled that from 1971–2 onwards, production from Libya and Kuwait, which had hitherto been expanding without any constraints, was levelled off and then cut back severely. They feel

---

[9] In 1991, the overhang of capacity that had been available at short notice was temporarily removed by the Iraqi firing of Kuwaiti oil wells and the UN control of Iraqi exports, which together put some 5–6 MBD of Gulf capacity out of action. Saudi Arabia and other Gulf exporters were producing close to *their* full capacity in winter 1991 and 1992, pending the return and redistribution of that spare capacity.

[10] P. W. MacAvoy, *Crude Oil Prices: as Determined by OPEC and Market Fundamentals* (Ballinger, 1983).

[11] R. Mabro, 'Opec after the oil revolution', *Millennium* (Journal of International Studies), London School of Economics, Winter 1975–6; I. Seymour, *Opec, Instrument of Change* (Macmillan, 1980).

those reductions, along with disputes in Iran and Saudi Arabia that threatened the tenure of the companies there, suddenly reduced the constantly advancing margin of spare capacity upon which Middle East concessionaires had been accustomed to count, by mid-1973 to nearly nil. Only that sharp reduction in spare or rapidly available capacity, they argue, along with general perceptions of a tightening market, allowed the Gulf Opec producers to force prices up before and during the Arab oil embargo of 1973. (Many of those market pressures had indeed come from Opec governments; but individually, not acting as a cartel.)

As to the 1979 price shock, much of the responsibility can be apportioned between Iranian politicians, panicky OECD consumers, spot market traders and speculators. Opec governments simply took advantage of this confusion and manipulated it somewhat (once again, hardly in unison). Later in the decade, almost incidentally, another school of economists was rediscovering a 'fundamental law' that the prices of extractive resources such as oil, quite regardless of cartel pressure, 'should' always rise over time (see Chapter 8, pp. 184–5)

There is no shortage of political and economic explanations of what has been happening to the oil business since 1973; indeed there is a surfeit of plausible theories. As was observed some years ago in much the same context: 'Unfortunately but not untypically, both sets of predictions can be readily validated, suggesting that both doctrines could be true or, even more distressingly, that the system is in technical terms overdetermined.'[12] Most of these explanations, also, were offered essentially as rationalisations in hindsight, once the sequence of surprises was already in train. Certainly no shift in trend from exponential growth of the oil industry had been generally foreseen by economic or political analysts.

Once that sequence of dramatic short-term changes began in the early seventies, however, everybody began frantically revising whatever forecasts they had previously been making. Ironically, almost the only forecasts that ever predicted a possible peak and levelling off in world oil as early as the 1980s were some of those frantic revisions, more political than economic, and gripped by fear of an 'energy gap', with an 'oil crunch' emerging before the mid-1980s as surging demand was expected to outrun the supply that Opec might be politically willing to make available.

In the event, reality turned such forecasts upside down. Long before the mid-1980s arrived, the concept of an 'oil gap' between demand and supply constrained by Opec had disappeared almost without trace. (A

12 R. Eden *et al.*, *Energy Economics: Growth, Resources and Policies* (Cambridge University Press, 1981), p. 374.

few of the same prophets, admittedly, remain convinced that it will re-emerge in the late nineties.) The only practical meaning that energy 'gaps' or 'crunches' could ever have had would have been times when demand exceeded supply and forced prices up rapidly. But the prices had already shot up again in 1979. The gap that actually emerged in the eighties was between surplus capacity and inadequate demand. The oil industry did show signs of levelling off at roughly the time that some of those ominous forecasts had predicted. But it appeared to be doing so for precisely opposite reasons.

## A different kind of forecast

But all analyses focusing solely upon the short-term political and economic turmoil affecting the international oil trade since the seventies may leave out some underlying factors of longer-run change affecting world oil supply. At this point, one also needs to take note of the longer-term forecasts made by earth scientists.

Geologists and geophysicists who make long-term predictions about oil have seldom concerned themselves with how politics affect the industry. Some of them, indeed, have specifically disclaimed any direct concern even with the industry's economics. These scientists' reckonings begin with the industry's history (which commercially goes back to about 1860): the record of additions to reserves through discoveries, and the subsequent development of production from those reserves. Looking forward, they draw upon estimates of the area, volume and rock qualities of sedimentary strata underlying the world's surface, petroleum province by province,[13] and assessments by geologists using 'Delphi survey' techniques of the probabilities that given volumes of petroleum resources will be found. The content and form of their projections have usually been wholly isolated from the analyses and forecasts of energy and mineral economists, and often in sharp conflict with them. The earth scientists are often, understandably, accused of crying 'Wolf'. Certain of their predictions about the peaking of production in the US, however, turned out to be far more accurate than those of any economist.

Many geologists have been predicting for years that world oil supply, too, might peak before the end of the century, at 70–100 MBD (which may be compared with the 65 MBD actually achieved in 1979 and again in the early nineties). The profession has gone on echoing the warning, though less specifically. In October 1986, for example, Dr Charles

---

[13] A petroleum province can be defined as 'an area in a sedimentary geological basin or uplift in which oil or gas occurs in a fairly predictable manner'.

Masters of the US Geological Survey emphasised 'our belief that we have but a few decades to enjoy the convenience of crude oil as our major energy fuel ... There is every indication that it will become ever more difficult to obtain in years to come ...'.

Oil predictions from most earth scientists, however, have usually been of *technically practicable* supply, not of actual production at any given time. They were estimates, essentially, of the production *capacity* that it would be practicable to develop from the world's underlying oil reserves. In fact, world production capacity had already been around 70 MBD since the early 1980s, even after some slight reduction of effective capacity in the Iraq–Iran war and a quite severe rundown of the capacity already installed in Saudi Arabia. Iraq sabotaged some 2.5 MBD of production capacity in Kuwait in 1991; but that destruction, like the embargo on its own exports, only temporarily reduced effective Middle East capacity.

Technically, it would still not appear difficult to raise capacity in the Gulf countries by a further 5–10 MBD within a few years, though even there the costs of rehabilitating rundown production systems and adding new capacity appear to have risen sharply. It might indeed even be practicable to raise total world capacity by another 5–10 MBD beyond that, before approaching technical constraints or sharply rising supply costs. That would imply a plausible world capacity approaching say 80–90 MBD by about the end of the century, well into the middle of the range for peak supply predicted by earth scientists. In prevailing oil circumstances, however, neither Opec governments nor private companies in non-Opec areas have yet been prepared to develop anything like as much.

## Shaving off the peak?

Nothing that has happened has invalidated the earth scientists' estimates of the practicable world supply. History has not yet tested them. (Probably it never will.) Demand for oil has not peaked yet. It could rise significantly further, if world economic growth quickens, and if oil prices fall again and stay low enough for long enough. But it would take a very powerful demand recovery indeed to call upon production by the end of this century approaching even the mid-point of the range of practicable supply first forecast well over thirty years ago.

The abrupt deceleration of growth in the early seventies and stagnation in the eighties may thus be followed by only slow and uncertain recovery, towards a levelling of world oil demand and production early next century for a decade or two, perhaps several. This would have arisen from a range of different causes. However much underlying technical factors contributed, one major cause of the premature slow-down was a continuing sequence of political and economic choices throughout the postwar era, choices about the comparative political advantage of developing low-cost and higher-cost oil, and about prices.

Opec inherited responsibility for those choices two decades ago, and gained much temporary wealth from the central distortion of comparative costs in international oil development. Its attempts to allocate production between member countries have in effect sought to avoid the principle of comparative costs, as other managers of world oil supply had sought before. That helped to restrain demand for two decades. So as the history of the oil industry continues to unfold, the Organisation's most significant influence upon it may perhaps be seen only as a matter of timing. It may have shaved off the peak predicted for oil supply by holding prices high enough to postpone a good deal of demand; and may thus have lengthened the trajectory of oil's development over time. (Earth scientists would perhaps add: 'But not by very long'.)

Prospects for all fossil fuels in the nineties will be powerfully affected by political concern with how much harm burning them may do to the global environment. Nobody at the time this book was written could be sure about this, or any practicable alternatives. Undoubtedly, many other factors external to the oil industry – again, economic, political and technical – will also influence the oil business during the nineties. Macroeconomic performance in the world's industrialised countries, in the political aftermath of Communism, certainly will. So will population growth in the developing countries, driving the divergent rates of economic growth they achieve. Further regional wars may – perhaps over water supply, as readily as over oil – unless peace imposed by American hegemony can be made to last. So will political choices regarding other energy technologies during the coming decade.

Nevertheless, the industry's own internal fundamentals – and fictions – will continue to shape its performance in detail. Whether its growth continues or levels off will depend largely on the continuing imbalance of oil demand and potential supply at a price high above medium-run incremental cost. There is no way yet of proving or disproving the hypothesis of levelling off onto dome or plateau. But what does actually happen will be decided by expectations in the oil business now, rational or irrational, and actions taken because of them.

During the eighties this industry entered upon a period of more short-term instability in its supply patterns than it had ever been accustomed to before. Its older-established managements have reorganised their reduced share of those patterns, learning to pay more attention to the avoidance and hedging of the short-term risks. This will remain an essential skill in managing the oil industry during the rest of this century. Some of the new managers inside Opec are beginning to learn it too. That short-term balancing act is undoubtedly manageable; and can be highly remunerative too.

## Balancing the risks

It is easy to argue that 'risk management' is needed for the longer term too. But in an industry with the economic time-lags inherent in oil development, that concept is easier to invoke than to implement. Insurance has been taken out against certain risks to oil supply. Importing governments are holding higher strategic stocks. Exporters have laid additional pipelines to move their crude to terminals outside the Gulf, and are maintaining significant stocks themselves close to export destinations. The region's longest war passed with hardly any immediate effect upon world oil supply or even price; and the short sharp conflict of 1991, after provoking brief spikes of panic in spot and futures markets, ended with crude prices lower than before the Iraqi invasion.

But regimes there, and their willingness to meet export demands, have still to be considered deeply at risk. Over the whole postwar period, the region has produced at least one war or political crisis every seven years. Its own governments still look unable to improve on that bloodstained record – though American dominance might. So far, at any rate, nobody has proved capable of managing the political risks of the Middle East. What turned out to be the world's ideal place to produce oil was never developed to full comparative advantage by the industry's earlier controllers there. But the governments who seized that unique opportunity for development two decades ago have since given importers every additional incentive to avoid dependence on it.

This international industry is passing through a climacteric. Following a series of shocks it has paused, and has not yet regained confidence. Much of it is under entirely new management, whose commitments are national rather than multinational, and at least as political as economic. The former multinational managers remain active, but their scope of operations has been curtailed. The two sets of managers have many interests in common, but some in conflict with each other. They share a fundamental dilemma – extreme disparities of cost beneath a price level that may still be inhibiting the full recovery of demand towards the supply readily available. Their like interests as oil suppliers, again, have some elements in common but others in zero-sum conflict with those of oil consumers. In their current commercial performance, all the industry's managers are beset with extreme short-term instabilities of price, and face medium-term uncertainties of a kind that the industry has never encountered before. What may look from outside to be levelling onto a plateau has become a balancing act on a precarious slack wire.

# CHAPTER 2

# A discontinuity in trade

It is hard to think of any business that is more international than oil. Yet in one sense, for a decade, its operations have been less international than they had been for many years, since long before the slowdown in growth began. Throughout the eighties, less than half of the oil that the world used was supplied through interregional trade. That had not happened since the early sixties. Very few people close to this business[1] had expected this situation ever to recur. In 1973, 60 per cent of world oil consumption had moved in trade between regions. In 1990, even after the belated upturn, that trade was still less than 49 per cent of consumption (Figure 2.1). Counting in intra-trade within regions, oil movement across national frontiers probably did still supply nearly 60 per cent of world consumption at the end of the eighties. But in 1973, by that same measure, it had been as high as 84 per cent (Table 2.1).

Indeed, international trade was what slowed down most in the oil business after the early seventies. It stopped growing earlier than world production or consumption; it fell much more sharply in the early eighties; and up to the early nineties it had still not fully recovered. From 1979 to the mid-eighties, world oil consumption dropped 10 per cent and production 14 per cent. By the measure most widely used in this business – the volume of oil movement between the main *regions* of the world – the decline in trade between 1979 and 1985 was nearly a third. The somewhat larger trade volume crossing all *national* frontiers, which includes 'intra-trade' between countries within the same regions, fell by about a quarter.[2]

Changes in the regional flows of oil movement are more significant

[1] Professor Peter Odell of Erasmus University in Rotterdam was the first analyst to note this development, in his arguments from 1981 onwards that the world oil trade would become increasingly 'regionalised'.
[2] Here the trade matrix considered is from BP's annual *Statistical Review of World Energy* (adjusted to continue long-run comparisons). Data for oil trade across *national* frontiers derives from the UN annual *Yearbook of World Energy*.

Table 2.1. *Consumption and trade: energy and oil, 1970–1989 (million tonnes oil equivalent)*

| | World primary energy consumption | | Energy imports | | Oil imports as % of consumption | |
|---|---|---|---|---|---|---|
| | Total | Oil | Total | Oil | Total | Oil |
| 1970 | 4640 | 1920 | 1676 | 1499 | 32.3 | 78.1 |
| 71 | 4828 | 2036 | 1779 | 1595 | 33.0 | 78.3 |
| 72 | 5058 | 2177 | 1933 | 1731 | 34.2 | 79.5 |
| 73 | 5307 | 2344 | 2177 | 1957 | 36.9 | 83.5 |
| 74 | 5354 | 2312 | 2126 | 1877 | 35.1 | 81.2 |
| 75 | 5409 | 2303 | 1993 | 1734 | 32.1 | 75.3 |
| 76 | 5691 | 2461 | 2187 | 1918 | 33.7 | 77.9 |
| 77 | 5875 | 2539 | 2281 | 1997 | 33.9 | 78.6 |
| 78 | 6060 | 2591 | 2270 | 1969 | 32.5 | 75.9 |
| 79 | 6284 | 2636 | 2358 | 2018 | 32.1 | 76.6 |
| 1980 | 6371 | 3093 | 2230 | 1871 | 29.4 | 60.5 |
| 81 | 6232 | 2921 | 2062 | 1719 | 27.6 | 58.9 |
| 82 | 6180 | 2806 | 1948 | 1579 | 25.6 | 56.3 |
| 83 | 6392 | 2525 | 1952 | 1557 | 24.4 | 61.7 |
| 84 | 6650 | 2563 | 2020 | 1580 | 23.8 | 62.6 |
| 85 | 6948 | 2542 | 1964 | 1491 | 21.5 | 58.7 |
| 86 | 6874 | 2591 | 2096 | 1667 | 23.9 | 64.4 |
| 87 | 7030 | 2939 | 2157 | 1670 | 23.8 | 56.8 |
| 88 | 7327 | 3073 | 2274 | 1753 | 23.9 | 57.0 |
| 89 | 7427 | 3112 | 2383 | 1833 | 24.7 | 58.9 |

*Source:* United Nations.

than the absolute volumes involved, which obviously depend upon how many and just which regions one chooses to separate out in any trade matrix. But regional trade statistics for oil run back longer on a consistent basis than those for trade between nations. Geopolitically, too, changes in interregional trade are the more important, since they include most of the crude oil imports from Opec. However, trade within regions has grown in importance during the last decade, notably with the rise in North Sea oil exports within Western Europe (and, arguably, with the resurgence of Mexican oil exports).[3] In 1985, the total oil trade recorded by the UN as crossing national frontiers was about 25 per cent larger in

[3] Mexicans dislike being classed as part of North America, though they may be part of a free trade area with the US and Canada. Many regard their country as in Central and/or South America, and they are unambiguously Latin American. BP tactfully ranks their trade with the US as *inter*regional, not intraregional. Even so, the gringos buy 50–60 per cent of Mexican oil exports.

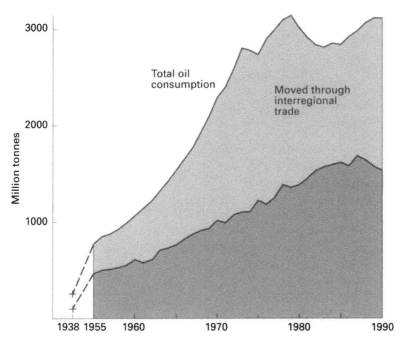

Figure 2.1. World oil consumption and interregional trade, 1938–1990. (*Source:* BP.)

volume than interregional trade. Statistics of world oil imports and exports never quite match (even allowing for changes in stocks and oil in transit), any more than totals for world production and consumption do. However, the volume of oil trade is only indirectly related to totals of world supply and demand (although it may be somewhat better measured, nowadays, than either);[4] and all three volumes are continuously changing. This chapter, assessing trade as an economic mechanism of adjustment between the other two, is concerned with the overlapping geographical patterns of oil demand, reserves and supply, and the flows of oil across the world that link these contrasting patterns. Chapter 3 considers the diversity of production costs in different oil-producing regions; the costs of transport to markets; and the extent to which trade flows reflect comparative costs.

Oil is, and will probably always remain, the cheapest form of energy

[4] *Imports* have to be declared whenever they cross a frontier. Statistical records of *production* (and *exports*) are at times nowadays manipulated for political purposes, e.g. to conceal performance outside Opec quotas. *Consumption* is only ever reckoned as the difference between *deliveries* (fairly well reported) and *changes in stocks* (partly reported, partly guesstimated).

Table 2.2. *Known reserves of fossil fuels, 1990*

| | Oil | Natural gas | | Pet-roleum | Coal | | All fossil fuels |
|---|---|---|---|---|---|---|---|
| *Units*[a] | BT | TCF | BTOE | BTOE | BT | BTOE | BTOE |
| US | 4.3 | 166 | 4.3 | 8.6 | 260.3 | 130.0 | 147.2 |
| Canada | 1.0 | 98 | 2.5 | 3.5 | 6.7 | 3.5 | 10.5 |
| Latin America | 17.1 | 242 | 6.3 | 23.4 | 18.5 | 10.9 | 57.7 |
| Western Europe | 1.9 | 175 | 4.6 | 6.5 | 98.5 | 44.1 | 57.1 |
| Middle East | 89.5 | 1324 | 34.4 | 124.3 | — | — | 248.2 |
| Africa | 7.9 | 285 | 7.4 | 15.3 | 62.4 | 41.7 | 72.3 |
| Asia and Australia | 6.7 | 299 | 7.8 | 14.5 | 324.4 | 195.0 | 224.0 |
| *of which:* | | | | | | | |
| China | 3.2 | 35 | 0.9 | 4.1 | 166.1 | 106.2 | 114.4 |
| USSR | 7.8 | 1600 | 41.6 | 49.4 | 239.0 | 113.9 | 212.7 |
| Eastern Europe | 0.3 | 19 | 0.5 | 0.8 | 68.7 | 33.0 | 34.6 |
| World | 136.5 | 4208 | 109.4 | 246.3 | 1078.9 | 572.1 | 1064.3 |
| Opec | 105.1 | 1750 | 45.5 | 150.6 | 3.4 | 2.0 | 303.2 |

*Note:* [a]BT    billion tonnes
BTOE  billion tonnes oil equivalent
TCF    trillion cubic feet
*Gas:* 1 TCF = 0.026 BTOE; *Coal:* anthracite and bituminous, 1 tonne = 0.667 TOE; sub-bituminous and lignites, 1 tonne = 0.333 TOE.
*Source:* BP.

to move over long distances. Moreover, reserves of coal and natural gas are neither as concentrated into any one region[5] (Table 2.2), nor as geographically removed from patterns of consumption, as those of oil. Nearly two-thirds of the world's huge coal reserves are in the US, China and the ex-Soviet Union; these are also the three top consumers and producers. The former USSR possesses nearly 40 per cent of the total gas reserves so far identified; it is also the world's largest consumer, producer (and exporter). The Middle East may possess nearly 30 per cent of total gas reserves,[6] but accounts for only 10 per cent of world production; and so far, it has exported very little gas beyond the region.

[5] Some analysts conjecture that the Arctic circumpolar region may eventually turn out to possess a concentration of *gas* resources comparable to that of the Middle East for oil.
[6] Quite apart from differences between national classifications of reserves, such figures are even vaguer than reserve estimates for oil or coal. Most of the gas resources yet 'measured' have been found in exploration for oil.

International trade in coal in 1990 was more than double the tonnage in 1973. The world's natural gas trade had much more than trebled since then. Yet even after close on two decades of expansion in both trades, while energy importers were reducing their dependence on oil, only about 11 per cent of the coal produced in the world and about 17 per cent of the natural gas were being exported at the end of the eighties.

Hence oil still accounts for three-quarters of the total volume of world trade in energy. After being so long the main growth element in energy trade, its substantial decline from 1979 to 1987 far outweighed the increases in coal and gas. As a result, the proportion of energy moving through world trade had fallen from more than 40 per cent of world energy requirements in the mid-seventies to only about 30 per cent by the late eighties.

Even so, oil, transported in bulk over longer distances than most other commodities or manufactures ever travel, has remained the largest single commodity in world seaborne trade. In the seventies, it accounted for 85–90 per cent of international trade in energy, and for no less than 60 per cent of total world seaborne trade. The main reduction in oil trade in the eighties occurred in the long-distance crude oil trade, particularly round the Cape to Western Europe, which needed less imported crude because of North Sea supply. So a higher proportion of the crude exported became what the industry calls 'short-haul', moving along shorter tanker routes to foreign markets. Also, trade in refined products continued to grow, taking a larger share of total oil trade. Products trade, even between regions, generally moves shorter average distances than crude. So the total tonne-mileage of oil movement fell by as much as a half. In spite of this, in 1989 it still accounted for about 38 per cent of total seaborne tonnage and for 44 per cent of total tonne-mileage.

*Break in the trend*

That sharp reduction in world oil trade after the seventies represented an abrupt break with trends established over the whole postwar era, during which the development of this industry had been primarily international, based on the growth (and extension) of world trade in crude oil. From 1950 to 1973, oil trade had grown faster than oil consumption, which itself was growing faster than energy consumption. *Imported* oil was the world's preferred energy option (Table 2.3).

Thus during the first twenty-five years after World War II a steadily increasing proportion of total world energy demand had come to be supplied by trade in oil. That trend was extremely welcome; it facilitated

Table 2.3. *Regional consumption: energy and oil, 1965–1989 (million tonnes oil equivalent)*

| | Commercial primary energy | | Oil | | |
|---|---|---|---|---|---|
| | MTOE[a] | % share of World | MT[a] | % share of World | % share of regional energy use |
| *OECD* | | | | | |
| 1965 | 2471 | 63 | 1101 | 72 | 45 |
| 1973 | 3627 | 61 | 1939 | 69 | 53 |
| 1979 | 3883 | 56 | 1973 | 63 | 51 |
| 1985 | 3738 | 51 | 1589 | 56 | 43 |
| 1989 | 4052 | 51 | 1730 | 56 | 43 |
| *Other market economies* | | | | | |
| 1965 | 362 | 9 | 199 | 13 | 55 |
| 1973 | 620 | 10 | 379 | 14 | 61 |
| 1979 | 856 | 12 | 499 | 16 | 58 |
| 1985 | 1134 | 16 | 587 | 21 | 52 |
| 1989 | 1365 | 17 | 691 | 22 | 51 |
| *CPEs* | | | | | |
| 1965 | 1112 | 28 | 230 | 15 | 21 |
| 1973 | 1668 | 28 | 479 | 17 | 29 |
| 1979 | 2215 | 32 | 652 | 21 | 29 |
| 1985 | 2500 | 34 | 650 | 23 | 26 |
| 1989[b] | 2677 | 33 | 676 | 22 | 25 |
| *World* | | | | | |
| 1965 | 3945 | 100 | 1530 | 100 | 39 |
| 1973 | 5914 | 100 | 2798 | 100 | 47 |
| 1979 | 6916 | 100 | 3125 | 100 | 45 |
| 1985 | 7372 | 100 | 2827 | 100 | 38 |
| 1989 | 8103 | 100 | 3098 | 100 | 39 |

*Notes:* [a] MT    million tonnes
MTOE  million tonnes oil equivalent
[b] Taken as the sum of 1989 consumption in Eastern Europe plus China and 1988 consumption in other CPEs.
*Source:* BP.

faster economic growth everywhere. The additional oil then surging into Western European and Japanese markets, in particular, was priced cheaply enough to undercut any other fuel incrementally available, and its real price steadily went down. Between 1955 and 1979, more than half the additional energy used throughout the world was oil; 36 per cent of it was imported oil. By the mid-seventies, oil trade had risen to account for more than 35 per cent of total world *energy* consumption. In the discontinuity that followed, that share dropped to only about 20 per cent.

In volumes of oil moving, the reversal of trends in world trade has perhaps been only a pause. By the end of the eighties, with demand recovering slowly, trade was turning up again more sharply. Until the embargo on Iraqi and Kuwaiti oil exports was imposed by the United Nations in August 1990, the proportion of oil consumption moving through world trade was once again growing. But oil consumption is still not growing as much as total demand for energy. The shift in oil supply patterns has gone along with complementary changes in the provision of other forms of energy in many countries. The changes that have been taking place in patterns of *total* energy supply across the world seem likely to be longer lasting.

## The overlapping patterns

At any time, international oil trade is mainly a function of geography, and of the radically contrasting patterns of world demand and supply – though the maps of oil are constantly open to revision. Fundamentals of oil geography derive from patterns of underlying petroleum *geology*, which are unchanging; from our imperfect *knowledge* of these patterns, accumulated irregularly during the last century and a quarter through *technology*, which usually changes for the better; and historically, since early this century, from *economic and geopolitical relationships* between nations and international power groups, also constantly changing for better or worse.

Oil is consumed in all the world's 200-odd countries, though up to now mostly in only a few of them. It is produced in commercial quantities in about seventy countries, but again mostly in a few. The degrees of concentration in demand and supply are indeed quite similar. The top five consumers and producers account for more than half of each world total, and the top ten of each for around two-thirds of world consumption and production. These cores of demand and supply overlap, mainly because the US and the ex-Soviet Union were until 1990 the world's largest oil consuming and producing nations. But only three others out of the ten largest consuming countries are large producers; and none of the others among the world's ten largest producers yet consumes much oil (Table 2.4). That geographical dispersion of demand and supply outside the US and the USSR, in the postwar decades, was what generated most of the international oil trade. But

Table 2.4. *Oil: largest producers and consumers, 1989 (million tonnes)*

|  | Consumption | | Production | |
|---|---|---|---|---|
|  | volume | ranking | volume | ranking |
| US | 793 | 1 | 434 | 2 |
| USSR | 435 | 2 | 608 | 1 |
| Japan | 233 | 3 | 1 |  |
| China | 117 | 4 | 138 | 6 |
| West Germany | 108 | 5 | 4 |  |
| Italy | 94 | 6 | 5 |  |
| France | 88 | 7 | 4 |  |
| UK | 81 | 8 | 92 | 8 |
| Canada | 77 | 9 | 80 | 9 |
| Mexico |  |  | 141 | 4 |
| Venezuela |  |  | 99 | 7 |
| Iran |  |  | 142 | 4 |
| Iraq |  |  | 139 | 5 |
| Saudi Arabia |  |  | 257 | 3 |

neither, nowadays, is in any sense isolated from this trade. The US is the world's largest oil importer; the USSR was at times the second largest exporter.

At the beginning of the nineties, the world was consuming about 65 million barrels a day, or 3,100 million tonnes a year. That was just under 40 per cent of all the commercial energy used in the world (Figure 1.3). Its share is down from over 45 per cent in the late 1970s, and will continue to decline proportionately, even presuming that oil consumption goes on slowly rising in absolute terms. But oil is likely to remain the world's most important single source of energy for a few decades into the next century. (Whether some other fuel may then surpass it, which one, and when, have of late become increasingly difficult to guess. Nowadays, each form of energy has to confront its own uncomfortable assortment of environmental complaints, which continue to alter its relative acceptability.)

All of the world's largest oil-consuming nations except China are industrialised countries. All of these but the former Soviet Union are rich ones. They are indeed the most important member countries of the Organisation for Economic Co-operation and Development, the 'rich countries' club' of the postwar generation. These collective labels, along with the political-economic groupings of nations, are now becoming obsolescent. Not all OECD member countries are industrialised or particularly rich. Some developing countries have become relatively rich, not only within Opec but also, perhaps more dependably, around the Pacific Rim.

More than half the world's oil (plus nearly half of all other commercial energy) is consumed by the twenty-four member countries of OECD, which contain only about 15 per cent of the world's population. In 1990 oil represented about 43 per cent of these countries' total energy consumption, as against the 40 per cent or less to which they had earlier hoped to reduce it by that date. (Their self-denying ambition had later been officially postponed by a decade, to the end of the century. Nowadays, the limits that such high consumers of energy are considering may apply to all fossil fuels generating carbon dioxide, not to oil alone.) These rich countries had levelled off their oil consumption during the eighties. Their total energy consumption was about 10 per cent less than they had expected for the end of the decade. National incomes in their economies had risen more in line with their hopes. (But after nearly a decade of macroeconomic virtue, their inflation rates had also risen at least temporarily.)

Even the other rich countries of OECD are dwarfed in oil consumption by the US, whose 5 per cent of world population use a quarter of total world supply. That considerably exceeds the nearly 20 per cent of total consumption used in the seventeen OECD countries of Western Europe. Japan, the second largest national consumer in OECD, uses about 8 per cent of world oil (and its consumption, after a decade of saving energy very effectively, has of late been rising more than in the rest of OECD).

Comparably, what used to be the Soviet Union consumes about 13 per cent of world oil, out of the 19 per cent used by all the formerly Communist economies. China, with four times as much population, uses only 3 per cent of world oil. Soviet oil consumption levelled off during the eighties, with its command economy pushing through a determined switch to natural gas. Indeed, the whole Communist bloc managed to stabilise oil consumption for a decade. Like the OECD countries, their demand in 1989 was only about the same as in 1979. But none of the countries then labelled as 'centrally planned economies' (CPEs) has achieved nearly as much energy conservation as most of the member countries of OECD. With far lower national incomes per head, they consume oil and other fuels much less efficiently.

All the 150 or so other non-Communist nations, comprising 75 per cent of world population, consumed only about 24 per cent of the world's commercial energy in 1989. Their energy consumption per head, varying from only about 125 kilogrammes to say one tonne of oil

Table 2.5. *Commercial energy consumption among rich and poor,*
*1965 and 1989*

| | Kg of oil equivalent per head | | Annual growth rates of total energy consumption (%) | |
|---|---|---|---|---|
| | 1965 | 1989 | 1965–80 | 1980–89 |
| Low- and middle-income economies | 275 | 575 | 6.9 | 4.0 |
| Sub-Saharan Africa | 72 | 73 | 5.7 | 2.5 |
| East Asia | 164 | 487 | 9.4 | 5.1 |
| South Asia | 99 | 197 | 5.7 | 6.1 |
| Europe, Middle East and North Africa | 909 | 1658 | 5.7 | 3.1 |
| Latin America and Caribbean | 514 | 1010 | 6.9 | 2.6 |
| High-income economies | 3641 | 4867 | 3.1 | 1.2 |
| OECD members[a] | 3748 | 5182 | 3.0 | 1.0 |
| Other[b] | 1397 | 2131 | 6.5 | 6.5 |

*Notes:* [a] Except Greece and Portugal, classed as 'upper-middle-income economies'.
[b] Including Saudi Arabia, Kuwait, Qatar and United Arab Emirates.
*Source:* World Bank.

equivalent annually, was tiny compared with over five tonnes per head in the OECD countries (Table 2.5). But these poorer countries' energy consumption went on growing rapidly during a decade and a half of sharply increased and then unstable crude oil prices, while OECD's levelled off in the early eighties, fell, and has recovered only slowly.

Oil has remained the form of energy that nearly all developing countries have mainly relied on to achieve high rates of economic growth, and to maintain them. (For a few, those growth rates have been spectacular; for some, almost zero; in most, impressive but from pitifully low levels). These countries generally use so little per head that they can hardly achieve any energy saving. Also, economic growth is their main priority, well above any concerns about the world environment that richer countries urge upon them. So most of the continuing growth in world energy and oil demand during the nineties is nowadays expected in these poorer economies – provided that they can find the money to pay for it. (That prudent proviso was equally justified at the beginning of the eighties. However, and regardless, many of the developing countries *did* achieve faster growth then, in GDP as well as oil consumption, without ever really appearing able to 'afford' it. Fortunately, in that decade, the rich provided loans as well as virtuous advice. In the nineties, bankers are less eager to press such 'sovereign loans' on poor countries.)

## Where oil is – and isn't

It is customary, and may ultimately become crucial, to contrast the geographical pattern of world oil consumption with that of oil reserves, because the two differ so radically. Where the oil is known to exist under the soil can be illustrated on maps of the world that are quite unlike any projection to which one is accustomed (Figure 2.2a).[7] It might be equally instructive to draw another map illustrating relative consumption patterns, blown up in quite the opposite way. But if one did, everywhere except the OECD countries and Russia would shrivel out of recognition, and the world's most important oil-exporting region would effectively disappear.

However, consumption is a day-to-day voracious appetite. Reserves are an imperfectly assessed stock-in-trade, drawn from underlying resources. In between the two, in practice, two other elements are interposed. The first is supply *capacity*, a matrix of current mechanical access to that underlying stock. The second is *current production*, the extent to which the industry chooses to use that capacity. Geographical patterns of capacity and production also differ significantly from that of world oil consumption. But today, they do not differ from it quite as much as they did before the 'Opec decade' (Figure 2.2b). So far in the industry's history, oil capacity and production patterns have never differed from the consumption pattern nearly as much as the pattern of reserves does.

The concepts of fuel resources and reserves, which are complex even to define, are discussed in Appendix 1 of this book. In practical terms, they are relevant mainly for the medium-term supply possibilities outlined later in Chapter 10. But even the limited portion of world oil resources that the industry has so far discovered and identified as 'recoverable' is huge (Box 2A). At the end of 1992 the 'proved reserves' of conventional oil – usually defined in the industry as 'those quantities which geological and engineering information indicate with reasonable certainty can be recovered in the future from known reservoirs under existing economic and operating conditions'[8] – were estimated to be about 136 billion tonnes, or just under a trillion barrels.

---

[7] British Petroleum pioneered this mapping of world oil patterns in its annual *Statistical Review* of the industry, using steadily more ingenious graphics. (It used the form of map followed here until 1989.)

[8] Here cited from BP's *Statistical Review*, 1991. Definitions of recoverability vary considerably between oil-producing countries. US definitions, which are the most precise, exclude oil which is not in fields already developed or known to exist in fields contiguous to these, and make no allowances for expected improvements in technology.

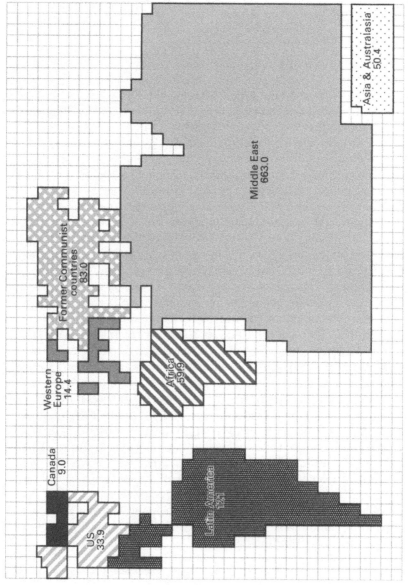

Figure 2.2a. Oil reserves (billion barrels), 1990, by regions: map redrawn to show Middle East predominance.

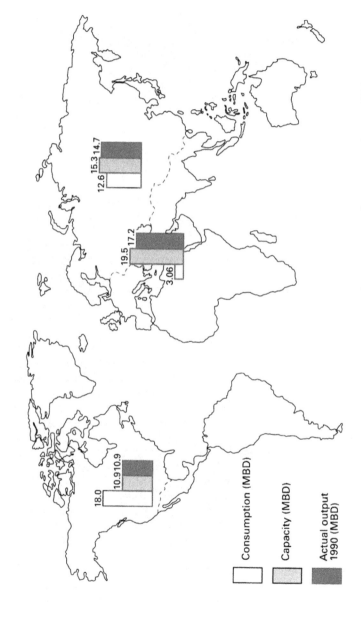

Figure 2.2b. Oil consumption and production capacity, 1989, and output, 1990, by regions. (*Source*: BP.)

## Box 2A.   **Where oil is found**

Oil and gas were formed prehistorically from organic marine sediments under calm seas protecting them from decomposition by oxygen. Over millions of years, some of these sediments were converted by anaerobic bacterial action, heat and pressure into source rocks for hydrocarbons. A sedimentary *basin* is an area under which petroleum source sediments could have been deposited.

Most of the hydrocarbons formed in source rocks gradually escaped into more porous and permeable 'reservoir rock' strata nearby, where oil drilling *may* reach them. Any form of trap within these rock strata in which oil and gas migrating upwards are sealed by some impermeable layer of 'caprock' (or, in some Arctic areas, of permafrost) is known as a *reservoir*. One or more reservoirs formed in the same trapping circumstances constitute an oil or gas *field*. Within a sedimentary basin, there may be one or more petroleum *provinces* containing oil or gas fields.

'Worldwide, there are about 600 sedimentary basins where source rock could have formed. About 200 of these are virtually unexplored, generally because of difficult physical and environmental circumstances. Another 240 have been explored, but there have been no commercial finds. The final 160 have yielded petroleum, but only 26 of them have yielded significant amounts; a mere 7 basins account for 65 per cent of total discovered petroleum.'[a] Studies for the US Geological Survey suggest that 'no new major basins (that is, with 20 billion barrels or more of recoverable oil) remain to be discovered'.[b]

In order to develop the oil production now taking place worldwide, exploration had to take place in all the unproductive sedimentary basins tested and found wanting across the world; in all the producing basins that did not yield significant oil; and even now, in the significantly productive basins, in plenty of places that turn up mostly dry holes. For the oil industry as a whole, this unsuccessful exploration is an unavoidable cost of continuing production worldwide. Eventually, the industry's total revenues from production are called upon to cover all these costs. But most of the costs of unsuccessful exploration, by definition, have been incurred where petroleum is *not* found, even later.

Persuading host governments to share those costs of exploring unsuccessfully elsewhere has always been difficult for international companies. (Some governments felt they were being called upon to contribute to the cost of dry holes across the US, drilled to maintain a large fringe of uneconomic high-cost production, protected from the competition of their own exports.) In the nineties – when a wider range of governments is engaging in various kinds of joint petroleum ventures with foreign companies – such arguments will continue to be heard.

[a] E.C. Macrae and J.E. Evered, *Exploring for Oil and Gas* (US Energy Administration, 1984).
[b] C.D. Masters et al., 'World resources of crude oil, natural gas, natural bitumen, and shale oil', in *Proceedings of the 12th World Petroleum Congress* (Wiley, 1987).

Those proved reserves of oil represented about 45 years' world production at the 1992 rate. This latest global reserves-to-production (R/P) ratio[9] was far higher than during the 'OPEC decade' (Table 2.6). In 1973, the world's proved reserves had been equivalent to about 30 years' production; by 1979, to only about 27 years' production. The ratio increased during the eighties partly because exploration had continued to discover new oil; and to a greater extent because the estimates of reserves in existing oilfields had been revised upwards very considerably. Also, the rate at which oil was being drawn from those reserves had not increased. Production in 1990 was no higher than in 1979, after having been lower for ten years. So the 'stock' of reserves left represented a higher ratio to the current 'turnover' of production.

As a stock known to be readily available, any of those world R/P ratios would have sounded ample enough. Globally, they are. At this point in what some American historian may eventually call the industry's 'mid-passage', it is the *location* of oil reserves, and their concentration in the Middle East and a few other regions, that complicate matters for the industry and the world's consumers.

Out of perhaps 40,000 oilfields in the world, just over 300 'giant' fields are reckoned to contain up to 75 per cent of the recoverable conventional oil yet discovered. (A giant field is one defined as having originally contained a minimum of 500 million barrels of recoverable oil or a billion barrels in place.) Almost all those giant fields had been found by the beginning of the 1970s. Among them, thirty-nine 'super-giants' (each having originally contained at least 5 billion barrels recoverable) account for between a third and a half of all the oil resources yet discovered and proven as reserves.

However, it is the geographical concentration of oil resources that matters more geopolitically than their concentration in field size. The Middle East accounts for twenty-seven of the super-giant fields and for three-quarters of all the giant fields. Indeed, some 66 per cent of the world's proved oil reserves, over 660 billion barrels at the end of 1992, lie under the Middle East. Another 11 per cent, over 100 billion barrels, are owned by the rest of the Opec countries (Box 2A). But at the beginning of the nineties, the Middle East appeared to have under 30 per cent of world production capacity, and the whole of Opec only about 40 per cent.

The pattern of current production, the extent to which world capacity

[9] This ratio is frequently expressed as a number of years' production. Although this is not inaccurate, it can be misleading. The years of production measured are at the current year's rate. If the production rates are growing, the reserves would cover significantly fewer years' output. The R/P is strictly just a numerical ratio, not a number of anything.

Table 2.6. *Oil reserves to production ratios, 1979 and 1990 (number of years' supply at current production rates)*

|  | 1979 | 1990 |
|---|---|---|
| World | 27.3 | 43.4 |
| World excluding Opec | 15.8 | 16.1 |
| USSR | 15.5 | 13.9 |
| China | 25.5 | 22.7 |
| World excluding Opec, USSR, China and Eastern Europe | 9.6 | 18.6 |
| US | 8.6 | 10.3 |
| Canada | 12.8 | 10.9 |
| Mexico | 57.0 | 49.9 |
| Norway | 40.9 | 12.2 |
| UK | 26.3 | 5.6 |
| Non-Opec LDCs | 10.9 | 43.4 |
| Opec | 38.6 | 87.2 |
| Middle East |  | over 100 |
| UAE: |  |  |
| Abu Dhabi | } 44.0 { | over 100 |
| Other emirates |  | 36.6 |
| Iran | 50.1 | 81.6 |
| Iraq | 24.4 | over 100 |
| Kuwait | 75.1 | over 100 |
| Qatar | 20.3 | 27.8 |
| Saudi Arabia | 47.8 | over 100 |
| Algeria | 22.7 | 21.8 |
| Libya | 30.8 | 46.5 |
| Gabon | 6.7 | 8.0 |
| Nigeria | 20.7 | 27.1 |
| Ecuador | 15.1 | 13.9 |
| Venezuela | 21.1 | 71.0 |
| Indonesia | 16.5 | 20.5 |

*Sources:* BP, OGJ and Opec.

was actually being used, differed yet again. Little more than a quarter of world oil production in 1990 was in the Middle East, and not much over 35 per cent from the whole of Opec. At those rates, reserves in the whole of Opec would have covered nearly ninety years' production, and the Middle East had R/P ratios averaging more than 100:1! Yet nearly two-thirds of world production was occurring elsewhere, from the remaining quarter of world reserves. That afforded non-Opec oil an average R/P ratio of only about 16:1.

Even that non-Opec ratio of stocks to production has not of late been uncomfortable in terms of current performance (for anybody, perhaps, but Opec). For each oil-producing region, this ratio, after all, summarises an aggregate of producers' choices. The 16:1 ratio signifies only that producers outside Opec are choosing to draw down the reserves that they are prepared to declare as proved by an average of about 6–7 per cent each year. That is not out of line with the rules of thumb ratios that producers in the longest-established oil industries such as the American and Soviet ones would traditionally have thought worth while in deciding how much to produce from any given total of reserves. Indeed, the R/P ratio for all non-Opec producing areas has hardly altered over the past decade. The US ratio has been around 10:1 ever since production there peaked in 1970. It should be borne in mind that producers are often very conservative in most of the reserve estimates that they publish. Also, the proportion that they consider recoverable is gradually being revised upwards as reservoir technology advances.

Changes in some of these R/P ratios during the last decade may be more significant, though these too arose from a variety of factors. One major reason why the ratios in Opec more than doubled was that large increases in reserves were reported in many member nations. But another, of comparable importance, was that their production fell sharply. The decline in the ratios of producers outside Opec, essentially for the opposite reason, may be of greater significance. Maintaining any chosen R/P ratio *during a period of rising output* remains a demanding exercise for the fortunate producers involved. Every year, it requires their exploration to succeed in finding significantly more oil than they produce.[10] Non-Opec output rose rapidly during the eighties, faster than their annual additions to reserves. So their average R/P ratio was slipping downwards throughout the decade following 1978. Ever since the late seventies, most non-Opec oil production has been operated as close to full capacity as its operators have found practicable.

Outside Opec as well as inside, of course, reserves are not spread evenly; and the rates at which reserves are currently being depleted vary considerably across non-Opec oil supply. The largest and most mature non-Opec producers have the lowest ratios. By 1990 the USSR, the world's largest producer, was operating at a reserves-to-production

---

[10] A reserves-to-production ratio is measured as the reserves remaining at the end of any year, divided by the production in that year. When annual production is rising, in order to maintain any given R/P ratio the producer will need to prove additional reserves of the same multiple of the year's increase, over and above replacement of the reserves drawn down during the current year.

ratio of 14:1, and the US ratio was down to 10:1.[11] The US ratio is fairly stable, but the USSR's was run down severely for two decades. Both countries have considerable reason to be anxious about their industries – but immediately, more about sustaining their current rates of output than about their R/P ratios. In the former Soviet Union, oil production may have peaked and is temporarily at least in quite sharp decline, facing rising costs even to maintain capacity in being. In the US, output has been in decline for two decades – perhaps irreversibly, at the levels of price currently expected and given the environmental restraints that preclude exploration in some 'frontier' areas. (The most notable decline in non-Opec R/P ratios outside the USSR has occurred in the North Sea, particularly the UK sector, where governments have favoured more rapid depletion of reserves than in Norway. The most notable increases were in Mexico and a large assortment of other developing countries.)

On the other side of the world oil maps, the extraordinarily high R/P ratios for most of Opec, essentially concentrated under the Gulf, are for any *current* purposes largely irrelevant. (They will probably – not quite certainly – become fully relevant early next century.) All the main Gulf producers, and some other Opec member countries, reported huge additions to their proved reserves during the late 1980s. Few details or definitions of these reserve estimates were published, but the additions appeared for the most part to have come from the 'up-rating' of earlier conservative estimates for the same fields, rather than finding many new ones. Initially, elsewhere in the world, there was some scepticism about those additions – including suggestions that the new reserve figures were disclosed mainly in order to boost the various countries' short-term production quotas within Opec. (But the higher reserve estimates have not often been challenged technically as exaggerated. Some Western oilmen believe they could still turn out to be conservative.)

Whether technically or politically estimated (or both), few of those huge additions made any difference whatsoever to these Gulf countries' *immediate* circumstances as oil exporters. For the nineties, selling enough oil to raise current production levels back towards present and planned capacity – at prices high enough to restore oil revenues – may be what will matter to the main producers in Opec. Successful or not, that process could not draw down Gulf Opec's R/P ratios to anywhere near the world average. Even the highest recent projections of world demand by the early years of next century[12] appear to call for pro-

[11] The two countries' R/P ratios are not directly comparable. US reserve figures include only proved reserves. Soviet figures appear to include what in the US would be ranked as proved probable, and some possible reserves.
[12] For example, OECD/IEA's '$21 constant real price case' in *World Energy Outlook to 2005* (OECD, 1991), which projected demand for Middle East output in 2005 reaching 46 MBD.

duction between now and then of less than a third of the Middle East reserves that had been proved by the end of 1990.

The only additions to Gulf reserves that can usefully affect current production there during this decade are certain recent discoveries of light, low-sulphur crudes that may improve the *quality* of some member countries' export offtake. Most of the main Gulf export crudes have been medium in gravity, but with higher sulphur content than refiners prefer.[13] Most of the non-Opec crudes developed in the last two decades – along with some Opec crudes discovered outside the Gulf, notably in Venezuela – are lighter and 'sweeter' (i.e. with lower sulphur content). This was one competitive disadvantage for the Gulf in selling to refiners with a wide range of crudes to choose from. Now Saudi Arabia has discovered several new fields containing much lighter and lower sulphur content crudes than most in its older-established reserves, and is developing another light crude field that it already had 'on the shelf'. Some known but undeveloped fields that could be developed in Iraq, as and when production there is restored and allowed to expand, might also offer crudes with relatively low sulphur content.

Such minor changes in quality might improve the Gulf's potential competitive situation. In terms of quantity, nothing that happens there could do so – unless its competitors elsewhere fail to maintain *their* output levels.

---

[13] Oil gravity as measured by the American Petroleum Institute (API) is defined as '(141.5 / specific gravity at 60 degrees Fahrenheit) minus 131.5'. It thus works in the opposite way from measures of the ordinary specific gravity of a liquid. Heavy crudes that may be almost too viscous to move through a pipeline without heating have low API gravities, of say 10–20 degrees. Very light crudes with high natural yields of the lightest fractions boiled off by simple distillation have high API gravities, say 40 degrees or more.

# CHAPTER 3

# Cost: concepts and comparisons

As well as their prodigious reserves, the main Gulf producers have so far enjoyed lower production costs for oil than those of any other energy in the world. These two elements of their rich natural endowment are distinct, though associated. The amount of oil in place in any reservoir depends on the total volume and the porosity of reservoir rock that it contains. The proportion of this resource that can be recovered, and the rates of production one can achieve from it, depend mainly on:

the permeability of the rock by which oil can flow through the reservoir, and the viscosity of the particular oil contained there; and

the natural energy contained in the reservoir that drives the oil up towards the bottom of the well, such as surrounding or underlying water; gas compressed within a 'cap' above the oil in the pores of the reservoir rock; or gas bubbles forming within the oil reservoir.

But many other factors also affect costs. Not all the world's super-giant fields have low production costs: two of those most recently discovered, Tenghiz in the former USSR and the much-debated Chicontapec in Mexico,[1] up to the time this book was completed, had not proved economic even to begin developing.

It is hardly surprising that the Middle East's lion's share of world reserves has so far been developed more cheaply than the smaller reserves elsewhere. The huge concessionary areas granted to companies from the beginning, often nationwide, allowed 'unitisation' of the development of large reservoirs under single management, without the wasteful sub-division that had often occurred in the history of the US oil

---

[1] Chicontapec, discovered in 1974, is the main source of controversy about Mexican petroleum reserves. It has alternatively been credited by some geologists as a super-giant with 12 billion barrels of crude oil in place, and dismissed by others as an area containing a lot of small shallow fields likely to have an average productivity of only about 10 b/d. The national company Pemex has not yet produced crude from it, and may never do so.

industry. The large proportions of Gulf output coming from super-giant and giant fields would in any case have allowed straightforward technical economies of scale in pipelines, gas separation plants, and many other ancillary surface facilities. But other factors making for low costs of production from much of the Gulf matter more in any short run than its abundance of reserves. These cost advantages derive essentially from a group of inherent natural advantages found in combination almost nowhere else.

Arab producers in the Southern Gulf tap wide areas of thick sedimentary strata in the Gulf geosyncline. To the north, Iraqi and Iranian structures are folded and more broken, but have comparable sedimentary 'pay-zones' and extremely high rates of oil flow. Some of the Gulf's giant fields are still on 'natural drive' by surrounding water, though in parts of the largest such as Ghawar, seawater now has to be injected (after desalination) to maintain the underground reservoir pressure, and Iran's largest fields need gas injection on a large scale. Most of the giant Middle East fields are onshore, close to Gulf terminals – though in recent years, following military confrontations, other Gulf exporting governments as well as Iraq have invested in long overland pipelines to bypass the Straits of Hormuz. Producing strata under the Gulf generally lie somewhat deeper than the average well depths for development elsewhere, and in deep drilling costs per foot rise very sharply. But this depth factor is far outweighed by the region's other advantages in technical cost.

The most important technical factor affecting oil production costs is productivity per well. Most Gulf producing countries enjoy *average* productivities across the whole of their national production that are achieved only in a few individual oilfields anywhere else. In 1992, Saudi Arabia produced about 8.2 MBD from 1,400 wells, an average well productivity of 6,000 b/d; Iran averaged roughly 5,000 b/d, Iraq and Kuwait (before the Gulf war and UN embargo) each about 2,500–3,000 b/d.[2] Outside Opec, only the North Sea, Alaska and Mexico have at times achieved average well flow rates anywhere near those (and inside Opec, for that matter, only Libya and Nigeria are remotely comparable). By contrast, in the US, more than 600,000 producing wells have an average productivity of about twelve barrels a day; and the former USSR's average per well had probably never exceeded 80 b/d.

---

[2] Traditionally, Iraq and Iran used to have the highest well productivities in the region, though from fields farther inland than in the Southern Gulf. In 1992, Iraqi production was still limited by a UN embargo upon its exports; Kuwait and Iran were recovering from damage to their oil facilities in the two wars with Iraq.

*The sequence of costs*

There are three main stages of cost in oil production, incurred in an overlapping sequence. First comes exploration, which includes two layers of cost: not only a direct cost chargeable to each operation, but in addition a continuing overhead cost for the whole industry. In any particular area, exploration usually takes a year or two of preliminary surveys from the surface before the sedimentary strata beneath are considered worth drilling, and as long again before any oil is found. After discovery, further detailed seismic surveys and perhaps more exploration drilling may be necessary, followed by a few appraisal wells to delineate the reservoir before one can decide whether it will be economic to develop production from it (Box 3A). Whether the producer treats this specific exploration as part of the investment in the particular field that may be developed is partly a matter of accounting practice.

However, in economic terms that specific exploration expenditure is not the whole exploration cost of the oil production actually developed. In order to develop the oil production now taking place worldwide, exploration has taken place in the many unproductive sedimentary basins tested and found wanting across the world; in all the producing basins that did not yield significant oil production; and even now, in the significantly productive basins, in plenty of places that continue, much of the time, to turn up mostly dry holes. Any company operating worldwide may regard that unsuccessful exploration as a continuing overhead cost of its total production everywhere – comparable perhaps to the scientific research constantly required in advance to maintain technical progress in manufacturing.[3] In any case, the company's, or at any rate the industry's, total revenues from production will eventually have to cover all those costs.

The second stage, capital investment in developing any field once it has been discovered and appraised, is usually an order of magnitude higher than the direct costs of exploration that led to it. Drilling risks continue even after the investment decision: in the US, up to 20 per cent even of development wells turn out dry. But in general the technical risks in oilfield development are far lower than in exploration. By comparison with the casino gamble of exploration, development involves far higher stakes but much better odds (Box 3A). The commercial risks are comparable with those of any other highly capitalised

---

[3] The French oil industry indeed calls exploration 'recherche'. The term goes elegantly to the essence, like its phrase for the whole process of petroleum and other mineral extraction, 'la mise en valeur des richesses du sous-sol'.

## Box 3A.   Exploration

Development of any oil or gas field requires several, sometimes many, years of previous exploration before the successful discovery. Given recent rapid progress in supercomputer interpretation of data from three-dimensional seismic surveys, some experts believe such surveys can now at times directly identify the presence of hydrocarbons from the surface. But, so far, the indications they offer cannot be confirmed without drilling, which is where the heaviest exploration costs begin. From the first 'wildcat' exploration well onwards, an explorer has to venture very large expenditures with a continuing high risk of finding nothing.

It is often said that only one exploration well out of ten finds oil, and perhaps only one out of forty finds oil worth developing commercially. Such 'average success ratios' are cited to demonstrate – correctly – that petroleum exploration is a high-risk business. Beyond that, published success ratios mean nearly nothing worldwide. Only a few countries publish drilling statistics on any comparable basis. The definitions of exploration wells are seldom clear or consistent. And the criteria of success vary wildly.

Almost the only rigorous statistics available come from the US, where indeed more of the world's drilling has always taken place than in any other single region. There, in recent years, only 10–15 per cent of 'new field test wildcats' have discovered any oil at all. In the early 1980s, only about one US wildcat in a hundred was finding 'significant oil' (by the very modest US standards).[a] In the North Sea, one of the few other petroleum provinces where exploration statistics are adequate (though not quite comparable), only one of the first twenty-seven wildcats drilled found commercial oilfields. But during the seventies and eighties, the average success ratio of new field wildcats discovering oil was about 20–25 per cent.

Elsewhere, nearly all oil industries are immature compared with the US; and neither historical statistics nor current data are adequate or comparable. Opec governments report the numbers of wells completed in their countries for each of oil and gas, and the number that are dry holes – in 1990, 134 were dry out of a total of 1,657 drilled. However they hardly distinguish between wildcats, extensions to existing pools, development wells, and even wells for gas or water injection. In many countries, a few of them in Opec, the actual operations are conducted by international companies, in association with national companies. These would be perfectly capable of producing adequate data about exploration and its successes. But they often appear no more anxious than host governments to reveal these results.

The USSR in 1989 reported drilling about 24,500 wells, not so far short of the 31,500 drilled in the US. But from abroad there was no way of distinguishing exploration wells from others, or of really assessing the success ratios achieved – save to note that up to the late 1980s the Soviet industry was still managing to find super-giant gasfields in remote locations offshore.

[a] 'Significant oil' there being defined as discoveries confirmed after six years' production history as promising an *ultimate* recovery of at least 1 million barrels of oil. As of 1989, the latest data available covering that much production history was for discoveries up to 1982.

business investment abroad. The political risks used to be higher; nowadays, perhaps, they are ceasing to be.

Once the investment decision is made, it may take another two or three years to develop even a medium-sized field to its full planned 'plateau' capacity.[4] Outside the Middle East, that plateau capacity will be planned for say 5–7 years; afterwards, the total production declines gradually over time (Box 3B). Typically, a field will be capable of continuing production for twenty years or more. But under the time profile of development and production planned at the outset, more than half of the cumulative production would probably be recovered in the first ten years. This is as much a matter of economics, and of the developer's 'cost of waiting', as of the volume of reserves involved.[5] Any investment required later to delay the eventual production decline can be appraised and decided upon as and when it becomes practicable. In some cases, it may be decided from the beginning to develop fields in more than one stage. But in general the developer of any field (particularly offshore where the investment is usually higher) seeks the fastest extraction of reserves that can be made at the outset, to gain the best economic return over time from the original investment decision.

Oil production accounting depends crucially upon the technique of discounted cash flow analysis, and the intertemporal comparisons this facilitates. The technique began to be accepted throughout the US oil industry during the 1940s, and by the international companies during their surge of postwar expansion. It enables the value of cash outflows in investment early on to be equated with revenue inflows (net of operating costs) from production generated later, according to the cost of waiting, expressed as the discount rate that any given investor applies. This rate will be the percentage return that the investor can expect from other investments of comparable risk. For international comparisons of oil costs, the basic analysis was first fully defined in a 1965 Ph.D. thesis at the Massachusetts Institute of Technology by Paul D. Bradley, later professor of economics at the University of British Columbia. (MIT's Energy Laboratory, under Professor Morris Adelman, has been the world's foremost academic centre of research

---

[4] In principle, each production well in a field begins to flow at peak productivity and declines slowly over time. Since additional wells are steadily being drilled, offsetting decline in the earlier ones, total field production builds up to a peak and is maintained on a plateau for as long as new wells brought in cover the accumulating decline of those drilled earlier. Then the total field production comes off plateau and declines exponentially over time, until it reaches an 'economic limit' when current proceeds cease to cover current costs, and is shut down.

[5] Oilmen developing the field are aware that the reserves will almost always turn out to be larger than their original estimate, thus prolonging the working life of production there somewhat beyond the twenty years or so usually assumed to begin with. This is unlikely to make much difference to the original plan or investment decision – if only because at any significant discount rate, differences in cash flows from fifteen years onwards have very little effect upon the initial appraisal of any investment.

## Box 3B.    Production

**Real terms**

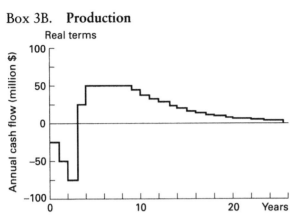

Once an oilfield is discovered and its likely reserves are initially appraised, production is usually planned over a working life of say 20–25 years. (For small fields, depletion may be planned over much shorter periods.) In practice, the working life of most fields stretches out longer than was initially planned, because the reserves turn out to be larger than the first appraisal. But the time value of money, reflected in discount rates, renders income and costs long distant in the future much less relevant to the initial investment decision.

From that decision, it may take 2–4 years to construct and install production facilities and drill the number of production wells decided upon. In principle, each well completed begins at its peak production rate, which then slowly begins to decline. As more and more wells continue to be brought in, total production from the field builds up in the first few years, then reaches a 'plateau' lasting say 5–6 years before it too slides into gradual decline. The field development plan usually provides to produce about 75 per cent of the reserve (as originally appraised) within the first ten years.

The investment is highly concentrated into the first few years before any oil can be produced and sold. (The planning also covers investment later to offset production decline, for example to maintain underground reservoir pressure by water or gas injection. But that will be mostly in the future, when output has built up net inward cash flows too.) The producer's return, adjusted for inflation and discounted for the time value of money, is essentially on the heavy 'front end' investment.

**Discounted**

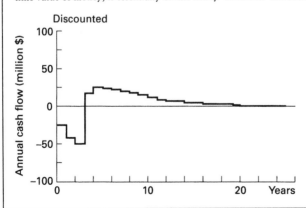

into petroleum economics since the early 1960s.)[6] Annual cash outflows to develop production, first investment and later operating costs, are discounted from the investment decision in 'year zero' onwards at the investor's chosen rate. So are the cash inflows of revenues from crude sold, once production begins. The same discount factor, applied to production from the field over time, provides a discounted total of barrels to compare with the discounted net cash outflows of the venture. Another physical factor reinforces the discounting: the actual decline rate of field production from its plateau level, once this sets in.[7]

Oil production costs anywhere thus have a characteristic 'time profile', associated with high investment at the outset to find and develop the capacity chosen; and with the third stage of costs, current operating costs that remain fairly stable annually, and thus become very low *per barrel* while output from a field is on its plateau, but rise steadily later as annual output moves into decline. Once production starts, all the 'front-end' investment becomes a sunk cost. Continuing production involves only current out-of-pocket operating costs; maintenance, involving limited continuing investment to 'work over' existing wells and replace some of those, successively, taken out of operation, so long as the reserves – and crude prices – justify this; and, where relevant, any percentage royalty on the current revenues per barrel of output that the producer may be committed to pay the subsoil titleholder or government. (Similar time profiles of cash flows, with heavy initial investment and low operating costs, apply to several of the other energy industries with which oil competes. In nuclear and above all hydro-electric power generation, investment is even relatively higher and operating costs are relatively lower still than in oil. Deep-mined coal, with its high proportion of continuing and often inflating labour costs of current operation, is the main exception.)

## Costs outside the Gulf

So far, this discussion of comparative advantages and of timing in oil production costs has been only qualitative, not quantitative. This is partly because precise and reliable figures are hard to come by; but also because the whole concept of production cost tends to be hazy, depending upon the purposes for which the producer (or his accountants) may wish to use it.

[6] P. G. Bradley, *The Economics of Crude Petroleum Production* (North-Holland, 1967).
[7] During the period on plateau, the decline is steadily offset by new wells coming into production – outlays on which have to be set against the cash inflows from sales revenues. (These outlays are sometimes classified as further investment, sometimes as operating costs.)

Whenever the development of any new oilfield is announced, nowadays, some estimates of the total capital investment expected and the rate of production it is hoped to achieve are usually published. However, such announcements seldom specify the development planned in much detail. Eventually, when production begins, those total figures may be given again, in hindsight. More often than not, they differ from those given earlier. This is seldom simply because of inflation in the meantime. (Indeed, in recent years, capital requirements per barrel of output, at any rate outside Opec, have quite often come down in real terms.) It is because a good deal of what was initially planned will have been altered in practice. The alterations quite often include the volume of production that it proves practicable to develop (and nearly always, as a matter of course, reserve estimates for the field).

Such total figures, announced quite honestly, therefore seldom allow clear cost comparisons with other current projects. Nobody but the producing organisation involved is likely to know enough about the project, and its technical requirements, to offer general comparisons. (Oil reservoir engineers behave individually. So, for that matter, do oil reservoirs.) At any one time, the projects in train that are publicised can suggest approximate ranges of capital requirements for production being developed in particular regions. But these can only be very broadly indicative, because the developments involved differ so much in detail.

Such comparisons are usually set out in terms of the *capital investment required per daily barrel (db) of the plateau production* to be developed from new capacity, sometimes called its 'investment intensity'. That is a definable outlay of hard cash, though the drilling, reservoir management and surface facilities involved vary widely from one development to another (and 'ancillary investment' can at times cover a multitude of sins).

Of late, investment plans reported for *new* commercial production in the OECD and non-Opec developing countries where development has been concentrated since 1973, much of it offshore or in hostile environments, have shown averages of $11,000 to $16,000/db of the production planned. The upper extremes of the range (excluding one or two experimental or partly subsidised ventures), some $30,000/db, and the lower, $5,000 or less, were both as it happens offshore in the UK North Sea.[8]

[8] The highest costs were $30,000/db for Alba, a UK North Sea field promising 70,000 b/d of oil at plateau level. The lowest were for small 'short-life' fields that can be produced without platforms and tied in to existing pipeline systems. For example, the tiny Staffa and Chanter fields beginning to be developed in the North Sea in 1991 appeared to involve investments of only $5,000/db or less. ('The costs of future North Sea oil production', *Global Energy Report*, Centre for Global Energy Studies, London, January/February 1992, p. 31.)

Sometimes such comparisons are expressed in terms of *unit cost per barrel* – or in terms of the ruling crude price at which such new capacity will become worth developing. These may seem easier to understand, but have little meaning unless the components of cost are precisely defined and sorted out. (Quite often, oil companies publish vague estimates or graphs of both kinds of cost comparison, blurring any clear distinction between the two.) Details of specific out-of-pocket *operating costs*, the only other figures of fairly hard cash in all these comparisons, are seldom disclosed, but are perhaps more practicable to estimate from outside.[9]

From those two sets of cash outlays, any reckoning of comparative unit costs per barrel will depend on two factors – the discount rates that each producer applies, and the decline rate of production expected for the field. The discount rates applied will vary according to the 'normal' rates of return that different developers expect. When oil companies are developing the field, also, the rate of return they seek will normally be net of the royalties payable on revenues, and the tax rates on their profits. When a national company develops the field, it or its host government may ignore these. An economist seeking to compare costs in different regions, likewise, may exclude all payments to government from the strictly technical costs. (That does not mean ignoring the difference that tax regimes and levels of 'government take' in different countries can make. It is a question of trying to build up 'like with like' supply costs on a standardised basis for comparisons between different oil-producing regions.)

Such questions of comparison are constantly posed by observers and analysts *outside* the industry; less often by those inside. Analysts inside the industry are normally concerned with particular fields that they (or their immediate competitors) are developing. They often know most of the relevant details and can estimate the rest directly; and have little incentive to publicise the details of any particular field. (The readers likely to be interested analytically will usually include the tax departments of one or more governments.) Their past history of operations in many different regions and circumstances allow them to call on invaluable technical and economic databases. They hardly need hypothetical

---

[9] In operation, the out-of-pocket continuing costs begin with labour, which involves high but relatively stable annual salaries; services and maintenance, which nowadays will often be done by outside contractors, where competitive rates for the jobs become known; and insurance for what is often a hazardous activity – unless the producer 'self-insures', bearing the unavoidable cost of risk as an internal contingency rather than a cash outlay.

'standard fields' for their planning; nor are they necessarily interested in other, more academic concepts of cost.[10]

The 'natural' decline curves expected in production from every petroleum reservoir derive primarily from its technical characteristics, determining the loss of underground pressure as cumulative output from the field increases over time. The decline rate that is actually experienced in every field reflects these underlying technical conditions; but also a history of commercial decisions. It is strongly affected by the sequence of producers' earlier development plans, and their later, continuing decisions about *how* to go on depleting whatever reserves remain to them.

In the US domestic industry, from which as ever most of the reliable data becomes available for analysis, the average decline rate is generally assessed as about 10 per cent per year. Not surprisingly, that is very close to the reciprocal of the country's reserves/production ratio. In the US, more simply than elsewhere, the R/P ratio reflects the number of years' 'stock' that, on the average, domestic producers choose and can manage to keep in hand. (Nowadays, they cannot always do so, year by year; thus national output is declining.) The UK North Sea, to take another example, had at the beginning of the nineties the lowest R/P ratio published for any significant oil-producing region. The decline curves occurring in production there are said to be unusually steep, as most of the larger fields have come off plateau. Broadly similar relationships between R/P ratios and the decline curves in oil production are found in most producing countries outside Opec. Developers everywhere else, during the last two decades, have been anxious to produce any oil reservoirs they find as soon as possible, allowing for conservation standards. That has usually also meant as economically as possible. Since the mid-seventies, non-Opec crude has been relatively easy to sell.

*In the Gulf, plateaus extend ...*

One important geographical distinction comes in here too. Plans for the development of any oil discovered outside the Middle East are generally calculated to deplete the *whole* reserve that the field is initially appraised

---

[10] In principle, the 'economic cost' of production in an extractive industry such as oil should also include 'user cost', the present value of the resource forgone when a barrel is produced today rather than in the future. This concept is a fruitful source of academic controversy between economists concerned with petroleum and other minerals. The industry is seldom directly concerned with it, though there is an active market in buying and selling the rights to produce already known reserves in North America; and elsewhere, given government consent, rights can also be 'assigned' between companies.

to contain, within about 20 years. In the Middle East, that has almost never been practicable. The reserves of major fields in the main producing countries of the Gulf are so large that no producer has ever been able to plan depletion of the whole field within the periods customary elsewhere. Even as early as 1949, the Middle East R/P ratio was 65:1, and the reserves appraised were building up much faster than production could be developed. The region's highest output levels so far, in 1973 and 1979, did not bring the ratio there below 45:1. Upward revisions of reserve figures in the late eighties have resulted in extraordinary R/P ratios, now well over 100:1 for all the main producers there.

The region's largest fields, which probably still produce the bulk of Gulf output, have been in operation for many years – for example, in Iraq since 1927 and in Iran since 1937. Among the super-giant fields of the Arabian peninsula, Saudi Arabia's Abqaiq began producing in 1946, and some fields in the complex that was eventually linked to constitute Ghawar, the world's largest, in 1948. Production from Kuwait's Burgan structure, the second largest, dates from 1948. In 1991, it was reckoned that about half of the production capacity in the Gulf had come on stream 30 years ago, and as much as 86 per cent of it over 20 years ago. Though total capacity there greatly increased up to the early seventies, not much more was added later in that decade. During the eighties, capacity in some countries was partly destroyed in war; in others, it was allowed to run down.

The Gulf producers concerned when Middle East fields were initially being discovered and developed were of course not the countries' governments. They were foreign companies, most of whose main business interests in oil were elsewhere. The governments with most influence on their initial investment decisions were the British and French, with imperial interests in and around the region, and the American, whose domestic and other foreign oil-producing interests seemed then of much greater importance to it. Even when the potential importance of Middle East reserves came to be recognised, from the beginning of the 1950s onwards, production there had to be fitted into the international companies' existing and prospective networks of producing capacity and downstream marketing opportunities across the world. There was no prospect of developing these unprecedented reserves within the time-spans chosen in oil development elsewhere.

Companies, and their host governments, appear then to have been concerned mainly with increasing the levels of Gulf production that they could sell abroad without disturbing the rest of their businesses too much, and with the periods over which they could maintain these increasing levels of output. In the early postwar years, production in some of the major fields experienced virtually no natural decline in production at all. Development continued to be extended, sector by sector, but it took a long time to reach plateau level for such huge fields considered as a whole. For reservoir management there, it seemed practicable to postpone longer and longer the date when they might be expected to move off their plateaus. 'Workovers' of existing wells and continued development drilling steadily offset any decline; alternatively, as and whenever it appeared more economical, other fields, discovered already and awaiting development, could be brought in.

The plateaus of production that concessionaires and Gulf governments then had in mind were to run for 15–25 years or more, not the five or six years usually envisaged in developing smaller fields elsewhere – until the end of the century or at any rate the term of the original concessions. In Saudi Arabia for example, as late as the mid-seventies, Aramco and its host government were discussing the technical and economic practicalities of reaching a plateau of 20 MBD in the early 1980s and maintaining it for fifteen years, or one of 25 MBD for eight years. Later, using more optimistic reserve estimates, they considered a plateau of 12 MBD, maintainable until perhaps the year 2014.[11] ('Possible' Saudi reserves were then estimated as 248 billion bbl; 'probable' reserves as 178 billion bbl; 'proven' reserves as 110 billion bbl. At the end of 1991, the Kingdom was reporting 'proven reserves' larger than its highest, 'possible', reserve estimate of 1978. But the level of sustainable capacity that it was considering for the late nineties, perhaps 12 MBD, was no higher than it had contemplated fifteen years before.)

None of the main Gulf exporters has been publishing details of production from particular fields, drawing down their reserves, separately since the early 1980s. Also, the huge upward revisions of national reserves by these exporters in the late 1980s will presumably have raised reserve estimates for most of those largest fields too. A few of the earliest fields developed in Iran and Iraq have passed into history. If one or two of their remaining super-giants, such as Agha Jari and Marun, had not moved off plateau into decline before the 1980s, they probably did so during the two countries' eight-year war, when neither government could afford the investment required to maintain its existing capacity fully. So it is hardly possible to judge from the outside how far depletion of reserves from those northern fields, let alone the extraordinary

[11] United States. Senate Committee on Foreign Relations, *The Future of Saudi Arabian Oil Production*, April 1979.

structures to the south in the 'Arabian platform', has yet proceeded.[12] But some of these fields could only ever be developed sector by sector, sequentially, and Opec has reported that output from the earliest-developed portion of Ghawar *has* now peaked.[13] Most of the region's super-giant fields have been using secondary recovery techniques such as water injection for decades now; lately they have been discussing more complex methods of 'enhanced oil recovery' (EOR). Iranian giant fields need considerably more pressure maintenance (mostly by injecting gas from other fields) than anyone has ever yet managed to organise.

For production capacity in the region as a whole, or for aggregate capacity in some of these nations, the development of a succession of giant fields during the early postwar decades thus served to postpone the prospect of 'coming off plateau' that smaller-scale production developed elsewhere in the world has to reckon with from its beginnings. In the seventies, production in giant fields such as Abqaiq and Safaniya was expected to move into decline during the nineties. As it happened, Gulf production and hence the depletion of reserves there have been much lower in the meantime than was foreseen then, while national reserve estimates have been raised considerably. But from the early eighties onwards, unable to sell all the production from their existing capacity, producers there cut back even their normal maintenance schedules. Some fields were shut in; capacity in others was allowed to move into decline by not drilling enough replacement wells; pressure maintenance plans were postponed. For the first time, moving off the plateaus of total capacity in the Southern Gulf countries began to become a practical consideration.

The concern is not primarily with *depletion* of the huge reserves proven there, a large proportion of which have never been brought into production. (In principle, depletion is no doubt continuing. But so far it has been more than offset by new discoveries, or by further upward revision of reserves in existing fields.) Decline rates in the region's existing *capacity* to produce, not its reserves, are what practically matter.

Moreover, the neglect of investment during that decade when prices fell and reduced Opec revenues seems to have been particularly severe for the Gulf industries' multifarious infrastructure of facilities above ground

[12] In mid-1992, Ghawar reserves were unofficially reported still to be some 70 billion barrels, which was about the same figure as reported in 1975 (though one estimate of the crude 'recoverable' there in 1984 had been as high as 83 billion barrels). Reserves in the huge field, therefore, may have been uprated at least sufficiently to offset sixteen years' production in the meantime. The same report (*PIW*, 25 May 1992), however, indicated reserves for two smaller fields, Berri and Zuluf, of 11 and 8 billion barrels respectively, which were much higher than even the 'recoverable' figures estimated for the same fields in 1984.
[13] Ibrahim A. H. Ismail, 'Opec production capacity: the need for expansion', *Opec Review*, Autumn 1991, pp. 197–214.

– gas/oil separation plants, water injection and pressure maintenance, pipelines and tankage of every kind, export terminals with all their ancillary equipment. Following upon the huge build-up of Gulf production in the late sixties, a large proportion of the oil infrastructure installed up to then may have been reaching the end of its scheduled working life. Most of it never had been replaced; nor was it during the eighties.

In oil production where much of the investment is to maintain capacity, the capital requirements often quoted per daily barrel of *net* additions to capacity have no clear meaning unless one knows the decline rates in existing production. Capital investment develops *gross* additional capacity, part of which will be required simply to hold production level; any *net* addition has to be developed over and above the decline thus offset. Decline rates in capacity are not necessarily published as such; but national rates can be broadly inferred from production statistics, when these are comprehensive and continuous. In the Gulf nowadays, they are neither. That makes development costs there even more difficult to compare with oil investment elsewhere.

Producers throughout the whole industry worldwide seek to maintain their capacity so long as this is practicable and economic; and the capital cost of doing so is no doubt higher everywhere else than in the Gulf. But nowhere else is there such an accumulation of capacity in giant fields that may now, more or less simultaneously, be moving towards decline. Moreover, the Gulf governments are indeed promising a net increase in production capacity – to about 25 MBD by 1995, against some 21 MBD in 1990. The gross additions to capacity involved must be considerably larger than that net increase. For example, an annual decline rate of 5 per cent in capacity would mean that over five years more than 22 per cent of the initial capacity would have to be replaced to keep production level, before providing for the net addition intended. For Gulf capacity of about 21 MBD in 1990, assuming such a decline rate, a net addition of nearly 4 MBD by 1995 might require a total gross addition to capacity of 7.8 MBD, nearly twice the net addition, during the five-year period. In most Opec countries outside the Gulf, decline rates are much higher: in Venezuelan production, perhaps as high as 22 per cent annually. So Opec capital requirements reported per daily barrel of net new capacity may in some countries be several times as high as those per daily barrel of the much larger gross additions to capacity that the programmes will in practice actually require (Table 3.1).

In very few oil industries in or out of Opec, admittedly, are any published statistics of oil capacity and investment adequate to allow clear estimates of the gross capacity that has been added in recent years and what this has cost. Prominent exceptions are, predictably, the US

Table 3.1. *Decline rates in existing production, and the gross additions required for net additions to capacity*[a]

| Annual decline rate (per cent) | Capacity decline implied over period (years) (per cent) | | Gross additions to capacity (per cent) required for net additions to capacity of: | |
|---|---|---|---|---|
| | | | 10 per cent | 20 per cent |
| 2 | 5 | 9.6 | 19.6 | 29.6 |
| | 10 | 19.3 | 29.3 | 39.3 |
| 5 | 5 | 22.6 | 32.6 | 42.6 |
| | 10 | 40.1 | 50.1 | 60.1 |
| 10 | 5 | 39.1 | 49.1 | 59.1 |
| | 10 | 65.1 | 75.1 | 85.1 |
| 22 | 5 | 71.1 | 81.1 | 91.1 |

*Note:* [a]Decline rates in existing production, and the gross additions required for 10 and 20 per cent net additions to capacity (in percentages of the original production.

and the UK North Sea in the one camp; less predictably, Venezuela, Abu Dhabi and Oman in the other. (Unlike most other Opec national oil companies, Petroleos de Venezuela SA publishes annual reports that actually provide adequate financial details. According to such figures published *ex post* for recent years, the capital expenditure to add gross additional capacity worked out at a little less than $11,000/db in the US in 1989–90; at just under $13,000/db in the UK North Sea in 1990; and averaged just over $1,600 in Venezuela in 1988.[14] In a few Gulf Opec countries, notably Abu Dhabi, private equity partners in joint producing ventures publish full accounts from which actual capital investment/db for net additions to capacity can be checked *ex post*. But even then, estimates of investment for the gross additions to capacity involved need judgemental assessments of the field decline rates – about which expert analysts from outside can disagree significantly.[15]

During the rapid expansion of Gulf output in the sixties, the capital investment required to add capacity in the main Gulf fields had been of

[14] M. A. Adelman, 'Modelling world oil supply', *Energy Journal*, 14(1993), no. 1 (special issue *in memoriam* David O. Wood).
[15] *MEES*, 25 January 1993, for example, quoted figures from a CGES report, *Oil Production Capacity in the Gulf*, vol. I, 'The United Arab Emirates', which implied an annual decline rate for Abu Dhabi of about 2–3 per cent. In the same issue an article by Dr Thomas Stauffer, 'Crude oil Production costs in the Middle East: Abu Dhabi, Omen and Egypt', suggested a decline rate there of 7 per cent.

the order of only $100–150/db of extra production, as compared with some $2,250/db in the US and roughly $1,000/db in Venezuela. Decline rates in the major fields of the Gulf were then reckoned as no more than 1–2 per cent annually; additions to capacity there could be taken as effectively identical with the increases recorded in production. In 1978, a team from the US Congress was told that the 'historical cost' of development in Saudi Arabia (possibly adjusted to current dollars after four to five years of exceptional inflation in development costs?) had been of the order of $455/db. But the same Aramco and Saudi government informants told the Senate investigators that the cost of adding further capacity from 1978 onwards *would be* $2,280 per daily barrel.[16]

Just how much it will cost to achieve the net increase planned for Gulf capacity in the nineties – as well as rehabilitating all the capacity damaged in the Iraq–Iran and Iraq–Kuwait wars – has been the subject of much recent controversy. (Of the main producers there, only Iraq developed any significant extra capacity after the late seventies, and did not disclose any costs.) Technically, Saudi Arabia and Iraq would almost certainly have the lowest investment costs; in Iran and the UAE, with much of their prospective development offshore, costs might be significantly higher.

The various kinds of 'decline offset investment' involved in maintaining existing capacity levels in the Gulf were forecast in 1990 to take $50 billion by 1995, a large majority of the total capital expenditures on production in the Gulf region to be expected during the period.[17] This could have been taken to imply either a surprisingly steep decline rate in production capacity in the Gulf; or alternatively, an annual decline rate there of say 5 per cent, but extremely high capital investment, averaging $7,000/db or more for gross additional capacity. The same analysis, however, reckoned that developing 5 MBD of 'new' production capacity would cost $20 billion, or only $4,000/db. In practice, in a region with so many known fields awaiting development, those two ways of maintaining capacity should be fairly simple alternatives, as a geologist in the Opec secretariat noted in 1991.[18] If developing extra capacity in new fields offers a better return on investment than maintaining old capacity, or vice versa, Saudi Arabia at any rate could readily take either course. (Iran, Iraq, Kuwait and the Emirates have fewer options.)

[16] Senate Committee on Foreign Relations, *The Future of Saudi Arabian Oil Production*.
[17] 'The cost of additional oil production capacity in the Gulf', *Global Energy Report* (Centre for Global Energy Studies, London), January/February, 1991, reckoned that from 1990 to 1995, capacity maintenance in the region might require $50 billion of decline offset investment, while investment in additional capacity would require $20 billion. (But even at such costs, it may be noted, maintaining a Gulf capacity of say 20–25 MBD would mean only about $1.37/bbl. Given prices of say $15–20/bbl, that would take no more than 8 per cent of total oil revenues for the region.)
[18] Ibrahim Ismail, 'Opec production capacity'.

Few of the investment budgets published for Gulf countries in recent years differentiated between the maintenance of existing capacity and making net additions; one list published from within Opec in 1991 did so, but not clearly. Capital expenditures for the period 1990–5 implied by member countries reporting to Opec in 1991 ranged from $2,000–9,200/db for Saudi Arabia to sums of $10–15 billion for Iran and $5 billion for Iraq for the rehabilitation of facilities without much net increase over their pre-war levels of capacity (Table 3.2). Even Venezuela weighed in with a need for $6–10 billion of investment needed to develop only 450,000 b/d of net extra capacity – reflecting, presumably, its extremely high decline rate in existing capacity. In setting out national claims for petroleum envestment, no member government understates its case. Dr Subroto of Indonesia, Opec's Secretary-General, has frequently spoken of average capital requirements to expand capacity across the whole of Opec in the nineties in the range of $10,000–15,000/db. Nearly all these figures were derived from dividing total investment budgets by increases per daily barrel of *net* additions to capacity, which as noted above cannot be clearly interpreted without the decline rates involved. For the Gulf in particular, these figures also suggested great increases over those reported up to the late seventies.

Opec has not been slow to announce one of the conclusions it draws from this figuring – that its member governments will need considerable outside finance to support these increases in supply, which they believe the world will have no alternative but to demand from them during the nineties. But its member governments in the Gulf may have paid less attention to another conclusion that international financiers might reach from such figures – how much they suggest that the gap between average costs in the Middle East and the rest of the world industry may have narrowed over the past decade. The capital requirements per daily barrel of output reported for some of the Gulf producers now appear to overlap quite significantly the lower figures in the cost range reported for non-Opec oil development. In nearly all other areas, private oil companies can get easier terms, including equity interests in production, than in much of Opec and almost anywhere in Gulf Opec. They may still consider the other places politically safer, too.

Figure 3.1 is designed to indicate very approximately the ranges of development investments reported for some Opec and major non-Opec producing regions at the beginning of the 1990s. (These too, except for the *ex post* US, UK and Venezuelan figures, appear to be effectively for *net* additions to capacity. Capital requirements for *gross* additions to maintain existing capacity in the other regions would no doubt be significantly lower, depending on the relevant decline rates.) Also, in

Table 3.2. *Various estimates of comparative oil production costs, 1988–1991*

All figures represent capital investment in 1991 US$ per daily barrel of plateau production added.

| | |
|---|---|
| *Ex-ante capital programmes* | |
| **Net additions to capacity**[a] | |
| In existing or new fields: | |
| Saudi Arabia | |
| Onshore | 1,400–2,000 |
| Offshore | 3,000–9,200 |
| Average[b] | 2,000–4,000 |
| Iran | |
| Onshore | 3,000 |
| Offshore | 5,890 |
| Iraq | 6,200 |
| Abu Dhabi | |
| Onshore | 1,300 |

*Decline offset investment to maintain existing capacity (per daily barrel of total current capacity)*[c]

| | |
|---|---|
| Worldwide | up to 3,000 |
| Gulf | 500 |

*Ex-post averages of actual capital expenditures (per daily barrel of capacity added)*[d]

| | | |
|---|---|---|
| **Gross additions to capacity** | | |
| US 1990 | 12,021 | (1990) |
| UK North Sea 1990 | 12,901 | (1990) |
| Venezuela 1988 | 1,602 | (1988) |

*Qualitatively estimated ranges of capital cost, 1990*[e]

| | |
|---|---|
| 'Low-cost oil': Middle East, some Venezuelan and other Opec fields, Mexico, Brazil, Colombia | 500–7,000 |
| 'Medium-cost oil': North Sea, Latin America, 50 per cent of US and former Soviet production | 5,000–20,000 |
| 'High-cost oil': other 50 per cent of US and former Soviet production, high-cost North Sea, new fields Alaska | 20,000–30,000 |
| Frontier areas, Arctic | over 30,000 |

*Sources:* [a] Governments and/or Opec.
[b] Saddad al-Husseini, Saudi Aramco.
[c] Centre for Global Energy Studies.
[d] US and UK Departments of Energy; Venezuelan Ministry of Mines; CGES; T. Stauffer, 'Crude oil production costs'; M. A. Adelman, MIT.
[e] Oxford Institute for Energy Studies.

most of the oil industries and regions compared, 'average' costs would probably be closer to the bottom than to the top of the ranges shown. The same could not necessarily be said of centrally planned ex-Soviet and Chinese oil production. Communist accounting bore no relation to capitalist oil accounting, having been developed with entirely different investment incentives and criteria. The former Soviet industry has as wide a diversity of fields and producing environments as exist in North America. In Figure 3.1 its range of costs is assumed to be broadly comparable with those of the US and Canada; but possibly ranging somewhat higher, as a much larger proportion of Soviet output came from Siberia than of American from Alaska. (However, Western oil companies now eager to develop production there argue that entrepreneurial management of ex-Soviet oil could considerably improve on the costs achieved under Soviet management.) Development costs in the much smaller Chinese oil industry may perhaps be lower than *averages* in the former USSR.

### Are Gulf costs comparable?

From the outside, one is reluctant to believe that oil production in the Gulf has lost as much of its natural cost advantage as the budgeting recently reported suggests. But even if per daily barrel investment costs for gross additions to capacity might be not much more than half those quoted for net additional capacity, the net additions *will* probably be required during the coming decade. However, almost all of the capital requirements discussed above arise from statements of future intentions. Very few such budgets, particularly within Opec countries, are nowadays followed up with any detailed figuring of what actually becomes of the intentions and what the costs turn out to be. Moreover, how comparable are all these published capital costs, when the physical facilities involved vary so widely? Can they be considered in any real sense as 'like with like'?

Up to the early 1970s, figures of actual investment in some of the Gulf fields were very occasionally available from concessionaires operating there. Also, until the mid-1980s, there were certain very broad statistics of actual capital expenditures in world oil, compiled after the fact, against which it was possible eventually to check the totals of *ex ante* statements of investment intentions. Certain US banks operating internationally, notably Chase Manhattan, published annual summaries of oil industry investment by regions and for different stages of the business.[19]

[19] 'Capital investments of the world petroleum industry', Chase Manhattan Bank, New York, annual series, 1956–87.

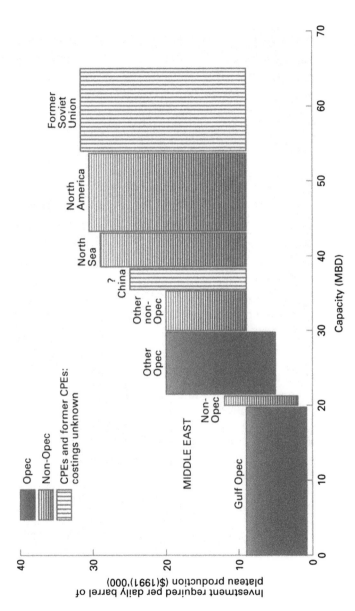

Figure 3.1. Reported ranges of development cost for *net* additions to world oil production capacity, early 1990s. (These are not directly comparable. The amount of *gross* capacity added to achieve these net additions in any region – which *would* allow direct cost comparisons – depends on existing production there and its 'natural' decline rate.)

An ideal way to check all these statements of investment requirements might be to build up more objective comparisons of development costs for oil in different regions, taking the various activities involved stage by stage and item by item. Attempts to do so are frequently made. Is this ideal really practicable?

There is only one region where statistics of oil expenditure are comprehensive and reliable enough to use for any international standards of cost: this is, inevitably, the US. The largest element of cost in oilfield development everywhere – and in exploration – is always drilling. Up to the late eighties, more drilling was done in the US than in any other oil region; innovations in technique come mainly from there; and much of the drilling elsewhere in the world is done by US drilling contractors. So techniques are fairly standardised, and follow US practice. In the US, moreover, drilling costs are on the public record, analysed in elaborate detail; the variations of cost with increasing well-depth are constantly monitored. Across the world, average well productivities for production in each country are published, along with *average* well-depths everywhere; so are the numbers of wells drilled, and the annual totals of 'rig-time' spent by drilling crews in different producing countries. In search of 'like with like' comparisons between production costs in different countries and regions, should not US costs per foot drilled to different depths, onshore and offshore, offer a standard from which, using appropriate multipliers for local circumstances, 'surrogate' drilling costs in other producing areas can be extrapolated? If so, by reckoning all other elements of production investment as rules of thumb 'percentages of the drilling costs' involved, it may be practicable to build up estimates of the total investment/db in each area.[20]

Ambitious 'surrogate costings' of this kind for oil development costs internationally have been offered – since the mid-1960s – by Professor Adelman and various colleagues at the MIT Energy Laboratory. Their calculations of investment per daily barrel for nearly all non-Communist oil-producing countries have always been for gross additions to capacity. So they are not directly comparable with investment costs reported for net capacity added. But even if the gross additions to capacity averaged twice the net additions, and the investment per daily barrel gross only half those reported figures, the capital requirements quoted of late for development of Opec and some other Gulf production

[20] Some analysts take this attempt to develop objective standards for international crude oil production costs further. Annual operating costs of production are generally stable, and may be reckoned as standard percentages of the original investment. It is possible to assume standard rates of return that oil investors might expect internationally. But unit costs *per barrel* then still depend on the production decline rate assumed for each field. Those can hardly be standardised.

would still be much higher. Professor Adelman, in particular, believes that production investment requirements in Gulf Opec, on a strictly comparable basis, could still be, proportionately, almost as far below capital requirements elsewhere as they were up to the early seventies.

Such MIT standards for oil investment, built up theoretically from the statistical database of the US domestic industry, accorded fairly well up to the mid-seventies with the capital requirements per daily barrel occasionally reported for production development plans in some Gulf Opec countries (and with the data reported *ex post* for the North Sea and Venezuela). They appeared rather lower than, but not far out of line with, the annual regional estimates of capital investment for oil development worldwide published during the following decade by Chase Manhattan. However, Chase Manhattan ceased to publish its annual estimates of capital expenditure in world oil in 1987.

From the mid-1980s onwards, the MIT calculations – using standards of about 2.4 times the capital costs of US production investment, built up from drilling costs there – have suggested far lower capital requirements for oil development than most of those published by governments in Opec countries, in some non-Opec countries, and indeed on occasion in certain departments of the US government itself.[21]

One is reminded of the preconceptions of US oilmen in the early postwar decades – that operating abroad would cost 'anything from two to four times' the cost of operating in the US. But many more US oilmen have gained practical foreign experience since then, and many more people in the Gulf practical experience in bargaining about oil. Drilling and completion, onshore at least, has become a specialised but highly competitive international contracting business. Albeit largely US-owned, it should be competitive enough throughout the world industry to squeeze out uncompetitive tendering anywhere. Indices of US drilling costs showed a sharp increase in the early seventies, through to about 1981–2, then a slackening of business and a collapse in contractors' drilling charges; by 1990, they were still nearly four times as high as in 1970. Few Opec governments were major customers for contractors in drilling and other field development in the eighties; so arguably they might have been less well-informed bargainers when they began planning to expand production capacity again. After years of under-invest-

---

[21] United States. Department of Energy, *Performance Profiles of Major Energy Companies*, 1991, estimated that twenty-three large oil companies invested $36,800/db for new production in the US in 1987–9, and in Canada, $59,300/db. Yet the 1989 *Survey on Oil and Gas Expenditures* of the American Petroleum Institute showed that oil development investment in that year, right across the US industry, averaged only about $10,700/db for (*gross*) additional capacity. (There was no *net* addition to US capacity in the year. The gross addition was reckoned as the annual production of crude, plus the small net decline recorded in the country's reserves.)

ment, production departments have huge arrears of postponed development, especially pressure maintenance, to make up; no doubt they insist
on the latest 'state of the art' technology. Foreign tenders may allow for
more wastage and lengthier delays in construction (and even payment)
there than elsewhere; fees and commissions to local agents and partners
can be high. But given the competition among contractors in a recession,
it is hard to see why Gulf governments seem to be suffering so much
more inflation in development costs than producers elsewhere.

None of the governments or companies reporting much higher figures
for the 'investment intensity' of development programmes there has ever
felt obliged to comment upon Adelman's or other independent costings
of development or explain away the differences. In practice, there would
anyway be problems in extrapolating cost relationships from the most
mature oil industry in the world (with almost all reservoirs on a smaller
scale and development seldom unitised) to oil-exporting areas like the
Gulf, where all the circumstances – technical, economic and political –
are so vastly different. In the US oil industry, endowed with the longest-
established oil infrastructure anywhere, development costs can be rigor-
ously defined, and strictly delimited to production alone. In countries
that had no industrial base at all (nor much significant national investment) before oil, the industry's capital budgeting has never been nearly
as tightly defined, and probably never will be. Port terminal capacity in
the US, for example, even including storage tank farms, is a quite
separate business from oil production. In the Gulf, define it how you
will, the national oil industries have to pay for it.

Those MIT estimates, if they could be realised in practice, would
once again restore the gap that used to be apparent between comparative costs in the Gulf and most other areas. They suggest that at any
level of crude oil prices at which oil production is worth developing
elsewhere, the lowest-cost producers in the Gulf *could* gain even greater
economic rents[22] than the cost figures generally published imply.

In a period of uncertain world demand for oil, even that would not
mean that low-cost oil exports could immediately price higher-cost
production elsewhere out of business. In competitive circumstances,
during a period of growth, low-cost oil can be developed to provide all
the *additional* supply required by the market. But if total production is
not increasing much, low-cost development will not be able to displace
*existing*, higher-cost production until its full costs including capital
charges are lower than the operating costs alone of the older capacity.
The rule is normal for any industry; but the timing of cash flows in the

[22] Economic rent can be defined as any extra payment over and above the earnings (including a
'normal' return on capital) required to supply a factor in a competitive market.

development of oil and some other energy industries might prolong its effect. This is one of the reasons why low-cost Middle East production, accounting for so much of the industry's growth in the postwar decades, hardly ever actually displaced much higher-cost oil production elsewhere. But during and since the Opec decade, the main reason has been that some governments have restrained production, and prices have been high enough to keep oil with much higher costs profitable for companies to develop elsewhere.

## Moving oil to markets

The comparisons between regions discussed above are for production costs and the infrastructure of gathering and primary trunk pipelines, gas separation plants, etc., through which crude moves to export terminals. (In some 'frontier' oil provinces, such as Siberia and Alaska, the pipelines become a large proportion of the front-end investment, even to reach seaboard and enter the world oil trade.) However, the comparisons that are commercially relevant include also the costs of shipping the crude oil to where it is wanted.

In the early postwar years crude transport costs were high enough to afford US domestic oil production some commercial protection from imports of Middle East oil, but not from Venezuelan (which was usually shipped in as one product, fuel oil). But increases in the average size of crude oil tankers from the sixties onwards dramatically reduced these vessels' costs of long-distance crude movement. In 1950, a vessel of 28,500 tonnes deadweight (dw) had ranked as a 'supertanker'. By 1970, most of the world's crude trade moved in VLCCs (very large crude carriers) of 250,000 tonnes dw or more. Several 360,000-tonners were put into service in the early seventies, and a few ULCCs (ultra large crude carriers) of 400,000 tonnes or more were built. The largest tankers ever built, of 550,000 tonnes, were never put into service, and were scrapped in the 1980s. That rapid development of the supertanker was one of the most dramatic examples of economies of scale ever achieved in industrial history. In terms of marine engineering, the vessels were less remarkable – and most of them were over 15 years old by 1990. A second generation of them, which would have been built in the 1980s if oil trade had not stagnated, would no doubt have corrected many of the faults and special problems that they encountered in operation. But that second generation has not yet been built. (In the US and some other importing countries, also, terminal facilities and internal distribution systems were never adequate to handle these huge vessels and their cargoes efficiently.)

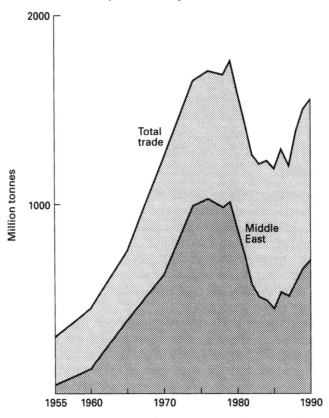

Figure 3.2. Middle East proportion of world interregional oil trade, 1955–1990. (*Source:* BP.)

So the advantages of oil sources closer to markets were steadily becoming less important even before 1973. Then, suddenly, transport costs were rendered for a time almost irrelevant by the sharp increases in the price of crude to all markets in 1973. The reductions in oil demand that followed in the mid-seventies, and again in 1979, were concentrated on seaborne trade, bringing about a slump in tanker business and freight rates for more than a decade. In the early 1990s, with long-distance trade increasing again, many of the VLCCs have been brought out of lay-up. A few oil producers – mainly, so far, national companies of Opec countries – have ventured to order new ones. (In the meantime, accidents, oil spills and the resultant costs of cleaning up have made governments insist on much tighter design criteria, such as double hulls, and impose penal fines and virtually unlimited compensation liabilities.

But up to the early nineties freight rates had not risen enough to cover the extra costs involved. And some of the international companies have become much more chary of heavy reliance on the supertanker.)

In 1973, crude and refined products moving from the Middle East made up nearly 60 per cent of world trade in oil (Figure 3.2). Its exports, 18.8 MBD of crude and 1.2 MBD of products, had almost doubled in five years. More than half of its exports went to Western Europe; 22 per cent to Japan; only four per cent to the US. Importers outside OECD, mainly the developing countries, took less than 20 per cent. Most of those exports, then, were still moving through the 'integrated channels' of Western concessionaires.

As the main oil-exporting region, the Middle East took the swings of the oil trade whether its governments wanted to or not. It bore the brunt of the trade slump between 1979 and 1985, its exports falling by more than half. That was the nadir: by 1990, Middle East exports were back to about 60 per cent of the 1979 level. But they represented less than 45 per cent of the still reduced world oil trade. Western Europe was taking only about 30 per cent of these shipments, because of its own North Sea supply; Japan, again, about a quarter; and the US, after a few years of stabilising its total imports in the early eighties, was taking 14 per cent of Middle East exports. But close on 30 per cent of the region's exports were going to Africa, Asia, and other developing countries – where the main growth of oil demand now seems to be.

# CHAPTER 4

# Ambitions of autarky?

In the early seventies, when development of the first few oilfields discovered in the North Sea had only recently begun,[1] one was sometimes
asked by friends in Middle East governments whether its production
would need to be subsidised.

It was a fair question. Oil produced close to the heart of the world's
largest oil-importing region would obviously enjoy a very large transport advantage over crudes usually moving some 11,000 miles around
the Cape to reach north-west Europe; and at that time transport costs
were representing close on a third of the landed price of Middle East
crude. But against that, 'frontier exploration' in the North Sea and the
development planned to exploit commercial discoveries had to be conducted almost beyond the limits of existing offshore technology. Every
company was on a learning curve. From the Gulf, producing with
operating costs of a few cents a barrel and able to add capacity for about
$100–150/db of extra production, it was hard to believe such operations
could be commercially worth while.

At the time a barrel of Gulf crude was being landed in Western
Europe at a price of about $2.50 a barrel (after taxes and royalties of
about $1.35). The largest and first British field to be developed, BP's
Forties, was due to come into production by mid-1975. If prices in the
meantime were assumed to rise by no more than the escalation then
already agreed between Gulf governments and concessionaires against

---

[1] One small oilfield, Hewett, was discovered in 1966, during exploration primarily for gas in the
southern basin of the North Sea, but not developed. A discovery offshore of Denmark in 1967
encouraged exploration in the much deeper waters of the northern basin; then came the giant Ekofisk
field (Norwegian sector) and the smaller Montrose (UK sector) both in December 1969. Ekofisk was
brought into partial production as early as July 1971, Montrose not until 1976. Of the three other
giant North Sea oilfields, Forties was discovered in November 1970 and began producing in
September 1975; Brent, discovered in July 1971, began producing in November 1976; and Statfjord,
found in 1974 beneath the boundary line between the Norwegian and UK sectors, began producing in
1979.

inflation and currency fluctuations, say 5 per cent annually,[2] the price for Middle East crude landed in Europe in 1975 could be taken as around $3.00 a barrel, giving a value after pipeline costs of say $2.75–2.80 at the wellhead for North Sea crudes. Reckoning the development costs envisaged in 1972[3] for sizeable North Sea fields – perhaps $2,500/db of plateau production from a field expected to reach 150,000 b/d or more, with average well productivity approaching Gulf standards and higher-quality crude than most imported from there – such giant fields in the North Sea *did* look economic to develop commercially. (That was not simply a matter of covering operating costs once the capital investment had been sunk. The notional prices that producers might in that case have obtained for crude from large North Sea fields would have implied perhaps a 10–15 per cent DCF rate of return on investment in the fields, after a then 'normal' 50 per cent rate of Western European tax and expensed royalty.)

So the answer to the Middle East question, strictly, was 'No'. Production being developed in the North Sea then did look likely to be genuinely economic. But personally, one was inclined to add a proviso. If by mischance North Sea oil *should* need to be subsidised – or more likely, protected in some more genteel way – it almost certainly would be. By 1972, Western importing countries were certain to put a premium on politically safe oil.

Everything quantitative in such an answer turned out wrong, except that the first oil was shipped from Forties on time. Soon after development began, it began to become obvious that development costs for North Sea oil were still being underestimated. When BP, for example, raised £360 million (then worth $850 million) from a syndicate of banks in 1972 to finance the development of Forties – it was the largest sum ever borrowed until then by any British company – its firm development plan implied more than $2,000 per daily barrel from a plateau production then reckoned at 400,000 b/d. But later estimates of the actual investment in bringing Forties into production ranged from £600 million to £850 million. The plateau production actually achieved, in 1978, exceeded 500,000 b/d: that still meant an investment of $4,000 per daily barrel in 1974 dollars. Investment for the other giant fields in the North Sea, all discovered by 1974 but mostly developed later than Forties,[4] was

---

[2] After the sharp increases under the Tehran agreement, an annual escalation factor of 2.5 per cent plus 5 cents in posted prices per barrel of crude had been agreed against continuing inflation in export prices of world manufactures.
[3] The initial estimates, published in 1971 shortly after the first fields had been declared 'commercial', had been of $1,000–1,500/db.
[4] Ekofisk, which lies under the seabed 'median line' but is mainly in the Norwegian sector, preceded Forties. In all, nine fields were under development by autumn 1973.

generally of the order of $5,000–8,000 per daily barrel of plateau pro-
duction, two or three times as much as one could estimate in 1972.
(Capital costs for some of the medium-sized fields eventually turned out
to be of the order of $10,000 per daily barrel.[5] But development of those
hardly began before 1973.)

Costs overran the initial estimates partly because weather and seas in
the North Sea turned out far worse than anything in the industry's
previous experience offshore. Average well productivity was lower than
originally hoped, which involved drilling more wells than had initially
been assumed. Moreover, only a few firms in the world were competent
to design, construct and install the huge production platforms and
undersea pipelines required. After 1973 all those constructors soon
became overstretched with demand from most oil provinces outside
Opec. (They were among the earliest Western firms to be able to cream
off *their* share of the economic rent that Opec in 1973–4 conferred upon
everyone connected with petroleum production elsewhere.)

If prices had risen only as much as Middle East governments and
concessionaires were committed to in mid-1972, then those huge cost
overruns later might have choked off further North Sea oil development.
The fields coming in earliest would have gone into production, and
development already in train for some others would have been worth
completing. (Operating costs in most of the big fields would have been
little more than a dollar a barrel.) But whether such prices would have
offered returns on capital sufficient to maintain exploration and development of new fields at what North Sea costs *had turned out to be* looks
in hindsight very doubtful. (Most of the companies involved, moreover,
had borrowed heavily to finance North Sea development, with loans
charged in one way or another against their early field production.)

## Opec to the rescue?

But in the meantime, of course, the landed prices that importers round
the North Sea had to pay for Gulf oil had more than trebled. Opec's
price lift-off in 1973–4 made almost every field discovered there up to
the mid-1970s highly profitable (although the price rise helped fuel cost
inflation). At the same time, for North Sea exploration, it substantially
reduced the minimum size of discovery that was worth developing into
production.

So the question of subsidy or any other kind of protection never in

---

[5] Exceptionally, costs for one or two of the smallest 'short-life' fields, with reserves that did not
justify installing production platforms and where oil was loaded directly from drilling barges into
tankers, were much lower.

fact arose. Admittedly, in both the UK and Norway the tax regimes as originally designed had been fairly favourable compared with Opec's 'going rate' of terms for foreign exploration and development. Royalties and tax were related to the prices actually realised, not to artificially high tax reference prices. British provisions allowed rapid and generous recovery of capital outlays, in comparison with more usual depreciation allowances.

After Opec lifted prices off, both North Sea governments did raise 'windfall taxes' of varying kinds over and above their basic oil tax regimes. (Norway also created a national oil company that took a large practical share of the production, costs and profits.) When production came on stream in the late seventies, the two countries gained consider-able balance-of-payments advantages over the other Western Euro-peans, who had to go on importing nearly all their crude requirements. Oil taxation made a substantial contribution to their budget receipts. There may have been a few unpalatable side-effects on other parts of their economies, akin to the 'Dutch disease' that followed upon devel-opment of, and exports from, the Groningen gasfield during the same period.[6] But on balance, both governments could reckon North Sea oil as having been of enormous benefit to their economies.

In the early eighties, when prices began to fall, all governments with production or hopes of it around the North Sea *did* begin to moderate their terms for companies operating and exploring there. Special pro-visions began to be made for remission of royalty on small new fields and those discovered in deeper water; there were successive modifi-cations of the rates and timing of taxes on oil production. There was never any question of subsidy. Oil taxes remained higher than those on other industries. But this also meant that governments accepted a major-ity share of the decline in prices and profits. When a price collapse was precipitated by Saudi Arabia in 1985–6, no North Sea production needed to be shut down. Even if the price of Gulf crudes landed in Europe had then fallen as low as $5 a barrel (it did not in fact decline below about $9), that would have covered operating costs for over 90 per cent of North Sea production[7] and kept that output economic to continue.

There could not have been a more opportune time to become more than self-sufficient in oil. (Britain continued to import the Middle East crudes for which its refineries had been designed, but exported its own

[6] An export boom in Dutch gas was argued to have made the country's other exports uncompetitive, because of a rise in the guilder against other European currencies.
[7] R. Mabro *et al.*, *The Market for North Sea Crude Oil* (Oxford University Press, for Oxford Institute for Energy Studies, 1986), citing figures from Wood Mackenzie & Co.

lighter crudes, soon becoming a net exporter. Norway, with limited internal demand and refining capacity, became an exporter straight away, because laying a submarine pipeline to its shore, across a deep 'trench' in the seabed, was long delayed. At the outset, it delivered its North Sea petroleum to Britain.) This transformation of oil balances for the two countries sharply reduced import dependence for the whole of OECD Europe, increasing its degree of regional self-sufficiency. Limited exports from the North Sea to the US did not alter Western Europe's import dependence; but they helped moderate its reliance on Middle East supplies for about two decades.

*Greater self-sufficiency*

Indeed, a mirror-image of the decline in international trade in oil during the Opec decade was an increase in self-sufficiency for the main oil-consuming regions. Throughout the eighties, more than half the oil used in the world was consumed in the same regions as it was produced. This had always been true of total energy consumption; but the degree of self-sufficiency increased for that too (Table 4.1). From 1974 until the present, energy consumption has grown faster than oil. Oil imports have been drawn upon only as the energy option of last resort.

One reason why regional self-sufficiency in oil and total energy across the world increased during the Opec decade had nothing to do with Opec's price increases. It was macroeconomic, a matter of comparative economic growth. The economies then commanded by Communist governments were growing faster than the capitalist industrial economies, or at least purported to be; and in aggregate they were more than self-sufficient in all forms of energy. Soviet oil production, together with, later, some in China, had exceeded total oil consumption in all the then 'centrally planned economies' (CPEs) ever since the Second World War. While those economies were growing faster than the rest, that contributed to reducing *average* import dependence right across the world. Indeed, until the nineties, those centrally planned economies, with a very large share of world oil and energy consumption, were only peripherally concerned with the world oil trade.

Until the internal collapse of central economic planning began in 1989, the international oil trade had been mainly concerned with the rest of the world, the market economies that it then called acronymically WOCA or NCW (the 'world outside Communist areas', or 'non-Communist world'). Sometimes it further separated out WOCANA, leaving out also North America (which had also been for a time 'semi-detached' from the international oil trade). From 1989 onwards, poli-

Table 4.1. *Regional self-sufficiency: oil and energy, 1965–1989*

| (a) Oil | (million tonnes) | | % self-sufficiency |
|---|---|---|---|
| | Production | Consumption | |
| *OECD* | | | |
| 1965 | 491 | 1053 | 47 |
| 1973 | 661 | 1939 | 34 |
| 1979 | 700 | 1973 | 35 |
| 1985 | 806 | 1589 | 51 |
| 1989 | 735 | 1730 | 42 |
| *Developing countries outside Opec* | | | |
| 1965 | 90 | 199 | 46 |
| 1973 | 136 | 300 | 45 |
| 1979 | 164 | 397 | 41 |
| 1985 | 289 | 498 | 58 |
| 1989 | 321 | 574 | 56 |
| *Former CPEs incl. China* | | | |
| 1965 | 269 | 230 | 117 |
| 1973 | 503 | 479 | 105 |
| 1979 | 716 | 652 | 110 |
| 1985 | 743 | 650 | 114 |
| 1989 | 766 | 676 | 113 |
| **(b) Energy** | (million tonnes oil equivalent) | | % self-sufficiency |
| | Production | Consumption | |
| *OECD* | | | |
| 1965 | 1764 | 2332 | 76 |
| 1973 | 2271 | 3525 | 64 |
| 1979 | 2565 | 3853 | 67 |
| 1985 | 2865 | 3744 | 77 |
| 1989 | 2895 | 4052 | 71 |
| *Developing countries outside Opec* | | | |
| 1965 | 158 | 216 | 73 |
| 1973 | 272 | 330 | 82 |
| 1979 | 427 | 515 | 83 |
| 1985 | 449 | 816 | 55 |
| 1989 | 573 | 1087 | 53 |
| *Former CPEs incl. China* | | | |
| 1965 | 1099 | 1010 | 109 |
| 1973 | 1598 | 1466 | 109 |
| 1979 | 2175 | 1939 | 112 |
| 1985 | 2360 | 2117 | 111 |
| 1989 | 2645 | 2345 | 113 |

*Sources:* United Nations and BP.

tically and economically, such collective labels for groups of nations rapidly became obsolete. But the distinction had been all too real for more than forty postwar years, and most historical series of statistics remain classified in these ways up to 1990. (In energy statistics, all the acronyms had always slightly overlapped. Some peripheral trade in oil had always continued across the political divides. Oil balances for WOCA, for example, always needed to count in net export/import trade with the former CPEs, essentially imports from the Soviet Union.)

However, it was in the world outside the then Communist bloc that the *specific* sharp reduction of dependence on oil imports really took place from the mid-seventies onwards. In the main consuming regions of WOCA, indigenous oil production never quite reached 50 per cent of total consumption. But from more than 70 per cent of total non-Communist world oil consumption in 1973, interregional imports into non-Communist countries fell to only about 53 per cent in 1985 (before recovering to about 60 per cent in 1990).

That reduced dependence on oil trade arose partly from deliberate policies of governments at both ends of the business. These were initially most purposive and successful in the development of new primary electricity production, through nuclear power and hydropower. Increasing regional self-sufficiency in energy supply, while it lasts or when nations can regain it, is usually considered desirable as reducing political risk. For oil, imports within regions are also generally considered politically safer than those from outside. However, the biggest reductions in oil import dependence during the Opec decade arose simply from luck in the exploration game.

*Extra capacity – at home*

As it happened, three of the four important new oil provinces brought into production during the 1970s – West Siberia, the North Sea and Alaska – were within the national jurisdictions of major energy-consuming countries. At their peaks during the mid-1980s, the three new provinces within major consuming areas produced in total about 13 MBD. Allowing for the decline in other US production that Alaskan development offset, these new oil provinces added about 11 MBD during the two decades, accounting for well over half the net increase in world oil production during the period (Table 4.2).

None of the main oil provinces brought into production in the seventies was easy or cheap to develop. Siberia and Alaska were in exceptionally low temperatures and harsh conditions onshore. The North Sea environment turned out to be in unexpected ways more

Table 4.2. *Oil production outside Opec, 1965–1990 (MBD)*

|  | 1965 | 1973 | 1979 | 1985 | 1990 |
|---|---|---|---|---|---|
| *North America* | | | | | |
| US (incl. NGLs[a]) | 9.0 | 11.0 | 10.1 | 10.5 | 8.9 |
| of which: Alaska | — | 0.1 | 1.4 | 1.8 | 1.8 |
| Canada | 0.9 | 2.1 | 1.8 | 1.8 | 2.0 |
| Latin America | 1.2 | 1.6 | 2.9 | 4.7 | 4.9 |
| of which: Mexico | 0.4 | 0.6 | 1.6 | 3.0 | 3.0 |
| Western Europe | 0.4 | 0.4 | 2.4 | 4.0 | 4.1 |
| of which: North Sea | — | — | 2.0 | 3.0 | 3.7 |
| USSR | 4.9 | 8.7 | 11.9 | 12.2 | 11.7 |
| of which: Siberia | — | 1.8 | 5.7 | 7.6 | 7.4 |
| Total Non-Opec | 15.8 | 27.3 | 34.3 | 40.4 | 40.1 |
| Opec | 14.4 | 31.3 | 31.5 | 17.3 | 24.8 |

*Note:* [a] NGL natural gas liquid.

hostile than any offshore conditions that oil developers had encountered before, even though it was wonderfully close to markets. Siberia and Alaska were remote from actual centres of high consumption, and needed complex, dedicated transport systems to move their oil to market.[8] Companies developing production in Alaska and the North Sea encountered exceptional inflation in the costs of drilling, oilfield development, pipelines and equipment; and Soviet oil developers too cannot entirely have escaped that.

Nevertheless, all these were major oil provinces by any standards, containing giant and some super-giant fields, and there was never much doubt that all of them would be developed. The first discoveries in all of them were made by the end of the sixties, and their development was initially decided upon before Opec took over control of world oil prices and raised them sky-high. Nor, at the time the decisions to develop Prudhoe Bay were taken, was it even fully appreciated that domestic oil production in the US 'lower forty-eight' states was passing its peak. As to Siberia, no consideration of the likely alternative costs of imports would ever have entered the calculations of Russian oil decision-makers regarding the development of extra capacity there. They needed the oil (and gas) not only to meet rising demand at home and in other

[8] But they opened up new, vast and exciting prospective areas. As early as 1968, Walter Levy, the world's best-known petroleum consultant, said that the centre of gravity of North American and Soviet petroleum was shifting to the Arctic, and would become firmly settled there.

Communist countries, but as almost the only Soviet exports for which some Western countries would pay hard currencies.

The fourth big addition to world oil supply during that same period, the Reforma and later the Campeche oil provinces in Mexico, brought that country back to the front rank of non-Opec oil exporters, right next door to the US, the world's largest market for oil. Reforma, for its part, was the first major success in exploration for Mexico's state oil company Pemex since the government had nationalised American and European companies' oil operations there at the end of the nineteen-thirties. Its development was a feat of national self-assertion, as well as central to the country's economic development.

Mexico was glad to benefit from the prices raised initially by Opec. But it has always borne in mind the possibility of some new 'Western Hemisphere preference', formal or informal, in the US market – which indeed seems to be emerging during the nineties.

It was by happy chance, therefore, that production from the three non-Communist oil provinces of these four offered a considerable and welcome fillip to non-Opec supply just when the need for higher US oil imports had become generally recognised, and when Opec was exercising its power to raise world crude prices. Production from some of these new non-Opec oil provinces may have been accelerated by the price upsurge, though Alaska was delayed by one of the first major 'green' political campaigns ever to affect energy development anywhere, and came into production much later than had been planned.[9] (All these developments, as in the North Sea, proved to be much more costly than had originally been hoped. So higher prices were very welcome, making later expansion economic – but hardly critical for the earliest fields.) The new provinces' total output rates might never have risen as high if prices had never taken off, because a wider range of small fields became worth developing in later years. But in the short term, those giant field developments were the main factors in reversing the former established trends in the postwar supply pattern of world oil, indeed of total world energy.

That reversal too may have been temporary. The medium-term effect of these developments cannot yet be fully assessed. Several of the giant fields in these new oil provinces are already moving into decline. The powerful impetus to exploration elsewhere outside Opec has not discovered any comparable upturn of giant oilfields since those. Opec

[9] It was preceded by an oil 'spill' (actually a leakage from the seabed) off the Californian coast near Santa Barbara in 1969 during offshore exploration there, which precipitated passage of a National Environmental Policy Act in the US, and encouraged environmental lobbies to oppose, and succeed in delaying completion of, the Trans-Alaska pipeline from the Prudhoe Bay field to the Valdez shipment terminal.

analysts were glad to see non-Opec oil supply beginning to level off by the late 1980s; trust that it is now passing its peak; and hope that it may move into decline before the year 2000.

## Saving energy imports

It has been estimated[10] that in 1987 energy consumption in OECD was 600 million tonnes of oil equivalent lower than it might have been if it had gone on being used no more efficiently than in 1973. Such calculations can only be rudimentary, since so many factors were involved. But even if one were to halve the estimate, 300 million tonnes of oil equivalent would have taken up most of the capacity for energy supply that was in surplus worldwide at the beginning of the nineties.

The savings that have moderated oil import demand since 1973 resulted to a limited extent from switching to imports of other energy, gas and coal. Many importing countries have sought to diversify their sources of supply (from oil to other fuels, and, within oil, to sources other than Opec). But perhaps the most important factor that reduced oil trade was the development of local energy supply. Import dependence for energy in total declined. Most of the additional production of other forms of energy as well as oil developed since the mid-seventies has been within hitherto importing regions (Figure 4.1). This has helped to diversify their supply, and has somewhat increased the extent and degree of energy self-sufficiency across the world.

Degrees of self-sufficiency change over time, and are never easy to measure. Considering oil alone, in the 107 countries shown in UN statistics as having significant energy consumption,[11] there were 71 countries producing crude in 1989, 10 more than in 1973. Out of 78 countries in 'oil deficit', of which 40 including Japan have continued to produce virtually none at all, 28 had increased their levels of self-sufficiency, with 9 moving into oil surplus and net exports. Only 10 countries had become less self-sufficient during the period. (Those included the US, so that average oil deficits for all these countries, in terms of tonnage, did increase slightly over the sixteen-year period. But average oil deficits for the twenty largest importers went down slightly in tonnage.)

Thus a few more individual nations have become self-sufficient in oil, or even net exporters. A larger number have increased their degree of

[10] D. Heal, 'Efficiency or self-sufficiency: choices for energy consumers', *Energy Policy* 20 (1992), no. 10, pp. 942–9.
[11] Over a million tonnes of coal equivalent, or just over 650,000 tonnes of oil equivalent. These countries together accounted for over 99 per cent of world use of commercial energy.

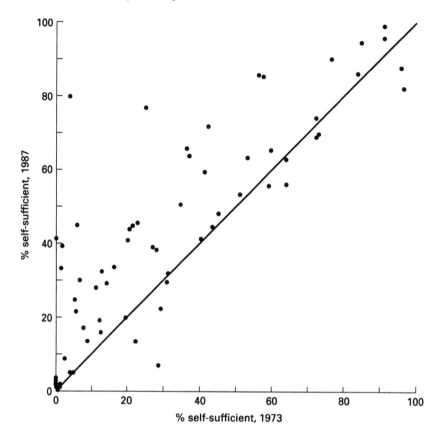

Figure 4.1. Changes in degree of self-sufficiency in energy supply between 1973 and 1987 for the 107 countries each consuming more than one million tonnes of coal equivalent, together accounting for over 99 per cent of world consumption of commercial energy. (*Source:* David Heal, 'Efficiency or self-sufficiency'.)

self-sufficiency in total energy supply. Of the same 107 countries, the number of countries in energy surplus, enabling net exports, had risen from 33 to 38 (Figure 4.2). For the others, the median proportion of national energy self-sufficiency had increased from 17 to 29 per cent of their (considerably increased) total energy consumption. Those reducing their energy deficits included seven of the world's ten largest energy-consuming countries (and seventeen of the member countries of OECD).

Some energy surplus countries (including all the Opec countries) showed reductions in their net exports between 1973 and the mid-eighties, but have shown increases since. In oil, the recovery was a response to lower prices from 1983 onwards and a collapse in 1986; in other fuels, exports began or increased under long-term projects set in train after the 1973 price increases. The Soviet Union, developing its gas supplies to Western Europe, supplanted Saudi Arabia as the largest energy exporter. Within OECD, Norway, the UK and Australia became significant exporters; so did a fringe of developing countries, some within the Middle East but outside Opec. Australia and Colombia developed large-scale coal exports.

Hence the diversification of supply and increased self-sufficiency in *total* energy that accompanied the decline in oil trade cannot be simply correlated with it. The imports reduced have been almost entirely of oil. Much of the extra energy production newly developed by nations 'at home' has not been oil. Between 1985 and 1989, when oil trade recovered strongly, it picked up only about 40 per cent of the accompanying increase in world energy demand.

Clearly the new power to raise prices demonstrated by Opec countries during the 1970s, exploiting their concentration of low-cost oil supply in the Middle East, accentuated the efforts everywhere else to increase self-sufficiency in energy. That concentration, although it did not become come fully appreciated until after the Second World War, had influenced the political history of this industry long before. Geopolitical rivalries in world oil stretch back to before the beginning of this century, and continue to this day. But another political factor, within individual nations but common to many, has also affected oil development. This is a recurrent and seemingly almost universal yearning for *autarky* in the provision of energy.

Within national economies, energy industries often command nearly as much and as special political concern as agriculture.[12] Most of the world's older-established rich countries had initially developed their national wealth through manufacturing industries based on large local energy resources. They used quotas, tariffs or excise taxation to protect those domestic energy industries – coal in Western Europe, oil in the USA – for decades after much of their production became commercially uncompetitive. Once they begin to become increasingly dependent on imported energy, the governments of such nations become uneasy.

---

[12] Coalminers in Britain sometimes gain but often lose public sympathy. They have never asserted as much political clout for as long as French peasants (or British landowners).

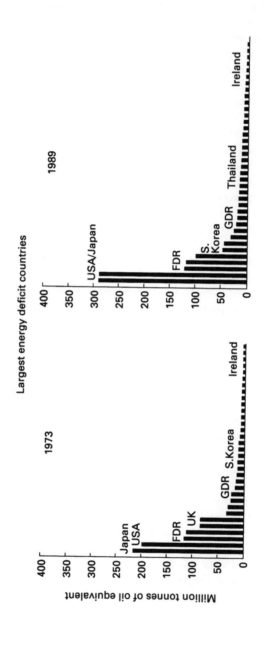

Largest energy deficit countries

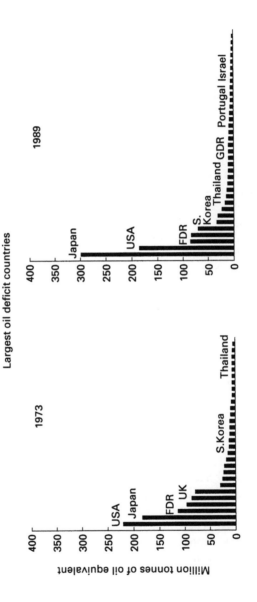

Figure 4.2. Largest deficit countries, energy and oil, 1973 and 1989.

Whether or not they can sensibly do anything about this, they tend to try.[13]

Long before Opec developed much leverage over oil exports, the decline of local coal industries and the seemingly inexorable postwar growth of import dependence had already stimulated anxieties in Western European countries. Any promise of substantial reduction in that dependence – initially gas in the Netherlands and later the UK North Sea, then North Sea oil for Norway and the UK – was politically prized. (Nuclear electricity in the UK and France inherited its initial political momentum from military ambitions, but commanded continuing support from governments as another localised energy supply that saves oil imports.) Some analysts oriented towards Opec have derided this almost universal desire to reduce oil imports as 'petrophobia'. But it remains a powerful motive within many countries' energy policies.

Not all members of the rich nations' club achieved much with efforts to develop 'their own' oil to offset imports. Geopolitically, Germany had been shut out of the main Middle East concessions from the First World War onwards. After the Second, neither it nor Japan were allowed to gain any significant foothold there. West Germany engaged for a time in substantial, partly subsidised exploration programmes for oil abroad, which were largely fruitless; Japan's efforts gained only a little more. Afterwards, both these highly successful industrial economies engaged in some nuclear development; but they resigned themselves mainly to diversifying the sources of their energy imports, in order to reduce risks of interruption in supply (which neither of them had ever in fact experienced). They were confident of their commercial ability and manufacturing prowess to pay whatever these diversified energy imports might cost. Later, most of the newly industrialising countries of the Pacific Rim, which like Japan started with virtually no fuel supply of their own, had to do the same. They focused on manufacturing, accepted heavy dependence on imported fuels, and were prepared to use these prodigally in order to achieve their own rapid industrial growth.

As it happened, much of the new plant and machinery that they installed was more efficient in using energy than comparable equipment in longer-established industrial nations; and certain of the manufactures

---

[13] Exceptionally, during some postwar decades, two countries sought autarky for quite the opposite reason – because it was hard for them to obtain oil imports. Israel and South Africa, subject to an oil embargo from Arab exporters, had costly difficulties in purchasing crude. During the dozen years after 1967 that Israel occupied the Sinai peninsula, one oilfield was discovered there; after it made peace with Egypt and returned the territory, that oil supply continued. South Africa had developed synthetic oil production from coal long before it too was embargoed in 1973; later, it invested heavily in oil synthesis from natural gas.

upon which they focused their new development were electronic and thus inherently less energy-intensive. But it is only of late that these economies have put much emphasis on policies to save energy.

Not all developing countries could be confident of emulating the Pacific success stories. Their ambitions to achieve oil production were doubly motivated. After 1973, the imports on which poor countries depended suddenly cost far more than they could afford. Anything that might reduce that cost was highly desirable. But beyond import-saving, there was always another hope: emulating Opec, with the chance that petroleum might be found to export, with high royalties and taxes. That ambition to develop oil at home was fostered by international oil companies eager to replace elsewhere the rights to reserves that they had lost through Opec nationalisation. But the poor countries had had those ambitions even before Opec raised the rewards of exporting and the costs of importing so high.

Expansion of energy supply in the Communist-controlled economies after the Second World War was dominated by the Soviet petroleum industry. Others among those 'centrally planned' economies needed to import oil, and could only get it conveniently from this overbearing superpower partner. For a time, initially because it happened to suit the Soviet central planners, the satellites got this oil (and later gas) on rather easy terms.[14] Import dependence for oil within the Communist satellite countries was somewhat less uncomfortable than other elements of Soviet domination. But as soon as any of those countries detached themselves from Soviet influence – China to begin with – developing their own energy became one of the political ambitions of their governments too.

China has sizeable oil reserves, significant production, and hopes of increasing it. Nearby, Mongolia is said to have significant reserves, but less hope of developing production. The Eastern European countries wishing to reduce dependence on ex-Soviet oil have limited prospects for oil exploration. Some of them have old-established coal industries, though much of their production consists of lignite or oil shales, often environmentally obnoxious. Whether they will seek greater self-sufficiency through developing extra coal production is an open question. They seem unlikely to get Western financial backing to do so. For them, the gas option might be simply a shift in the form of dependence on imports from the ex-Soviet republics.

[14] Soviet exports to their Warsaw Pact allies and for a time to China were priced at a past-five-years rolling average of world oil export prices. While oil prices were rising, notably during the 'Opec decade', that 'Budapest formula' gave those Communist customers a comfortable price advantage compared with buying from the world market. When world prices began to fall, they lost that planned advantage. But until 1991 they retained the continuing unplanned advantage of paying for Soviet oil in roubles at an artificially inflated exchange rate.

Throughout Eastern Europe, in the early nineties, governments were zealous in promising to reduce intervention within their economies. Most political parties in Western Europe and other OECD countries were already slanted in the same direction – but cautious in modifying their energy policies. In Britain, in winter 1992–3, for example, when the government decided to close down the half of British Coal's deep-mined production that was uncompetitive, public indignation forced it to back track and subsidise parts of this output for a few more years, obliging the electricity utilities it had privatised to burn extra coal, in preference to gas. Germany was already committed to coal subsidies under its comparable *Jahr-hundert* contract, which the European Commission has not found it easy to persuade the government to reduce. Also, most of these European democracies, however non-interventionist in political persuasion, have long been accustomed to exert considerable management of demand for imported fuels through excise taxes on oil transport fuels. It is too large an element in their budgets, and too easy to collect, for governments to dispense with. They apply such taxation differentially, and if ever carbon taxes are implemented, that will widen their options. (In Eastern as well as Western Europe, moreover, environmentalist lobbying is steadily becoming more professional.)

However, neither the developing countries nor those ex-Communist nations of Eastern Europe show nearly as much unease about global warming, nor as much public interest in saving energy, as the environmentalists *may* have managed to generate in some of the industrialised democracies. Nor, in spite of experience in places like Mexico City or Bangkok, do their populations display any misgivings about becoming part of the universal car culture. Nowadays, their appetite for oil is no longer being funded with loans pressed upon them by Western bankers. During the nineties, their demand for oil cannot grow much faster than their economies can afford. But their populations' craving for the satisfactions that oil can provide – and one in particular, personal transport – may remain insatiable.

# CHAPTER 5

# Still the prime mover

For millions of years, oil has been a fuel on the move. It is discovered not where it was originally formed from organic sediments beneath shallow prehistoric seas, but where its upward or lateral movement through strata of porous rock formed from such sediments was trapped or sealed in the remote past under some impervious layer of 'caprock'. It is produced when it moves through the pores of those underlying strata to the points where drilling has pierced and reduced pressure at the bottom of a well to allow the oil, driven by water or gas interfaced with it, to rise to the top. Once it has reached the surface, it can be moved more cheaply than any other fuel over the long distances that it often has to travel to where it can be used. Whether or not 'the economics of a liquid' makes the oil industry unique,[1] its readiness to flow naturally remains the dominant physical factor in all the myriad actions of this industry's technology.

Oil moves throughout the world mainly as crude, in huge physical volumes. Nowadays crude is bought and sold in yet far larger contractual volumes of 'paper barrels'. But it is almost never consumed as crude.[2] Final consumers use the petroleum products refined from it, in patterns that have often varied widely between and within different groups of countries, and that alter everywhere over time.

'Crude' signifies unrefined mineral oil. In any other sense, the adjective is a misnomer for intense complexity. There are about 40,000 separate oilfields in the world, all in principle producing individual crudes. Every crude is a mixture, mainly of hydrocarbons of differing molecular structures. In practice, most of these are commingled into a few hundred localised crude streams, and only about seventy different

---

[1] As argued by the late Dr P. H. Frankel, the most influential pioneer of petroleum economics, initially in his *Essentials of Petroleum* (Chapman & Hall, 1946).
[2] Limited quantities of certain Far Eastern crudes are burned 'entire', or after minimal processing, under power station boilers in Japan and some other countries of the Pacific Rim.

qualities move regularly in international trade. Even these traded crudes differ widely in quality, and hence in the yields of products that can be refined from them for final use.

Oil demand is for refined products, and the prices that final consumers pay are for those. That is one of the reasons why economic modelling of market responses to the only widely applicable and constantly publicised set of oil prices, those of crude, is so difficult. There are said to be over a thousand separate products derived (at several removes) from the refining of crude. But 85 per cent of the output of the world's refineries consists of four main energy products: gasoline, kerosene, gas/diesel oil, and residual fuel oil. All are saleable. So are a wide range of other products, low in volume though sometimes higher in unit value. Ultimately, very little of the crude barrel goes to waste (which helps to make it economic to transport over great distances before processing). But no single crude oil will provide all these energy products in the proportions and qualities that markets require. Nor is any of the main products producible alone. The refiner cannot meet extra demand for any one product without producing others too. (That problem of 'joint products' is another inherent complication for the economics and the management of this industry.)

Demand for these main oil products, and their relative values, depend essentially upon the extent to which other fuels can compete with each of them. Historically, the industry has generally commanded at least one market in which other fuels cannot compete at all. Nowadays, most of these 'essential' uses of oil are for movement. Modern transport is almost entirely dependent on it, and uses more oil than any other single sector of demand.

Technically, oil is even more indispensable for lubrication between all kinds of moving surfaces.[3] Lubricants involve almost a separate business, with its own techniques of refining and blending to fashion a wider variety of grades than are needed for most energy uses of oil. It is relatively high in value but minuscule in volume. It takes little more than 1 per cent of the total oil used, but is worth 3 per cent of the industry's turnover.

There are hardly any other uses of oil for which it is technically indispensable. As a general fuel, it has powerful advantages over some others. As a raw material for chemical intermediates, it is still the most widely used. (In both applications, its readiness to flow is technically valuable.) But technically, substitutes are practical and readily available. Oil needs to be economically competitive to retain its hold on these markets.

[3] Though some synthetic base oils for lubricants are under development.

*The only remaining growth?*

Since world oil demand began to recover in the mid-1980s, moreover, most of the increase has been in fuels for transport. In the industrialised countries of the OECD, there was indeed no growth in any other main sector of oil demand between 1973 and the end of the next decade. There, even transport demand fell between 1978 and 1982; but by 1989 it was 504 million tonnes, more than 21 per cent higher than in 1973. Total oil consumption in OECD had fallen by 50 million tonnes during the same period. So for everything except transport, oil demand in the world's richest countries was down by nearly 30 per cent (Table 5.1). OECD still accounts for well over half of world oil consumption, and for two-thirds of demand outside the USSR. Its transport sector, taking 60 per cent of the total, is still setting the pace. Sectoral demand in the rest of the world is not so well documented historically. At present, transport is much less dominant in Eastern Europe or the developing countries. But the current indications are that these transport fuels probably amount to around 40 per cent of the world total, and that the strongest resurgence of demand in all regions continues to be for them.

Much of oil's contribution to world energy supply nowadays is thus as a family of specialised transport fuels, outside the general fuel market where it competes with other forms of primary energy (Table 5.2). From the run of the last decade and a half, it looks as if this specialised market sector might be the main, if not the only, element of continuing growth. Oil has consolidated its commanding position, for the present still unassailable, in supplying these specialised transport fuels. That may have simplified the medium-term planning in which the industry, following the pause of the eighties, has once again begun to engage. But if so, it would also leave the scope for such planning somewhat shrunken. For during the same period, oil had to surrender much of its postwar gains as a general fuel. One net result is that the total oil volumes to which the industry is now looking forward are much smaller than used to be envisaged twenty years ago.

It looks quite probable, therefore, that the future of oil will depend essentially on specialised demands for which it is irreplaceable. However, it has looked like that before in the history of this industry; and it has not always turned out that way. The hypothesis needs critical assessment historically – and perhaps more important, geographically. There is not much doubt about the positive element of change involved, the growth of demand for automotive power, everybody's desire everywhere to move about more and to travel. But the negative shift, away from oil as a source of general power and heat, is not yet so firmly

Table 5.1. OECD: total oil consumption and transport use, 1960–1989 (thousand tonnes)

|  | Total oil consumption | Transport use |
|---|---|---|
| 1960 | 727 | 318 |
| 1965 | 1053 | 414 |
| 1973 | 1954 | 633 |
| 1978 | 2005 | 724 |
| 1980 | 1758 | 743 |
| 1981 | 1662 | 737 |
| 1982 | 1589 | 734 |
| 1983 | 1565 | 742 |
| 1984 | 1594 | 757 |
| 1985 | 1569 | 776 |
| 1986 | 1655 | 761 |
| 1987 | 1677 | 789 |
| 1988 | 1738 | 829 |
| 1989 | 1749[a] | 891 |

Note: [a] Includes Eastern Germany.
Source: OECD and IEA.

Table 5.2. Total energy and oil supply, and transport use, 1989 (thousand tonnes oil equivalent)

|  | Total primary energy supply | of which | |
|---|---|---|---|
|  |  | Oil | Transport |
| OECD | 3987 | 1735 | 885 |
| N. America | 2163 | 873 | 531 |
| Europe[a] | 1321 | 571 | 259 |
| Pacific | 503 | 270 | 96 |
| Ex-CPEs Europe[a] | 1842 | 535 | 182 |
| Developing countries incl. China | 1987 | 821 | —[b] |
| World | 7816 | 3092 | [c. 1250] |

Notes: [a] Eastern Germany included in ex-CPEs Europe, not in OECD.
[b] Data incomplete.
Source: OECD and IEA.

established, nor so widespread. It may not be happening in the regions where total growth has recently been faster. It might not go on happening in some other regions, if oil prices come down closer to the marginal *costs* of supply of other general fuels.

If this shift from general towards more specialised fuels can be taken as firmly established for the rest of the century, it should determine the patterns of downstream investment throughout the industry. Technologically, this poses no problems: various 'upgrading' processes to increase refinery output of the lighter products used in transport fuels have long been established. Even financially, the capital requirements may be relatively lower than the refining investments that were needed during the postwar periods of stronger oil expansion. (The US closed down a lot of inefficient refinery capacity in the eighties; other major importing regions cut back more slowly. In some regions, the industry is still left with more basic distillation capacity installed than it can be sure of utilising fully before the mid-nineties.) Nevertheless, the technical and economic choices that it poses are complex. Strategically, refiners have to decide how much adjustment to invest in; and particularly, when. Getting this timing right, in a period of accentuated economic and political uncertainties in some regions recently relied upon for most of the industry's growth, can make or lose fortunes. These questions of adjustment have recurred time and time again, in a stage of the industry that has no dependable record of profitability. And the world's oil companies remember uncomfortably that they have often been wrong about refinery investment before. (The cuts they had to make during the eighties and the imbalance of distillation capacity left in some regions is a memorial to their costliest set of past over-optimistic plans.)

If the hypothesis of oil's concentration onto specialised demand does turn out to be true, there will still be further uncertainties. For the nature of transport uses for oil in world energy demand is a focus of environmental fears about air pollution and global warming. Those are already imposing constraints upon road transport fuels in some countries. They could set eventual limits to this one dependably dynamic element in world oil demand.

## One purpose or many?

Oil has always been a specialised as well as a general fuel. It has usually commanded at least one market in which other fuels can hardly compete at all. In its initial half-century after commercial production began in Pennsylvania in the 1860s, kerosene became indispensable for lighting in the US[4] until electricity took over. With the rise of internal combustion engines, gasoline became the key specialised market, as simply an automotive transport fuel (it vaporises and can explode too easily to be burned as any kind of general fuel).[5] Yet the oil products used in competition with other forms of general energy, the distillate and re-sidual fuel oils, have accounted for more than half of total oil use during most of the period since the First World War.

Nowadays, gasoline is not the only transport fuel. In recent decades, distillate fuel (usually called 'gasoil' outside the US) has also been widely used in diesel-engined ships, rail and road vehicles, becoming partially a transport fuel. Kerosene has too; its most important and fastest-growing use is now for jet aviation. But even with those counted in – and if one counts out the large volumes of oil not used as energy – the transport fuels account for less than half of world oil consumption.

Residual fuel oil contributes little to transport, except at sea. It is used to power some marine diesel engines, and in the largest ships (mainly oil tankers) in marine turbines. There, as in its land uses, it is a general fuel burned under boilers. Apart from some extra convenience compared with coal, it can command no more than its thermal 'Btu value' in competition with other fossil fuels. After the oil price shocks of the seventies forced its heat value upwards in relation to other general fuels, fuel oil was the product that took the brunt of oil's competitive losses.

Aggregated statements about any 'world' patterns of oil demand have little practical meaning. Market patterns differ widely among economic groupings, regions, and individual countries within them. This enduring diversity seems to have arisen partly as a matter of historical and geographical timing, in the development of the oil industry itself and of the availability of other fuels.

It can be argued that different regions of the world are nowadays following a similar evolution of these patterns of oil product demand, but are at different stages in the process. The US, where commercial production and refining of oil *and* mass use of automotive transport all

---

[4] Oil production was almost called into being in Pennsylvania in the 1860s to replace tallow and lard for candles and axle grease. Camphene, the first refined product (from coal and shale) was an effective illuminant, but explosive and evil smelling. Oil, once drilling techniques had been borrowed from salt mining to discover and produce it, offered kerosene for lighting, plus better lubricants.

Lighting with gas manufactured from coal never developed widely across the dispersed rural communities of the US, because it was too costly to distribute. For the same reason, the spread of electric lighting was delayed.

[5] Until this kind of engine came into general use with the automobile early in the century, gasoline was flared off along with refinery gases as a dangerous by-product of kerosene. The rest of the barrel was burned for heating.

began earliest, is farther advanced along this path than any other region. Shortly after the First World War, gasoline became the oil product used there in larger volumes than any other. For a time in the thirties, at times in the sixties, and most recently during the eighties, its use there exceeded the total consumption of the distillate and residual 'black oils'. However, that did not occur simply because transport demand for oil was advancing so rapidly. It was partly because from the mid-thirties onwards more and more areas of the US were able to get natural gas. The development of long-distance gas pipelines made this possible. (In the forties, also, some trunk pipelines originally laid for oil were converted to move gas to the industrial North-East.)

Rapid development of this second form of petroleum commandeered much of the further general fuel expansion for postwar American economic growth that might otherwise have been supplied by the black oils. By the end of the Second World War, much of American industry was switching to gas. That enormously widened the market for a fuel which had mostly been discovered by oil companies in the search for oil; which was not always worth while to develop commercially where it had been found; and which was much more costly than oil to move to distant markets.

This substitution of gas for oil in other market sectors left the US industry happy to concentrate on gasoline, the product it had emphasised most since early in the century. Continued growth in US oil demand concentrated more and more upon the transport fuels, and primarily upon gasoline. Many US crudes are high in API gravity, yielding a larger proportion of light and middle distillates, even from simple refining, than most of the Middle East crudes used more widely elsewhere. They are also low in sulphur content. But as total US oil demand approached the limits of its production capacity, more of its heavier and high-sulphur crudes had to be used. Also, the predominance of oil in energy consumption there (including large amounts in electricity generation) raised objections and provoked regulatory limits earlier than elsewhere on the amounts of sulphur that consumers were prepared to breathe. (Japan, with its high density of population, was the next region to impose sulphur limits on oil. Consumers in Europe, accustomed to power stations burning coal, frequently with yet higher sulphur content, took longer to register their objections.)

Sulphur presents more technical problems for refiners than crude gravities do. Simple distillation, boiling off the lighter fractions, tends to concentrate the sulphur content of any crude into the residual fuel 'bottoms'. Gasoline, when boiled off, is relatively free of sulphur, and the content in middle distillates can be reduced as necessary by specialised processing. Desulphurisation of residual fuel oil is practicable, but only Japan has ever invested heavily in such processing (after a period when it was charged what it considered were excessive prices for low-sulphur Indonesian crude).

In the US that was not necessary: natural gas, free of sulphur, was already 'backing out' fuel oil. Refiners there preferred conversion processes to increase output of the lighter and generally more valuable products from any crude processed. They have always installed more upgrading capacity than refiners anywhere else. Since the fall in demand for non-transport uses of the black oils, the US industry has accentuated its extra conversion by the installation of higher conversion processes such as coking, which can reduce the yield of residual fuel oil from most crude qualities almost to nil.

### Abroad: a general fuel?

The greatest surge of oil consumption after the Second World War, however, was outside the US. And it was not primarily of gasoline.

After 1946, the United States virtually pumped oil into the Western European and Japanese economies. Aid in the names of Marshall and MacArthur, added to the commercial impetus of American oil companies, helped to promote and finance the switch to oil in those recovering economies. Initially, the oil involved was mainly American; but not for long. The US, along with the Caribbean refineries processing Venezuelan crude, had been the largest exporter as well as the largest producer before the war. World trade then consisted almost entirely of products. But the main surge of trade into Europe and later Japan was of crude from the Middle East. From the early fifties onwards that surpassed exports from the Western Hemisphere. Export growth there was left to the Caribbean; US exports soon moved into decline.

That switch to oil in Western Europe and Japan made room for the upsurge of Middle East production that had become practicable since the end of the thirties. Saudi Arabia had begun producing in 1938; Kuwait's fields had been discovered by then, but development was postponed throughout the war. By the early fifties, the magnitude of Middle East reserves – then as now enormous in relation even to world oil production – was beginning to be appreciated. With US domestic production still then growing fairly healthily, markets for this huge potential had to be found elsewhere. There was little that was healthy about Western Europe's coal industry, with its deep thin seams and high labour costs for sometimes sulphurous coal. Japan had almost no energy production to protect (and a strong US influence upon the planning of its recovery and further industrialisation). International oil companies entrenched in the Middle East could readily move oil into both those market areas at prices set conveniently just below the going prices for coal.

The pace of that switch to imported oil was measured, partly because European coal and, later, US domestic oil industries *were* protected during the postwar decades. Incomes in the regions newly switching to oil only gradually rose towards the levels of mass car ownership. Moreover, the development of Middle East production, tankers and refineries in these burgeoning markets involved a huge call on investment resources that were generally overstretched during postwar reconstruction.

Postwar growth in oil demand in those Eastern Hemisphere economies was less dominated by transport than the US market had been. Before the war European demand patterns had resembled the American, with gasoline accounting for about half the total. By the mid-fifties, gasoline was down to about a fifth of total oil demand in Western Europe. From 1960 onwards, clearer statistics are available for total consumption of oil products by market sector. In that year, gasoline was still about 20 per cent of oil demand, but the kerosenes and diesel fuels used in transport brought its share up to about a third of total oil consumption. Comparable statistics for Japan show transport taking about a quarter of oil demand in 1960.

During the 1960s, however, economic growth that was rapid in Europe and extraordinarily rapid in Japan was fuelled essentially by oil moving into industry and domestic heating, and to a lesser extent into electricity generation. Those sectors of demand grew faster than oil for transport. Between 1960 and 1972, transport use of oil in Western Europe nearly trebled in volume; but its share fell back to only 23 per cent, because the rest of demand was rising even more. In Japan, transport demand for oil rose nearly six times during the same period; but its share of total oil demand shrank to about 16 per cent. In these industrialised economies of the Eastern Hemisphere,[6] oil's main growth was then primarily as a general fuel.

Western Europe began to draw upon modest natural gas supplies in Italy and France shortly after the Second World War, and much larger supplies from the huge Groningen field onshore in the Netherlands and the UK North Sea during the 1960s. These supplemented the postwar

---

[6] In Australia and New Zealand, rich economies though exporters mainly of food and other primary products, oil demand patterns developed in much the same way, with transport taking about a third of the oil used in 1960, falling to about 20 per cent in 1972. By 1985, however, transport was again taking a third of these Pacific economies' oil consumption.

surge of oil consumption, but never substituted for it to the same degree that natural gas had in the US from the forties onwards. For a long time, European gas utilities were able to persuade their governments that gas should be marketed and priced, wherever possible, as a 'noble fuel' for specialised applications rather than as a general fuel.[7] Japan's first natural gas supplies, imports of liquefied natural gas (LNG), did not arrive until 1969. Its attitude towards gas was more cold-blooded, as befitted a voracious energy consumer with virtually no indigenous production of its own, having to import all its fuels. It developed LNG imports much more persistently than Europe or the US. From the beginning, it used the majority of its gas imports for electricity generation. (But gas has never yet exceeded 10 per cent of Japan's total energy consumption, as compared with more than 15 per cent, and still rising, in Western Europe.)

After 1973 the transport share of oil consumption in Europe and Japan began to rise again. This was not because of any very rapid growth in demand for transport fuels. As noted earlier, it was because demand for oil in all other sectors of those markets stopped growing or actually fell. Demand for transport by road (and in particular by air) went on growing, somewhat more slowly than before. By 1985, the nadir of total oil demand in OECD following the oil price shocks, transport was taking nearly 40 per cent of Western Europe's oil consumption and 27 per cent of Japan's. Price shocks in the seventies had given those economies extra incentives to follow the US and rely on fuels other than oil for their general energy supply.

### Patterns of processing

More than once since the war, industry planners have burned their fingers by extrapolating earlier trends and patterns of oil product demand. In the Marshall-Aided expansion of European refining in the immediate postwar years, companies assumed that patterns of product demand there would parallel those of the US (as before the war European markets had). Assuming that gasoline would lead the growth, they installed a higher proportion of upgrading plant (to increase yields of light products) than turned out to be necessary. That technological sophistication soon proved premature. By the end of the fifties, the region's demand for fuel oil was growing faster than for gasoline.

---

[7] Initially, more as a fuel consumed directly, *in competition with* the electricity sold by other monopolies, public and private, than as an alternative primary fuel for electricity generation. Most European governments, indeed, discouraged their power utilities from burning gas until the late 1980s. More recently, improved technology has encouraged generation from gas.

Catalytic crackers, put in as the pride of the new European refineries, were underutilised. Some, temporarily, had to be taken out of service.

During the next decade, demand for the black oils determined refiners' total throughput there. This left them surpluses of light products, traditionally higher in value but with local demand growing more slowly. Some of them were diverted into 'lower-grade' uses. Naphthas, products that hitherto would 'normally' have been reformed and blended to increase the gasoline yield, were for a time used in gas manufacture and even as 'low flash distillate' fuels burned under boilers. They found more enduring markets as feedstocks for cracking into petrochemicals in Europe and Japan (another departure from experience in the US, where that industry relies on natural gas liquids as feedstocks). To meet the continued rapid growth of general oil demand in these two regions, extra capacity continued to be needed; but simple distillation units were usually adequate. European refinery capacity more than trebled during the decade; Japanese capacity rose more than sevenfold. Refining in Europe was seldom a particularly profitable activity (so far as its profitability could be sorted out of largely integrated operations able to use arbitrary transfer prices). In Japan, restrictions on foreign ownership kept the degree of direct integration lower than in Europe. MITI, the ubiquitous Ministry of Trade and Industry, exerted a good deal of control over the prices that Japanese refiners paid for crude and charged for products; but also protected them from competitive imports of products. For international companies, one main purpose of developing refining capacity in both regions was to move what then seemed to be ever-increasing volumes of low-cost Middle East crudes that were comfortably profitable to produce. (Even on the crude, the profit margins were modest. The comfort came with the huge volumes.)

Then as now, practical oilmen knew that demand forecasts could always be depended upon to be wrong. The difference was that until then, for about twenty years, they had been dependably too low. That became part of the industry's conventional wisdom. From the late sixties onwards, up to about 1972, the demand experience that oil refiners in Europe and Japan had to look back upon consisted of annual growth rates over the previous ten years of 9 and 14 per cent respectively, with the growth seeming even to accelerate. There was little alternative but to extrapolate those trends. It was not surprising that refiners committed themselves to a continuing surge of refining investment, at comparable rates of expansion. In Europe, plans were for an increase of about 65 per cent between 1970 and 1975; in Japan, for almost a doubling of capacity.

Those plans were not quite fulfilled, but unfortunately they very nearly were. By 1974 the first Opec price shock had fractured the soaring demand curves. But some of the extra capacity was already on stream, and much of the rest was too far advanced to postpone. Indeed, in 1975–6 the growth in demand seemed resurgent. It was not until 1977–8 that recession and price responses became fully recognisable. In Europe and Japan some projects were postponed; by the mid-seventies, refinery capacity peaked and levelled off. Refiners had begun arguing about the need to 'rationalise' from the early seventies onwards. But the process of actual refinery closures took several years to commence, and quickened only after the second price shock of 1979.

In the US, refinery expansion went on throughout the seventies. Various perverse government reactions to the first Opec price surge included special advantages in crude allocation to small refiners. These actually encouraged the building of many new simple distillation units, 'entitlement refineries' without any conversion capacity of their own. (Much of their output needed further processing in other refineries to fit US demand patterns.) So until the entitlement programme ended in 1981, US distillation capacity went on growing. Then, suddenly, many of the 'tea kettle' refineries were closed down. Total OECD capacity peaked in 1981; by then, refinery utilisation rates were down, to under 70 per cent in 1982. Outside OECD, several Opec countries expanded their local refining capacity, to match rising internal demand and 'add value' to part of their exports;[8] and capacity went on expanding in the then Communist economies. The net effect of all these minuses and pluses was that total world *distillation* capacity peaked in 1981 at nearly 82 MBD, but came down to about 76 MBD by the end of that decade (Figure 5.1).

Measuring refining capacity simply in terms of distillation, however, had by then become as inadequate for many other OECD economies as it already was for the US.

Rapidly, the check to growth had transformed Europe's patterns of product demand; more slowly, Japan's. The growth that was checked first, and then reversed, was for fuel oil and for some stationary uses of the middle distillates. Both regions ceased to use oil primarily as a general fuel. Much of the extra distillation capacity installed there in the seventies, originally designed for high residual yields from Middle East crudes, simply could not manufacture the changed pattern of products required within a slackening total demand. (In effect, much of the net

---

[8] Though exports from the Caribbean declined sharply, and certain export refineries there were closed down.

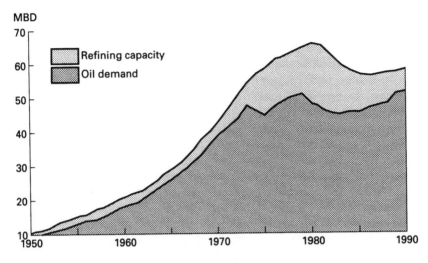

Figure 5.1. Refining capacity and oil demand, world (excluding Communist and former Communist areas), 1950–1990.

additional primary capacity put in there was never used.) During the same years, US import demand was increasing, to serve the world's most discriminating market for oil products. In refining jargon, the OECD 'demand barrel was getting whiter'.

Around the late seventies, also, the crude import barrel appeared to be getting blacker. Exports of the low-sulphur African crudes that had lightened the average gravity of crude supplies to Atlantic markets during the sixties seemed to be peaking. The volumes likely to become available from the North Sea were then perhaps underestimated. Late in the decade, moreover, Saudi Arabia gave its customers notice that it would reduce the proportion of Arabian Light crude in its exports, and supply more of its heavy crudes. This Arabian crude is 'light' only by comparison with most other Gulf crudes. It is a medium-gravity crude of 34 degrees API gravity, and fairly high in sulphur. But it comes from Ghawar, the world's largest oilfield. It can be produced – and was then being exported – in greater volumes than any other crude produced anywhere. So the Saudi announcement confirmed fears that all OECD refiners, henceforth, would need to make the additional light products they needed out of generally heavier crudes.

A further wave of refining investment in Europe from the late seventies onwards, therefore, added no primary distillation, but was concentrated on upgrading. Refiners put in several different kinds of unit, varying widely in their degrees of conversion.[9] All, however, can be measured in terms of standardised catalytic cracking capacity (which in its various forms remains the most widely used of all these conversion processes). The US remained ahead of all other regions in its proportion of conversion, over 68 per cent of primary capacity in 1990. Europe achieved the biggest increase, from 12 per cent in 1979 to 28 per cent by 1989. The degree of conversion in Japanese refineries, hitherto able to import enough light sweet crude from established suppliers such as Indonesia and Brunei, has remained lower (except for the desulphurisation of certain sour crudes). For OECD as a whole, the degree of conversion reached 45 per cent of primary capacity. But refinery upgrading is no longer confined to the more industrialised countries. Gulf Opec exporters, led by Saudi Arabia and Kuwait, have installed complex refineries; so has Indonesia, mainly for the internal consumption of its huge population. Singapore, the Far East's oil entrepôt and refining pool, is adding more sophisticated units to its large export refining capacity.

Even some of that upgrading investment, in the event, could have been premature. In Europe, the proportionate shift towards lighter products coincided with a larger drop in total demand than anyone had expected. So for some years the light crudes from the North Sea, supplementing imports from Africa, proved sufficient to maintain the regional refining balance. However, the more sophisticated refineries generally achieved better margins on refining – during a decade of surplus and weak profitability – than the older straight distillation capacity.

*Where the growth is*

From now on, however, OECD will not be where the oil growth is. Its patterns of product demand may cease to be dominant. What have begun to become more important are the patterns of oil demand *outside* OECD – in the developing countries, and in the formerly Communist economies (Table 5.3). During the 1980s, those economic groupings expanded faster than the OECD countries, and their growth exceeded the net growth in total world consumption.

At present the ex-Communist economies, together with China, consume much more energy, including oil, than the developing coun-

---

[9] From *visbreaking*, the simplest conversion process, through *fluid catalytic cracking* and *hydrocracking*, with higher conversion of residual bottoms into light products and middle distillates, to *coking* processes, which effectively convert all the fuel oil into lighter products and solid residues of petroleum coke.

Table 5.3. *Patterns of oil consumption, 1989, main products by regions*
*(percentages)*

|  | North America | Other OECD | Former CPE Europe | Developing countries incl. China | World |
|---|---|---|---|---|---|
| LPG/naphtha | 7 | 12 | 4 | 8 | 8 |
| Motor gasoline | 39 | 19 | 19 | 16 | 24 |
| Aviation fuels | 9 | 4 | 6 | 4 | 5 |
| Gas/diesel oil | 19 | 31 | 23 | 28 | 25 |
| Fuel oil | 10 | 20 | 31 | 30 | 22 |
| Other | 17 | 13 | 18 | 15 | 16 |
| All products: regional percentages of World total | 28 | 29 | 16 | 27 | 100 |

tries. In Eastern Europe, macroeconomic growth is almost in abeyance. Its energy consumption is still more coal-oriented than elsewhere, and is characteristically wasteful. It might easily go on growing even if the economies stagnate; but could probably more advantageously be reduced for a time than grow further at all. Moreover, the petroleum-exporting republics of the ex-Soviet Union *may* be able to go on exporting more petroleum than all the others need to import. *If* these republics can produce enough, regardless of high resource costs, they probably will, since they have little else to export that is worth hard Western currencies. (The other ex-Communist countries may choose to stop buying oil and gas from the ex-Soviet Union. But whether they do or not, their petroleum has been costing them world prices, in dollars, since the beginning of 1991.) So on balance that collection of formerly subjugated nationalities, restored to independence if not yet to prosperity, may not make much *net* difference to international oil supply and demand over this decade.

The developing countries – themselves, yet again, extraordinarily diverse – will probably have a much greater impact on patterns of demand for oil between now and the end of this century. The share of oil in their energy consumption is far higher than in the ex-Communist countries – and indeed of late, at around 50 per cent, higher than its share in OECD energy use. Up to now, transport has taken a smaller share of these countries' oil consumption than it does in OECD; but now their transport demand is growing faster. Much of this is concentrated within relatively few of them – notably the richer 'newly industrialising countries' of the Pacific Rim and some oil exporters inside and outside Opec. Everywhere from Bangkok to Mexico City, their populations have avid expectations of motorised living. But while their transport demand goes on growing apace, oil demand in other sectors has not yet levelled off as in OECD. So far, developing countries still rely heavily on middle distillates and liquefied petroleum gases (LPGs) for industrial and domestic consumption; and generate much of their electricity from fuel oil.

One new general fuel appearing in the markets of both the industrialised and the developing countries during this decade has intriguing possibilities in relation to oil, technically, economically (and even politically). Venezuela's state oil company, Petroleos de Venezuela SA (PDV), has developed and is now exporting 'Orimulsion', a mixture of very heavy crude oil with water (to make it flow through pipes and pumps more readily), as a power station fuel. This is produced from one of the more accessible parts of the country's vast Orinoco 'tarbelt', a reserve of 'unconventional oil'[10] that is probably the earth's largest single accumulation of petroleum, but until now had remained unexploited. Production of this particular fuel from heavy crude has been claimed to cost no more than $3 a barrel, which would be comparable with Middle East crude costs. (Technically, the possibility of producing any usable fuel so cheaply from these unconventional oil deposits is astonishing. Such very heavy crudes had traditionally been relegated to the remote upper range of very costly substitutes to be developed only around the middle of next century – and within Opec, as noted in Chapter 3, Venezuela has gone on emphasising that development of the tarbelt will require extremely high capital investment per barrel.) Orimulsion could compete only with fuel oil, the lowest-value product refined from conventional crudes; PDV is insisting that it will in practice compete mainly with coal (how effectively, will depend on the comparative costs of flue-gas scrubbing from the two fuels at power stations). But no refining cost at all is involved (in contrast to the very expensive processing that some international companies had developed in order to process a fuller range of more generally acceptable refined products from other heavy oils and bitumens, such as Canada's tar sands).

Politically, Orimulsion is also no doubt interesting as a petroleum fuel that Venezuela can export free of Opec quotas, since it is outside the gravity range classed as crude oil. (Indeed, its reserve source may not

---

[10] 'Extra heavy' crude oils heavier than 10 degrees API gravity are technically not included in 'conventional oil'. 'Heavy' crudes between 10 and 20 degrees API are. Gravities in the Orinoco heavy oil belt vary from 4 to 17 degrees API, but are probably mostly under 10 degrees API.

always be included in Venezuela's reported oil reserves.) But it is a reminder that *some* kinds of oil may remain quite competitive in the range of general fuels even if most refined products retreat to their specialist markets.

## *Alternative transport fuels?*

If transport continues to expand faster than any of the other ways that humans use energy, then refining worldwide must follow US practice and technology towards yet higher conversion of the crude barrel. But another sequence of petroleum evolution is already in train, and may partially overtake this further evolution of refining technology. Natural gas is beginning to enter the range of transport fuels. So are a range of alcohols and ethers derived from vegetable sources such as sugar cane. Most of those so far introduced have needed direct subsidy, or at any rate fiscal advantages over the established oil transport fuels with which they compete, to render them commercially worth marketing. But such encouragement has been forthcoming in the most advanced industrial societies such as the US, as well as in less-developed oil-importing countries such as Brazil. The political motives are a mixture of environmental concerns and the lingering fear that oil prices *might* just take off again some time during the coming decade.

Alcohols and ethers have a long history of use as additives to improve the octane[11] quality of gasolines. Now some of them are being used much more because the form of additive most widely used for this purpose since the 1920s, lead compounds, has already been phased out in the US and soon will be in other industrialised economies. This is not simply because the compounds used hitherto are toxic, but because after improving combustion they deposit lead upon the catalytic convertors now generally fitted to reduce exhaust pollution. Unleaded gasoline is now standard throughout the US, Japan and Australia, and rapidly taking over motoring markets in Europe and the newly industrialised countries.

To replace lead in improving gasoline engine efficiency, one of the ether additives, methyl tertiary-butyl ether (MTBE), has come widely into use. Brazil engaged in a lengthy and commercially unsuccessful experiment with pure ethanol as a gasoline substitute in the eighties, and still uses large amounts of it blended with gasoline. But the most

---

[11] The *octane* number of a gasoline measures the extent to which 'knocking', premature explosion of fuel in the combustion chamber, reduces the efficiency of an engine. For diesel engines, the *cetane* number measures the delay after fuel is injected into the chamber before it ignites simply by compression.

powerful political support for this alcohol fuel during this decade is coming from US federal and state governments. California has ambitions to phase out gasoline completely, and President Bush pushed through legislation stipulating much more use of 'clean fuels' such as ethanol in major American cities. (Predictably, the US oil industry argued that this legislation was ill-conceived. Less predictably, it added that if any such fuel had to be imposed on the automotive market, the governments had chosen the wrong one. It should have been methanol.)

Methanol, a liquid fuel that can readily be produced from natural gas and is easier to transport by sea than LNG, the ultra-cold liquefied form in which gas can be shipped, has many advocates for gas competition with international oil. As yet, large-scale processing and export of it has hardly begun. The liquid gases so far best established as transport fuels are the LPGs, propanes and butanes derived from the liquids often produced with natural gas (as well as from the lightest fractions boiled off in oil refining). These are becoming quite widely used as automotive fuels in some countries; another form, compressed natural gas, is used in a few gas-producing countries.

But the main advance of gas into road transport fuels from now on may eventually come from synthetic gasolines or diesel fuels converted directly from natural gas. Major oil companies have developed several advanced processes to produce such fuels at fairly competitive costs – much more cheaply, particularly in capital cost, than any of the conversion processes for liquids from coal. Such fuels may command some political encouragement from the producing end of the business, quite apart from consumers glad to reduce dependence upon imported oil. Countries with local gas reserves that they cannot use fully at home, but which do not justify capital-intensive export schemes, may be even more glad of a new chance to produce high-grade transport fuels from their own domestic petroleum. Also, most of these liquid fuels converted from gas are claimed to be cleaner in terms of most forms of atmospheric pollution than similar fuels refined from oil.

One of the myriad unanswered questions surrounding the controversy over climatic change at the time that this book was completed was whether any of these potential road transport fuels generate demonstrably less carbon dioxide than all of the others. Road transport has been reckoned to contribute perhaps 20 per cent of all carbon emissions.[12] Comparison of the carbon content of the main *primary* fuels we use is

[12] 'Between 70% and 80% of anthropogenic $CO_2$ emissions are estimated to come from the burning of fossil fuels, more than half of which is oil. Since about half of the world's oil is used for transport, about a fifth of the world's anthropogenic $CO_2$ emissions can be attributed to the transportation sector'. *Motoring and the Environment* (Shell, 1992).

Table 5.4. *Carbon content of the different fossil fuels (tonnes of carbon per tonne of oil equivalent)*

|  | Carbon content TC/TOE | Degree of uncertainty |
|---|---|---|
| *Primary fuels* | | |
| Natural gas | 0.61 | ± 1% |
| Crude oil | 0.85 | ± 3% |
| Bituminous coal | 1.09 | ± 5% |
| *Oil products* | | |
| Gasoline | 0.80 | ± 2% |
| Kerosene | 0.83 | ± 2% |
| Diesel/gas oil | 0.85 | ± 2% |
| Fuel oils | 0.89 | ± 2% |

*Source:* M. Grubb *et al.*, *Energy Policies and the Greenhouse Effect* (Aldershot, UK, Dartmouth for the Royal Institute for International Affairs, 1991), appendix A.

relatively simple, if necessarily approximate (Table 5.4). But comparison of the carbon dioxide emissions that arise from their processing and combustion is more uncertain.[13] Producers of all these new or modified transport fuels have to assess these debated technical comparisons; also, to assess the extent to which politicians will use them to justify discrimination between the fuels by regulation or differential excise taxation.

*Pollution and congestion*

If coal is readily identifiable as the worst polluter of all the fossil fuels, will that imply a resurgence for fuel oil? So far, the only signs of this have occurred in the US, although not so much for environmental reasons, but simply as a response to the 1986 price collapse and further falls in some years since. Most other industrialised economies have less flexibility for short-term fuel switching in their power generation[14] and other energy-intensive industries. In the eighties, those economies had

[13] Other greenhouse gases are negligible by weight compared with carbon dioxide, but contribute much more 'radiative impact' per molecule to the greenhouse effect. Methane from natural gas operations and coal seams is over 20 times as radiative as carbon dioxide; nitrous oxide 290 times as powerful per molecule. But the volumes of methane actually released from either primary fuel industry are matters of much debate.
[14] In countries with a higher degree of interconnection through transmission networks, such as the UK, switching can be carried out simply by load despatching, bringing in different stations higher up the rank order. But there and in Germany, longer-term contracts for coal use have so far limited the use of such flexibility.

greater hopes than the US of large incremental supplies of competitively priced gas, from abroad. In the early nineties, however, the US was once again becoming confident of ample supply from its own continuing 'gas bubble', with freer markets in gas driving its delivered prices down below those of fuel oil or even coal.

Quite apart from air pollution and global warming, automotive transport of course accumulates another inherent problem, ever-increasing traffic congestion. (Technologists have been promising the electric inner city vehicle for decades now, but the problems of battery bulk and weight seem hardly yet to have been solved commercially. Also, its most practicable application might come back into *public* city transport.) None of the industrialised democracies has yet ventured to set really significant constraints upon the use of private cars in cities. In government – and equally in opposition – politicians are uncomfortably aware of just how venturesome, and electorally risky, any moves to do so by regulation might turn out to be. As sampled by opinion polling, voters often sound fairly responsive to green economists' proposals such as 'carbon taxes' or 'tradeable pollution permits', whether or not they fully comprehend the notions. They, or at any rate the politicians they elect, have so far sounded more uneasy about the comparable idea of road pricing (perhaps because its potential direct inconvenience for them is easier to comprehend and fear).

There is even less chance of moderating the expectations of mass motoring in the varied array of countries across the world that are experimenting anew with versions of democracy. For many decades, the USSR's central planners discouraged private car ownership. This was not simply because its citizens were too poor to afford the vehicles; they often had enough savings, because the command economy delivered so little else to buy. Ostensibly at least, it was a matter of deliberate policy, to take advantage of the higher efficiency of public transport in cities. Proponents of the same virtuous social engineering in more advanced industrialised countries may note how unconvinced Soviet citizens were by this good advice. Their ambitions to exercise the divine right of driving one's own car seem as unquenchable as those of the populations of the other countries that discarded Communism – preferably, no doubt, a bigger and better car. (No television image caught the tenor of the 1989 revolutions in Eastern Europe as clearly as those long dreary queues of Trabants inching steadfastly towards the West German border – towards democracy, a united Germany, and the dream of a BMW.)[15]

---

[15] Second-hand BMWs, in 1991, did indeed become a significant element in trade between the reunited Germanys.

If world economic growth continues as at present hoped, then measures to control congestion (and perhaps pollution as well) seem liable to be overwhelmed in most developing countries by the linked growth of personal incomes, car ownership and road use. That is less likely in the rearguard of the poorest small countries; but given the tiny demand those exert to start with, their bad luck will hardly affect the world oil market much anyway. Two outstanding exceptions, which must eventually matter enormously, are the world's two centres of largest population, China and India. If and when either of these advance towards comfortable levels of average income, their citizens may exert a massive demand for personal transport fuels too. That hardly seems likely this century. But if China continues its recent rates of growth and if India could achieve any similar take off, their total demand for oil must rise anyway. It remains skewed towards the middle distillates and fuel oils, still for use mainly as general fuels. The huge potential of those two markets, and the industrialisation they will need to undergo to approach any threshold of mass automotive transport, may prolong the strength of demand across the world for the black oils.

Across the world, indeed, demand for the middle distillates seems likely to remain stronger than for gasolines or fuel oil. They are the most commercially versatile of oil products, spanning the transport and general fuel markets. Aviation jet fuel, of late the fastest-growing of all refined products, is essentially the same oil that lit the way out West as oil's key specialised product at the turn of the century. (It still is oil for many of the lamps of China.) Diesel fuels are growing more than gasoline in the world's most sophisticated market, the US, as well as in the developing countries, where they serve a diversity of small-scale power uses as well as most forms of transport.

For the rest of this decade, then, the hypothesis that world oil demand may concentrate increasingly upon specialised transport fuels still looks well founded. But gasoline may lose its star role. Some at least of the blacker oils may hold their relative share across the industry's diverse markets. And beyond the turn of the century, the transport fuels will no longer come exclusively from oil.

# CHAPTER 6

# An industry restructured

During the first half of the Opec decade, member governments of the Organisation took over, by stages, the declaration of prices in the world oil trade, the ownership of production in their countries, and the setting of formal limits to output there. During the second half, they took over the actual selling of most of the crude oil traded physically in the world oil market, along with most of the operational responsibility for producing this crude.

That sea-change transformed the structure of international trade in oil. Directly, it involved only just under half the world's production capacity. But most of the other half was in North America, a formerly self-sufficient region already becoming more import-dependent, or in the then Communist landmass, more than self-sufficient in oil but exporting relatively little. The production that Opec governments took over represented about three-quarters of the production capacity in what the industry used to call 'WOCANA'. More significantly, it accounted for about 80 per cent of world crude oil exports.

Within the former matrix of international oil, private companies owned outside the exporting countries had not only produced about 90 per cent of the crude moving through world trade. They had transported it through their own integrated channels for refining and marketing as products downstream. Vertically integrated supply through the systems of the eight companies regarded as 'international majors' then dominated the trade.

Those eight were the four Aramco shareholders, Exxon, Mobil, Texaco and Socal (later renamed Chevron), plus British Petroleum, Gulf and Royal Dutch/Shell – three other largely private companies, ranked in order of their entitlements to Middle East production. These were often described as the 'Seven Sisters'. The eighth was France's Compagnie Française des Pétroles. CFP, later called Total, was seldom listed in the sisterhood, partly because it was sometimes regarded as one of its parent government's chosen corporate instruments.[1] The first seven were reduced to six in the early eighties: Gulf was taken over by Chevron in 1984. But in fact none of them has remained an international major in quite the same sense. That status effectively disappeared when ownership upstream passed to the Opec governments.

When the world oil trade was dominated by those eight vertically integrated companies, most of the crude that moved internationally was never sold at all. It was simply transferred between subsidiaries of these groups, at prices that could be adjusted to minimise the total tax exposure of the parent company across all the countries where it operated. The crude oil did not change ultimate beneficial ownership until, refined into products, it reached consumer markets downstream – the one point at which all oil, finally, does change owners.

As well as their own integrated supplies, these companies then also produced and sold most of the crude purchased at arm's length internationally by other refiners. The bulk of world trade in crude, non-integrated as well as integrated, moved at one or more points through the major companies' channels (Figure 6.1). In 1972, just before government participation in the operating companies of these concessions was agreed upon in the Gulf, only about 6–8 MBD out of the total 25 MBD of crude moving in interregional trade was sold at arm's length. About 6 MBD of that volume was sold to others by the integrated major concessionaires, out of the 22 MBD that those majors then produced outside the US. (Their non-American production in 1972, incidentally, was roughly five times as high as in the late eighties, and roughly three times as much as these major companies' total production of crude worldwide in 1990.)

Between 1972 and 1985, the volume of crude sold at arm's length doubled, although total world trade in crude had fallen by nearly 30 per cent. As a proportion of the total crude moving in this trade, the importance of arm's length sales had trebled. At present, probably 85 per cent of the crude moving in interregional trade is sold at arm's length, almost all of it at prices available to all comers.

Most of the crude lifted by the former concessionaires, as well as by other customers, nowadays represents sales by the exporting countries' national companies, no longer private equity offtake. This is a mirror-image of the decline of vertical integration in the world movement of

---

[1] In fact, until 1983, the French government had a lower shareholding in CFP than the British government had in BP. Which government shareholder wielded more influence in key periods over the behaviour of the company that it partly owned is a matter for historians' conjecture. (Companies have no rules for eventual publication of their records, and often commit less to paper than governments.) BP has now been fully privatised and the state shareholding in Total further reduced. But their governments still display some special national interest in each.

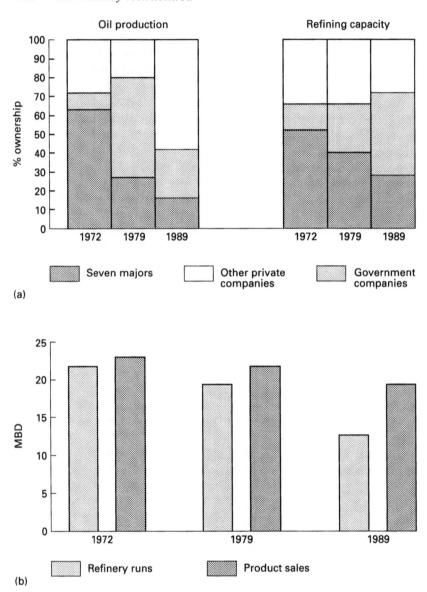

Figure 6.1. Oil market structure, 1972, 1979 and 1989: (a) transfers of ownership in international oil between seven international major companies, other private companies, and government companies: crude oil production and refining capacity and (b) major companies' refinery runs and product sales. (*Source:* Kelly, 'Restructuring of the world oil market'.)

crude. It is not a direct measure of decline in these majors' crude supplies, nor in their importance in the business – though both *have* been eroded since the Opec takeovers. (The governments who took over ownership had no objection in principle to vertical integration, only to the foreign owners who controlled it before.)

## *The formerly favoured few*

The international major companies always differed widely in size, and never included all the world's largest privately owned oil companies. Indeed some of them, as we have seen, were at the time themselves partly state-owned. Their degrees of integration, and their balance of operations, geographically and between different stages of their business varied considerably. So did the importance of international operations to their total business, partly because their parent countries applied quite different import and tax regimes to oil. But in their heyday in the sixties one simple common factor distinguished those eight companies from all the rest. Each of them shared control of the crude oil offtake from, and the development of capacity in, the main concessions of *two or more* of the longer-established producing countries bordering on the Persian Gulf.

So during that era the international companies' vertical integration was complemented in practice by a degree of informal but effective *horizontal* integration. Their joint ownership of operating companies in the Middle East, and their voting rights under the complex operating agreements through which they controlled exploration, development and offtake there, gave them a unique degree of knowledge of each others' opportunities to increase crude offtake, and some leverage to influence each others' opportunities.

The crude oil reserves to which these eight companies had concession rights seemed at the time to constitute the only source of energy sufficient, and in technical terms dependable, to power economic growth in the industrialised oil-importing countries of Western Europe and Japan for the rest of the century. From the seventies onwards, they were then expected to contribute a similarly essential ingredient to the economic growth of the US. Also – it seemed at the time almost incidental – these Middle East reserves constituted the basic supply of commercial energy to the developing countries of the Eastern Hemisphere.

Hence the informal degree of horizontal integration that they then enjoyed in the Middle East applied to the most important incremental supply of energy available anywhere. It was not the only powerful influence on that supply. Long before nationalisation and indeed before

Opec, the host governments had always to be satisfied financially. That was a primary concern that none of the international major companies could avoid. But that obligation once met, they had strong commercial incentives to compete 'responsibly' amongst themselves in the many markets where they met – so long as they could move increasing quantities of low-cost Middle East crude downstream. (Up to 1972–3, their responsible competition *did* move rapidly growing volumes of low-cost oil into the world market without severely undermining price levels. Opec has never managed as much.) Their situation afforded them a further advantage over competitors at all levels in the trade: the sheer volume and quality of information moving back, forth and sideways throughout their integrated systems.

That complex situation afforded the international majors considerably more advantages than might be expected from any textbook definitions of vertical integration. One could quite as logically (quoting different textbooks) argue that the advantage which the majors exploited so successfully during twenty-five postwar years arose from elements of oligopoly ('competition between the few') in the horizontal linkages upstream rather than from vertical integration as such.

These companies were all strongly affected, directly or indirectly, by concern about American anti-trust laws. They had to lean over backwards, nearly always, to avoid being suspected of collusion. (Very occasionally the American companies among them were given dispensations to consult with each other and even negotiate as a group with host governments. Those occasions, as it happened, were not among the companies' most impressive negotiating performances.)

Nevertheless, their shareholdings in joint operating companies in the Gulf permitted and indeed necessitated a good deal of effective consultation without too much fear of anti-trust vapourings.[2] Over the years, that web of mutual influence, leverage and two-way flow of shared information probably did more to sustain their advantage over other companies than their structural patterns of organisation.

## Was the co-ordination optimal?

In theory, vertical integration could *ideally* have offered optimal cost savings:

A fully integrated firm would have the advantage of being able to plan capital investments in different phases with perfect coordination. Adaptive sequential decision making can best be implemented by an integrated firm with full

---

[2] Of late, none of the investigations mounted fairly often in the US and occasionally elsewhere has achieved much. But no US oil company ever forgets the high-water mark of anti-trust, when in 1911 the original Standard Oil was dissolved. (Three of the 'Seven Sisters' are descended from it.).

intrafirm information flows regarding divisional opportunities and plans. Integrated companies have pronounced advantages in the logistics of handling fluid flows. These advantages are largely informational and are lost without the data base that integration gives.[3]

In practice, the international majors did some of those things very effectively. Their performance never depended on *complete* ownership of the physical operations at all stages throughout their systems. For example, they normally contracted out the drilling within their exploration programmes. They depended to a considerable extent upon an independent (and highly competitive) tanker business, not only for current logistics but for the technical development of future capacity to move oil. In refining, wherever it became politically advisable (for example, in Japan and some European countries, as well as in developing nations), they accepted joint ventures with local capital. In the marketing of various 'black oil' products, they used independent wholesalers. Even in gasoline marketing, where they are most visible to the final consumer, they depended to a large extent upon franchised service stations. Effectively, their vertical integration was exercised in the central planning of all these functions.

Whether the international majors performed better then than some theoretical multitude of non-integrated competitors might have, nobody will ever know. From the experience of American exploration, one of the few parts of the industry where a multitude of competitors has regularly been evident, it has often been argued that US majors (a wider group than the Seven Sisters but including all of them) had *not* historically been more successful than independent explorers in finding oil. Changes in exploration technology, primarily in the accumulation in databanks and improved computer interpretation of geophysical data, could now be improving the major companies' chances. Also, they now have far more experience of planning the development of large fields, particularly offshore, than smaller companies anywhere. But those are pluses and minuses of scale in particular stages of the business, not of integration.

The international majors' logistic programming of world oil supply often appeared to observers from outside[4] to be the most sophisticated and impressive function of their vertically integrated management. From the inside, however, it did not always look so perfect:

We had supply departments, not trading departments. There were small units dealing in exchanges so as to balance supply and demand at the margin and improve logistics; but the main emphasis was on a centralised system dis-

---

[3] J. M. Griffin and H. B. Steele, *Energy Economics and Policy* (Academic Press, 1980), p. 295.
[4] E.g., J. E. Hartshorn, *Oil Companies and Governments* (Faber & Faber, 1962; revised edn, 1967).

tributing in as rational a manner as possible supplies from the company's production ... or brought in under long-term contracts ... refineries around the world were told by the parent organisation what they were to process. The 'centre' would arrange shipping. It was not a particularly efficient way of allocating resources, but in a blunt sort of way it worked.[5]

A vertically integrated company's ability 'to plan capital investments in different phases with perfect co-ordination', again, could at times simply mean that all the 'adaptive sequential decision making' went wrong the same way. The international majors had a period during the 1960s when their forecasts always turned out to be underestimates. Continuing expansion was taken for granted, and only the timing was ever doubted. Investment never seemed likely to be mistaken; at worst, it might turn out to be premature. On that basis, they planned huge, co-ordinated investment programmes for the seventies to expand super-tanker fleets and basic refining capacity in Europe and Japan. But it was just then that the trend of forecasting errors happened to flip over. Huge surpluses of both kinds of capacity were left to overhang the industry for a decade.

*From simulation to competition?*

Within their vertical integration, these companies logically sought to minimise costs by simulating a quasi-competitive pattern, postulating the 'right' supply values at which crude and products could be transferred interdepartmentally. That was intended to optimise the allocation of resources, and minimise costs, through the systems of each integrated company. The international companies were extremely well-informed, particularly through the Middle East joint companies, about each other's plans and capacities. They were prepared to exchange large amounts of different crudes and products, and to share transport and processing capacity at different points around the world, where this might reduce costs. It could be argued that these several companies, each sub-optimising its own operations, might together not have diverged far from some optimal allocation of resources throughout the whole international business. (Even if true, that would have said nothing about the degree of competition involved. The same logistic allocation to minimise costs could in theory have come about through perfect competition at all stages; through the operations of an efficient monopolist owning the whole system; or possibly through the behaviour of a well-informed and diligent oligopoly – as in practice, then, it did.)

[5] M. S. Robinson, 'Oil trading: yesterday, today, and tomorrow', in *The Oil Market in the 1990s*, ed. R. G. Reed and F. Fesheraki (Westview Press, 1989), p. 163.

Since the end of the seventies, for these international companies, vertical integration has largely become confined to their operations outside Opec. That has reduced the two-way flow of internal information up and down their integrated systems. The mutual leverage across interlinked joint operating companies has largely disappeared along with the equity shareholdings in the largest Gulf producing countries. Nobody in the companies now has as much information about the Gulf upstream as the majors had then (but kept largely to themselves). Certainly none of the Gulf governments has.

Thus, there has been a loss of inside information that used to have directly operational effects upon the whole crude trade. Its loss has been to some extent offset by a widening, perhaps deepening, and certainly accelerating flow of public information about and through the trade, via its open markets (Figure 6.2). The new avalanche of market information through the computer, with its proliferation across video screens worldwide, is provided far faster, almost instantly, though the information is seldom as accurate. It certainly has directly affected internal behaviour within the vertically integrated companies, providing more continuously reliable criteria for inter-departmental transfer values and 'make or buy' decisions. It should be improving management flexibility and the speed of response throughout these companies.

Nevertheless, this constant flow of market information is in the public domain. Integrated companies have more than one stage of the business in which to make use of it. Because they may have deeper judgement and more comprehensive databases, or can devise their own expert software to carry out particularly sophisticated analyses, these companies *may* be able to make better use of all this instant information than the rest. This remains to be seen. For the international majors, now much less vertically integrated than before, faster market information may therefore largely offset the lost advantage of inside information:

Integration (apart from a few groping attempts by Kuwait and Venezuela) is out. The trading function is needed to keep the flows going. And it adds value in two ways. First, it reduces supply costs: through freight optimisation, back hauls, and exchanges, and by relentlessly searching out particular markets that can make the most of a particular crude or blend of crudes or by meeting specifications by blending two off-specification products. The market and trading are a more efficient mechanism for doing this than central supply allocation, with its calculated-value structures. Second, trading adds value by price arbitrage, by perfecting markets.[6]

But even if trading in open markets helps internationally integrated companies to respond more efficiently to selected information, that may not make it attractive to Opec governments who are uneasy about

[6] Robinson, 'Oil trading', p. 169.

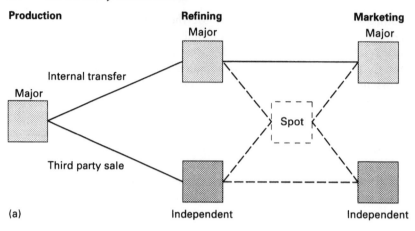

**Production**    **Refining**    **Marketing**

(a)

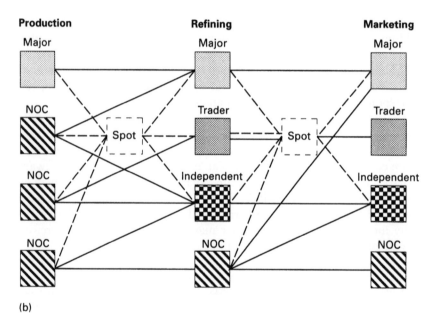

(b)

Figure 6.2. Dominant oil market structure: (a) 1972, (b) late 1980s.
(*Source:* Kelly, 'Restructuring of the world oil market'.)

various aspects of open markets anyway, and to some of whom vertical integration seems the 'natural' way to exploit the huge low-cost oil reserves that are their countries' underlying wealth.

In the seventies, the loss of equity rights to produce from those incomparable reserves had deprived the former concessionaires of the upstream profits (and shares of economic rent) that they had had before. But at the same time, it put large amounts of spare cash into their hands, and made exploration for oil at much higher technical costs look potentially quite profitable. So it turned out to be.

Most of the new development in the eighties outside Opec (and the former Soviet Union) was equity oil. For the companies, tax-paid cost outside Opec was generally cheaper than paying nearly full price for crude from Opec. The companies of course needed a degree of confidence that they would be able to hold onto equity rights to any production that they could develop in such new areas. But Opec's price increases had also made the companies' parent governments much more concerned to encourage exploration and development in their own or other politically safer areas.

Non-Opec host governments were not slow to tax the resultant production at the high percentage rates then fashionable. But when world prices began to drop, those high rates meant that the host governments' royalties and taxes suffered more of each price reduction than the equity producers did. Also, since prices fell, some of these new host governments have been careful to moderate their terms and taxes, in order to keep licensee companies interested in further exploration within their territories.

### Seeking reinforcement upstream?

In the heady Opec decade while they were gaining control, the takeover of ownership and, later, of management upstream did not demand much entrepreneurial skill from most Opec governments or their national oil companies. Largely because of their success in raising prices in the seventies, they were *not* called upon to increase capacity upstream in the eighties. Most had ample reserves, with little need for exploration in the short term. Their learning curve as managers upstream was dependably lucrative and not technically demanding in terms of oil production, though some carried through huge development schemes to reinforce their industries' infrastructure, such as gathering systems to reduce the wasteful flaring of gas produced along with oil. Drawing upon or extrapolating the investment planning that former concessionaires had left, they could afford to hire or buy in all the technology they wanted.

In the early eighties, the problems these national companies encountered were essentially commercial, trying to market crude that customers were reluctant to buy. It was not until the end of that decade that they saw much need to rehabilitate and perhaps expand production capacity. By then, the renewal of oil development was no longer as easy

to finance as it would have seemed in the super-riches of the seventies –
even in the Gulf. None of the main exporters there was as rich as a
decade before. Moreover, at least two of them had found another way
to waste their reduced oil revenues.

In the brief interval between the two Gulf wars that it launched
against its neighbours in the decade to 1990, the government of Iraq had
spared a little attention to its own oil industry. In February 1990, it
announced that it had invited certain foreign oil companies to participate in financing the development of new oilfields, beginning with one
discovered in the 1970s near the Iranian border, where it had halted
development after launching the first Gulf war. But the government
soon pre-empted any constructive ideas that its oil technocrats might
have had there by choosing the military option once again. Its invasion
of Kuwait in August that year took as one excuse among others their
dispute over rights to an oil reservoir that underlies the frontier between
the two countries.[7] The Iraqi aggression, however, no doubt had wider
purposes than the seizure of any single set of oilfields. If the US and its
allies had not evicted its forces from Kuwait in 1991, Iraq might have
gained more potential control over Gulf oil exports than any single
government in the region has ever exercised.

A technically effortless Western victory in 1991 destroyed those pretensions, along with much more besides in Iraq and Kuwait. It devastated Iraq, and may have put paid to any hopes of Western co-operation
in oil development there for the rest of this decade. The second Gulf war
deeply damaged Kuwait's oil installations as well as polluting its lit-
toral. It also, for a time, plunged the Emirate into as weak a short-term
financial position as most other hitherto oil-rich Gulf states.

The first Gulf war, over seven-and-a-half years, had already nearly
ruined the economy of Iran as well as that of Iraq. Even before incurring
the further interminable burden of reparations to mortgage the oil
production that it is allowed, Iraq had been heavily indebted. Iran was
less so, because political enmity between it and the US had shut it out of
world financial markets for a decade. But that enmity had also frozen its
substantial assets in US banks; and its current oil revenue from production was far below its current aspirations. It too had a huge national
programme of postwar national reconstruction to preoccupy it – which
could be financed only with oil revenues, from an industry severely
damaged through the 1980–8 war. Even before Iraq's overtures in early

---

[7] This is a fairly frequent occurrence beneath contiguous areas of surface rights to oil. It can readily
be resolved by independent technical assessment, provided that the adjoining surface landlords show
sensible goodwill. In this case, there were few signs that either government did; moreover, they had
long-standing disputes over sovereignty and frontier demarcation.

1990, the Iranian government had announced that it was discussing, also with a consortium of foreign companies, the joint development of two gasfields offshore in its Gulf waters, discovered long before but with their development further postponed by the danger of attack.

These two countries have the oldest oil industries in the Middle East. They were also the first to nationalise all or part of those industries, long before 1972–3. Both had revolutionary governments (of bitterly opposed kinds, secular as against religious), and have usually been more hostile to foreign enterprise operating there than any other governments in the region. Both have long-established national oil companies, and would claim a high degree of competence in running their oil operations. (INOC, the Iraq National Oil Company, was perhaps technically the stronger. It had announced the discovery of thirty-eight new oilfields, and trebled its oil reserves, since 1970.) But neither, during their war of the eighties, can have kept up with Western advances in oil technology.

Both of these revolutionary governments would have had to call in foreign capital to finance the increases in output that they needed so desperately. For the present, Iraq's government may have forfeited INOC's chances of doing so. NIOC, the National Iranian Oil Company, can promise to service the return on the new foreign investment that it requires, and pay for the companies' technical assistance with part of the proceeds of the gas to be produced, eventually, from these fields. But gas exports usually take several years to organise.

Until it was invaded in 1990, Kuwait had been expanding its production capacity too, with no need for external finance. Its healthy revenues from oil had been sufficient to finance its own expansion of capacity, and to develop the production of some oil and gas that it had discovered through exploration abroad. Moreover, it could afford to expand the downstream operations that it had acquired in North America and Europe, and was still seeking opportunities to buy into Japanese refining and marketing. The war might have undermined all those ventures. But to finance recovery, the government of Kuwait wisely chose not to sell off direct investments in foreign industry, but instead to run down some of its huge investment portfolio abroad. (Part of this is held formally in the name of the country's future generations. Getting back into production as soon as possible was a sensible trade-off.)

After the country's rescue by United Nations forces, the fires that Iraqi troops had started on most of the country's 900 oil wells were extinguished, mainly by Western specialists, in a matter of months; production, too, recovered much faster than anyone had expected. But not all the wells could be started up again simply; many needed re-drilling and the rebuilding of surface facilities. Kuwait has had to renew much of its producing capacity. Technically, this may have been fairly straightforward; but today's capital costs are much higher than those embodied in other existing and undamaged onshore capacity elsewhere in the Gulf. Financing this, even with the debatable assurance of repar-ations from up to 30 per cent of Iraq's oil revenues, is making enormous demands upon the severely wounded Kuwaiti economy, and upon the oil revenues earned in its recovery.

Even before the other Gulf exporters, the government of Saudi Arabia had been reported as discussing with 'certain European companies' co-operation in the development of some of its known but undeveloped oilfields. But nothing was ever divulged about any such negotiations; in December 1989, the government was stung into a denial that it was 'considering swapping some of its oil reserves for downstream acqui-sitions', and has often said the same since. Such co-operation as it appears to have in mind is technical, and not necessarily financial.

The Kingdom's huge oil production comes essentially from only about fifteen fields, almost all of them discovered before 1960 and none of them anywhere near depleted. (In 1979 those fifteen had been able to produce nearly 10 MBD, almost twice the country's total production in 1989; and in 1990 it took only a few months' rehabilitation to raise production back to 8.5 MBD.) The government had ceased publishing details of production by individual Saudi fields after 1982, but in 1989 it listed the names of thirty-five fields, more than it had ever reported to be in production. During the 1980s, also, it raised its estimates of national proved reserves by some 90 billion barrels.

Most of the fields that Saudi Arabia could consider developing as new joint ventures are likely to be very large compared with anywhere outside the Gulf. Development there to the highest modern standards will involve huge financing projects. But, technically, it may not be particularly demanding, compared with new fields elsewhere that need 'frontier technology' in exploration as well as development. There and in some other parts of the Gulf, in newly developed fields as well as old, the underlying advantages should still offer the world's lowest oil costs.

Even the Kingdom, albeit still extraordinarily rich by some standards, was less comfortably placed financially than at the end of the Opec decade. During the late eighties it had perhaps 60 per cent of its 1980 volume of exports, at about 60 per cent of 1980 nominal prices. The royal government had been running budgetary deficits, and drawing heavily on the surpluses it had accumulated earlier. With the 1990 embargo on Iraqi and Kuwaiti crude exports, its production rebounded, and prices were high for a time. So its oil revenues recovered sharply. But after helping to subsidise Iraq in the first Gulf war, it provided logistic support for all the UN forces *against* Iraq through the second war, and paid the US $13.5 billion in cash for military protection during that period.

Given its extraordinary oil reserves, and the second highest output in the world, all those tribulations did not weaken the country's creditworthiness with international bankers. But on principle, the Saudi government is still averse to borrowing more than the minimum required to finance current expenditures.

Thus, of the four main Gulf exporters at the beginning of the 1990s, three were seeking foreign corporate partners and two of them foreign finance for further upstream development of the oil industries that they had nationalised about fifteen years before. Those four Gulf exporters, along with Venezuela, had been the founder members of Opec thirty years before. They had effectively brought to an end the traditional concession system under which foreign companies had originally discovered and developed their oil. Venezuela too was committed to increase its productive capacity, and was deep in debt after lower oil prices in the second half of the 1980s. But whether it should invite foreign investment back into oil upstream has remained a subject of considerable political controversy there. In operational terms, it hardly needed any assistance (except in technology for the development of its enormous reserves of 'heavy oil', most of which are hardly producible by conventional methods). But it was already involved in joint refining and marketing ventures in Germany, the United States, Sweden and Belgium; and it was consolidating its stronghold of Caribbean refining and storage terminals to serve US markets.

All of the founder-member countries of Opec, thus, were toying anew with the idea of foreign investment in their oil industries upstream; or with vertical integration downstream; or with both. None, however, was specifically inviting former concessionaires back, or restricting its choice of foreign partners to them. There were some signs that their national companies preferred co-operation with smaller foreign partners than with the former international majors. These common shifts in policy raised a different question. Were the new policies intended as, or would they promote, a reintegration of the international industry that their nationalisation had helped to split apart? That question was less easy to answer – both in terms of intentions and of practicability.

In the other main Gulf producing area, the United Arab Emirates, more modest extensions of existing production capacity were also being planned by the governments of Abu Dhabi and Dubai. But they had no need to seek new foreign finance. Neither government had ever nation-alised their producing operations fully. Both therefore retain foreign equity partners in their oil operations, with commitments to put up part of whatever investment is agreed upon. (In the early nineties the finan-cial troubles of Abu Dhabi were only indirectly related to the oil business. The Bank of Credit & Commerce International, of which 65 per cent had been owned by that government, was engulfed in failure and recriminations over long-term systematic fraud.)

A similar involvement with foreign oil companies upstream continues in most of the rest of Opec. In Ecuador, Gabon, Nigeria and, in effect, in Indonesia, foreign oil companies remain as operators with minority shares in oil production. That gives them a continuing special status as offtakers of crude, getting their percentage entitlements of oil with profit margins that are effective discounts below the prices that other crude buyers pay. But it also involves them in putting up their shares of investment in developing extra production. (Libya, as so often, was a special case. It has foreign equity shareholders in several producing operations, but the American companies among these were forbidden by their government to take part in operations.)

### Integrated gas exports?

Two other Opec countries that had nationalised parts of their petroleum industries in their own fashion, Algeria and Nigeria, were also once again enlisting foreign investment partners in the late 1980s. Algeria was discussing joint operations with Shell and Total/CFP to rehabilitate its natural gas liquefaction trains and export terminals. It had already modified its nationalisation law to allow joint ventures in exploration once again. In 1991 its then prime minister, himself from the country's oil business, announced plans to offer several years' oil deliveries in advance to foreign companies prepared to finance, and then develop, extra oil and gas liquids production from the country's huge Hassi Messaoud reservoir by enhanced recovery techniques.

Nigeria, in preparations for an ambitious but long-delayed liquefied natural gas export project, had been reported as 'selling its foreign partners in the project gas reserves in the ground'. That is quite a common practice between private oil companies, and indeed is often preferred as an alternative to finding new oil. But it is not usual in many host countries, and as described it sounded almost unprecedented for any Opec country.[8] What had in fact happened was that the Nigerian

---

[8] Traditionally, concession rights gave the foreign enterprise the rights to all petroleum 'won and saved'. This was often interpreted as leaving ownership of the oil in the ground vested in the host

National Petroleum Company, which had owned 80 per cent of a long-standing production joint venture with Shell, sold another 10 per cent to Shell and 5 per cent each to Elf and Agip, retaining 60 per cent itself. There is considerable oil production from this acreage already, with gas reserves intended to contribute to the LNG scheme when it finally commences. But the transaction between shareholders hardly involved selling off 'dedicated' national reserves.

One other Opec country, Qatar, is already planning to develop gas for export by pipeline around the Gulf and has firm intentions to export LNG worldwide later. Its relatively small oil production is entirely nationalised, and its pipeline gas exports may be financed jointly with the other Gulf countries that will import its gas. But if and when its government develops LNG exports, Qatar is committed to work with private foreign companies experienced in the trade, including former concessionaires such as BP.

The export of natural gas, particularly in the form of LNG, has developed its own peculiar rules during its brief postwar history. Exporting gas in any form involves even heavier 'front-end' capital investment than oil, because gas is far more expensive to transport; LNG involves costly liquefaction as well. Indeed, gas exports have so far only become worth while to develop under very long-term contracts linking all the enterprises concerned, at both ends of the business and in between. Typically, LNG export projects involve joint ventures in lique-faction and transport between a governmental gas producer and one or more private foreign partners, committing sale and specialised transport of the whole of the gas reserve over a period of twenty years or more to an importing utility at the foreign destination, which also has to become equally tightly involved contractually before any of the development starts.[9] The ownership is not identical all the way along the supply chain. But in a sense, gas exports as LNG (or even through pipelines) have so far tended to involve more exclusive vertical integration or longer-term contracts than are nowadays practised in oil, where exports move into an established pattern of uncommitted trade offering con-tinuing flexible options at all stages.

These particular joint ventures to develop or expand LNG exports during the 1990s – and similar expansion of Indonesian export projects

government. Only when the crude was brought to the surface at the wellhead, accordingly, was its ownership said to pass to the concessionaire. (For what it is worth, some oil company lawyers have always disputed that interpretation.)

[9] In complete contrast to the pattern of the world's largest (capitalist) gas market, the US, where a myriad of gas producers have access to an established network of pipelines, nowadays trading very competitively. (Whether the world's largest gas supply and consumption, in the former Soviet Union, can be described as a market is debatable. Its pipeline *exports* have involved long-term contracts and heavy initial investments more akin to the LNG export patterns.)

– are in no sense new departures. They carry on in the only way that such exports have ever been developed so far. In one way, however, they do resemble the Gulf countries' renewed flirtations with foreign companies upstream. They involve investment to develop known petroleum fields, *not* exploration to find new ones. (Nobody can plan LNG exports until the gas is found and its reserves appraised, to see whether they will allow the minimum volume and term required to make an export project worthwhile.)

### Developing known reserves

Joint development of oilfields that are already known and may be fairly well appraised is a different exercise from exploration and production in general. The essential difference, as noted in Chapter 3, is in relative risk. Technical risks continue in production, as illustrated by terrible accidents such as Piper Alpha. Investment in oil and gas development, however shared, is far higher than the amount spent on exploring for any given oilfield. But the commercial risk is far lower.

Quite frequently, the development costs of 'frontier' oil development have turned out to be much higher than the initial estimates. That does not imply that the commercial risks of oil development are peculiarly high; it means, rather, that the initial assessment was inadequate. (In the seventies, oil was not alone among capital-intensive industries in suffering such cost overruns. Indeed, in some energy industries the actual capital investments required turned out to be much larger multiples of the capital originally budgeted than in oil – and ruled some nuclear projects, for example, out of business even before they were completed.)

Host governments in countries lacking any oil may haggle over the rates of return that explorers stipulate they will need to develop whatever petroleum may be discovered. But they are not normally capable technically or financially of taking the exploration risks themselves. So they usually have to settle for whatever is currently the 'going rate' of exploration terms. But where no exploration is involved and the known reserves are ample, the case is altered. Opec governments inviting foreign companies in to share the much lower risks of developing known fields will hope to offer significantly less than the going rate for ventures elsewhere that include exploration. They may also have a wider range of choice among foreign joint venturers. (In the prolific known fields of the Gulf, some may be tempted to rely almost entirely on drilling contractors.)

Development of proved oil reserves in undoubtedly low-cost areas, even in a period of price instability, would also usually appear to be eminently 'bankable'. Governments inviting foreign partners to co-operate in developing such known fields, therefore, are seeking partly technical expertise and partly low-risk capital. Several of the Opec governments now inviting foreign companies in once again have proposed forms of development contract designed to offer an 'adequate' return on the expertise, but one which is closer to financial borrowing rates on the element of bankable capital. Ultimately, this must come down to bargaining about the value of technical expertise and comparative political risk, together with any advantage that a foreign partner may be able to offer in disposing of the extra petroleum production envisaged. *If* some of the capital is bankable (which will vary according to the government involved), then one partner or the other can raise it. The rest of the bargaining will depend upon the international market for technical expertise in planning field development. As it happens, that planning is *not* one of the activities that companies ordinarily contract out, even though they too use contractors to do much of the work that they plan. They usually manage the complicated process of field development themselves.

During this decade, the market for expertise in field development has tightened somewhat, because the oil industry of the former USSR needs help. It is the only one outside the Middle East with super-giant fields of conventional oil (and gas) already known and awaiting development – though with far more difficult technical conditions and higher costs. (Further, it also has exploration opportunities in some regions that oilmen consider 'highly prospective'.) Also, in a state of political remorse and anxiety to re-invent capitalism, the former Soviet republics are not in an ideal negotiating situation. They are competing for exactly the same scarce resources of knowledge and technology in the international oil industry, as well as for finance. That may weaken the chances of Opec governments to drive hard bargains.

## Following older integration

Known fields in the Opec countries, also, might appear eminently developable by the foreign partners who had originally discovered them, *if* those partners happen to have remained around. In Saudi Arabia, the discoverers have retained rather more presence on the ground than nationalised ex-concessionaires in most other Gulf countries. But up to the time this book was completed, the Aramco partners had not been invited back to develop new production from the country's many known but undeveloped reservoirs.

Saudi Arabia, after long advocacy of 'participation' in a country's oil operations as an alternative to nationalisation, had in fact taken over 100 per cent ownership of its main oil concession by 1976, earlier than most other host countries in the Gulf. But its relationship with Aramco and that operating company's former corporate shareholders remained extremely close and apparently amiable, though not to the exclusion of other foreign companies. The government constructed several refineries and petrochemical plants from the mid-1970s onwards as joint ventures with other companies as well as the four 'Aramco partners'. But upstream, within the Kingdom, it had continued to work exclusively with them, using contracts for technical services that offered the former shareholders an effective discount on their purchases of crude. Technically, those arrangements appear to have worked well. Commercially, in the turbulent market circumstances of the mid-1980s, they came under more strain. (It was through bargaining with those ex-shareholders that the Kingdom originally had recourse to 'netback contracts', selling crude for whatever the products from processing it could later fetch. In 1986, those sales punctured inflated crude prices for everybody in the business.)

In autumn 1988, it was with one of those partner companies, Texaco – suddenly and fortuitously rendered financially the weakest[10] – that the Saudi government, preparing to act upon a newly declared policy of vertical integration, entered into its first significant downstream venture abroad, purchasing 50 per cent of a sizeable portion of the company's US refining and marketing interests.

The linkage between Saudi Arabia and the Aramco ex-partners is thus no longer symbiotic, but still close. Formally treated in the same way as other customers for crude, they remain *primi inter pares*. Their technical services to Saudi Aramco in the management and extension of its existing production capacity may still be indispensable. But for the development of new production within the Kingdom, some but not necessarily all of it within the original Aramco acreage, they may no longer be the only foreign contractors considered.

In the other Opec countries that went to full nationalisation – Iran, Iraq, Kuwait, Qatar and Venezuela – former concessionaires continue as crude buyers, often on a large scale. During most of the 1980s those companies enjoyed no special favours, beyond their bargaining power as large-scale customers in any given state of the market. By the end of the decade, just under 20 per cent of Opec exports consisted of equity crude 'offtaken' by their foreign shareholders, or on specifically preferential terms by former concessionaires such as the Aramco partners.

[10] The independent US company Pennzoil took legal action to challenge Texaco's takeover of Getty Oil, and eventually obtained huge damages from Texaco in a remarkable Texas court decision.

(The proportion was in fact higher than a few years before; partly because total Opec exports had fallen, and partly because these customers could buy crude on easier terms than most others.)

If Opec governments in general invite foreign joint venturers to invest in expansion upstream, it would somewhat dilute the degree of state ownership in Opec countries that nationalised their industries fully[11] in the 1970s. How much it may do so will depend on the proportion of new capacity being added, and on the shares of production from this new capacity that the government and its new private partner may agree upon. At the current 'going rate' for terms in oil agreements, 80 per cent or more of any additional oil or gas produced will probably accrue to the government. So government ownership of the Opec countries' total oil production seems unlikely to be much diluted.

Nor would such development necessarily lead to greater vertical integration of the oil business of the government involved. Iraq, for example, always seemed to be more interested simply in increasing its output of crude for export (in one way or another) than in securing refining and marketing assets. Iran needs to develop gasfields for internal use (including the 're-pressuring' of its main oilfields) as well as for export. Both need any extra petroleum revenues more to finance national reconstruction than to acquire downstream assets abroad. (At the same time, in order to export LNG at all, Iran would have to become involved in the particular form of vertical integration which that business requires.)

Any foreign company involved in such ventures *is* likely to become somewhat more vertically integrated than before, by adding to its guaranteed supply of equity crude or exportable gas. But the net effect will depend on what is happening to its other equity production, inside and outside Opec. For the industry as a whole, as non-Opec production levels off or as it peaks, these new additions may not fully offset some continuing decline in the integrated share of world trade.

## The impulse to reintegrate

Saudi interest in new joint ventures upstream, *if* the government should choose those rather than other ways of financing its expansion of output, may be deliberately linked to vertical integration. The Kingdom has already declared its intention to follow such a policy, ultimately, to the point where 'without putting a time frame, probably all' Saudi oil

---

[11] Neither Saudi Arabia nor Kuwait ever nationalised the concession held by the Arabian Oil Company (of Japan) offshore in the Neutral Zone between their two countries.

would move through its own or jointly integrated channels. In 1989 its oil minister Hisham Nazer argued:

the oil world is an integrated world by definition. And while some historical and economic anomalies were straightened out in the 1970s, I feel with hindsight that the delinking between producers and the oil companies should perhaps have not been so severe. The present impulse to reintegrate, therefore, is merely a result of the inherent tendency of the oil industry towards global integration.[12]

Presumably, therefore, in selecting any new partners to help add capacity upstream, the Saudi government would always be interested in their abilities to move the resultant extra crude through integrated refining and marketing abroad, preferably with Saudi partnership there too. The government, indeed, has said much more in public about seeking more partners downstream than it has about inviting partners in upstream.

In some senses, this harks back to the previous Saudi preference for participation rather than nationalisation. Both policies reflected an even longer-established trust within the Kingdom that major integrated companies can nearly always dispose of oil, even in soft markets, without as much price-cutting as weaker or less integrated resellers are forced into. That often did seem true to some degree before the Saudi and other governments severed that linkage in the majors' dominance of the trade in the 1970s.

But should one ascribe the advantages of that past, rather extraordinary, but in its time widely beneficial situation of the international majors simply to inherent advantages of vertical integration in oil? Whether it arose in the past only from their vertical integration is highly debatable, as noted above. Whether it could now be restored by new vertical linkage is even more so.

Kuwait and Venezuela have always explained their moves abroad more specifically, in relation to particular projects and purposes. Both are already much more integrated than Saudi Arabia, in terms of home and foreign refining capacity compared with their crude output (Table 6.1). Venezuela, since long before nationalisation, had exported a large proportion of its oil as products, notably residual fuel oil processed in its own or Caribbean refineries, to the north-eastern United States. Both countries produce mainly heavy sour crude oils, unsuited to the recently increasing demand for 'a whiter products barrel' in the other main OECD importing regions as well as in the US. Their crudes need conversion refineries at home or abroad to process what refiners call the 'slate' of lighter products now more in demand. The particular form of

---

[12] Hisham Nazer, 'The players in the oil market', *PIW*, 23 October 1989.

Table 6.1. *Downstream ventures abroad of Opec governments,*
*1990–1991 ('000 b/d)*

|  | Saudi Arabia | Venezuela | Libya | Kuwait |
|---|---|---|---|---|
| Crude production capacity | 9,000 | 2,800 | 1,600 | (2,500)[a] |
| Crude production quota, 1990 | 5,380 | 1,945 | 1,233 | 1,500 |
| Refinery capacity |  |  |  |  |
| At home | 1,863 | 1,167 | 347 | (819)[a] |
| Abroad | 383 | 777 | 199 | 232 |
| Total | 2,246 | 1,944 | 546 | (1,051)[a] |
| As per cent of production capacity | 25 | 69 | 34 | 42 |
| Integrated supplies to foreign refineries[b] | 640 | 630 | 300 | —[c] |

*Notes:* [a] Capacities in Kuwait shown as in early 1990, before Gulf war damage.
[b] Refining capacities abroad shown as percentage share with foreign partners.
Hence integrated supplies may exceed governments' ownership in b/d.
[c] Kuwait was not producing or exporting crude in the last half of 1990 and most
of 1991.

downstream investment that Venezuela chose, joint ventures, had been
successful in a number of petrochemical developments with local private
partners in the 1960s. (Similarly, Saudi Arabia probably chose this same
form of downstream venture abroad because of local experience with
jointly owned refineries within the Kingdom.)

One minor additional incentive to downstream integration (at home
or abroad) for all these Opec members was that no one ever tried
seriously to establish quotas for refined products. What they refine and
export escapes any limitations on crude production. Quota discipline, in
practice, has seldom been very binding on crude exports either. But even
if the Organisation ever puts any teeth into its monitoring of performance against quotas, products exports would probably remain immune.

So far, these moves into downstream integration abroad have not
given Opec or other crude exporters any sizeable share of the international refining business. In 1990, their refining capacity abroad
amounted to only about 5 per cent of the total capacity of the countries
importing their crude.[13] The export refineries *within* Opec countries

---

[13] Measured, roughly, as total world refining capacity *less* the capacity in countries with net exports
of crude.

were more significant: they accounted for about a quarter of world trade in refined products.

Historically, integration *has* been the recurrent mode and tendency of organisation throughout this business. Most small oil companies as well as large have usually sought to become or to remain integrated whenever they have had the chance. Not many large and successful companies have stayed strictly in one stage of the industry, even in the US, the most mature and diversified arena of the world oil business. However, there is an enormous diversity in the degree of integration among different highly successful oil companies, even the largest ones such as the international majors.

In their heyday these varied from Shell and Mobil, which traditionally produced far less crude themselves than they refined and marketed, to BP, Socal/Chevron and Gulf, which produced far more. (Some of these international companies have now reversed their patterns and rankings.) Texaco was at one time admired for maintaining a nice balance of crude self-sufficiency. Whether that ever really mattered much is debatable.

During certain long periods in the history of this industry its average degree of integration has appeared to increase (though this is not easy to measure). But these increases have been interrupted from time to time by sharp reductions in integration, usually through government pressure or action. Historically, the most important of these was in the US industry, the splitting up of the original Standard Oil Trust ordered in 1911. The most important in our time has been outside the US – the Opec takeovers in the 1970s, which cut the established links between their production, world exports, and the processing downstream.

## The intention of permanence

Whether or not 'global integration' is an inherent feature of this oil industry, any player in the market who engages in it does so for his own chosen reasons. But all the low-cost producers with extremely high reserves in the Gulf have one overriding incentive to practise in all stages of the industry. They expect to be able to stay in the business longer than the rest.

Saudi Arabia, the producing country with the lowest costs and potentially the largest volume of current output anywhere, is uniquely placed in all market circumstances, whichever structure it chooses for its operations. At almost any level of price 'netted back' from final markets, it can capture some economic rent on its crude exports. The supply costs of all other production that demand requires will be higher, and the most expensive required to match demand will determine the price. If it were thoroughly confident of strongly increasing demand – or if it were prepared for price competition *à outrance*, one possible way of bringing that about – Saudi Arabia would be able to combine a comfortable economic rent with a high volume of exports, whether it invested downstream or not. That could conceivably be the simplest way to maximise its oil revenues. But it would provoke powerful opposition from higher-cost producers, inside as well as outside Opec. After trying that course once in 1985–6, the Kingdom has usually drawn back from the brink.

When contemplating a promising but inherently uncertain oil market for the nineties, the incentives for even the lowest-cost producer to invest in marketing abroad may look stronger. (Continuing market uncertainty, however, may derive mainly from the yawning gap between its production costs and those of the higher-cost producers setting the price level. That is one of Saudi Arabia's, and all countries', problems, and it is not easily surmountable.)

*If* the lowest-cost producer has reason to believe that investment in marketing downstream can 'move more crude' for it without drastic price-cutting and still increase the volume on which it can gain this rent, then taking only a minimum return on the downstream assets may become financially worth while. That was good enough reasoning for much of the refining capacity installed in Europe and Japan after the war. The concessionaires who put in that integrated capacity never enjoyed nearly as high a proportion of the economic rent on Middle East crude as the governments have since. Also, the netbacks then available on products from that crude were tiny by comparison.

With the more uncertain market prospect of the nineties, investment in refining capacity to process the extra crude moved might be unnecessary. Processing can usually be hired at no more than the variable costs of existing capacity, whenever that pays better. The flexibility that one's own refining capacity and storage in various downstream locations can offer may be commercially interesting. But arguably the most valuable element in investment propositions downstream may be brand names, and the marketing prowess of the chosen joint venture partners (though Kuwait has succeeded alone with Q8). So far, that commercial expertise in final markets has been largely outside the domain of the governments who now control most of the industry upstream.

CHAPTER 7

# Governments in the oil business

One consequence of the cumulative Opec takeover in the 1970s was to extend state ownership to about 85 per cent of world oil-producing capacity. The member countries' nationalisations altered the ownership of about 50 per cent; other state-owned companies in the market economies rose to about 10 per cent of the total; and production in the then Communist countries, which had been only about 17 per cent of world output in 1970 but was rising much faster, reached nearly a quarter of the total by 1979. In 1989, even outside the Soviet Union, the proportion of state ownership was close on 60 per cent. Much of the 40 per cent of world capacity of which private owners retain sole or partial ownership is in North America.

That is capacity. The ensuing shares of actual production were somewhat different. Most of the extra capacity developed since the Opec nationalisations has been by private companies. Nearly all the capacity producing private 'equity crude', ever since, has been fully employed. During the early 1980s some of the state-owned capacity, notably in the Soviet Union, China and Mexico, was fairly fully employed too. But by 1985 the rest, essentially in Opec, was not much more than half-employed. By the end of that decade, recovery in world demand, setbacks in some non-Opec supply, had brought Opec production back to some 85 per cent of capacity, even before the Gulf war. That was mainly due to higher output in member countries. But it was also partly due to sizeable downward revisions in Opec capacity, mainly in the Gulf, and after 1990–1 the removal of Kuwaiti and Iraqi supplies from the market.

There was nothing new about government ownership of oil companies. Two of the international majors had been backed by government shareholdings and support since the beginnings of Middle East oil production, and had had their operations extended when Germany was effectively shut out of that industry after World War I. Other state companies had been set up downstream in the interwar years to import refined products from American and Anglo-Dutch companies, and were encouraged to develop local refining industries and limit the imports to crude. In some cases, the governmental motives may have been autarkic, as discussed in Chapter 4. On occasion, as in France, Italy and Spain, these state companies were created to implement 'delegated monopolies' of local refining or of gasoline marketing. But the French state-backed companies obtained a significant share of production from existing Middle East joint concessions; and after World War II they found and developed a completely new petroleum industry producing oil and gas in Algeria. France's Compagnie Française des Pétroles (with originally 38 per cent state ownership) and its Elf group (originally 100 per cent) thus lost significant shareholdings when Opec governments took over in the Middle East and North Africa. The proportion of total government ownership did not necessarily change; the governments involved did. As oil began to be exported to the developing countries in the postwar years, some of their governments also developed national oil companies to import, market, refine, and when possible combine with international oil companies in exploration and in the development of any more oil found.

That recently overwhelming majority of state ownership did not last. Waves of privatisation, however defined or organised, have swept across the former Soviet petroleum industry, once the only massive bastion of nationalised petroleum. In the West, also, some formerly state-owned oil companies have been sold to private shareholders, and shareholdings in others are likely to be. Moreover, in several Opec countries, as noted in the last chapter, foreign private oil companies are being invited to co-operate in increasing production.

*Privatising the Gulf?*

The wave of privatisation across world oil *production* during the early nineties, up to the time this book was completed, was still breaking just short of the industries that Opec had nationalised in the seventies. Several member countries, were inviting international companies back into joint ventures to develop new fields or additional capacity in old ones – seeking the capital such companies could contribute or help to attract, as well as their technical expertise. Some Opec governments have invited local private businessmen to invest in their internal distribution networks and into oil-related businesses such as petrochemicals. However, their oil-producing industries remain so central to the national economies of most Opec countries that it is hard to envisage their governments reselling large equity shares in their *existing* production to any private owners, foreign or local, for at least the rest of this century.

Devotees of privatisation as a panacea in itself are to be found in the Gulf as elsewhere, advocating the transfer of oil production there to private local investors as a solution preferable to joint ventures with foreign oil companies.[1] Certain among them proposed to leave the Gulf governments to perform within Opec simply as representatives of their privatised national companies. That proposition sounded rather unworldly, and not simply because Opec had never been anything but an organisation of sovereign *governments*. The nationalisation of Opec oil industries had had little in common with the ideological nationalisations of public utilities and a few manufacturing industries carried out in some European countries after World War II. Nor would privatisation of Opec national oil industries necessarily resemble the privatisations elsewhere, which resulted from ideological change as voters in many democratic countries became disillusioned with the incompetence, bureaucracy and lack of accountability of state-owned public utilities.

The moves to nationalisation in the Opec countries had rejected over-mighty enterprises exploiting the nations' natural resources not because they were privately owned, but because they were foreign – and backed by foreign parent governments with histories of imperial dominance or pretensions. In some countries, the Opec takeovers had represented the assertion or consolidation of national identity and independence. In another sense, particularly in the Gulf, the oil industries taken from foreign ownership in the seventies were at a stroke converted into forms of family business. Ownership passed from remote foreign shareholders to a few local ruling families, who had originally been placed in control, or whose territories had been arbitrarily delineated, by European imperial powers or under American influence. (That was as true of Iraq as of Iran, Saudi Arabia, Kuwait and the Emirates. All the frontiers around the Gulf, until the Iraq–Iran war of 1980–8, had been demarcated by European powers during or after two world wars.)[2]

The oil production and exports developed within those Gulf frontiers now constitute the main element of internationally recognised legitimacy for the ruling families of these Gulf regimes. The ruling families are unlikely to hand these core businesses over to other private owners, local or foreign, so long as they believe their Gulf oil reserves retain their

---

[1] W. al-Mazeedi, 'Privatising national oil companies in the Gulf', *Energy Policy* 20 (1992), no. 10, pp. 983–95.

[2] In the early nineties, a commission of foreign countries wearing United Nations labels again redrew these frontiers to reduce direct Iraqi access to the Gulf seaboard even further. This seemed liable to become a dependable recipe for future disputes, whoever rules Iraq.

unique underlying national value. There are plenty of rich and commercially-minded entrepreneurs in the Gulf. They can perhaps claim more legitimacy for local privatisation than for the joint ventures that foreign oil companies seek in Opec oil. But they have no comparable technical expertise to contribute. As to their ability to muster foreign financial backing, the performance of local Gulf enterprises in other businesses during recent decades – from the Souk el-Manakh to BCCI – would not necessarily encourage the international financial community. Politically, it is doubtful whether importers would trust local entrepreneurs to guarantee security of supply from Gulf oil industries more than the same export industries run by NOCs on behalf of their government masters.

(*If* in any case the privatisation of existing Gulf production ever does become politically on the cards, it would present fascinating but perhaps baffling problems of valuation. Putting a 'present value' price on relatively limitless reserves of oil that could be produced more cheaply than other energy whatever happens, as noted earlier, might in any case strain the scope and rationality of the techniques of investment appraisal that the world's accountancy profession presently has to hand.)

Government shareholdings *per se* had never made much discernible difference to the performance of international companies in the world oil trade before the Opec decade. Certainly, government backing had often been demonstrably influential in the development of world oil trade, ever since the beginning of the century. But that had been as true of the wholly private American international major companies as of Anglo-Iranian-cum-BP or CFP. If some European state companies had enjoyed a degree of protection against imports in the interwar period, so had the US domestic industry then and later. The international major companies, in particular, all traded in much the same (admittedly peculiar) way, regardless of the nature of their shareholdings. Soviet oil developed in its own even more peculiar way, occasionally frightening the international majors with its lurches into exporting. But it overlapped only a fringe of the international market, remaining mainly isolated in self-sufficiency. (Nor was its impact upon oil markets necessarily strengthened by being Communist. If the Russian oil industry had historically remained in private hands – say Shell's – would its impact upon oil trading since the twenties have been less, or more?)

So how much difference did the later shift into Opec government ownership (and eventual control) really make? Much more, in fact, than state ownership in oil anywhere else. The difference turned out to be profound, mainly because Opec produced such a large proportion of internationally traded oil, but also because most of its member countries

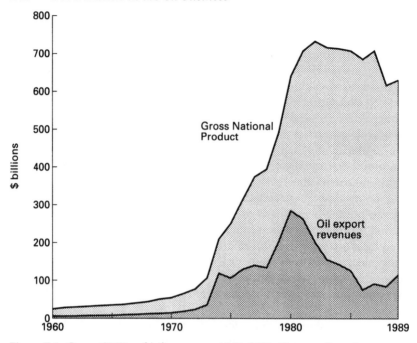

Figure 7.1. Opec: GNP and oil revenues, 1960–1989. (*Source:* Opec.)

produced very little else. Some of the structural changes in oil trade – and in the development of private equity oil outside Opec – that followed from those Opec takeovers were outlined in the last chapter. This one is concerned with the nature of these new actors in the world oil performance, and how they have played the principal roles that they then took over.

The largest exporters in Opec are monoculture economies. They have little national income, and almost no foreign earnings, other than their petroleum revenues. But they own absolutely the oil and gas that they produce, and the underlying reserves.[3] Nowadays they get the whole proceeds of crude oil sales directly, not through royalties and taxes on production. Certain of the Opec governments, indeed, levy few other taxes. They have very little other current revenue in their budgets (Figure 7.1). That underlines their dependence on oil. It also highlights one larger social and economic peculiarity of these countries. They are state capitalist economies of an unusual shape.

---

[3] Outside the US, subsoil rights are generally owned by governments. Even where the oil production is wholly private, royalties are therefore payable to the government. That applies in Alaska and the US offshore, too. Elsewhere in the US, private landlords own the rights and the royalties.

Instead of drawing their revenues from taxation of the incomes generated by their citizens' economic activities, these Opec governments initially get a large proportion of the national income themselves, as their oil revenues. Then each government distributes much of this down to its people. The usual economic pyramid is inverted. Most of their national income flows downward, the opposite way to elsewhere. Before the takeover of ownership, this revenue reached the government as royalties and tax upon the foreign concessionaire. After the takeover, an Opec government may still, formally, gain its oil revenues by levying tax upon its national oil company. But that is a matter of internal accounting. Whatever the form, the government still creams off all the economic rent earned over and above a normal return on its oil industry capital. In one way or another, all its citizens are partly dependent upon the direct and indirect distribution of shares in that rent.

Incidentally, few Opec governments are fully democratic or (simply) 'free market' economies. One of them, Iraq, professed a despotic form of 'Arab socialism'; Algeria, Libya and Iran each carried through their own forms of national revolution; but even those seldom countenanced Communist parties within their own countries. All but one of the most prominent governments in Opec are Islamic states – but each in its own way. And in most, the opposition comes from Islam too.

## *From influence to responsibility*

Before the change of ownership that they imposed in the seventies, the Opec governments' influence on the business had rested simply on sovereignty. It was powerful but indirect. Having once conceded exploration and development rights to foreign companies, any further influence that host governments chose to exert could then only be negative. If necessary they might be able to prevent things being done – in the end, by expelling the foreign enterprise – but not positively do other things themselves. This negative power of governments, potentially capable of being used collectively through Opec, was often compared with the influence of an effective trade union, 'managing discontent'. The Opec governments' negative influence, however, was in fact more often exercised effectively by particular governments acting alone, rather than being used collectively through the Organisation.

In practice, that earlier insulation from transactions in the marketplace had never been to these governments' financial disadvantage. Host governments had achieved steady gains in total oil revenues from growth in the volumes of exports from their countries, revisions to their

fiscal formulae and revenues per barrel that almost never went down.[4]
(The only time the latter were actually reduced, in 1960, led to the
foundation of Opec.) From the late 1960s onwards, using the political
leverage of sovereignty on their concessionaire companies, the governments were able to supplement those total gains with increases in
revenues per barrel. Those were usually applied as increases in tax, far
removed from the consumers who finally had to foot the higher bills.
That seems to have made them more acceptable.

Increasing tax demands appear to have been accepted as fairly legitimate by all those who paid. Legally this was debatable, given the
somewhat remarkable 'tax-binding clauses' that some initially un-
sophisticated host governments had been persuaded by concessionaire
companies to accept.[5] However, these governments did not remain
naive. Sophistication, and financial appetites, grew in line with their
total revenues. Ultimately, the concessionaires could not refuse rising
tax demands if they wanted to go on operating, in general very profitably. Moreover, faced with the threat of *force majeure*, they were able to
pass the extra taxes on to consumers and consumers' governments as
unavoidable 'costs' of supply. (In 1971, Sir Maurice Bridgman of BP said
that the major companies had become 'international tax collecting
agencies'.)

Final consumers were never happy to pay more for oil. But many of
them had a predisposition to believe that oil companies were probably
not paying enough tax anywhere. Nor were Opec governments the only
ones levying high taxes on oil. Up to 1975, for example, importing
governments in Europe took more than half the total tax revenues
included in the prices that final consumers paid for oil. This did not
make it particularly easy for such importing governments to lecture
Opec about moderation. They could always argue quite logically that
their excise taxes on oil products represented 'transfer payments' within

---

[4] In nominal dollars of the day. At times during the fifties the governments' revenues per barrel went
down in real terms, since oil prices were held down below general inflation (in consumer markets).
But that contributed to sharply rising export volumes and *total* oil revenues for the governments.
[5] Most of the host governments that eventually joined Opec had levied no income taxes at all when
they originally granted concessions to foreign oil companies. They were content, and indeed
preferred, to accept simpler royalties per barrel (at fixed rates, but often denominated in gold). From
the early fifties onwards, payments to governments in the Middle East were generally amended to
include income taxes as well. Often these taxes were at rates 'bound' by the agreements with
companies for the whole remaining term of the concession.

Longer-established fiscal authorities in more developed countries would probably never have
accepted such limitations on the tax levels that their future governments would be able to set or
change. Venezuela never accepted tax binding either. But the Middle East taxes levied on oil
companies were always elements in negotiated (and constantly renegotiated) concession agreements,
and not general income taxes. At that time nobody else in those host countries paid any income tax at
all.

their national economies, and were not directly comparable with Opec taxes on exports. Opec governments, with equal logic, always argued that the final prices including both kinds of tax were what final consumers were prepared to pay (particularly for the transport fuels in which oil products enjoyed a monopoly), and that *they* gained less of the difference between those final prices and supply costs than importing governments did.[6]

## From multinational to national oil

From the mid-1970s onwards, however, the Opec governments chose to exert their influence more positively and directly, as full participants in the business. That made them more visible to consumers as suppliers getting, perhaps monopolising, most of the profits. So it also made them more internationally unpopular; and more vulnerable financially. Their royalties and taxes per barrel had lately been irreducible. Profits per barrel, however, they eventually discovered, could go down as well as up (Table 7.1).

Opec governments have never wholly enjoyed their peculiar economic posture. They know their oil reserves cannot last forever. They are seldom content with the prospect of simply investing oil wealth elsewhere and becoming rentiers dependent upon economic activity abroad. They would prefer to develop other productive activities in their economies, lasting or renewable, as soon as possible. In the words of two former officials of Opec:

From the point of view of oil-exporting countries, oil prices must be viewed in terms of the material collateral they get in lieu of the finite resource they deplete … In the long term this means that a production and depletion policy would be judged efficient to the extent that it succeeds in serving the purpose of bringing the economy of the producing country to the highest possible level of economic development sustainable without further need for oil revenues at the time when petroleum is no more available for export.[7]

These governments are also aware that any such desirable shift to sustainable economic development based on more than mineral resource depletion – *if* it ever becomes practicable in their countries – will take many years to achieve.

[6] In the mid-seventies, Opec governments' extra earnings on the equity shareholdings that they took over in the rapid transition towards majority or complete ownership increased their total oil revenues much more than the importers' tax revenues. But after the 1986 price collapse, Opec was soon again able to argue that importing governments' excise taxes on products were exceeding their own *total* revenues per barrel from crude sales, even before charging costs. In 1988, total Opec oil revenues were $86.3 billion. Total excise taxes on oil products in eight OECD countries were reckoned at nearly $124 billion.

[7] F. al-Chalabi and A. al-Janabi, 'Optimum production and pricing policies', in *OPEC: 20 Years and Beyond* (Westview Croom Helm, 1982), pp. 229–58.

Table 7.1. *Value of Opec petroleum exports and current account balances, 1963–1989 ($ millions)*

|  | 1963 | 1974 | 1980 | 1986 | 1989 |
|---|---|---|---|---|---|
| *Algeria* | | | | | |
| petroleum exports | 439 | 4,267 | 12,647 | 4,819 | 7,000 |
| current a/c balance | 32 | 136 | 249 | − 2,229 | − 1,260 |
| *Ecuador* | | | | | |
| petroleum exports | — | 613 | 1,551 | 983 | 1,147 |
| current a/c balance | 3 | 38 | − 670 | − 613 | − 472 |
| *Gabon* | | | | | |
| petroleum exports | 10 | 773 | 1,745 | 723 | 1,200 |
| current a/c balance | 5 | 219 | 384 | − 1057 | − 107 |
| *Indonesia* | | | | | |
| petroleum exports | 269 | 5,211 | 15,595 | 5,501 | 6,059 |
| current a/c balance | − 169 | 597 | 2,865 | − 3,911 | − 1,100 |
| *Iran* | | | | | |
| petroleum exports | 799 | 20,904 | 13,286 | 7,183 | 12,500 |
| current a/c balance | 273 | 12,267 | − 2,438 | − 3,029 | − 3,200 |
| *Iraq* | | | | | |
| petroleum exports | 579 | 6,534 | 26,296 | 6,905 | 14,500 |
| current a/c balance | 286 | 2,618 | 15,836 | − 3,043 | 2,850 |
| *Kuwait* | | | | | |
| petroleum exports | 1,029 | 10,394 | 17,678 | 6,378 | 9,306 |
| current a/c balance | 813 | 9,066 | 15,301 | 5,379 | 8,445 |
| *Libya* | | | | | |
| petroleum exports | 392 | 8,149 | 21,378 | 5,438 | 7,500 |
| current a/c balance | − 414 | 2,700 | 8,212 | − 155 | 1,280 |
| *Nigeria* | | | | | |
| petroleum exports | 57 | 8,640 | 25,290 | 6,010 | 7,500 |
| current a/c balance | − 131 | 4,878 | 5,104 | 373 | − 143 |
| *Qatar* | | | | | |
| petroleum exports | 138 | 1,979 | 5,406 | 1,720 | 1,955 |
| current a/c balance | 80 | 1,720 | 2,647 | − 189 | 180 |
| *Saudi Arabia* | | | | | |
| petroleum exports | 1,004 | 35,476 | 105,813 | 16,975 | 24,093 |
| current a/c balance | 268 | 23,026 | 42,752 | − 11,796 | − 8,500 |
| *UAE* | | | | | |
| petroleum exports | 47 | 6,948 | 19,558 | 7,453 | 11,500 |
| current a/c balance | 9 | 3,568 | 10,069 | 1,852 | 3,870 |
| *Venezuela* | | | | | |
| petroleum exports | 2,155 | 10,548 | 18,248 | 6,653 | 10,020 |
| current a/c balance | 564 | 5,760 | 4,728 | − 1,471 | 2,497 |
| *Total Opec* | | | | | |
| petroleum exports | 6,918 | 120,436 | 284,491 | 76,741 | 114,280 |
| current a/c balance | 1,619 | 66,653 | 105,039 | − 19,889 | 4,340 |

*Sources:* IMF, OECD and Opec.

The economic interests of each Opec government are national, not multinational. Each is concerned to exploit its own natural resource, not to select from an assortment of such resources to produce or to trade internationally. Hence none can pretend to optimise its supply at any level wider than the national one, as certain of the international major companies could, and within narrower limits, still do. All these governments may recognise the increasing interdependence of the world's economies, and the vulnerability of their own national economies to external influences, particularly financial. Politically and militarily, some of them are now deeply dependent upon the US, if not quite client states. Several were at one time in a position to seek favours from the USSR as well, and manoeuvred to play off the superpowers – while there were two – against each other. But those are simply external conditions that the government of any country has to bear in mind in attempting to optimise its own national performance, political and economic.

Has this recent change of role made Opec governments (or even their national oil companies) behave quite like private equity producers or internationally integrated major companies, let alone independent oil traders? They operate in the same international oil trade. This trade makes up most of their nations' economic base, which no government anywhere can ever escape. But the medium-term opportunities of this particular set of governments in Opec, and the production policies they have chosen, differ significantly from those of other operators in the trade. So do their difficulties.

### Different time horizons

No foreign private concessionaire developing the same petroleum resources would have to concern itself directly with those future national difficulties (or indeed with occasional current local preoccupations such as going to war). Even in peace, some economists inside and outside Opec would argue, this difference in time horizons might logically imply fundamentally different production policies for governments from those of private companies developing the same oil resources.

Any private company's rights to produce oil abroad are limited to the term of its concession or licence. In principle, that gives an incentive to produce all it economically can (of whatever oil reserves it discovers) before the terminal date. In many Opec countries the operative concession periods were very long, to around the end of this century, and extensions were envisaged. Though the terminal dates approached inexorably, they were hardly imminent. But during the postwar period, no private concessionaire could be certain that its concession would run the full term without at least partial expropriation. After the foundation of Opec, that uncertainty increased. Other things being equal, it might have been expected to increase the incentive for concessionaires to deplete whatever reserves they discovered as soon as practicable. One Saudi Arabian economist, Dr Ali M. Johany, suggested in 1978 that the fear of nationalisation 'led the firms to act "as if there were no tomorrow"'.[8]

Quantitatively, it is customary and may be sufficient to express this simply in terms of the discount rate that any developer uses to help decide how rapidly to deplete any oil reserve that he has discovered. A barrel produced today means one less to produce at some time in the future. In order to maximise the total gains from developing and depleting the whole reserve involved, any developer needs to equate the value that he expects for the barrel forgone at some future date with the value of the same barrel if taken today. In principle, this leads him to discount the per-barrel income expected in later years (expected prices net of taxes and expected costs throughout the whole depletion period) at the rate of interest that he could get from producing and selling the same oil straight away and investing the cash proceeds.

The basic discount rate that a private oil developer would apply would presumably be his 'opportunity cost' of capital for projects of comparable technical and commercial risk, say the development of reserves discovered in his parent country. But in foreign countries there remains the possibility of expropriation before the concession term expires. That alters whatever risks he normally allows for in such oil development, and adds another factor of uncertainty. Many investors would allow for this by using a higher discount rate to appraise the project,[9] allowing for the less-than-100 per cent certainty of the oil's continuing to be available.

Once the host government takes over, Johany's argument continued, that particular uncertainty disappears:

Since the oil-producing nations need not fear the loss of their property rights (excluding foreign invasion) or the expiration of the concession terms, their decision as to how much oil to produce in each period is influenced by their discount rates (which are much lower than those of the companies) and the expected future prices, as well as by the current and future costs of exploitation.

[8] A. M. Johany, 'OPEC is not a cartel: a property rights explanation of the rise in crude oil prices' (Ph.D. dissertation, University of California, Santa Barbara, 1978).
[9] Strictly, this may not be ideal accounting practice in investment appraisal. In theory, raising the discount rate can distort comparisons between projects that are more or less capital-intensive, or have differing time profiles of cash flows. Some purists advocate using a single discount rate, and assigning different probabilities to more or less risky prospects. In practice, however, many business decision-makers *do* raise discount rates as a rough and ready adjustment for higher risk.

This argument did not simply draw upon the theory, widely held, that governments should always apply lower rates of 'social time preference' than the discount rates of private investors. Johany argued, further, that Opec governments have few opportunities for direct investment in their own countries offering returns that exceed world market rates of interest. They can invest their surplus revenues abroad at the market rate. But 'then they are uncertain that their property rights in financial assets will not be threatened ... These host countries have a problem of insecure property rights in their investment in foreign nations which is qualitatively similar to the problem faced by the oil companies in the Opec states.'

The first half of that basic argument, about concessionaires' using higher discount rates abroad, would be accepted, in principle, by most oilmen and many Western economists. There is no doubt that major international oil companies, ever since nationalisation in Mexico in 1938 and in Iran in 1951–4, *did* take account of the possibility of expropriation in other host countries where they had developed substantial production. In practice, whether or not they adjusted for political risk in quite the way that theory might have suggested, oil companies operating internationally certainly did often argue that they needed rates of return on capital in foreign oil development of the order of 20–25 per cent, sometimes higher. Political risk was nearly always one of the reasons that they quoted.

Many Western economists have expressed the same view on this issue as Dr Johany. For example, Professor Colin Robinson wrote:

my own experience indicates that they [oil companies producing in the Middle East] also subscribed to the general expectation of the time that real oil prices would remain approximately constant or decline for many years. The resulting coincidence of high discount rates and low price expectations appears to have resulted in a strong tendency to produce oil sooner rather than later, thus holding prices down.[10]

(Johany's view appears also to have been blessed, at least cursorily, by as eminent an economic authority as Paul Samuelson.)[11]

Indeed, at the time he was developing his thesis Johany might also have cited in support of it Professor Adelman of MIT, who as noted in Chapter 3 has been specialising in international oil longer than any other academic economist. He did not, which was just as well. Adelman had argued in 1972[12] that apart from political risk, the acceptable rate of return for an American company developing oil abroad ought to be

---

[10] C. Robinson, 'The changing energy market: what can we learn from the last ten years?' (University of Surrey, 1983).
[11] P. Samuelson, *Collected Scientific Papers*, ed. K. Crowley (MIT Press, 1986), pp. 896–7.
[12] M. A. Adelman, *The World Petroleum Market* (Johns Hopkins University Press, 1972).

lower than the 9 per cent mid-point rate they might require inside the heavily depleted domestic industry of the US. But taking account of political risk, he guessed the rate for their operations abroad might be higher – say 20 per cent. On the other hand,

> Let us now consider the costs of the national company of a producing nation. Since they do not face any political risk, their cost of capital is governed by commercial and technical risk added on to what it costs them to borrow, or what they can expect to get by lending ... The greater the political risk, the greater is the competitive advantage of a national company.[13]

However, Adelman has since changed his mind. He still believes that the two kinds of developers' discount rates should differ. But he now thinks that these governments' discount rates should be higher, not lower.

### Risks for governments

He now thinks so partly because most Opec countries, as noted above, are overwhelmingly dependent on oil revenues. Even whatever local revenue-earning activities they can invest in tend to be strongly oil-related, all in the same basket. This makes an Opec country's whole portfolio of assets far less diversified than those of any prudent private investor, because the earning power of its oil capacity usually greatly exceeds the return on all its other investments. An Opec government's net revenues from oil, moreover, are nearly always tightly committed to the current needs of its population. Those needs constitute 'leverage' on the income from the government's national assets. A high proportion of its flow of income is committed in advance to serve its population (rather as part of a private company's total income is usually committed to the prior service of debt).

Neither of those characteristics of the national assets that Opec governments manage can be altered in anything but the long term. The two together, in Adelman's present view, ought to add a significant 'risk premium' for these governments when they invest in their oil production, over and above the discount rates that a diversified and less-leveraged private investor might reasonably apply to developing the same oil.

Further, Adelman nowadays argues that many Opec regimes face considerable risks of political overthrow, from external or internal enemies. He feels that should logically imply an additional risk premium to be added to their discount rates. On his analysis, it would be the governments, having taken over control, who should logically act as if

[13] Ibid., p. 57.

there were no tomorrow. For this and other reasons,[14] he feels that 'the cartel gravitates towards a policy of "take the money and run"'. This argument, of course, is a mirror-image of Johany's.

Adelman's views about the investment leverage and life expectancy of these regimes reflect one economist's professional and political judgements, the latter perhaps guaranteed to affront some of them. In Indonesia, Iraq, Nigeria, Libya, Iran and certain Emirates, particular governments or even whole regimes have indeed been overthrown during the years since Opec was formed. In 1990 one Opec regime was temporarily overthrown by another, and did have to 'take its money and run'. (Indeed, Kuwait had always invested a lot of its money outside of the country; and a remarkable proportion of its citizens were either fortunate enough to be abroad already, or able to run.) On the other hand, some of the governments overthrown had lasted much longer than any government ever does in developed industrial countries.

It is perhaps difficult for a citizen of any Western pluralist democracy to appreciate just how unstable and subject to rapid change the political procedures in *his own* country may look to royal and other non-elected rulers of some Opec states. Whether such regimes are inherently riskier than those in states where governments have no pretence of lasting tenure, and disappear at more predictable intervals, is a matter of political opinion. In 1992–3, Saddam Hussein and George Bush had to face that moment of truth. (Assassination or departure forced by one's ministerial colleagues, of course, can happen alike to all kinds of ruler: Kassem, Kennedy, Faisal, Palme; Saud, Shakhbut, Nixon, the Shah, Thatcher and Gorbachev.)

## Too fast or too slow?

Should foreign companies with time-limited concessions, and the risk of expropriation, thus develop and deplete the reserves they discover faster than their host governments whose interests in the development of their oil will be longer-lasting? Or should it be these governments themselves, so overwhelmingly dependent on oil revenues in the medium term, and so vulnerable to internal or external overthrow, who should develop faster, take the proceeds, and run? Theoretically, both arguments are logical and cogent. (In a sense, they are the same argument turned round, demonstrating the old political dictum that 'Where

---

[14] The higher their discount rates, Adelman also argues, the less Opec governments need worry about demand elasticity to the prices that they may force up. Demand responses take a long time to work through. Given higher discount rates, the present value of reducing demand later might matter less to an Opec government than to a purely commercial operator.

you stand depends on where you sit.') What, however, is the practical evidence for either, about private and governmental development of the same oil provinces?

Historically, to begin with, it is impossible to demonstrate that during the postwar period to the early seventies, private concessionaires developed and produced reserves in oil-exporting countries at any abnormally rapid rate, or any faster than their host governments would have preferred. Most of the evidence points the other way. Several host governments spent the fifties and sixties complaining that the companies were developing the reserves they had discovered too slowly, not too fast. They complained that the companies were extracting only 1 or 2 per cent of Middle East proven reserves each year, as compared with the annual rates of 6 to 10 per cent at which the companies were drawing down their proven reserves everywhere else (including the most important host country outside the Middle East, Venezuela). The sharp difference between reserves-to-production ratios in Middle East producing countries and those elsewhere in the industry, mentioned in Chapter 2, long preceded the advent of Opec. It reflected an established practice of oil development there, decided upon, and later left as a legacy, by international major companies. So far from acting as if there were no tomorrow, the companies were frequently accused of 'drilling for dry holes' and delaying the development of reserves already proven.

Each host government then argued that others were being unduly favoured in the expansion of output for export. They complained, too, that multinational companies allocated incremental production and developed additional capacity according to their own patterns of comparative economic (and especially fiscal) advantage, rather than according to the comparative costs of supply from different oil sources. Host governments felt that influenced the companies to develop higher-cost oil elsewhere in preference to low-cost oil in Opec countries.

Up to 1972, therefore, the government pressure was nearly always for more output and capacity, not less. It is true that through royalties and tax the host governments were then getting only about 70–80 per cent of the economic rents earned *on the crude*, rather than the 100 per cent that they received later as owners.[15] They would also argue that those economic rents were depressed during the period because the companies were keeping prices too low. But those were separate arguments, specifically about revenue. Almost all the governments wanted higher

---

[15] Opec governments, as noted earlier, dispute both percentages. If the economic rent is reckoned in terms of the prices that final consumers have to pay for *products*, then governments of consuming countries get a large percentage, and the producers' share of the total economic rent captured by governments becomes much lower.

production, too. It was not until 1972 that any Opec government showed signs of a different attitude. Then, within a year, two of the most important ones did.

## The first allowables

In March 1972, crude oil production in Kuwait reached a record of 3.86 MBD. The next month, the government of Kuwait imposed an official limit of 3 MBD on its annual average production. The government did so with the avowed intention of moderating the depletion of its reserves, then estimated to be the second largest of any oil-producing country, 'in the interests of future generations'. At the time, this cut in output also meant a deliberate sacrifice of continued growth in the country's national oil revenues. The cutback did not cause any increase in world market prices for crude oil. Moreover, Kuwait's oil revenues per barrel were not then linked to market prices.

That was the first time that the interests of future generations were invoked by any major oil-exporting government to set limits to its level of output.[16] Kuwait's limit to production in 1972 was of immediate significance to the world oil market. Fortuitously, its timing was striking. It was announced in the same month as the Texas Railroad Commission went to a '100 per cent allowable', permitting all the wells in the state to produce as much crude as they could. Texas was the prime mover of the US oil 'proration' system, which then effectively regulated US crude oil production to the country's oil market demand (at comfortably protected prices). So its action confirmed publicly that American oil demand could no longer be fully met except by increasing imports. The Kuwaiti decree, simultaneously, gave the first warning that host governments in the world's most important oil-exporting region would not necessarily remain content to meet demand from importing countries *ad lib*.

Kuwait's decision had extra market significance because of the special role that the country then played in Middle East production. It was at that time the third highest producer in the Middle East (and Opec). It had reputedly the lowest technical costs per barrel of production. Its output from the Burgan field, the second largest oil reservoir ever found anywhere, was rapidly flexible. Most important, its joint concession to BP and Gulf was free of the 'offtake agreement' restrictions that limited

---

[16] Venezuela, since the fifties, had imposed conservation on the output of certain fields, for technical reasons. Libya had set limits to output by certain companies during negotiations in 1970, and had maintained them. But both governments were then concerned with their *current* national interests, not those imputed to their descendants.

individual shareholders' liftings of crude from Iran and Saudi Arabia. For that last reason, other major companies as well as BP and Gulf had frequently taken Kuwait crude during the 1960s as their 'swing supply', to make up their total offtake from the region to whatever they reckoned market demand for Middle East oil would be.

Kuwait's limitation confirmed the switch that was already taking place to Saudi crude as the region's residual supply. The Kingdom has the largest reserves of any country, and several of the world's largest oilfields. It was then and probably remains the country in which additional production capacity can be developed most cheaply and rapidly. (Its sole but significant limitation as a 'swing supplier' was then contractual, between the concessionaire companies. No Aramco shareholder was as free to increase its offtake independently as BP and Gulf were in Kuwait.)

Saudi Arabian output had already exceeded Kuwait's by 1966, and had gone on expanding faster. In the years from 1970 to 1973, Saudi Arabia's *annual* increases in output had averaged 1.25 MBD. In 1973, however, the first intimations surfaced of any official concern to limit the expansion of Saudi Arabian output – eventually. The government had been considering proposals put up in 1972 by the foreign shareholders of Aramco to develop Saudi capacity to 10.5 MBD by end-1974; to 13.5 MBD by the end of 1977; and possibly to 20 MBD by around 1980. That objective would have meant nearly trebling the 1972 level of Saudi output. It would have meant raising the Kingdom's output to more than twice that of the largest oil producer then, the USA (and to 65 per cent more than the record output that the USSR achieved during the next decade).

Initially, the Saudi government raised technical questions about the effect that such an expansion of capacity might have on reservoir pressures in its largest oilfields. Then, without more ado but with no immediate public explanation, the government turned the long-term proposal down. In 1978, however, the then Crown Prince, later King, Fahd did comment, '... our feelings of responsibility towards future generations also claim careful consideration and the establishment of a calculated balance between the present and the future'. In later years, Saudi officialdom tended to dismiss that stated objective of 20 MBD as 'fanciful'. That is not an adjective that would readily have come to mind in seeking to fathom the mental processes of Aramco management. Moreover, the country's then oil minister, Shaikh Yamani, had already mentioned the possibility of 20 MBD in a speech in Washington in autumn 1972 seeking US–Saudi trading co-operation.

(From the outside, technical doubts were soon expressed whether such a prodigious expansion would ever be practicable, even given Saudi Arabia's range of super-giant oilfields. In the event, King Faisal's 'No' was not a halt to further production development. Saudi capacity went on being increased during the seventies, by well over 50 per cent during the decade. In 1979, its peak year, output there averaged nearly 10 MBD, from a capacity perhaps approaching 12 MBD. During the eighties, the government appeared anxious to play down its capacity figure, to even below its earlier allowable figure of 8.5 MBD. With output around 4 MBD in the late eighties, it was embarrassing to admit how far below capacity its industry was operating. Technically, Saudi capacity was undoubtedly allowed to run down to a considerable extent. Nobody could be sure how rapidly wells shut in and facilities mothballed could be brought back into production – until 1990, when Saudi Aramco achieved it in a few months.)

Thus there *is* historical evidence that some Opec governments, indeed the two Middle East swing suppliers, did eventually demonstrate different policies in production and development from those of their private concessionaires. But it does not quite fit the theory that would attribute this to a takeover of property rights. Kuwait's decision to limit production was made before its government owned any part of its oil operations. The Saudi decision not to aim at a far-off production objective was made when its government had only just, in principle, gained the right to buy 25 per cent ownership of the operations of Aramco.[17] Both those limits, to current production and to future development, were thus decided upon before the governments concerned had any experience at all as owners of their oil industries.

Nor can it be shown that from 1973 onwards these and other Opec governments, 'taking over' in a *de facto* nationalisation, immediately began to apply different depletion criteria, reducing output and restricting the expansion of capacity, from those applied by the companies. Once the Arab political embargo was lifted in early 1974, most Opec governments did not practically limit production for several years. Rather more of them than before did take to publishing national 'allowables', which set limits to their country's maximum current output. But those limits were almost never reached. In 1974–5, and again in 1977–8, the market was relatively weak. Production was effectively limited by demand, not by the exporting governments. As to capacity, some member governments continued to invest in increasing

---

[17] Kuwait took part in negotiating the General Agreement on Participation in 1972, but never ratified the agreement. Eventually, it took over 60 per cent ownership in 1973 and 100 per cent at the end of 1975. Saudi Arabia did ratify the 1972 General Agreement, gaining the right to buy 25 per cent of Aramco. It agreed to take over 100 per cent (dated back to 1976) in 1977, and paid for the assets in 1980.

this – Saudi Arabia, Iran, Iraq and Abu Dhabi, for example. Others did not. Each exporter acted according to its national circumstances – all of which in the event had been transformed financially by the 1973–4 price surge.

Admittedly, these host governments' influence upon their production levels had not suddenly come into being when they signed their participation agreements. They had had some influence on output levels ever since production began in their countries, generally seeking higher output, not lower. Fiscally, too, these governments had become deeply if involuntarily involved in financing the development of additional capacity in their industries long before they gained any participation in ownership. Depreciation charged against tax rates that were effectively far above the nominal rates of 50 or later 55 per cent made the governments substantial contributors to their concessionaires' handsome net cash flows. (Not all the governments may have fully appreciated this.) Those depreciation provisions were adequate to self-finance the expansion of capacity even at Aramco's pace. Formally, also, concessionaire companies usually went through the motions of consulting the host governments in planning the expansion of their operations. But that approval, too, was often a formality.

The accumulation of Opec government influence was thus gradual over a period. Also, it was uneven in effect. The takeover in 1973 was essentially of the publication of crude prices, not of any positive control of production. In several of the largest Opec exporting countries, current production continued to be determined mainly by the former concessionaires' offtake under their long-term supply contracts. Also, in the countries where expansion of capacity did go on, it mostly continued development programmes set in train earlier by concessionaires (and often continued to be managed by them). Thus *de facto* nationalisation was not a single act in 1973. It did not become effective in terms of operational control until, at the earliest, 1979.

Johany first put forward his 'property rights' theory, in 1978, as an alternative explanation of price changes in 1973–4. He felt this explanation made it unnecessary to regard Opec as an effective cartel then. Even if prices were competitively determined, in his view, the lower rates at which governments 'ought' logically to produce their reserves would have been sufficient to explain the price increases of 1973 and after. Adelman, who has long identified and criticised Opec as an effective though clumsy cartel, believes it began taking over control even earlier, indeed from 1971 onwards. But, in fact, the only *collective* restriction imposed on production up to 1973 was a political embargo by the Arab member governments of Opec alone, which was ineffective and soon over. So experience in the seventies did not really test either theory so far as output and development of reserves were concerned.[18] Production rates were not reduced by anything but demand; and in any case the governments were not really making the relevant production decisions then.

## Discount rates and development

Both these economists at the time appeared to assume that decisions about development and production in oil-producing countries are determined largely by time preferences regarding depletion, and can be expressed completely in terms of discount rates. The rates, argued to be objectively measurable from outside, 'must' really (even, if necessary, subconsciously) govern the decisions made. This was argued to apply regardless of the actual discount rates, or other criteria, that the people concerned might themselves imagine they were applying in their investment decisions.

Adelman was quite confident that *he* could specify the discount rates that Opec governments ought to use, whether they could or not. The argument became piquant when it is considered that discounting represents essentially the reciprocal of compound interest rates – a concept not always openly acceptable throughout Islamic business behaviour. In principle, Muslim rulers may or may not recognise time discounting as a technique of measuring their concern for the interests of future generations in their countries. In practice, they do not have to. They employ plenty of competent economists who can draw eclectically upon a wide array of techniques for investment appraisal. (First-hand impressions suggest that sets of expected future cash flows are presented to them, in making decisions about oil as well as other development projects, which *do* incorporate a conventional range of discount rates, say from 10 to 25 per cent.)

Such calculations, for all scenarios of oil investment, are in any case subject to huge uncertainties regarding price expectations. Discount rates are unlikely to be critical in these governments' decisions, except as cut-off criteria to exclude the least remunerative options. It is rather doubtful, for that matter, whether discount rates are often *critical* in the major corporate decisions about oil development made in private oil companies.

It is also worth noting that the largest single programme of petrol-

---

[18] After 1973, it was in some *non-Opec* countries where new oil was discovered that companies, encouraged by governments such as Britain's, really *did* accelerate development and produce (albeit 'consistent with good oilfield practice') as if there was no tomorrow.

eum development ever carried out anywhere *was* by a government – and one that in principle abhorred the concept of interest at least as much as Islam does. That was the Soviet expansion of oil output nearly twenty-fold after World War II, followed by its creation of the world's largest gas industry. The economics of Soviet petroleum development under central planning have remained opaque to Western understanding. Its petroleum investment decisions clearly involved laborious analysis of capital intensity and timing. But its planners hardly seem to have used discount rates in ways that Western economists recognise. The Soviet energy industries were essential pillars of a 'military-industrial complex' of even more central importance within the Soviet economy than its counterpart became in the US. Managers in Soviet oil and gas appear to have operated under command to fulfil output targets within given planning periods and 'campaigns'. They concentrated on rapid development of extra production as soon as possible, and are said to have neglected exploration (albeit finding more super-giant oilfields within their own frontiers than the world's most technically accomplished oil business, in the US, ever has). Perhaps that too could be interpreted as having applied a high discount rate?

However, as Adelman has since acknowledged, it *cannot* be taken for granted that the higher its discount rate, the faster it must be logical for any developer, private or governmental, to deplete a reserve. If costs could be ignored, that proposition would logically hold good. But the theoretical proposition would never sound self-evident to ordinary businessmen who use DCF simply as a practical tool of investment appraisal. To them, any development involves heavy exploration and development expenditures in the early years, before the eventual sequence of cash receipts from drawing down the stock of oil reserves begins. At first sight, they might expect an investor with a higher discount rate (or cost of borrowing the capital) to be *less* inclined to make any given investment, not more so.

Practical investment decisions cannot avoid the question of costs and the time profiles of cash flows in and out.[19] Oil development is highly capitalised, and a large proportion of the capital has to be put in as front-end investment in the initial years, before production and cash inflows begin. Whether applying a higher discount rate will make one more or less inclined to go ahead with investment will depend on the time patterns of cash flows expected in each case that arises. When the principle is applied to the private developer considering the possibility

---

[19] P. G. Bradley, 'Production of depleting resources: a cost-curve approach' (MIT Center for Energy Policy Research, 1979).

of nationalisation before his concession runs out, 'there is on the one hand an incentive to deplete the fields quickly, but on the other a disincentive to undertake exploratory activity and invest in extractive capacity. The net bias caused by the presence of risk, as compared with the risk-free case, is in general indeterminate.'[20] Arguably, moreover, the effectiveness of discounted cash flow analysis in choosing between different time profiles of development and production for very large reservoirs may have inherent limitations. Almost every oilfield, small as well as large, turns out to have significantly larger recoverable reserves than can be assessed at the time the initial decision is made to develop it. When this likely but unquantifiable factor of 'reserve growth' is applied to such giant or super-giant reservoirs as occur in the Gulf, the idea that developers' different discount rates would make a crucial difference to the way they should be developed appears implausible.

It is perhaps worth entering the further caveat that any such comparison of private and governmental discount rates applied to development and depletion of the same known reserve would be strictly theoretical. In planning such development, would the two operators face the same sequence of cash inflows and outflows? Only, presumably, if the private entrepreneur could be assumed to have no tax liabilities over the whole period envisaged (or perhaps if the government planned to debit its own prospective cash flows by some simulated tax on a hypothetical private entrepreneur?). Either such assumption would require a considerable suspension of disbelief – and could make the comparison meaningless.

## Depletion decisions and prices

There is however a further and even more cogent reason why differences in discount rates would *not* have had much influence upon any decisions about current production, or development of future capacity, made by certain key Opec governments in most of the years since 1973. During those years Saudi Arabia, Iran, and perhaps Kuwait could probably make such decisions without much reference to discount rates at all, whichever rates they might choose to apply. These countries (and their major offtakers of crude) could hardly increase or decrease current production without immediately and sharply affecting the world price of crude oil, and consequently their own total oil revenues. They had to be much more sensitive to those immediate potential consequences for

[20] A. M. Khadr, *Fiscal Regime Uncertainty, Risk Aversion, and Exhaustible Resource Depletion* (Oxford Institute for Energy Studies, 1987), p. 3.

prices and oil revenues than to the application of debatable discount rates to their future depletion opportunities.[21]

In countries with such potential influence, depleting more rapidly – or even the announcement of decisions to raise exports – might simply have collapsed the price (as it eventually did in 1986). Regimes fearing revolution could not run away with the reserves, which take a long time to develop, let alone deplete. They might do better to hold down output and force up prices while they had the chance. That could raise the revenues to run away with – if they should ever choose to – considerably faster. Assuming short time horizons (alias high discount rates?), the moves by which they nearly quadrupled crude prices in the last few months of 1973 were at least as logical as trying to develop extra production capacity that would have taken years of heavy investment to bring in and might have been underutilised once it was installed.

That quandary, however, was neither new nor simply political. It applied just as awkwardly to major international companies in the past as it does to governments producing the same super-giant fields nowadays. Those concessionaire companies had a much wider range of oil interests abroad to consider than any national government ever will have – also a wider range of government pressures on those widely deployed vested interests in oil production. A price collapse might have hurt them more in those days than it would later have hurt any single government, whose low-cost oil export volumes ought *eventually* at least to have gained from the cutting prices.

The quandary has not disappeared. It has simply been transferred. It continues to compound the problems of those few Opec governments whose decisions on developing capacity, as well as on current production, are likely to affect the general level of prices now and in the future. The major companies, in the late sixties, had been gradually facing up to the problem of introducing growing volumes of low-cost oil into markets that they and other producers were accustomed to supply with much higher-cost oil. The lowest-cost Opec producers chose not to face that problem. Not many of the other Opec member governments, since 1979, have had the surplus revenues, or in some cases the reserves, to consider heavy investment in further capacity to produce crude at future prices over which they can have little individual influence.

## In the banks or in the ground?

In considering arguments why Opec might deplete reserves more slowly, it is not easy for outsiders to judge the political risk that some of its

[21] Bradley, 'Production of depleting resources'.

member governments may attach to investing spare revenues in foreign capital markets. Sequestration of financial assets deposited abroad has in fact happened since the formation of Opec to Iran, Libya, and briefly in 1990–1 to Kuwait as well as Iraq. Until that war period, funds had been frozen only by one country, the US. (The US government did however try to get Iran's and Libya's assets frozen in other countries too, somewhat to the embarrassment of European banks traditionally averse to such a politicised code of banking conduct. It may also have exerted some influence that affected their later sales of sizeable holdings in European industrial companies.)

Other Opec governments as well as these have long had similar suspicions. (Johany, indeed, argued that Saudi Arabia had anxieties of this kind about the political influence to which its build-up of currency reserves in dollars was liable to expose it.) In a report on long-term strategy that Opec commissioned in 1980, its experts said 'the placement of those funds in financial investments in the industrialised countries exposes them to erosion in value through inflation, and is facing a multiplicity of growing legal and administrative restrictions of a discriminatory nature which tends to throw doubt on their ultimate security'.[22] That phrasing was probably drafted before the US government ever froze Iranian funds or leaned on Italy to discourage Libyan investment there. It certainly preceded the only really blatant example of such discrimination in Europe – when Britain in 1988 obliged the Kuwait government to resell to BP more than half of the 22 per cent shareholding that it had legitimately bought in the company during the previous twelve months.[23]

Another set of arguments about Opec governments' depletion policies surfaced rather often in the late 1970s. This was whether they did prefer, or ever logically should have preferred, oil in the ground to money in the bank. In some years of high inflation during the seventies, a valid case could be argued for risk-averse Opec governments to hold back from producing rather than invest surpluses abroad. Inflation in the prices of manufactured goods that Opec countries imported from Western industrialised countries did indeed reduce the unit purchasing power of Opec oil revenues between 1974 and 1978 (though not nearly back to 1973 levels). There were a few years in which the rate of return obtainable in world capital markets on low-risk investments (which some though not

[22] Opec, 'Report of the Group of Experts submitted to and approved by the Ministerial Committee on Long-Term Strategy' (London, 1980). (This report has never been published, but was privately circulated quite widely.)
[23] By the early nineties, nothing might have suited BP better than a substantial shareholder able to guarantee low-cost crude supplies.

all Opec governments tended to prefer)[24] was lower than the accompanying rates of inflation, however measured. In such periods, the real rate of return on such foreign investments did become negative.[25] (Some Opec governments felt that foreign currency depreciation at times exacerbated this for them. In principle, they were free to convert their holdings, arising and largely held in US dollars, into whichever currencies they preferred. But in practice, because the size of their holdings was large and identifiable enough to affect exchange rates, some Opec surplus governments felt effectively locked into the dollar.)

During the eighties, that argument disappeared. All those indices and expectations came down. Real rates of interest rose sharply, making any such proposition highly dubious even at face value. In practice, too, Opec governments have had little or no surplus oil revenue to invest since then.

Some of these governments' unease about investment abroad probably extends beyond any specific fear of sequestration or even discriminatory restrictions. As one Western analyst has put it, 'the objectives of most Opec states are not consistent with creating a nation of rentiers dependent on "coupon clipping" for their economic survival, even if this were the wealth-maximising strategy'.[26] His comment formed part of a 'target revenue' theory of Opec motivations and behaviour as a cartel. That theory, whatever its general application, did become highly relevant during the mid-eighties. All Opec governments have at times since been hard put to generate enough oil income to cover their national revenue requirements.

## Politics and oil policies

Further, one needs to widen this comparison between companies and governments as developers of petroleum to include the huge array of political factors that governments anywhere may always have to take into account. Any single decision, especially about anything as important on its own as oil in an Opec country, may affect the government's expected 'return' on its whole national economic and political system. Even some petroleum exporting countries that are neither monocultures nor at risk of revolution, such as Canada, Norway and Britain, have

[24] Saudi Arabia is reputed to have been an ultra-cautious investor in long-term fixed-interest securities, and Kuwait to have been much readier to invest in equities. Each, however, had highly respected Western financial advisers; and both probably invested significantly in real estate abroad, which in some countries at least, until the late eighties, kept up with general inflation.
[25] G. M. Heal and G. Chichilnisky, *Oil and the International Economy* (Clarendon Press, 1991).
[26] D. J. Teece, 'OPEC behaviour: an alternative view', in OPEC *Behaviour and World Oil Prices*, ed. J. M. Griffin and D. J. Teece (Allen & Unwin, 1982).

from time to time laid down depletion policies or influenced exploration and development in the light of the repercussions of oil development that they expect on the rest of their national economies.

This assessment of incremental return on a complex and interlinked system arising from single development decisions that cannot sensibly be assessed alone is familiar in large organisations everywhere. (It is most carefully quantified, perhaps, in the investment decisions of large-scale electricity utilities, which have to measure incremental returns over very long periods ahead to a whole integrated system, rather than the returns on individual increments of investment.) For governments it applies more widely, across non-economic as well as economic consider-ations affecting their countries.

To summarise, there is *some* firm evidence that Opec governments have occasionally demonstrated quite different attitudes from private oil companies to the production and development of capacity from the same oil reserves. But so far the conclusions to be drawn from this are uncertain. There have been other quite sufficient reasons for the pro-duction policies that these governments have followed since 1973. Over time, the governments may choose rather different depletion policies from those that private developers might have applied, whether or not these would seem logical or wealth-maximising to friendly or hostile economists. But attempts to deduce their future depletion behaviour simply by assigning them lower or higher discount rates have so far yielded indeterminate results – and probably always will.

It may perhaps be wiser for outside observers simply to be ready for occasional Opec government policies regarding current and future pro-duction that they will not quite be able to rationalise for more than brief periods in terms of their own preconceptions.

## Different approaches to trading

In the meantime, as practical oil producers and sellers, Opec govern-ments are in a commercial sense too quite differently placed from other operators in the trade. They get *all* the profits plus any economic rent obtainable through their sales of crude.[27] So every increase in the crude price benefits them far more than private equity producers, who pay up to 85 per cent tax. By the same token any fall in price hurts their income far more than it does the private producer, whose net income bears perhaps only about 15 per cent of the reduction. Most Opec govern-ments, again, have only their own country's crude to sell. Usually, they

---

[27] Though importing governments can later capture additional 'rent' through excise taxation of refined products that final consumers regard as indispensable, notably gasoline.

have no access to crude supplies from anywhere else. The variety of crudes they have to sell, therefore, is less diversified than many producers operating in several countries can offer, or than traders can obtain for a customer's requirements. Buying any other crude for resale is a far less profitable business for an Opec supplier than purveying its own.

If Opec governments explore elsewhere and find crude, they will never be able to produce that crude supply on the same terms as their own. Kuwait and one or two other member governments, during the eighties, did invest in exploration abroad; Kuwait achieved a few discoveries. Not enough production from any of these ventures had ever been achieved up to the time this book was completed to show how such agreements between visitor and host governments would work out in practice. But quite apart from the unusual experience of paying royalties and tax, any Opec government finding oil abroad will presumably come under pressure from its host to develop and maximise local production there, even at much higher costs than its own production at home. If the country in question is one that has previously been importing the Opec government's own crude, the substitution could become doubly unprofitable. In any event, whatever production it develops abroad will compete with its own exports somewhere in the world market.

Kuwaiti motives for these foreign exploration ventures were probably mixed. They were direct investments abroad in the one industry that the government felt it understood well. They offered a potential diversification of the crude qualities Kuwait could offer; and possibly extra supply sources closer to markets. Any production they could develop abroad would be free of Opec quotas. And in general, these ventures would help establish the image of Kuwait as more than just a passive investor of rentier income. Both the exploration and each individual venture represented a mixture of commercial and political considerations.

## The delegated monopolies

This chapter has discussed the nature of Opec countries' decisions in oil operations as if these were taken and implemented directly by the governments now owning their petroleum. That is of course an oversimplification. Opec member governments and most other oil-exporting countries, like many oil-importing countries, employ national oil companies to manage all or parts of their industries.

The national oil companies within Opec have now built up considerable technical experience in producing, refining and transporting oil.[28] Few of them have had much success in exploration, partly no doubt because they took over the management of ample capacity during a period when demand was hardly expanding at all. They are engaged, perforce, in selling crude on a large scale; but as yet they seldom appear as flexible commercially as private companies. Nevertheless, their national rather than multinational scope, as well as their special positions within national economies, have set various limitations to this invaluable process of learning on the job.

These Opec national companies are as diverse as the member countries themselves. So are their relations with the governments, their sole shareholders. They usually enjoy monopolies of their countries' internal oil businesses, and almost by definition manage their countries' largest industrial enterprises; neither special advantage makes for competitive efficiency. When oil is their country's sole major industry, they may have first call upon more of its educated elites than any single business can have in more diversified economies.[29] Some national oil companies, offering effectively an alternative ladder to local advancement, have at times gained great political influence within their countries. But their positions of power are more vulnerable than those of the top boards of private oil companies. Directors are appointed, and their salaries are set, by their sole shareholders, their governments; they are quite often subject to direct interference from them in commercial operations; and they can always be dismissed at a moment's notice. One or two Opec national companies have had executives forced out with allegations of corruption. But as often as not, a government has not bothered to explain.

In financial terms, these national companies' revenues are determined mainly by the prices that their Opec member governments are able to secure or sustain, commercially or politically. How the revenues are (or should be) allocated is always a matter of debate. Of late, national company executives often complain, governments have left them too little of the national oil revenues they recoup to cover the investment that they consider essential to maintain the national industry, let alone expand it. Ultimately, there is no escaping the fact that these Opec national companies are instruments of state ownership and government policy. However much their expert advice may be listened to, they lack the powers of decision that private oil executives carrying out the same

[28] In 1990, there were ten Opec national oil companies, plus Mexico's Pemex, among the twenty largest oil companies (measured in terms of production) in the world's market economies.
[29] More priority, indeed, perhaps, than international oil companies in their parent countries, where in the eighties financial services were for a time able to outbid almost every other employer for potential talent (not that the Opec elites, either, were backward in entering finance).

industrial and commercial operations can normally exercise. To the extent that Opec oil industries differ from their private counterparts, governments make the difference.

Some of the Opec governments' policies reflect predictable national preferences. Already, they have developed more refining capacity 'at source' to export oil products from their countries than the concessionaires producing there before ever would have. That keeps more of whatever 'added value' can be gained in refining at home, within the producing country. Whether this refining capacity will ever be able to compete commercially on equal terms with marginal refining capacity in importing regions is debatable. Refineries in the Opec countries can usually count on cheap fuel, the 'associated gas' produced along with crude. This may be virtually costless to produce (though gathering it through national pipeline networks, in several Opec countries, has turned out to be extremely expensive). Unless it can usefully be re-injected into the substrata to maintain reservoir pressures, the only alternative may be to flare this gas wastefully. The governments often prefer to use it as cheap refinery fuel (and sometimes its associated liquids as petrochemical feedstocks). Certain Opec governments have invested in very large product tankers, seeking to match the economies of scale that have given crude oil transport to refineries in import destinations an overriding cost advantage. But the capital costs of Middle East refineries appear to have been distinctly higher than they would have been elsewhere. And since the early 1980s almost nobody else in the world has been investing in new 'green-field' refineries.[30]

The Opec governments concerned, however, probably never expected to get a fully commercial return on that refining investment. They are concerned to add value, and increase employment and related skills in their economies. That is a legitimate national consideration for any government, but not one which might ever have interested multinational investment decision-makers. In practice, international companies did venture jointly in some of these Opec refineries, and engage to market the products exported. (Their equity investment was very low. Most of the investment was financed at very low interest by the governments concerned. The companies' main concern at the time was probably the promise of secure crude supply contracts.)

Historically, the international companies too had frequently been required to install and finance refineries – first in Europe and Japan,

---

[30] One exception in Europe (an extension that virtually amounted to a new refinery) was built by a non-Opec oil-exporting country's national oil company, the Norwegian Statoil. That ran into financial and managerial difficulties. But even apart from these, this highly sophisticated refinery had always been promoted partly on grounds of employment opportunities in the relatively depressed coastal area concerned.

later in developing countries – to secure access to markets and import contracts for crude. As compared with those importing governments, politicians in Opec countries have at least been prepared to put up most of the capital.

As noted in Chapter 6, several Opec governments did decide during the 1980s to 'integrate downstream', buying storage depots, refineries and products marketing chains in the regions that import their crude. This remains an interesting option for those with low-cost crude and sufficient commercial self-confidence. They can at times earn large economic rents from crude even when prices are weak in final markets for products. It might pay them to invest downstream even with little or no return on the downstream investment involved there. However, this option arises from their control of low-cost crude production, mainly in the Middle East, *not* because they happen to be governments. (It was indeed the way that their major concessionaires had originally developed exports from the same low-cost oilfields that these governments now own.)

External politics, also, may sometimes affect these governments' approaches to trading. When the market is strong they often engage in government-to-government deals with political overtones, either to gain favour from industrialised countries or to assist poor developing countries that cannot afford high prices. When the market is weak, they may go in for counter-trade, in effect bartering crude for desirable imports such as armaments. These deals may also offer the advantage of secrecy – for a time – concealing both the low prices that the governmental crude sellers may concede and the terms on which the governmental arms salesmen are doing business. All the advantages are debatable and transitory. But they will probably never quite disappear while governments remain significantly involved in the oil business – at both ends.

## The most important difference

Probably the most obvious difference between governments and private companies operating in the world oil trade, however, is another aspect of national sovereignty. No anti-trust laws exist internationally to discourage governments from forming cartels.[31]

International organisations, from the United Nations on downwards, have become more assertive politically in the last few years. Economically, the IMF and the World Bank have an even wider assort-

---

[31] Prosecutions under US anti-trust laws do not necessarily recognise any frontiers, as foreign oil companies have often found out. One attempt was made in 1979 to invoke these laws against Opec (by an American trade union!). But a Federal court accepted that it had no jurisdiction.

ment than before of financially embarrassed countries ready to promise competitive free-market capitalism in exchange for loans. GATT, also, may be able to whip in many poor countries to accept the free-trade principles of mutual treatment that its industrialised member countries always promise but often contrive in large part to slant. But up to the time of writing, none of these monitors of international capitalist probity had yet proposed rules to prohibit cartels such as Opec.

Initially, that freedom from anti-monopoly rules did not free the governments that founded Opec from being considerably embarrassed about the label. It was remarkable, throughout the Organisation's first two decades, how regularly oil ministers felt it necessary to declare that Opec was *not* a cartel. In private as well as public, economists from member countries assiduously pointed out how many of the textbook attributes of a cartel it lacked – even while at the same time boasting of Opec's role as 'the controlling power' in world oil pricing.

There seemed sometimes to be, in those years of success, a desire to be awarded a vote of thanks for their willingness to supply, while setting ever-higher prices. After prices began to decline in the eighties, however, Opec governments became readier to take the cash and let the credit go – *if* behaving like a fully-fledged cartel could still get them enough cash.

Readiness to be seen as a cartel, however, did not guarantee success or even competence in behaving like one. When it comes to actual perform- ance, sovereignty may even have some inherent disadvantages.

# CHAPTER 8

# The Opec performance

Opec has only ever used one of the traditional mechanisms of a cartel trying to hold prices up; and that one, never very effectively or for very long. Just before the second Gulf war, some of the Organisation's leading member governments – in a temporary state of mild euphoria because prices were rising – felt they could do without that one too. This was not because they believed this chosen cartel mechanism technique had clearly succeeded, and could henceforth stabilise prices at the level they chose. (Their euphoria, while premature, was not naive.) They simply thought it had turned out to be more trouble to apply than its results were worth.

This mechanism was the Opec production ceiling and quota system. There had only been three serious attempts to use it in the Organisation's first thirty years. The first lasted four months; the second, two years. The third began in August 1986; the system was still formally in being until quotas were suspended in September 1990 because of the war; and after February 1992, member governments began going through the motions again. But even before that war several member countries had been paying no more than lip-service to the system, and most had been exceeding their quotas.

Shaikh Ali Khalifah al-Sabah, then the Kuwaiti oil minister, had summarised the prevailing attitude in February 1990: 'Everybody who could [exceed the quota], did. Everybody who couldn't, complained about it.' For some years, Kuwait had been one of the countries exceeding its quota, which it considered far too low. Shaikh Ali admitted that it was going on exceeding the higher one that Opec had eventually allocated it. 'I would like to see the Opec quotas scrapped as soon as possible. From a practical standpoint they are already irrelevant, so all that is needed is a recognition of that fact.'[1]

---

[1] *MEES*, 12 February 1990.

Not everybody in the Kuwaiti government was as outspoken as the sardonic Shaikh Ali. (Shortly afterwards he was moved sideways to become finance minister, and did not join the next government, appointed after the Gulf war.) One of Kuwait's Opec neighbours, however, *had* recognised the fact of its disregard of quotas, and reacted brutally. This was another of the several excuses that Iraq advanced for its invasion that summer. And certainly envious resentment of its rich, sometimes arrogant-sounding neighbour was not difficult for Saddam Hussein to invoke in his own and some other Arab societies.

After the Iraqi invasion was defeated by an international rescue of Kuwait, Opec member countries went through the motions of agreeing their total production from within a total capacity from which Iraq and Kuwait had been temporarily removed. Whatever they 'decided', however, was for a time subject to a quota set by governments outside Opec. Production for export from Iraq did not depend upon what its government might choose or Opec might agree upon. It was controlled by the UN Security Council; in effect, ultimately, by the United States. The production level was ostensibly related to the needs of the Iraqi people for internal sustenance (and to a continuing 30 per cent reparations rake-off, primarily for Kuwait). What the control imposed on Iraqi exports reflected most was probably President Bush's determination to drive Saddam Hussein out of power, and chagrin at not having achieved that already from his overwhelming military victory.

When Opec quotas appeared to matter, few other member governments had ever been as frank about their 'overproduction' as Kuwait. But another large-scale exporter in the Gulf, the United Arab Emirates, had refused to accept any quota at all in 1989. Opec output in 1989 and early 1990 had been running at least a million barrels a day above the agreed total production ceiling. Moreover, that agreed total included up to 800,000 barrels a day of quotas larger than the countries concerned appeared capable of producing. So the rest of Opec were certainly not taking much notice of their allocations either.

At an Opec conference in November 1989, several other governments from the Gulf had also expressed their confidence that production quotas 'would soon be a thing of the past', by 1991 if not before. They could point to an increase in demand for Opec crude of more than a million barrels a day in each year since 1985, close on 6 per cent annually. Opec had also begun 1990 with its average prices very close to the level of $18/bbl that its member governments had been seeking since 1986. In the meantime, inflation and the dollar exchange rate had eroded that price slightly in real terms. But since the price collapse of 1986, Opec had not been too ambitious about pricing in real terms. All that some of the larger Gulf producers were hoping for was price stability, in a range of say $18–20/bbl in nominal terms, for a few years.[2] Even some hope of that prospect, at the turn of the decade, was enough to generate euphoria.

Nobody, however, could claim that as a result of successful Opec policy. Indeed, there remained some mystery about the causes for it, proximate or underlying. One immediate reason appeared to be that everyone, inside and outside Opec, had for a time been underestimating demand for oil. The International Energy Agency in Paris, from whose published estimates most other analysts draw for their own, had revised its demand figures upwards in several winters of the late eighties. As to underlying causes, there had been some signs that oil production outside Opec had levelled off and might even decline, greeted eagerly by those member countries that still had capacity to spare or could readily develop more. If the world economy could continue to increase its oil demand as much as it had since 1983, they reasoned, the extra oil could only come from Opec. (That was conventional wisdom, which the oil business has good reason to distrust. But few people disagreed with the direction of the change expected, only with the timing.)

The levelling off expected in production was not all outside Opec. At that conference in 1989, the government of Indonesia had renounced its quota share of the increase in the total production ceiling because it could not produce the extra crude. This was the first time that any member government had ever admitted that it was producing to the limits of its capacity. But at the same meeting the Nigerian oil minister, while accepting an increased quota with no immediate doubts about increasing capacity, also commented, 'We are 100 million people and if we are not careful we will have to import oil in the next twenty years.' A fundamental division, predictable long ago but delayed in the doldrums of the 1980s, is widening within Opec.

Several Opec member countries were at the time claiming increases in quotas that they could not immediately produce (Figure 8.1). Not all of them appeared to be in, or even approaching, the situation of Indonesia. Certain of the producers believed to have been overstating their immediate potential at that 1989 meeting were certainly committed to raising their production capacity, from ample reserves. For them it was simply a matter of time and money – though even among some oil exporters reporting very high reserves, it can be technically difficult to increase production (Figure 8.2). But there are several other member countries with relatively low reserves and reserves-to-production ratios, and with sharply rising local consumption. (As it happens, some of these have gas

[2] Hisham Nazer, Saudi Minister of Petroleum and Minerals, *PIW*, 23 October 1989.

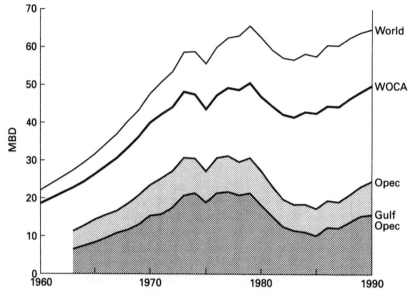

Figure 8.1. Oil production: world; world excluding Communist and former Communist areas; Opec; and Gulf Opec, 1960–1990.

exports or good chances of developing them soon, which should prolong the petroleum contribution to their economies. But that gas trade, which is steadily becoming more important in world energy supply, is beyond Opec control and certain to remain so.)

Indonesia's oil reserves are down to only about eighteen years' current output, and the ratio is declining. Algeria, like Indonesia a major gas exporter, and Nigeria and Qatar, which hope to become the same, have R/P ratios for oil comparable to say Norway, with reserves representing 25–30 years' output. Gabon, Opec's smallest producer, has reserves equivalent to only 14 years' output, down towards the low R/P ratios characteristic of production in the former USSR, US or UK. (But with its tiny output, relatively small new finds could at any time improve that ratio sharply.) Only one member country, Ecuador, had left Opec up to the end of 1992, with output declining and hopes of privatisation. Such departures had been predicted frequently during the eighties, but had never come to pass.

### Opec's fractured core

But basically the oil circumstances and some of the interests of that outer fringe of Opec have little in common with those of an inner

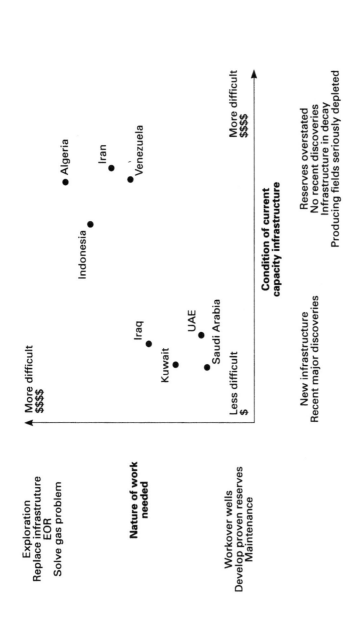

Figure 8.2. Opec's capacity expansion problems, early 1990s. (*Source*: Gochenour, 'Coming capacity shortfall'.)

grouping, mainly in the Gulf. Seven member countries count on reserves representing many times their current annual production. These producers include all the five founder members of the Organisation. They have often been called its 'core' – though at the beginning of the nineties, this core was fractured. Three of the seven – Saudi Arabia, the UAE and possibly Venezuela – could increase their output rapidly once they think the investment would be economically worth while. Kuwait's production capacity, burnt down in 1991, was very soon largely restored, but with some continuing unease about damage to its reservoirs; Iraq's production is financially mortgaged for reparations and under UN control; Iran's exports still suffer from residues of US hostility. (Technically, in terms of reserves-to-production ratios, Libya might rank with this upper crust of Opec. But politically it is at odds with almost everybody, and has suffered even more than Iran from a continuing American blockade, political, economic and on occasion military.)

Most governments of the Opec core shared Kuwait's impatience with Opec's failure to control production effectively. All of them appear still to agree on one objective – that crude prices should not fall. But that is as far as any agreement throughout the Gulf ever went. Few governments there have ever fully accepted the Saudi proposition that prices should not rise significantly, either. Some, too, doubt whether another oil game, with fewer players, would serve the ultimate objective of Opec pricing any more certainly than the arrangements that the 'clumsy cartel' has employed so far.

### The unchosen instrument

The quotas that Opec once again decided temporarily to abandon for the duration of that minor war were not only the sole traditional instrument of cartel practice that it had ever applied. As it happened, this had been the *only* definite policy initially recommended for Opec when the Organisation was set up thirty years before. Under the name of 'production programming', it had been written into the first resolution of the conference that set up the Organisation in September 1960 by Perez Alfonzo, then Venezuelan oil minister, the conservationist 'philosopher of oil' who provided the main intellectual stimulus to Opec's foundation:

1.i.3.    That members shall study and formulate a system to ensure the stabilisation of prices, by, among other means, the regulation of production, with due regard to the interests of the producing and of the consuming nations and to the necessity of securing a steady income to the producing countries, and efficient, economic, and regular supply of this source of energy to consuming nations, and a fair return on their capital to those investing in the petroleum industry;

Having committed themselves to study such a system, the five signatory governments then effectively put it on the shelf for more than twenty years. Historically, that may have been partly because Perez Alfonzo moved to another ministry within a few years, and the only other founding-father of Opec who liked the idea, Abdullah Tariki, lost his post as Saudi oil minister in 1962. But it was mainly because Middle East governments were uneasy about the idea – as some of them have always remained.

To restrict everybody's production and drive prices up could in theory have gained all host governments extra revenue in royalties and taxes. That would have suited Venezuela, which in 1960 was the world's largest oil exporter, but had relatively high costs and (then) only limited chances of increasing production. But Middle East host governments were gaining what then seemed to them large revenues, steadily increasing, from the rapid expansion in export volumes of their low-cost oil. They wanted their exports to be increased yet faster, not to be restricted to protect Venezuelan exports from competition. (The verbs are advisedly passive. At that time, the governments' influence was indirect. The export policies of both regions were influenced by their governments, but finally set by international major companies, usually the same set. Comparative 'tax-paid costs' to the concessionaires were what mainly mattered in oil logistics then.)

Initially, host governments in the Gulf just went on competing for volume. Their attitudes towards production programming varied a little at times during Opec's first decade, according to how each happened to be placed in the current exporting order. (There was one half-hearted experiment in programming production *increases* during the years 1965–6 and 1966–7. It came to nothing, except perhaps to increase the Shah's megalomania.) But Saudi Arabia, after Tariki's departure, opposed the idea implacably for twenty years.

During the seventies, busy with taking over the pricing, ownership, and, finally, the sale of their crude, Opec member governments hardly mentioned production programming. After the first upsurge of 1973–4 they concentrated on what they called the 'administration' of prices at their new high level (Figure 8.3). They never found this easy to define, agree upon or organise. Since pricing rather than volume is what most Opec governments hope to benefit from during the coming decade, some of the techniques they toyed with then (not altogether unsuccessfully) are examined later. Enormous intellectual effort by Western economic and political analysts was devoted during the rest of the seventies to

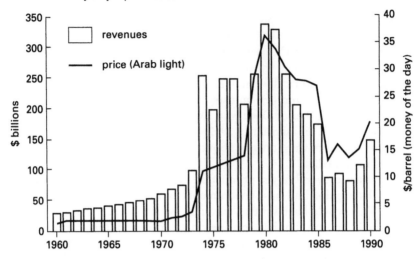

Figure 8.3. Crude oil prices and Opec's oil export revenues, in real terms, 1960–1990 (adjusted for export price inflation in OECD countries). (*Sources:* Opec, CGES.)

examining the Opec governments' strategies and performance (as well as pontificating about their motives, as noted in the last chapter). All the serried analyses were inconclusive – like the results of the Opec pricing performance.

Then came the second price shock of 1979, in which Opec needed to do little more than ride the price wave. It was followed by another two years of confusion in prices. Recession and price elasticity reduced demand sharply, and there was almost no panic in oil markets when Iraq invaded Iran. Saudi Arabia kept its official prices well below those of the rest of Opec, and produced as much as it could (then some 10 MBD). But even with output from Iraq and Iran severely reduced by the war, and promises by some member governments to reduce their output (predictably not kept), oil demand continued to fall. In late 1981 Opec finally compromised on a 'reunification' of its official prices. That could not stabilise the market either.

### Quotas, perforce

At that point, in March 1982, Opec made its first serious attempt at a system of production quotas.[3] Even Saudi Arabia agreed that total Opec

[3] The agreement actually took place informally in Doha, Abu Dhabi, during an Arab Energy Conference and a meeting of OAPEC, the Organisation of Arab Petroleum Exporting Countries (a separate group formed in 1968 to promote development projects financed from Arab countries' oil revenues).

output should be limited, and grudgingly went along with a quota system – for the other member countries. For some years, its government still refused to accept any firm numerical quota of barrels set from outside for its own production. In practice it set its own production ceiling at or close to the difference between the total Opec ceiling agreed upon and the aggregate of all the other members' quotas. That saved face; but it also implicitly accepted the role that the Saudi government has nearly always been reluctant to accept explicitly, that of Opec's swing supplier. In any case, that first quota agreement did not survive the next Opec conference, which had Iran and Saudi Arabia in particularly bitter opposition, and other countries seeking higher quotas or price differentials. (Ironically, it was Venezuela, the initial proponent of production programming, which put an end to that first quota system by officially disavowing its own production limit.)

Another production ceiling and set of quotas was agreed upon in March 1983 – along with Opec's first-ever admitted reduction in official prices. (Until then, the actual reductions had been subsumed in 'reunification' of the various official selling prices.) Saudi Arabia was for once explicit about acting 'as a swing producer to supply the balancing quantities to meet market requirements'. That conference, which became peripatetic but ended in London, did also elicit a promise of export restrictions and price alignment from Mexico and even some muffled noises from the UK Department of Energy that Opec was unwise enough to interpret as sympathetic. However, the total Opec production that its quotas envisaged was 16 MBD for 1984, just over half what Opec had produced in 1979 (or for that matter 1973).

Continuing overtures to non-Opec exporters produced conciliatory words from Norway, but little price support in the Atlantic market. Member governments engaged in various forms of price discounting, open or hidden within government-to-government deals, countertrade deals paid for in crude oil with no values visible, and the like. Opec had its own word for these, 'malpractices', and one of its inevitable commissions to inquire into them. At the end of 1984, under pressure from Saudi Arabia and Kuwait, it agreed to set up a Ministerial Executive Council to monitor export sales, prices and production, and appointed a firm of Dutch accountants to audit all the figures they could get. (It is instructive to recall that in 1961, inspired with Perez Alfonzo's dream of production programming while devising its first administrative statutes, Opec had included an enforcement department in its secretariat. That had somehow got lost on the way – as had later its economics department.)[4]

---

[4] However, considerable economic expertise and a comprehensive econometric energy model are nowadays deployed in Opec's research department.

It has never been clear how much information, reliable or not, the Executive Council or its auditors ever obtained from member governments. Whatever it was turned out to be too little and too late.

It was not until early 1985 that Yamani mentioned in passing that Saudi Arabia *did* regard itself as adhering to a fixed quota (to which in autumn 1984 it had appeared to agree only with its usual reservations). He did so in order to complain that because other member governments were discounting below official prices, the Kingdom was finding itself unable to export the 4.3 MBD of this quota. A few months later, embarking upon their experiment in netback pricing, the Saudis torpedoed that particular version of the quota system. In December 1985, faced with this Saudi *fait accompli*, an Opec conference bravely announced that the rest of the membership, too, would 'secure and defend ... a fair share in the world oil market consistent with the necessary income' for their countries.

### Prices, production, or both?

Both those first two attempts to control Opec production by quotas had been tied firmly to a set of official government selling prices (defined in terms of a marker price, for Arab Light or some hypothetical surrogate crudes). Some among the sacred band of independent, critical but friendly intellectuals who often advise Opec were arguing, from this experience, that it should try to set prices, or production, but not both. (They did not always agree on which would be more practicable to control.)

In its experiment with netback pricing in 1985–6, Saudi Arabia temporarily dispensed with *any* official price for its crudes. After King Fahd brought that experiment to an end, and accepted a Saudi quota, (but once again rejected any swing producer role), Opec went through its customary motions of trying to do both things at once. It announced a price of $18/bbl; this time, for the average of a basket of seven crudes, on which all other member governments would hope to align their prices.[5] But there was a sharp difference, in practice if not in admitted principle. The basket price, and all others linked to it, were 'target prices' to be aimed at. Being averages of one's own and other sales, they could never be specifically charged, or even monitored except in hindsight. The targets, also, were a long way off; the price level in August

[5] Saudi Arabian Light; UAE Dubai; Nigerian Bonny Light; Algerian Saharan Blend; Indonesian Minas; Venezuelan Tia Juana Light; and Mexican (non-Opec) Isthmus. Differentials were recommended for seventeen other Opec crudes. Because none of its crudes was included in the basket, Iraq refused to adhere to the accompanying quota agreement.

1986 was about $10/bbl for the basket. There was no longer any set of official selling prices that Opec could hope to impose. Member governments emerging from a period of selling their crudes at netback prices or various other kinds of 'spot-related' prices had little chance of dictating any kind of new fixed prices to customers. Steadily, during the following years, more and more Opec governments agreed upon 'formula' prices for their term contracts which were escalated to the spot or forward prices of non-Opec crudes quoted from open markets abroad.

Under this new dispensation, all that Opec purported to control was its own production, in the hope of affecting pricing in those open markets. As we have seen, its collective performance in abiding by production quotas was not noticeably more impressive after 1986 than it had been in 1983–5. By the end of the decade, the member governments' oil ministers had plenty of reasons to be scathing.

Yet by the end of 1989, even though all of its quotas had been honoured more in the breach than in the observance, those market-related prices *were* indeed very close to Opec's basketwork target. The target, by the standards of a decade before, was admittedly not high. Member nations were then producing perhaps two-thirds of the peak volumes they had reached during the seventies, at prices about half as high in nominal terms and about 70 per cent lower in real terms. Their oil revenues were little more than half the triumphant levels of 1980–1, but twice as high as in the financially disastrous year of 1986. Nevertheless, given everybody's continuing malpractices with the quota system, the rewards in pricing were for a time impressive. (By 1990, however, the basket was spilling again.)

As so often before, the role of the Organisation in the world oil market remained ambiguous. Its direct leverage still seemed limited; its indirect influence, more than could be simply explained. Would Opec, yet again, turn out to be just lucky, and able simply to take advantage of external circumstances?

Economically, that renews a question that analysts inside as well as outside the Organisation have been debating ever since its first direct intervention in pricing in 1973. Some eminent economists continue to attribute the first oil price shock of 1973 entirely to the machinations of the Opec cartel. Others are equally convinced that most of the price increase then would fairly soon have occurred anyway, whether Opec had existed or not. Subtle and compelling arguments can readily be adduced on both sides.[6] Politically, the question goes back even farther – to the origins, and the changing nature, of Opec.

[6] For example, Adelman puts the whole responsibility down to Opec, while Mabro and MacAvoy think it simply took advantage of market forces in winter 1972–3.

*Levelling up to leapfrog*

Opec had crystallised two postwar elements of nationalist leverage in the countries where international major companies had concessions. The first was the insistence of host governments that all of them were entitled to whatever any of them could get. (Very often, that meant a little more. Levelling up, which was hard for concessionaires to refuse, usually developed into leapfrog.) The second lever was the readiness of some of these host governments, on occasion, to force through changes in concessionary relationships by fiat, backed by their national sovereignty. (An early postwar example of this, Iranian nationalisation in 1951–4, had failed.[7] But it left other host governments resentful and readier to plot together.) Use of these governments' political leverage was perhaps facilitated by the fact that after that Iranian failure most of the international major companies were operating in all the countries significantly concerned with oil exports – who became the founders of Opec. That joint coverage was a source of great corporate strength, but also of visible common vulnerability.

Corporate unease about that vulnerability conferred upon Opec the only genuine advantage that it achieved collectively in the first decade of its existence. Its initial demand was for the reversal of price cuts made by international companies in the Middle East in 1960. Those had cut government revenues unilaterally, at a time when the Opec founders' preliminary consultations had already begun. (The US companies did not try cutting prices for Venezuelan crude. That simply gave Perez Alfonzo the chance to show his interlocutors from the Gulf that being tough could work.) Opec never achieved the specific reversal of prices that it began by demanding. But what it did achieve was to put a floor under its member governments' unit revenues per barrel. The companies never again dared to cut their posted tax reference prices in the Gulf. Thus Opec's first assertion of influence came easily, and was negative. Nonetheless, it was valuable.

Nearly all Opec's positive gains had to await its second decade, and were *not* bargained through collectively. More often than not, one or a few governments drove the bargains. Occasionally they were deputed by Opec. At the most important times, they acted on their own. This was true of:

Libya's unilateral action against its concessionaires in autumn 1970.

---

[7] The Prime Minister who instigated that in 1951, Dr Mossadegh, was overthrown in 1954. National ownership of the concession of the Anglo-Iranian company (later BP) formally remained; but a consortium of European and US companies was brought in to manage Iranian operations on terms financially similar to those in concessions elsewhere in the Gulf.

This set off the sequence of host government gains in the Tehran agreement of 1971,[8] followed by further Libyan 'leapfrogging' in Tripoli;

the General Agreement on Participation in December 1972, which began the sequence of agreed government shareholdings in Gulf operating companies, eventually rising to 100 per cent in several of them;

a Gulf Ministerial Committee's decision to declare crude prices unilaterally in October 1973, and the effect on world market prices of the simultaneous Arab oil embargo;[9]

Saudi Arabia's decision, with Abu Dhabi and Qatar, to impose new royalty and tax rates, and limit company margins, in November 1974;

the move to 100 per cent participation, first implemented by Kuwait in December 1975.

Certain of the examples of direct action by Opec governments concerned their countries alone. The moves towards government control in Iraq in 1961 and 1972, in Indonesia in the early sixties, in Algeria in 1969–71 and Venezuela in 1976 hardly affected the rest of Opec. But one eruption of entirely national politics had profound repercussions across Opec. The Iranian revolution of 1979 overthrew an Opec member government. It blew up all the prices that Opec had decided upon shortly before; transformed all member governments' selling practices; and eventually, altered the whole structure of international trade in oil.[10]

One reason why so little Opec action during the 1960s was collective was that most of the founder members were reluctant to allow any power to develop within the central organisation they set up. One early set of negotiations to bring Gulf concession terms closer to Venezuela's

---

[8] Negotiations leading to the Tehran Agreement of early 1971 were collective in form, on both sides. Ministers of Iran, Iraq and Saudi Arabia conducted them for the Gulf states, with a team from the international companies. (They did, for once, include a threat of embargo by all Opec countries, except Indonesia.) The Shah, already wreathed in delusion, hailed it as a personal triumph, and it did provide for five years of increases in prices, escalating with inflation. But the financial gains it gave Gulf governments did little more than match those achieved alone in the Libyan breakthrough.

[9] The prices that these governments announced were at that time 'posted prices' – those on which royalties and taxes were charged, and to which various forms of 'buy-back' price under the participation agreements were related. The prices invoiced in integrated operations or charged to third-party customers by the international companies actually lifting the crudes for export were not necessarily the same. But henceforth the companies did pass on to customers all the *increases* in price (or initially in tax-paid cost) that Opec resolved upon.

[10] It triggered the shift to direct selling by many Opec governments, and brought to an end most of the international major companies' sales of their equity crude from within Opec countries to third parties. Incidentally, when negotiations between its revolutionary government and the ex-consortium companies broke off in autumn 1979, the oil nationalisation begun by Mossadegh twenty-eight years before was finally completed.

was delegated to Opec's first Secretary-General in 1963. It failed within a few months because the governments concerned, including his own, withdrew their support. At the time, that arose from lack of confidence, disunity and the effective bargaining power of international companies backed by Western diplomacy. But the reluctance would probably have developed anyway, as it has in many international organisations. What Opec is concerned with is overwhelmingly more important to its sovereign government members than almost anything that most international organisations have to consider. From then on, they arranged that no Opec official should ever have more than an advisory role. A sequence of always talented and sometimes forceful Secretaries-General have served in that role, appointed roughly in rotation by the member countries. But they have never been given the backing to develop as influential a collective analytical apparatus concerned with oil as even the IEA, let alone some of the international companies.

As a result, the essence of Opec has become not so much an organisation, more a series of conferences. The impression given by the avid and devoted media coverage that its conferences commanded in the 1970s, fading a little since then, is not artificial. Decisions *are* indeed taken there, not just formally announced. The crucial meetings are often informal, between smaller groups (in ministers' suites rather than in full session, and as often as not without any officials from the Opec secretariat present). The jamborees of text and video journalists, sometimes reduced to interviewing each other,[11] are indeed almost 'present at the creation' of whatever the member governments agree and *may* act upon later. Between conferences there is plenty of Opec activity, often at the headquarters in Vienna. But much of this too is between officials of member governments, only assisted by the secretariat.

*Sovereignty over prices*

Crude price 'administration' by Opec governments between 1974 and 1978 did involve collective agreement between member governments, but without any obviously effective sanctions. It never involved any production control beyond the 'allowables' of total national production that some but not all member governments announced from time to time. There were very few occasions when those allowables actually

---

[11] At times, to the general advantage. For years, it was not only other journalists who hung upon the interpretations of Mr Ian Seymour, editor of *Middle East Economic Survey* and the most devoted Opec-watcher of all. At the close of many of these cliffhanger conferences, some of the returning Opec delegates eagerly awaited the next issue of *MEES* for him to explain what really had (or should have) happened – and even make all the processes of decision sound relatively rational.

affected the export offtake from any of the countries. Offtake, and hence total production from most of the countries, was physically controlled during the period by the former concessionaires that were in process of being nationalised. Usually, they needed much less than the national allowables anyway. So that mild degree of quantitative control by the governments never became effective.

Demand was soft from late 1976 until the middle of 1978. The price increases achieved during those years did not always fully match inflation (however measured), so that at times the real price of crude fell. It remains intriguing, however, that the Opec governments, acting in unison but without any particular sanctions, were then able to push through any increases in nominal prices at all.

One possible explanation may have been simply that this price-fixing association's members happened to be sovereign governments. Moreover, they were governments engaging more directly in the oil trade than before, and able to influence most of their other national trade. In those early years after 1973, the bargaining weight of their sovereignty was enhanced by the continuing, ill-understood repercussions of that first price shock and a welter of forecasts suggesting that oil prices must inexorably go on rising. No other operators in the oil trade then felt able to deal on equal terms with Opec governments. The only bargainers accustomed to them, their concessionaires turned offtakers, remained deeply beholden as contractors *within* the national jurisdictions. As exporting agents, they had no difficulty in passing on any price increases that Opec announced. Their own profits on Opec oil were soon trimmed; but Opec pricing at a stroke increased their upstream profits and opportunities everywhere else. Most other oilmen from outside were highly uncertain about dealing with these new seeming masters of future world oil supply. Opec governments were emboldened by having become enormously richer almost overnight. Oil companies and OECD governments took a long time to get over the sheer shock to general business confidence that had been dealt by the oil embargo and the price increases imposed in 1973–4. They chose to be intimidated.

## Pricing without a policy

Curiously enough, Opec has never committed itself to any fundamental 'objective' defining what its members *want* to happen to oil prices. The only clear statement of such an objective by any member government came from the late Shah, at the end of 1973. He was pushing a second price increase through Opec, beyond the first that the Arabs had forced already in October. In justification of that move, he argued that oil prices should steadily be raised towards the marginal supply cost of alternative fuels.

That would perhaps have been a logical objective for a confident Opec monopolist. The rest of the member governments were not as confident of monopoly power as the Shah was then. But they have never gone any farther, or postulated any alternative formula. About the end of 1979, after the Iranian revolution and the Shah's death, a committee of experts advising the Organisation on the formulation of a 'Long-Term Strategy' elaborated essentially the same idea:

Basically, the ultimate objective is to achieve self-sustained economic growth with a high and balanced level of economic activity from the revenues of a finite resource ... This means that oil prices should, in the long term, approximate the level of 'the cost of alternatives'. Since the cost and nature of alternatives to petroleum are not only uncertain but also moving over time, the target has to be flexible and dynamic ... As substitutes for some petroleum products come about, the target itself shifts to less substitutable usages. At the same time, this target takes into account the increasing cost of marginal oil supplies and the replacement cost of the depleted barrel.[12]

The ministerial committee to which that expert report was addressed – representing Algeria, Iran, Iraq, Kuwait, Saudi Arabia and Venezuela – appears to have accepted its advice in February 1980. But the whole of Opec did not then commit itself to that long-term strategy, or to any fundamental pricing objective: nor had it since, up to the time this book was completed.

Many Western economists, as it happens, have conducted much argument in the years since 1973 about a rediscovered price objective that Opec might 'logically' have been able to borrow. As long ago as 1931, the late Harold Hotelling had postulated that over time the 'net price' of any exhaustible resource (i.e. its market price less the full cost of production) *should* rise at a rate matching current riskless rates of interest. Otherwise the producer could do better at any time by extracting the whole remaining resource, selling it at the current price, and investing the proceeds. (Hotelling's argument was about *change* in price over time. He never pretended to define, for any given time, the initial price from which prices should rise.) His theorem remains simple, elegant and powerful. Once stated, it sounds self-evident. In practice, it seems to have been forgotten or ignored for decades; then re-discovered,[13] just in time to influence arguments about a 'right price' for

---

[12] Opec, 'Report of the Group of Experts ... on long-term strategy' (London, 1980).
[13] R. Solow, 'The economics of resources and the resources of economics', *American Economic Review*, 64 (1974), pp. 1–14.

world oil. Many distinguished economists[14] have taken it to demonstrate that quite regardless of Opec power, oil prices *must* rise with the
passage of time, as the outcome of 'elemental economic forces'.

*If* the extent of the resource in question is not fixed, however, does
Hotelling's theorem still hold good? Lately this has become a subject of
academic controversy, again focused on Opec pricing. It can be argued
that the magnitude of any extractive resource such as petroleum can
never be known with any precision,[15] since increases in price and cost
reductions through technological advances can always be counted upon
to extend the proportion recoverable. If so, the counter-argument from
another school of economists runs, the Hotelling theorem remains
irrefutable but becomes irrelevant.[16] Whether it might still apply as a
useful second-best approximation remains a source of scholastic dispu-
tation. (Few theoretical propositions in economics or other disciplines
depend crucially upon precise measurement of the quantities involved.
But if the quantities are considered constantly extensible, and hence
'unknowable', can any theorem relating to them have practical
validity?)

This question has generated some academic debate and much
research. But it may have contributed more to the economic theory of
exhaustible resources than to the study of petroleum pricing: 'An initial
interest in oil diverted intellectual talent along a road on which progress
took us further and further away from the problem in hand.'[17]

Relevant or not, that Hotelling rationale is one that Opec, wisely, has
never chosen to appropriate. The Organisation and its member governments are not short of economists (or theorists of all kinds). But they
have more practical problems to concern them. (Opec indeed came into
existence after, and because, prices had fallen for a decade in real terms,
and were finally cut even in nominal dollars. During parts of the
eighties, again, its members had plenty of evidence that oil prices do
*not* always rise.)

[14] For example: J. Stiglitz 'Monopoly and the rate of extraction of exhaustible resources', *American Economic Review*, 66(1976), pp. 655–61; M. H. Miller and C. W. Upton, 'A test of the Hotelling valuation principle', *Journal of Political Economy*, 93(1985), pp. 1–25; P. A. Samuelson, *The Collected Scientific Papers of Paul A. Samuelson*, ed. K. Crowley (MIT Press, 1986); D. A. Starrett, 'Production and capital: Kenneth Arrow's contributions in perspective', *Journal of Economic Literature*, 25(1987), pp. 92–102; G. M. Heal and G. Chichilnisky, *Oil and the International Economy* (Clarendon Press, 1991).

[15] For example, M. A. Adelman, 'Mineral depletion, with special reference to petroleum', *Review of Economics and Statistics*, 72(1990), pp. 1–10. Also, L. Drollas and J. Greenman, *Oil: The Devil's Gold* (Duckworth, 1989).

[16] This counter-argument does *not* suggest that resources are infinite. If that were so, not only Hotelling's theorem but much else in economics might become irrelevant. It simply denies any practical relevance to Hotelling if the extent of the resource, albeit finite, can never be known with any precision.

[17] R. Mabro, 'OPEC and the price of oil', *Energy Journal*, 13(1992), no. 2, pp. 1–17.

If sovereignty was a potent contributor to the governments' power to increase prices in the mid-seventies, its spell soon wore off, never to be cast again. Another explanation was much discussed in those years, the price leadership of a swing supplier, who might be expected to 'act like Texas', balancing total Opec output to market demand so as to maintain a stable price level.

### Acting like Texas, or not . . .

When Opec was founded, proration in Texas was indeed one of the models it thought of emulating. Saudi Arabia's first oil minister, Tariki, studied the system run by the Texas Railroad Commission deeply, and remained intrigued by it. He was unable to persuade his royal masters that it would be practicable within Opec. They, like the Shah, were at the time interested in increasing their own export volume, as the only dependable way to higher revenues. The idea of modulating output in the hope of higher prices to benefit their competitors as much as themselves did not appeal.

Nor, in any case, was it obvious then *which* Opec producer might be expected to take the swing. Venezuela was the largest exporter when the Organisation was founded. But its capacity was then expected to pass its peak during the 1960s; it had higher costs than the other founder member governments; and Perez Alfonzo's panacea was production programming, by all rather than just one producer. No single Opec supplier then had, or seemed likely to gain, a predominance in capacity among Opec exporters to compare with the sheer weight of Texas within the oil-producing states of the US 'lower forty-eight'. Nobody has ever incontrovertibly defined the prerequisites of a swing supplier. But such a producer, in order to balance total output to estimated demand, probably needs to be able to accept fluctuations in output, up and down, larger than any of its competitors or possibly all together. It may also need to have the lowest costs, of current production or of adding incremental capacity. (Being qualified for such a role, of course, will not necessarily make any producer volunteer for it.)

There was, to begin with, an involuntary swing supplier in the Gulf. In the mid-sixties, Kuwait was the largest producer, with the highest figure of published proved reserves (though Saudi oil resources were already widely believed to be greater). Kuwait's tax-paid costs of current production were said to be the lowest anywhere. (The incremental costs of raising capacity in its one huge oilfield, Burgan, may not have been as low as in Saudi Arabia, even then; but its operating costs from developed capacity were said to be lower.) Perhaps more importantly, its offtake was less constrained by intercorporate agreements than anywhere else in the Gulf. So it was drawn upon as a residual supplier by its concessionaires and their long-term customers, Shell, Exxon and Mobil. Its higher capacity brought exceptional riches to the tiny shaikhdom, but also wider fluctuations in output than other Gulf producers experienced. Its larger neighbours did not necessarily covet the role, except as it might follow upon the increases they continued to urge upon their concessionaires. It was not until the end of the sixties that Saudi Arabia (and Iran, and briefly even Libya) passed Kuwait in output. Shortly afterwards, its government set a limit to national production, imposing the first 'government allowable' in the Gulf.

Saudi Arabia, producing somewhat more than Iran and able to expand output at much lower technical cost, became automatically the swing supplier for its concessionaires. When it and other Arab producers engineered the 1973 takeover of Gulf crude prices and raised them 70 per cent, it was asserting a degree of price leadership. But it was trumped by the Shah a few weeks later with another increase that redoubled Opec prices. That angered the Saudi government, which was seeking leadership – politically in the Gulf, and perhaps economically within Opec if that would help. Three months after it had set off the price surge, its oil minister Yamani was already complaining: 'We believe the present level of prices is higher than it should be, and something should be done about that.' He voiced Saudi fears that the price level set by Iran might set off a worldwide depression and prejudice even Opec's own economic development plans. The Kingdom's political ambitions within the Gulf were always tempered, even in that winter of embargo, by concern for a special relationship with the US that dated back to Roosevelt and Ibn Saud.

Would this have been an occasion to 'act like Texas', using the potential upward flexibility of Saudi exports to hold Opec prices down? (Texas, in fact, had never done anything of that sort. *Its* flexibility had always been employed to keep US prices up.) Yamani, who by then had been the Kingdom's oil minister for a decade, was still less enamoured with any swing supply role than his predecessor might have been. The Kingdom did not immediately or even soon do anything about that level of prices – except to camouflage its next move, which significantly increased prices to final consumers in late 1974, as a decrease.[18] But it did use its potential leverage as the largest producer to impose its own

---

[18] Saudi Arabia, along with Abu Dhabi and Qatar, purported to *reduce* posted prices. But at the same time it raised royalty and tax rates sharply and cut the margins that under participation its concessionaires were then receiving.

chosen pricing formula rather than others that Opec had been discussing. (Those other formulae would have served the same purpose – reducing company margins that had been fortuitously swollen by the Opec price increases. None of the governments disagreed about that.)[19]

After 1975, inflation and dollar exchange depreciation began to erode the real price level, and Opec wanted compensation of the kind that it had been able to exact (by agreement with the companies) between 1971 and mid-1973. But now the companies were out of that negotiating phase; the governments had the full responsibility for pricing. Saudi Arabia argued for lower increases than Iran and most other member governments; for 1976 it compromised on a 10 per cent increase, but for 1977 it refused to go beyond 5 per cent. That set off a brief period of 'two-tier pricing', with crudes from the Saudis and the UAE on offer for about 50 cents/bbl lower than comparable crudes from the other eleven members of Opec. The Kingdom cancelled its production allowable of 8.5 MBD, and instructed Aramco to produce up to 10 MBD from capacity then believed to be nearly 12 MBD. For the first time, Saudi Arabia said it was ready to use its potential as the swing supplier.

It turned out to have overestimated that potential. Aramco turned out to be unable to produce even 10 MBD; bad weather reduced tanker loadings from Ras Tanura; and a fire at one of the main field gathering stations in May 1977 also limited exports. The test of strength was inconclusive. Saudi Arabia did increase its exports much more than member countries that had gone for the higher price increase, particularly in the second half of the year. (That delay was predictable, given the timing of contracts and tanker scheduling.) But even the others, as it happened, were able to increase their exports somewhat too. And in the meantime, the stand-off had been resolved by compromise. The Opec majority cancelled a further increase that they had planned at the mid-year; the Saudis and UAE put their prices up into line with the original 10 per cent increase of the rest. At the end of that year, the Shah announced a sudden conversion to moderation in pricing, following a visit to the new US President Carter. His switch appears to have been purely political. So was much of the behaviour of other Opec governments during that interregnum.

Even economically, Saudi Arabia's test of the swing supply role had not been a clear failure. But it had not achieved what Yamani may have hoped. It left him reluctant to choose such a role again. Behind and above him, his royal masters seemed even more so. During the next

---

[19] At the same meeting Saudi Arabia was also able to demonstrate its bargaining muscle against the Aramco concessionaires – who were constrained to consent hastily to the principle of 100 per cent participation.

decade, at various times during the on-off exercise with quotas, the Saudis were forced to behave as a swing supplier (while usually stoutly denying it). Yamani once or twice had to admit this. Others in the government, including his eventual successor, had never done so up to the time that this book was completed.

## Sharing the swing?

If Saudi Arabia is not prepared to act as a swing supplier, and none of the member governments feels it can rely on a quota system, what can Opec do to maintain price stability at a level to suit their revenue requirements? One possibility was being discussed up to early 1990 during a lull in pricing anxieties (for producers). This was to concentrate Opec's pricing responsibility again – but among a few of the main suppliers, not just one. Once again, Shaikh Ali Khalifah was forthright:

What is the ultimate objective? ... If it is maintenance of prices, then I think that those producers which have spare production capacity at their disposal can indicate that if the average price goes below the agreed price of $18/bbl, they will get together and see what they can do to reduce their own production and, to a lesser degree, possibly also the production of others.[20]

That proposition would have implied sharing the swing supply responsibility between some members of 'inner Opec', and leaving all the rest to produce however much – or little – they can. To some members of that exclusive inner circle, it had appeal; but not all.

In all likelihood, the chosen few would have had to be in the Gulf. Of the seven countries with very high R/P ratios, Libya would be unlikely to volunteer or to be invited. Abu Dhabi at the beginning of this decade was not prepared to co-operate over quotas, or perhaps over much else inside Opec. Venezuela is a most responsible producer, and might be sympathetic to the concentration of pricing power; but its main commercial as well as political concerns are with the Western Hemisphere and the Atlantic market. Even within the Gulf, Iran remains politically isolated from all Arab states, militarily and ideologically in a state of armed truce.

In early 1990, that seemed to leave only three members of the Opec core, Saudi Arabia, Iraq and Kuwait. They were the most richly endowed in terms of oil resources, possessing together about 45 per cent of total world proved reserves. They then had 46 per cent of production capacity within Opec and perhaps close on 20 per cent of total world capacity.

[20] *MEES*, 12 February 1990.

Politically, these three Arab states were always most unlike each other. Nevertheless, both the Kingdom and the Emirate had helped finance the war that Saddam Hussein's Ba'athist ('Arab socialist') government of Iraq had waged with some success against Iran for much of the eighties. That first Gulf war left Iraq, for two years, the most heavily equipped military power with access to the Gulf. It was also, temporarily, on better terms with the US than for many years before (in spite of exchanging threats with the closest of US allies, Israel). Even in early 1990, that sounded ominous for Kuwait, and not altogether welcome in Saudi Arabia. During the next twelve months, the omens proved true. By 1991, Iraq had devastated Kuwait and had itself been devastated by the US. Any illusions about a 'super-Opec' based on these three had been bombed and burned away.

Saudi Arabia and Iraq, during the 1980s, had developed pipeline linkages to the Gulf of Suez making them much less dependent upon tanker transport through the Straits of Hormuz and, to a limited extent, also interdependent. Iraq had already, during the seventies, laid a 'strategic' pipeline to link its northern Kirkuk field[21] to its southern export terminals on the Gulf and another via Turkey to the Mediterranean. Those two replaced a line across Syria that had often been disrupted during political disputes between the two neighbouring countries. A third pipeline across Saudi Arabia to the Red Sea, financed jointly by the two governments, added yet another export option.

Technical opportunities of co-operation in export policy, therefore, were for a time in the eighties dovetailed into the government relations between those two countries – until the second Gulf war cancelled them. Kuwait, before the Iraqi invasion, had concentrated in its first decade of industry ownership on refining capacity at home and abroad. In 1990 more than half of its oil exports were shipped as refined products, free of any Opec quota. Only in the late 1980s did it talk of restoring its former crude production capacity of some 3 MBD, and possibly moving higher. That always appeared technically quite practicable. At times in the past two decades, Kuwait alternated between the price hawks and doves of Opec. In the few years before 1990, it became as cautious as the Saudis about pricing Opec crudes at levels that might inhibit demand growth and stimulate too much non-Opec petroleum development elsewhere. (In the nineties, high prices may once again attract it more.)

Iraq never seemed to favour that or any other kind of caution in Opec

---

[21] Kirkuk, which has been producing since 1927, is one of the world's super-giants, with productivity at times of the order of 20,000 b/d, unmatched anywhere else except in a few (smaller) fields in Iran. It is, however, 500 miles from seaboard; its crude has had to be moved by pipelines through Syria, Turkey or Saudi Arabia, incurring transit fees.

counsels. For a long time after it nationalised most of its concession-aires' acreage in 1961, it had taken little practical notice of the Organisation. (Indeed, it had suspended its membership for some years after being rebuffed in a first token invasion of Kuwaiti territory.) In the years following the Arab oil embargo of 1973, which it characteristically chose not to join, it decided on its prices and export volumes without much relation to the attempts at price administration over which the other member countries spent so much time arguing. During the eighties, understandably preoccupied after invading Iran, its government most often refused to accept any Opec quota at all. When it did, that did not seem to make much difference to the quantities that it sold, or the discounts it offered. (Iran, during the same period, argued a great deal more within Opec about quotas, but likewise went its own way when actually selling crude.)

In the interval between its two wars, for a time, Iraqi spokesmen did talk publicly about co-operation with Kuwait as well as Saudi Arabia. But their emphasis was usually on the market power of high-reserve producers to keep prices *up*:

There is a political element behind the co-operation of these three countries ... We have to play a bigger role. We have among us, and perhaps one or two other countries, the highest reserves, the highest production capacity, and we can get things done with due consideration for the legitimate rights of others ... We will be co-ordinating our positions and this will continue whether during the meetings or in between. This is an element that will have weight for the support of Opec and for the stabilisation of the market.[22]

For Iraq, any desirable stabilisation of Opec prices always seemed to mean *above* a certain price level. No doubt it still does. But no Iraqi government seems likely to get what it desires in Gulf oil during this decade.

## Stabilisation by super-exporters

Political co-operation between those hopeful super-exporters has been destroyed, probably never to return. So long as militant Islam continues to rule in Iran and foment disaffection elsewhere, it may pose some threats to all three. But it seems unlikely that co-operation to administer world oil pricing from the centre of Opec – say even between Saudi Arabia, Kuwait, the UAE and some politically de-natured Iran – would ever have worked anyway.

Joint management of the international oil trade by the largest export-ers *had* of course been exercised before, fairly effectively and for quite a

[22] Isam al-Chalabi, Iraqi oil minister. *MEES*, 15 January 1990.

long time. Opec indeed came into being because of it. It was not surprising that Opec oil ministers occasionally appeared to pine for such a system:

The seven majors did not fix quotas and divide production in that way. They went about it more by using first-hand experience and accommodating each other when a problem arose. They may have met together once in Scotland in the 1920s, but certainly they didn't make it a four times a year affair. Nor was their control exercised through mechanisms such as joint concessions – though of course those did exist – but it was a considerably more subtle business than that.[23]

Indeed, it had been. But the leadership exercised in the world oil market by the international major companies during the first three postwar decades still depended more upon the interlocking ownership of joint concessions in the Middle East, and the offtake arrangements within them, than on anything else, subtle or not. Their exercise was not simply one of price administration. It was the responsibility of accommodating the awesome anomaly of Middle East reserves within an existing international pattern of higher-cost energy industries, including most oil industries elsewhere. (The responsibility was discharged imperfectly. But nobody else has ever faced up to it.) Without their framework of joint control, the companies could not have exercised their degree of price administration. Nothing in Opec – or yet conceived for any inner super-Opec – compares with it.

The mechanisms involved were not only part of the history, the legendry, and the conspiracy theories with which this industry has long been festooned. They were in themselves subtle. More important, they were designed to be largely automatic, obviating the need for recourse to Achnacarry[24] (or Vienna). The mechanisms were

joint ownership in established concessions;

constraints, for a long time, on the freedom of participants to go elsewhere in the region to establish new ones;

offtake agreements that penalised over-lifting and under-lifting;

long-term contracts for crude from concessions that one did not partly own, particularly those with relatively free offtake (such as Kuwait).

All those contractual operating rules did not need constantly to be referred back for decisions at the top, let alone to be redrafted *ad hoc* every year or two.

[23] Shaikh Ali Khalifah al-Sabah, *MEES*, 12 February 1990.
[24] It was at Achnacarry Castle in the Scottish Highlands that in 1927 representatives of the international major companies concluded what came to be known as the 'As Is Agreement', which did for some years moderate their competitive behaviour not only in the Gulf concessions but across most of the world oil market.

To be sure, the companies, like Opec, tried to reach explicit agreements about maintaining price, production, and market shares. But these seldom held for long. Their greater oligopolistic achievement was to use moments of harmony to set up structures that, once in place, would *automatically* give preponderance to those with the greatest stake in long-term equilibrium, restrain the pursuit of short-term advantage, and penalise aggressive behaviour without the need for direct retaliation.[25]

Moreover, in that particular heyday of the international majors (some of them no doubt have others to come), their dominance of the business extended far more extensively, upstream and downstream, than Opec's ever has. They did not try to exercise it from one end of the business alone. (Nor should one fail to note, finally, that their dominance of exports from the Gulf was beginning to be eroded by market forces even before they transferred the title deeds of it to Opec.)

After inheriting that control of production, Opec has nearly always chosen to operate it on a short-term basis. It has hardly ever contemplated any reciprocal mechanisms that might offset the losses to particular members for being required to depart from their own interests for the Organisation's 'common good'. (There was one paragraph in its first 'Long-Term Strategy' report of 1979 that mentioned possible 'compensatory financing' arrangements. But it went on blandly to assume that 'With the expectation of rising prices (which is guaranteed by the price floor) it should not be difficult to administer prices during a temporary glut.'[26] That sample of Opec realism was swept away, along with the report, in the pricing welter of 1979–80.)

Given sufficient commercial and legal talent, such mutually restrictive and incentive arrangements might in theory be devised to make departure from what a few super-Opec governments might regard as the 'common good' disadvantageous, and to compensate other members' losses through conforming with it. But it is less plausible to foresee such arrangements becoming readily acceptable to all Opec governments. One comes back to the awkward fact of national sovereignty.

Companies, most of the time, can single-mindedly engage (innocently or not) in getting money. Governments with as narrow a set of economic interests as Opec's sometimes can, too. But could they ever guarantee to do so automatically, under binding agreements with even a few partners? Oil is so crucial to the sovereignty of these governments that automatic economic commitments regarding it sound impracticable

[25] T. H. Moran, 'Managing an oligopoly of would-be sovereigns', *International Organisation*, Autumn 1987. (Professor Moran's penetrating article, in laying stress upon these *automatic* mechanisms of the former joint shareholdings, ignored only the fact that today several of the Opec protagonists *are* sovereigns, not given habitually to automatic compliance.)
[26] Opec, 'Report of the Group of Experts ... on long-term strategy'.

politically. It is hard to see, therefore, that any super-Opec would ever find production or price administration much easier to manage than Opec has, unless the demand/supply balance develops so as to make the whole exercise easier, wherever the responsibility lies.

For some years, UN control of Iraq's exports may share the power to modulate Gulf output and influence Opec crude price levels. But that is unlikely to be used to hold down those exports for long. Kuwait, the main beneficiary of Iraqi reparations if those ever materialise, may want to maximise the new oil revenues that it will be receiving indirectly, as well as its own oil income. So Opec will soon have to take back on board the capacity of both these countries, and accommodate them within its total quotas. In the short run, the responsibility is likely to swing back to Saudi Arabia, however much the Kingdom seeks to reject the role.

Current unease about that, like the temporary euphoria about getting rid of quotas which it has replaced, arises from assumptions about medium-term supply and short-term demand. If world supply of oil and its acceptable substitutes outside Opec cannot be significantly increased at going prices, then increases in demand can be met only by the countries within Opec that have spare capacity and can increase it. If and when that comes to pass, Opec can be fairly confident of regaining its medium-run market power in one way or another. But even then, exactly how such market power over crude oil price levels could be exercised has of late become distinctly more complicated.

# CHAPTER 9

# A confusion of prices

During the Opec decade, Saudi Arabia was always reluctant to admit playing the role in which outside analysts, some of its fellow member governments, and indeed the forces of market circumstance tended repeatedly to cast it. It almost always[1] denied acting as a swing supplier to support Opec price levels. But it never took really decisive action to reject that role until it experimented with 'netback pricing' in 1985–6. That experiment, perhaps as much a matter of exasperation verging on fury as of fully calculated risk, effectively punctured the then inflated pretences of Opec 'price administration', as well as collapsing world price levels for crude. Even so, it was mainly a gesture of accommodation to changes in the oil market that were already irresistibly in train.

At a stroke, the Kingdom's oil decision-makers pulled the carpet from under the official price system for the whole of Opec. That had been founded upon the price level agreed at any time for the 'marker crude', Arabian Light or some surrogate for it. Prices for all other Opec crudes had been related, in theory at least, to the price of this marker by 'differentials' in their refining values and transport costs to key markets. (Arguments about keeping these differentials up to date went on interminably. But lip-service to the principle was there.) In July 1986, Saudi Arabia simply abolished any fixed price level for that marker crude at the time it was loaded. It began offering its crude for whatever the products refined from it would eventually fetch in final markets several weeks later – the 'gross product worth', at market prices reported ex-refinery, of the products that can be refined from it, less the costs of

---

[1] Only once, in March 1983, did the Kingdom ever go on record in an Opec resolution as agreeing 'to act as swing producer to supply the balancing quantities to meet market requirements'. How long it did so has been left deliberately vague. Yamani did not repudiate the role again until July 1985. But he then declared that since November 1984, 'we have had a fixed quota and are therefore no longer the swing producer'.

processing and transport, 'netted back' to the crude export terminals.[2] The generous allowance for refining costs in the Saudi contracts included a comfortable profit margin – in effect, guaranteed to each refiner involved. This meant, incidentally, selling the same oil at different (eventual) prices to different customers.[3] But neither the customers nor the Saudi sellers knew at the time of any particular sale what its netback price would turn out to be. So there was no FOB[4] price benchmark for Saudi crude left for other exporters to use in adjusting their own prices.

That action was (uncharacteristically) abrupt. Its effects made it the most important single move in crude pricing since 1973. But the market evolution to which the Saudis chose their own way to accommodate had been in progress at least since 1979. Most of what has happened to oil prices since has simply broadened and elaborated Opec's acceptance of the forces acting upon and indicated through open markets for oil.

### Open markets in the lead

An international spot market in crude had existed for many years on the periphery of the world trade, while that was dominated by international companies integrated from production in their concessions through to refining and marketing of products downstream. It was a useful if not very important mechanism for evening out minor imbalances between variations in demand – seasonal, quantitative and qualitative – and the rates of export supply. There are no *inherent* seasonal variations in oil supply.[5] Major international company producers generally chose and were able to keep crude production relatively steady for political and economic reasons. (The spot market for crude was less important, until 1979, than the similar market in refined products. That spot market was more widely accepted as providing references for regular price reviews or specific escalation clauses in long-term contracts for products. Changes there could persuasively be argued to have 'led', or strongly influenced, long-term contract prices for crude.)

Spot markets for crude did not become determinant in international

[2] Ironically, product netback calculations were probably familiar to most Opec governments mainly in terms of assessing the price differentials of their own crudes in relation to Arab Light. The Saudi formula, which temporarily deprived Arab Light of anything but a netback value itself, unhinged that rationale, as well as cutting prices by about two-thirds.
[3] The Saudis backed that 'price discrimination', moreover, by seeking to prohibit resales by customers to whom they sold the crude.
[4] I.e., loaded 'free on board' at the export terminal, as against delivered CIF, with 'costs, insurance and freight' included in the value at the destination.
[5] In operations with exceptionally difficult weather, such as the North Sea, Alaska and, presumably, Siberia, there is a tendency to concentrate maintenance schedules into 'windows of opportunity' during summer months. The difference this makes to total world production is tiny; but has at times been enough to affect market pricing.

pricing until the early 1980s. Looking back, it is tempting to associate this with the emergence of surplus. But in fact their sharpest rise into prominence had begun in 1979, a year when crude prices rocketed because customers and the trade perceived the danger of an oil shortage. (Objectively, none existed. But a shortage is always a matter of shared perceptions, fears, and expectations feeding on them.) The new prominence of spot pricing was probably associated more directly with the international major companies' final loss of the control of crude offtake from their former concession areas in the Gulf. That process of 'de-integration' had begun with their loss of ownership through nationalisation there. But the actual transfer of control of current production levels took longer, and was finally precipitated only by the Iranian crisis that began in late 1978.

Suddenly, in 1979, this brought a surge of demand from customers without assured contractual supplies of crude. There were major companies heavily dependent on long-term Iranian supplies, bereft by strikes and revolution; refining customers whom they and other majors had cut off on grounds of *force majeure*; and, more importantly than was obvious at the time, a wave of traders in oil and other commodities, fascinated to assume the risks of losses and gamble on the chance of huge profits within the six or seven weeks that a tanker takes to sail Gulf crude to market (or as much longer as they were prepared to store the crude).

In that revolutionary year, Opec governments could hardly raise their official selling prices fast enough to keep up with the surge in immediate market prices generated by this perceived shortage. (At times, to nobody's surprise, most of those in the Gulf diligently contrived to sustain the perceptions.) Even as the short-run upward pressures on price eased, several Gulf governments either reneged on supply contracts or refused to renew them. Long-term contracts became the exception. Most buyers had to pay the price at which the crude was available to everyone in the short term – alias the spot price. Traders had a strong incentive to 'go long', holding crude until they judged the time to sell to refiners was ripe.

After the 1979–80 eruption, crude prices began to weaken. The interest of traders in the spot market for crude did not. They had the chance to operate across a supply pattern much less committed than before. Opec was reluctant to abandon a price structure which was becoming full of rigidities and anomalies, but had less and less contractual leverage or market power to impose it. With spot prices below term prices, it was now the refining customers that did not want term contracts. That opened up a broad range of possibilities for commodity trading skills.

*Needing new signals*

During 1979, the proportion of crude traded at spot prices was reported to have risen from perhaps 5 per cent to about 35 per cent. In the early eighties this reported share grew further – to perhaps 45 per cent of crude trade moving at spot or 'spot-related' prices by 1984. The market terminology in this trade is not distinctly defined: it has been aptly described as 'a continuum' (Box 9A). Those proportions of spot trade by volume were probably exaggerated. It is impossible to verify them, because in open markets the same crude is often sold several times over. But nobody needed to verify them. The increases in percentages reported measured mainly the changes in perceptions across the business of the importance of spot market prices.

Such percentages purported to measure the spot share of world trade

---

**Box 9A.   Oil pricing**

The spot–term continuum

| Transaction | Description |
| --- | --- |
| Spot | Single cargo, fixed price, delivery generally within a month. |
| Forward spot | Single cargo, fixed price, future delivery (2–3 months). |
| Spot linked | Spot sale at some relation to published spot prices. |
| Term (1) | Now, but not traditionally, the dominant form of term supply arrangement, in which all the supply arrangements are fully determined but price is set, cargo-by-cargo, in relation to some open market price. ('Market-related' prices are usually derived by a formula from spot markets.) |
| Term (2) | Supply obligation at a fixed price but with frequent (often quarterly) price reopeners and with phase-out provision. |
| Term (3) | The more traditional sort of term transaction, over a period but with a price fixed at the time of agreement. |
| Evergreen | As for Term (2) but automatically renewable, with prices agreed at the time of renewal. |
| Life of field | A commitment to lift crude from a field during its life on a price basis fixed at regular intervals in relation to the market. Both this type and the evergreen contracts comprise integration with *de facto* equity supplies. |

*Source:* Roeber, *Risk Management and Oil Crises.*

in crude, primarily trade in Opec crude. But by the late seventies, new crude supplies outside Opec had been coming on offer, partly from non-integrated producers with nowhere to go but the spot market. Most of the international major companies, by losing Gulf long-term contracts, had become net buyers of crude. In North Sea development they also had the familiar but never simple problem of convincing tax authorities that the transfer prices at which they moved oil to affiliates were realistic in terms of arm's length bargaining. In Norway and for a time in the UK this involved them with state oil companies required to sell new, increasing entitlements of crude and hence to price these 'independently'.[6] Established international companies in the North Sea often had a selection of mostly local partners, with little oil experience save the gamble of having invested in successful North Sea consortia. Those suddenly had their shares of equity crude to dispose of, but no way of valuing it. Nor had newly important exporters like Mexico much recent experience of pricing crude for the world market.

However, in a period when Opec was trying and failing to 'administer' prices, spot prices turned out to be far more volatile as markers for the crude market than any of these suppliers were accustomed to or liked. All of them sought to reduce this uncertainty. Thus, there was room for development of forward and futures markets for crude, to underpin the spot market with risk management.

Certain of these fresh exporters, new entrants or returning to the oil trade, were in fact the first to link their official prices openly to spot prices after the world market moved into surplus in the early eighties. In late 1984 the Norwegian national oil company, Statoil, began to use various forms of 'composite' spot-related pricing in its term contracts, inserting occasional cargoes at spot prices into its delivery contracts, or charging prices that would be averaged subsequently between official and spot prices. That preceded Saudi Arabia's venture into netback pricing by nearly a year. (Similarly, later, the Mexican national company Pemex started setting export price formulas specifically escalated with changes in spot market crude prices in 1986. Saudi Arabia did not begin doing the same until October of the following year.)

After less than a year of netback pricing, by June 1986, the Kingdom tried to reverse its bold move, having achieved more than it had bargained for. It had roughly doubled its export volume; but the price level

[6] British National Oil Corporation (BNOC) was set up in 1975 by a Labour government and abolished in 1985 by a Conservative government. The ideological motives of the first always appeared somewhat half-hearted; those of the second, much less so. When set up, BNOC seemed little more than a political charade; but in practice it did play a functional role in North Sea pricing during its short corporate life. One of the few moves for which it may be remembered was that it was reported to be the first oil seller to raise its official prices in the Iranian crisis of 1978–9.

was down so far as to leave its oil revenues no higher than before. Hastily it announced its return to the fold of official pricing, agreeing to aim at higher Opec prices once again. The reunited price-fixers had some success for a matter of months; but by mid-1987 the price level was sagging once again. In October 1987, Saudi Arabia again announced different contract prices for term supplies of crude to North American, Western European and Far Eastern markets. But this time its contract formulas changed its crude prices not in line with final product values, but with changes in spot market prices for crude. Pricing one crude according to the eventual values that would be derived from products markets could not be sustained when other crudes were regularly being traded as such in the meantime. The two sets of market prices for oil are interrelated, but in the short term each displays some variations arising from separate influences.

Those moves towards the spot market by two non-Opec national oil companies and then by the most important Opec national company of them all were explicit and immediately visible. Behind and around them was an enveloping cloud of less visible 'market-related' and 'spot-related' pricing, in which most other Opec exporters had engaged since the market weakened in the early eighties. Saudi Arabia's netback pricing came suddenly. It was surprising because hitherto the Kingdom had held on more faithfully to Opec prices without discounting than probably any other member. But with its exports halved since 1982 and its production running about three-quarters below capacity, it could hardly have avoided one kind or another of accommodation to the spot market for much longer.

In that move in 1985, Saudi Arabia had accommodated not only to market instability, but also to geography and time. It takes up to forty-five days for crude from the Gulf to reach its main markets in Western Europe, Japan or the US. At that time, crude bought in the Gulf at *any* fixed price, whether an official government selling price (OGSP), a discounted or a spot price, had every chance of sizeable losses of value during the six weeks that it took to be delivered. In Atlantic markets, that raised a differential of uncertainty between the prompt supplies of North Sea and African Opec crudes and the long-haul crudes from the Gulf. As a result, refiners around the Atlantic had sharply reduced their demand for Middle East crudes.

In effect, Saudi Arabia decided to accept that risk differential, first in part and then entirely. Its initial netback contracts valued the crude on the basis of refined product realisations averaged between the date of loading and the date of delivery. Soon, in their bargaining with a widening circle of customers, the Saudis had to accept product values based solely on the date of delivery, or even a little later. In such contracts, the exporting country was accepting the risk of fluctuations in oil price over the *whole* period from crude purchase to final products sale.[7] The crude sales, in effect, were put onto a delivered, CIF basis. Other Opec exporters, and some outside Opec, had to follow suit in one form and another. Through the pricing vicissitudes that followed from 1986 onwards, a significant proportion of Opec crude has continued to be sold under formulas in which the risk of cargoes losing value *en voyage* is borne by the supplier shipping the crude rather than the refining customer.

That risk was not new. It has always been inherent in deliveries taking so long from crude export terminal to refining customer. It is among the various risks of logistics that any such trade has to bear. It may be hedged by insurance or futures contracts, or simply accepted as part of the cost of continuing operations, as it was in earlier years by the integrated international companies. (The cost, then as now, was always ultimately passed on to consumers. Those integrated companies, however, were generally more successful in minimising price instability than Opec has been. Crude prices changed much less often.)

When it once again adopted formula pricing explicitly related to spot markets in late 1987, Saudi Arabia linked its term contract prices with changes in the spot prices of North Sea Brent blend for deliveries to Rotterdam; with Alaskan North Slope crude to the US Gulf; and with Oman and Dubai crudes for Far Eastern destinations.

## Market marker crudes

None of these crudes is directly much involved in the international oil trade. Indeed, Alaskan North Slope (ANS) is not even the crude most frequently quoted in American spot markets for oil. There, the spot price most generally quoted is for West Texas Intermediate (WTI), a crude that does not enter physically into world trade at all (being available only from a landlocked pipeline terminal in Oklahoma). The Alaskan crude is much less representative of general US or Atlantic market conditions, being mainly consumed in California. But some of it happens to be delivered to the same US Gulf terminals as Saudi and

---

[7] This shift of the burden of risk occurs only once-for-all, with the first cargo priced CIF rather than FOB. So long as the shipments involved continue (at any rate, under the same kind of contract), there is no subsequent *extra* burden of risk upon subsequent cargoes.

other Middle East crudes; it is closer to them in quality than WTI or most other US crudes; and it may occasionally be sold at arm's length, offering a datum for spot price quotations.[8]

Brent blend is sold in the largest volumes of any single quality of crude from the North Sea. Its exports have seldom amounted to more than 5 per cent of the total world export volume of crude (though in the mid-seventies its export volumes ranked at times as the third largest of all crudes moving into international trade). Production of Brent, WTI, and now indeed ANS crudes, incidentally, is declining (and their combined output has never exceeded 10 per cent of the crude volumes moving in international trade). Nevertheless, Brent and WTI prices are the two most regularly quoted in open markets for crude oil. Movements in them signal, or will soon be followed by, changes in export prices for all other crudes across the international market.

That used to be true of the earlier form of 'marker crude price', which was used as an international benchmark by oil companies and later by Opec. But the prices of that marker crude, which for about twenty years from the mid-1960s was indeed Saudi Arabia's own Arab Light shipped FOB Ras Tanura, were set by producers in a market managed by sellers, and changed much less frequently, seldom more than once a quarter. Arab Light was indeed then produced and exported in the largest volume of any crude from anywhere. Its production capacity could rapidly be adjusted upwards to meet whatever demand for it might become. It was, effectively, the world's marginal supply of crude oil (as well as, paradoxically, its lowest-cost incremental source of commercial energy).

In the buyer's market when they took over as marker crudes, that was never remotely true of WTI, and only occasionally of Brent. The supply *cost* of Arab Light continued to be the lowest; but that had nothing to do with its price. Whether Brent could ever have been described as the world's marginal crude supply is a matter of economic terminology. In a falling market, the marginal supply is not the production that could be expanded at the lowest cost, but what is made generally available at the most flexible price. Brent could sometimes meet that criterion. In the soft market of the mid-1980s, there were times when production and export volumes from the North Sea as a whole exceeded those of Saudi Arabia. But the acceptance of Brent as a marker crude (WTI was always more debatable) has never really depended on availability; simply, on visibility.

Since the early eighties, at any rate, changes in those two prices have become the best price indicators available for the world crude oil trade

[8] At times, it is said, one of the producers of ANS crude sold a cargo at arm's length from time to time in the US Gulf simply in order to provide a price reference there for imported sour crudes from the Middle East.

as a whole. There are about seventy grades of crude that are sometimes bought and sold internationally. At any one time, the values that refining customers put on all these different crudes vary across the world, according to quality, regional demand patterns and location – the range and value of products that can be refined from each, the cost of doing so, and the freight cost of moving them from source to market. But across the whole range, crude prices change roughly in step with each other; and since the early 1980s they have kept pace mostly with these two crudes in these two markets.

Crude oils from Oman and Dubai, two of the smaller Arabian emirates of the southern Gulf, are also insignificant in world oil export volumes. But Oman is outside Opec; and Dubai's Fateh happens to be one of the few crudes nominally within Gulf Opec for which any open-market price at all is regularly quoted – often as a spot price for prompt delivery, sometimes as a forward price like those in London. (Dubai is one of the United Arab Emirates, which have a collective membership of Opec. But it has never taken much notice of Opec pricing.) Changes in the Oman and Dubai crude prices have become more direct indicators of what is happening to the prices at which the main volumes in the world crude trade, from the larger Gulf exporters such as Saudi Arabia, Abu Dhabi and Iran (plus once again Kuwait and Iraq), are being sold.

The main Gulf export crudes are mostly sold under term contracts, very seldom as single cargoes in the spot market. Since about mid-1988, contract prices for all crudes loading in the Gulf have been linked by general formulas or individual bargains to published open-market prices such as those for Dubai, Brent or ANS, and change in line with them. Nowadays, the main Gulf suppliers and other large-scale exporters openly publish their price formulas and escalation clauses.

The use of Atlantic market crudes as benchmarks for crude pricing across the world may look in some ways artificial. There is nothing new about artificiality in marker crude prices. But in the past, with Arab Light, it was not the choice of crude that was artificial, but the kinds of price attached to it. The historical record of crude oil prices shows that after wide fluctuations in the 1930s and price controls during and after the Second World War, for just over two decades international crude prices were dominated by a sequence of 'posted' tax reference prices set by major concessionaires in the Gulf. Those were held relatively stable even in nominal dollars. In real terms they slipped slightly downwards (Figure 9.1).

The next decade was Opec's. Its 'official government selling prices' (OGSPs), set by agreement within Opec, were more unstable than in any other decade of the industry's history (Figure 9.2).

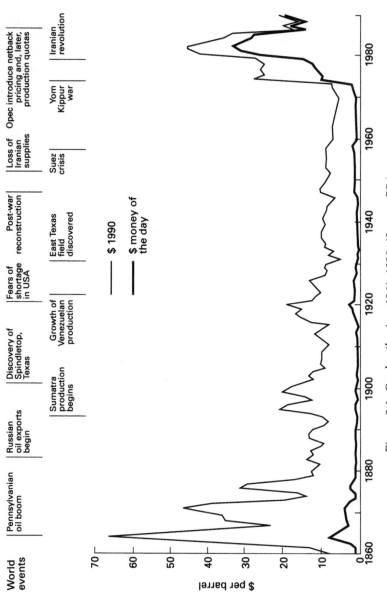

Figure 9.1. Crude oil prices 1861–1990. (*Source:* BP.)

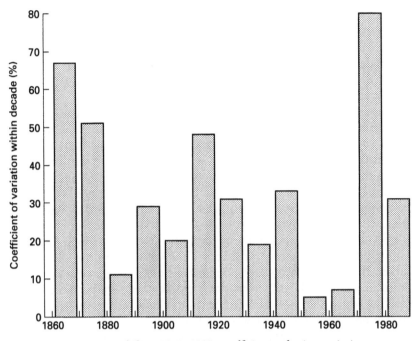

Figure 9.2. Price variability, 1861–1990: coefficients of price variation, ten years at a time. (*Variability* is measured as the standard deviation of a sample of oil prices about its average over each decade. A *coefficient of variation* is the standard deviation divided by the average over the decade, expressed in percentage terms.) In oil price history, volatility is seen to be the norm; price stability, as achieved by the major internationally integrated companies in the 1950s and 1960s, the exception. (*Source:* CGES.)

Neither of those sets of administered prices had much meaning beyond the fiscal purposes of setting government revenues per barrel. Few buyers ever paid exactly those prices for long. Each became festooned with an array of surrogate prices, reflecting the variety of terms on which different customers acquired Arab Light and other crudes linked to it by 'price differentials' of debatable validity. Usually, these prices served particular fiscal purposes at one or both ends of the oil trade. (Certain of the attractions of futures and forward markets in WTI and Brent, in their turn, arose initially from opportunities to establish, and minimise, tax values.)

The essential difference was that the former marker crude prices used to be administered by producers, and revised only at regular intervals (sometimes quarterly, often only annually). Today's market marker crude prices are set from day to day by face-to-face bargaining in open markets. (The fashionable term of art is now that these prices are 'discovered' there.) Neither process of pricing, almost needless to say, had or has anything *directly* to do with consumers. Consumers do not buy crude oil. The changes in oil product prices to which they respond consciously are as likely to derive from alterations in excise taxation as from crude price fluctuations.

Although American crudes such as WTI do not enter world trade, movements in their prices do represent market signals from the world's largest consuming and importing country. (For WTI, such signals from its internal markets can at times be wildly irrelevant to world prices. Crudes that can be quoted at coastal import terminals such as ANS are less insulated from the international trade.) The last time before the 1980s that the US had exerted any price leadership in world oil had been up to the mid-1950s, when it was also the largest market and importer. Its US Gulf market, fed mainly by domestic crudes, was then also the marginal import market for world oil. That was also in principle a spot market, though hardly a simply competitive one. Integrated companies controlling part of US domestic crude production simply 'posted' the prices at which they would *buy* from the independents producing the rest. Domestic crude supplies were controlled by state prorationing, and some voluntary restrictions were applied to oil imports. Later, for a time, the Caribbean became the world's largest exporter; but its largest market, predominant in price-setting, was again the US. The pricing of Middle East crude exports, however, steadily diverged from the values delivered to any American basing point. Gulf crude prices were increasingly aligned on deliveries to Western Europe, the world's largest oil-importing region. In 1958, statutory import quotas were imposed, which insulated the US market from the full growth of the international oil trade until they were removed in 1972.

### Managing price risks

Today, though many oil supply contracts specify spot or 'prompt' prices for Brent, Dubai and other crudes traded in open markets, the markets involved are mostly concerned with prices agreed upon in futures or other 'forward' contracts. These contracts are for crude oil bought and sold to be received and delivered (in principle) at dates varying from fifteen days to several months ahead.

Futures markets for crude oil have been firmly established in New York since 1983 and in London since 1988 (both after earlier attempts failed). Others have been opened in Singapore and most recently in Rotterdam. They are formally organised 'open outcry' markets working in much the same way as those for other commodities. Their trade is in contracts to buy and sell particular crudes (though in some cases substitutes are acceptable) and products of tightly specified grades. These markets are used mostly by buyers and sellers of the actual oil (often called 'physical' oil to distinguish their transactions from deals in 'paper oil' contracts where delivery is not necessarily intended to take place). For them, the markets' central function is to hedge trading risks between the time that a deal is made and the time later that the commodity can be delivered. For anyone else interested enough to take a view of future changes in the price of a commodity and back it, the markets' function is to facilitate speculation – which can also be argued to serve an extremely useful function in the 'discovery' of market prices.

The contracts traded in oil futures markets are commitments to deliver or accept standard quantities of a given crude oil or refined product at specified future times (on dates or within periods). All bargains in the open market are registered as to price and timing and are immediately communicated to all other participants in the market (and by media services to everyone else interested). The fulfilment of the contracts is backed by margin deposits from each member of the exchange, and guaranteed by an independent clearing house, which takes over all the commitments for its own account at the close of each trading day.[9] This clearing house matches all outstanding contracts to buy and to sell. At the end of each trading day some individual traders in the market will have 'long' positions (having bought contracts for oil that they expect to sell profitably when the eventual spot price exceeds the futures price they paid). Others have 'short positions' (having sold contracts to deliver crude that they hope to be able to buy more cheaply in the meantime).[10] These long or short positions and the contracts embodied in them may simply represent speculation; much more frequently, however, hedging against commitments in the opposite direction that traders have in the physicals markets.

Participants in these markets are buying and selling not so much crude as something that can be assumed to stay in line with the price of

[9] The clearing house assumes all the outstanding commitments itself, in a process legally called 'novation'. It receives the margin of paper losses or pays out the margin of paper gains to all the various traders. From then on, every contract to accept or deliver not so far offset by a reverse transaction is with the clearing house, no longer between the buyer and seller who originally agreed on the price for each contract.

[10] The oil futures markets of the New York Mercantile Exchange (Nymex) have a sizeable community of 'local traders' operating on their own account or for selected clients. These professionals are accustomed to balance their 'books' at the end of each trading day. They are adept enough to thrive by trading on price fluctuations within the day. As yet, few traders in European oil futures markets have emulated them.

crude. It has been neatly described as 'a kind of Platonic oil'.[11] As in most futures markets, only a small proportion of the oil contracted ever physically changes hands. Before delivery becomes due, the buyer or seller (or both) will usually reverse the commitments by reselling or repurchasing contracts for the same amounts of 'paper crude'. This can afford a physical trader the insurance against risk that he is prepared to pay for until his transaction is completed; or can test the speculator's backing of his price expectations against the actual later course of prices. Since both market participants may in fact buy and sell further contracts in the meantime, there is no hard and fast frontier between these two forms of trading activity. This is a traditional feature of futures markets, which had been established for other commodities for decades, perhaps even centuries, before they were brought into oil.

Although many crude sales contracts are linked to the *spot* price of Brent crude, that 'prompt' or 'dated' spot price arises in the '15-day Brent market', which is also mainly concerned with the 'forward pricing' of this crude. This is an informal market, in which deals are made by telephone between traders. It is not located in any particular place; there is no trading floor for open outcry bargaining. The Brent forward market has developed since 1981, as a trading activity in which contracts made by telephone are confirmed by telex, among a diverse range of oil producers, oil refiners, oil brokers and traders, and financial institutions interested in trading oil as well as other commodities. It works in broadly the same way as a futures market, allowing participants to buy and sell contracts for the delivery and receipt of crude on unspecified days of particular future months (up to several months ahead). But its contracts are for tanker loads of 500,000 bbl, worth say $5–10 million each, depending on the crude price, as against the 1,000 bbl standard contracts of the futures markets. So the financial commitments and risks involved are far larger. There is no clearing house to guarantee performance under these contracts; buyers are normally required to back their contracts with letters of credit.

Title to cargoes of Brent blend may be bought and sold on paper scores of times before each contract matures for physical delivery in a given month[12] at Sullum Voe terminal in the Shetland Isles. At any time there will be a number of contracts outstanding agreed between different

[11] P. Gal, 'Gas oil futures – how and why', *Europ-Oil Prices*, 3 April 1981.
[12] Actually a three-day range notified by the seller of the cargo to the buyer fifteen days before the first day of the range. Hence this forward market is often called the '15-day Brent market', as distinct from spot market transactions in 'prompt' or 'dated' Brent crude. In the first half of any month, say January, a 15-day deal can be done for delivery in February or later months. But from the middle of the month, 16 January, deals can only be done for deliveries beginning in the next month but one, i.e. March or later months.

participants in the market for delivery of the standard 500,000 bbl in the given future month, say August. Halfway through July, a seller who will have crude available gives fifteen days' notice to the buyer with whom he initially made his contract of the time during the next month when he requires the cargo to be lifted, thus 'wetting the contract' from that time onwards. If that buyer has also made a contract to sell August crude, he can give his buyer the same notice, and so on; the process becomes repetitive. In Brent market parlance, a series of contracts for August crude are thus sewn together into a 'daisy chain' of successive resales. Only the last-comer who is left without any sales contract to pass the obligation onwards – or may actually need the crude at that time – will actually take delivery within the specified period. The number of contracts outstanding need not always match the total amount of cargoes nominated for lifting. So on occasion the settlement of contracts for 'paper barrels' may oblige latecomers to buy in 'wet barrels' from the spot market, at a premium. This informal market may be more vulnerable to 'squeezes', manipulated by particular trading interests, than the formal futures markets. Occasionally traders have been unable to take and pay for delivery, and have been forced out of the market.

The Brent forward market lacks the instant, verifiable 'publication' of prices and deals registered that futures markets offer. Brent prices become known through word of mouth; of necessity, rather more approximately. Highly organised price reporting services are constantly telephoning traders and producers to assess the latest news (including rumours) of prices in deals done or discussed. The reporting services are also highly experienced and knowledgeable. But their coverage of details and timing cannot be as guaranteed as the registration of deals in a futures market. There will always be some deals kept confidential. At times of stress in the market, certain of the price services think, this admixture of secrecy tends to rise.

In practice, the two London markets for Brent crude are linked. The futures contract successfully reintroduced in 1988 by the International Petroleum Exchange (IPE) indeed allows for cash settlement 'at published average 15-day prices in the Brent forward market' for the future month concerned. But its standard contract is for only 1,000 bbl, which makes trading easier for participants in the market with relatively modest financial resources. This formal extension of the informal Brent market thus deals in lots that smaller market participants can afford, as well as being more transparent with more regularised financial settlement. In practice, subdivision of the standard Brent contract quantity had already begun before the formal futures market reopened in London in 1988, by the development of 'mini-Brent' or 'partial Brent' trading.

This was one of the first contributions to crude oil trading in Europe of the 'Wall Street refiners'.

It was never surprising that a number of finance houses highly experienced in other commodity markets, in arbitrage between different financial markets, and in other techniques of risk management should have become prominent operators in these open markets for oil. They were readier to handle 'basis risk' – the probability that the spot market prices of the crudes involved, for a variety of reasons, may often diverge from the futures and forward prices of the same crudes at the same future date – than the initial operators in the futures markets had been. (Such divergences can at times exceed the range of variation of the futures prices, and thus render a company's hedging in these markets useless.) The Wall Street refiners have experience of risk management techniques drawn from other comparable markets, such as foreign exchange.[13] Risk management in oil remains essentially a financial technique. Hence the financiers' prowess, and their capacity to enlarge the repertoire of futures trading. (It is a reminder that in ultimate value and scope financial services and manipulation, not oil, constitute the world's biggest business.)

Both these kinds of forward market draw upon computer systems and specialised software that allow almost instantaneous on-line analysis of what is happening in their own and other futures markets across the world, and access to an enormous range of industry and market data and selected general news that may in one way or another influence oil prices to some extent. The influence of any particular news item may be minuscule; but given the great volumes and values of oil involved in this trade, discerning any departure from expected patterns and acting upon it – for example in stocks, shaky though the statistics are – can be highly profitable.

The instant, dependable 'transparency' of the formal futures markets allows continuous analysis in depth. It has encouraged traders to diversify their dealing both in content and in form. They nowadays trade in the differentials between the physicals and futures markets; in various forms of 'spreads', between prices of the same crude for different months' delivery, or between the product values yielded from the refining of the standard crudes in particular markets and the spot crude prices; and in relationships between the prices of particular crudes and products. The new kinds of contract now being traded – for example,

[13] Foreign exchange markets were indeed the first in which major oil companies had to call upon or develop some expertise in futures trading. Among their other unforeseen problems of the 1970s was the floating of currency exchange rates, whereby currency fluctuations could at short notice greatly enhance or largely nullify the rewards of painstaking internal management of their own 'physical' oil businesses.

options (purchased rights to buy and sell futures contracts, without the firm obligation to do so) and swaps (contracts to buy or sell crude at a fixed price over a number of years, in exchange for the same quantity of crude sold or bought at a floating price related to the market at the time of delivery) – have become more sophisticated, along with the analysis. These 'derivative' forms of contract allow buyers and sellers to 'exchange risks' over medium-term contracts.

Each trader in these markets is concerned not with single contracts hedging the value of crude at different times, but with a 'book' of diverse contracts, perhaps matching net long and short positions in different trades: 'Within the totality of his "book", the trader may be net short or long when he considers it potentially profitable but will rapidly eliminate his net exposure on the futures markets if price trends change.'[14]

## Interaction with products

Long before the Opec decade, some parts of the oil business had had to take notice of spot markets – for refined products, even if the spot market for crude hardly mattered then. There were independent refiners who bought spot crude and sold their products largely into spot markets. Some independent wholesalers of products depended on those markets for supplies. Those competitors left the refining and marketing departments of integrated companies no chance to ignore spot prices completely in some at least of their own sales of products. These spot prices in entrepôts such as Rotterdam, also, had other implications. They could be used to reckon the values of crudes to refiners around the world, or more precisely their *relative* values compared with those of a particular marker crude (of which the price was then set otherwise, by company or Opec producers).

Up to the mid-seventies, the refining departments of the international major companies had little choice of the crudes they were going to run. Central supply departments of the integrated companies sought to optimise the logistics of crude movement around the world to the refineries where it could be processed to meet local patterns of demand most economically. Nevertheless, the products from those affiliated refineries had to meet local competition from products bought on the spot market from non-integrated refiners. A few big final customers for products such as public utilities, airlines and transport fleet operators had the chance to buy certain products in the spot markets themselves.

---

[14] W. Greaves, 'The current status of petroleum futures', Czarnikow Schroder, London, 1984.

They could bargain for parity with spot prices, or at any rate for price reviews taking some account of variations in them. By the late seventies, a large proportion of the term contracts made for products supplies in Europe, as in the US, contained clauses providing for escalation with the spot prices quoted by Platt's and similar price services. Again, ever since those spot prices began to be regularly reported in Europe from the mid-sixties onwards, fiscal and, on occasion, price control authorities have taken an interest in them, seeking to check the integrated transfer prices assigned to imported crude.

Until the eighties the importance of spot products prices to the international oil trade differed considerably between regions. During the period of US import controls, the open spot markets serving its markets – mainly with products, notably fuel oil – were primarily the Caribbean export refineries. Within Western Europe, then as now the main oil-importing region, the relevance of spot pricing was localised and varied considerably. It was particularly influential in Germany, the Benelux countries and Switzerland, served via the Rotterdam complex of oil terminals, refineries, and storage tank farms moving products by barge up the Rhine. Spot prices for products were less important in France and Spain because of the governments' 'delegated monopolies' of refining and limits on product imports; and in the UK because of the majors' dominance in products marketing. Italy played an ambiguous role. Its internal oil market was in principle as protected as the French; but it developed a fringe of refineries exporting products, primarily to Mediterranean destinations but also to the German market served through Rotterdam.[15]

Non-integrated refiners in Europe had gained a new source of crude supply with the development of production in Libya during the sixties, to a considerable extent by independent American companies. At the time, these were effectively shut out of the US home market by quota restrictions, and they had no downstream integration in Europe. They had no way to sell but at prices discounted below those that the integrated majors posted.[16] Italian refiners, in particular, processed large amounts of these newly available crudes, shipping the products from them to Germany via Rotterdam and the Rhine. The Libyan crudes had a high yield of gasoil, which particularly suited the German pattern of demand.

---

[15] Their patterns of product demand proved complementary, assisting this trade. Because of its early postwar development of natural gas, Italy did not consume much gasoil for heating purposes; apart from transport fuels, its demand was mainly for fuel oil for use in industry. German industry was accustomed – and suitably located – to use coal and coke-oven gas. For domestic heating, its growth of demand was for gasoil.

[16] Up to the late sixties, moreover, the Libyan governments encouraged their discounting by taxing them on the prices actually realised, not the posted prices used for tax purposes in the Middle East.

Major integrated companies established in Europe resented this competition, which reduced their market shares and rendered refining
unprofitable. But up to the time that their concessions were nationalised, some of them were primarily interested in low-cost Middle East
production, on which they could achieve upstream profits that their
competitors could not match, and satisfy their host governments as well.
They could hope to optimise their total profits by running their downstream refining and marketing networks with nil or even negative profit
margins, in order simply to 'move crude'. So they too were prepared to
sell products into the European spot markets.

Then, and indeed up to the time this book was written, an obvious
question could be asked. Why did it take so long before any spot market
for oil developed in Japan? This has become the second largest single
oil-importing country. One of the prime movers in the country's
uniquely organised capitalism has been its ubiquitous Ministry of International Trade and Industry, MITI, the world's only generally successful central planning organisation. The Japanese oil industry, an efficient
refining business with substantial but controlled part-ownership by
international oil companies, was firmly but rather cosily controlled by
MITI up to the late eighties. The ministry was always deeply concerned
with oil imports, since Japan had to build what became the world's
most efficient industrial economy with virtually no local energy supply
at all. It has been an adroit, though not particularly lucky, player in
various international oil games since the fifties (and has generally
managed to distance itself from the hostility often arising in Western
relationships with Gulf Opec exporters).

To the extent that Japanese refiners needed open-market price references, they drew them mainly from the Singapore spot market, which
like Rotterdam had developed around an oil entrepôt and export refining centre. Deregulation of the Japanese refining and marketing
business, announced in the mid-eighties, has been put into practice only
very gradually. Japanese operators – oilmen, trading houses, and banks
– were active in American and European forward and futures markets
for oil at times during the eighties. MITI is said to have carefully studied
the question, and decided yes, it would like an oil futures market for
Japan too – but not quite yet. That did not stop plenty of Japanese
operators becoming active from time to time, and perhaps rather ner-
vously, in the New York and London markets. Later, they became more
continuously active in the futures market opened in Singapore.

Just as spot pricing was accepted earlier for products than for crude,
so the earliest development of oil futures markets also occurred for
products, notably gasoil. Nymex established a successful futures contract

for 'No. 2 heating oil' (the US name for the same product) in 1979, and the IPE's first futures contract was for the same product. Futures contracts for gasoline have been fairly successful in New York, less so in Europe; and the trading of contracts for fuel oil, which would complete futures coverage across the main products of the crude barrel, commenced only at the end of the eighties in Singapore, New York and London. Some informal forward markets had developed earlier for particular products such as Russian gasoil and for petrochemical naphtha in north-west Europe; but at times several of these encountered problems with price reporting and with product specifications.

### Make or buy?

Since oil prices began to decline in the early 1980s, spot prices for products have become much more widely accepted and used throughout the Western European market, even within the downstream systems of the major companies.

While it lasted, the Saudi netback exercise was very comfortable for refiners, since the allowance negotiated for processing 'costs' in the contracts guaranteed them refining profits, with the crude supplier taking all the risks. Most other *producers* were glad when the netback experiment was abandoned. But it seems to have had lasting consequences for the refining and marketing management of some of the internationally integrated oil companies.

It tended to confirm and reinforce the shift, which had already begun in Europe within one or two of the major companies in the early eighties, to managing their refineries and marketing networks according to a 'make or buy' principle. Nowadays these companies use spot prices for European products as a basis for the transfer values at which the refining department supplies products to its marketers. In principle, the integrated refiners are then economically 'indifferent' between processing balancing quantities of each product themselves, or buying these quantities in from the spot market. They can choose whichever combination of making or buying optimises their margins over the *joint* operating costs of their supply operation. (There is no way of ascertaining a separate cost for any single refined product among the assortment produced jointly in distillation, the basic refining processes.) In meeting its demand, the marketing department too can take spot market values as the opportunity 'cost of product', over and above which it needs to earn its operating margin, regardless of whether it gets the products from its own company refinery or buys them in from outside. In the years of much fuller integration, some of the companies sought to simulate 'independent arm's-length values' for their interdepartmental transfer values. Nowadays departments have the option, indeed the obligation, to buy and sell whenever it pays better than transferring through their own channels. That can concentrate the mind wonderfully.

There are plenty of professionals downstream as well as upstream in this industry who distrust this recent, fairly complete acceptance of spot (and hence futures) prices as the only relevant opportunity costs for integrated management to consider. They feel that supply into or from the spot market could never really be depended on to cover all the various commitments and risks that any company planning to remain in business in the medium run has to handle. Also, if established refiners bought on a really large scale, these oilmen argue, their buying power would raise spot prices. If they sold large volumes, they would depress the spot market. Thus the opportunity costs of large-scale use of spot markets would not be identical in buying and selling.

It is certainly true that spot prices for products reflect only the variable operating costs[17] of some refinery somewhere, not the full costs (including depreciation and return on investment) of any refinery anywhere. The adoption of 'make or buy' management downstream in these integrated companies in the eighties enabled them to hold their shares of increasingly price-competitive products markets. It did not guarantee them margins adequate to cover capital investment in upgrading facilities to process the higher proportions of light products required and meet environmental standards, let alone replacement and fresh medium-term investment in new plant. But during the eighties, what was going on in downstream capacity, at least in the US and Europe, was *disinvestment*, not investment. The basic distillation capacity had to be reduced, not expanded. Even during the nineties, demand in the Western industrial economies is generally expected to remain fairly flat. Whether much investment in additional distillation capacity will be needed there or in Japan remains debatable, though tightening environmental regulation of product qualities will continue to require investment in extra upgrading capacity. Achieving refining margins to cover such investment, in any case, may simply not be practicable unless demand rises faster in these regions than is expected. (Faster demand growth elsewhere, in for example developing countries or Eastern Europe, will not necessarily affect refining margins within OECD.)

Thus the major companies' interest in spot and later in futures

---

[17] In established refining operations, a sizeable proportion even of operating costs – including, for example, labour – are in normal practice fixed, *not* variable.

markets, for both products and crude, did not remain simply a reaction to their losses of equity supply upstream, or a means of sharpening up their management accounting between stages of the business. It became a widening extension of their core business of physical supply, processing and marketing – profitable in its own right, and exploiting chances for managerial flexibility that may not have been noticed and were certainly not all acted upon before.

Academic students of oil markets have long pondered the chicken-and-egg question whether it is product prices that 'drive' crude prices, or the other way round. (Any practical marketer who could be confident of a continuing answer to this conundrum could profit enormously). It is not difficult to argue, quite logically, that over time the *relative* values of the different crudes imported for refining in the main regional markets must be determined in the trading that brings about products prices there. But econometric analysis seeking to decide which is the explanatory variable tends to reach the somewhat disconcerting conclusion of 'joint causality', with all the sets of prices considered appearing to 'cause' all the others.[18] Most oil marketers probably assume that in practice the influences work both ways, with each becoming dominant at one time or another. Moreover, judging how the *absolute* levels of price for crude are settled remains a matter of endless debate.

### Are these markets efficient?

There can be no doubt that these spot and futures markets are more open and transparent than the patterns of pricing in the international oil trade at any time since the 1920s. (The term contract prices related to them, at which the majority of trade in oil actually takes place, are not quite as transparent. But even those are susceptible to closer interpretation nowadays than the blurred array of intercorporate transfer prices and scrappily reported discounts off published prices that prevailed up to the late seventies.) The rise and acceptance of these open markets does not demonstrate that the trade they monitor has become any more competitive in the classical sense. Indeed, the world's largest exporters remain committed to, and hope to reassert, open cartel administration of world oil pricing. 'New classical' economists, nowadays, apply a more recent and businesslike criterion to these open markets. Are they efficient?

This criterion derives from the 'efficient markets hypothesis' developed in the analysis of stock exchanges. This hypothesis suggests that all

[18] Philip K. Verleger, Institute of International Economics, Washington: private communication, December 1987.

information currently available to an open market, and the average of rational expectations on the basis of this information, are instantly encapsulated in the current market price. Averaged over fairly short periods, the prices 'discovered' in such open markets should theoretically offer better possible indications of what will happen to prices in the future than any other data or analytical technique.

Stock market 'efficiency' does *not* depend upon the best-informed expectations available at any time eventually turning out to be right. It denotes the best analysis and judgement of what is generally known *at any time*. Buying any traded commodity – here crude, products, or various forms of 'spread' between their prices – at the current futures price and holding it for the chosen trading period 'should' be more profitable than any other market strategy at that time, whatever may happen in the meantime to upset everyone's expectations. In particular, it should be more profitable *ex post* than any market strategy relying on regular 'dependencies' observed up to that moment between price movements in past statistical series.

This hypothesis was highly controversial when it was first put forward for financial markets, since its underlying assumption was that prices followed a 'random walk', which could be taken to imply that the technical analysis of markets such as stock exchanges, the thriving activity of a small army of professionals, was largely irrelevant. But so far as the efficient markets hypothesis applies to stock exchanges, 'the vast majority of all empirical studies have concluded that there is no readily available information that the market neglects'.[19] Assessment of commodity markets according to this criterion, on the other hand, has been less conclusive. Some have been confirmed as efficient. In others, econometric analyses suggest that trading strategies drawing rules from past market performance, e.g. to buy when the price has fallen by some given proportion below a previous peak, or the reverse, *can* in many cases outperform 'buy and hold' strategies related simply to the current futures market price. The success of trading strategies exploiting rules of price dependencies, rendering such commodity markets 'inefficient', have often been attributed to too much 'movement trading' by speculators. This is a tendency for people trading in such markets to follow and exaggerate the 'natural' responses of the market to changes in supply and demand.

So far, studies of the efficiency of spot and futures markets in oil have come out with mixed judgements. For products, the spot markets were judged not to qualify as efficient, while the futures markets *did* meet that

[19] D. Begg, S. Fischer and R. Dornbusch, *Economics* (McGraw Hill, 1984).

criterion. (The London futures market price for gasoil was held to work better than any other single indicator as a predictor of what prices would be at later dates, though analysts felt its performance could be improved by taking account of other price data as well.) For crude, neither the Brent forward market nor the Nymex futures market for WTI have yet been judged to be efficient markets; the spot price average for any month appeared better than forward or futures prices in the same month as an indicator of next month's spot price. But in oil, any inefficiency can hardly have arisen from the exaggerated behaviour of speculators. Even Nymex, the longest-established futures market in oil, is sometimes argued to draw upon too few speculators, not too many. The Rotterdam and London markets appear to have even fewer of the individual speculators so beloved of the Chicago commodity markets. Europe, so far, has nothing comparable with their almost fabulous constituency of 'doctors and dentists', fascinated to gamble on the future prices of pork bellies and almost anything else.

No crude oil futures markets became fully established before the eighties. Spot markets for crude gained some central importance only in 1979 and after. Spot markets for products are older; but the debatably reliable recording of their price history goes back hardly beyond the late 1960s. So limited efficiency in the oil spot and futures markets is often attributed by analysts to this immaturity. They feel these markets may perhaps still be too 'dominated by physical traders, who react less than instantaneously to new information, thus generating trends and cycles in spot price movements ... [that] leave arbitrage and speculative opportunities which have yet to be fully exploited'.[20]

To many oilmen in the physicals business, the idea that a market *needs* more speculators may sound perverse. But to provide a satisfactory hedge, a market needs specialists in managing trading risk. Certainly the proliferation of new financial instruments for oil futures trading suggests that 'technically' the oil futures markets are still on a learning curve, with a good deal more sophistication to acquire. (The Wall Street refiners have imparted much of this already.)

In principle, as noted above, the quality of the information available to open markets need not affect their efficiency. So long as nobody has any better (or more up-to-date) information, current prices that represent average expectations in the market should predict what is going to happen better than any other approach can. No market anywhere is ever fully and instantly informed; if it were, everyone might accept the current price as right, and little trading would occur. But there may be inherent

[20] P. J. W. N. Bird, 'Continuity and reversal in oil spot price movements', *Energy Economics*, April 1987, p. 80.

differences in the kinds and quality of information available to different markets, which at any time may leave more room for disagreement, and hence perhaps greater volatility in pricing, in some than in others.

In oil markets, a very high proportion of the quantitative 'facts' that participants have to analyse are of dubious accuracy. Figures of crude production, products deliveries, and changes in stock are variously unreliable (and may be manipulated). Most other quantitative data, for example consumption, have to be derived secondarily from these. Time-lags in reporting are considerable; substantial later revisions the norm rather than the exception. What does become known arrives much faster. It remains doubtful whether all that is instantly transmitted across electronic trading screens in these markets is as deeply or as mutually effective as the information that used to be shared horizontally between vertically integrated companies with joint shareholdings in Opec concessions. The quality of that earlier shared information was far more reliable. (However, those companies were mainly linked by mutual leverage, not just shared information. Through voting in joint operating companies in the Middle East, some of the international majors could effectively control the incremental costs at which others could expand their exports. Perhaps that leverage made for the efficient performance of an oligopoly. It had nothing to do with the efficiency now hoped for in open markets.)

As to the qualitative information that influences market judgements, a sizeable element in it has so far been constant conjecture about the likely behaviour of a cartel of indecisive governments. In practice, since the mid-eighties, the consensus of expectations embodied in spot and futures market pricing has often looked from the outside less objective and neutral than traders may have been. At times, as a leading industry journal once put it, these markets 'were suffering from a bout of selective listening: word of bearish developments falls on deaf ears, while any bullish whisper comes through loud and clear'.[21]

It is only on the average that open-market prices – spot, forward or futures – could be hoped to offer the best possible prediction of what will actually happen. In practice, so far, these markets have never more than briefly served to bring going prices for crude down towards any fully competitive level. Perhaps to expect that would be more than they ever pretend to offer. Fairly often, trading behaviour in them has seemed to reflect a general wistful desire that the clumsy Opec cartel should prove itself able to go on rigging the market. This desire, admittedly, spreads widely beyond the oil trade. More generally, world financial

[21] *PIW*, 18 June 1990.

markets appear scared of any abrupt change in oil pricing, even down-wards, as liable to generate further unpredictable economic instability.

### Fluctuations and levels

Major integrated companies that had first lost ownership and then control of their main upstream supply had no alternative but to secure a higher proportion of their crude requirements in spot markets, or from suppliers stipulating spot-related prices. The process, in the early eighties, was gradual, and uneven as between companies. Later, vola-tility in spot pricing and more general uncertainties made these com-panies move, gingerly to start with, into futures markets too.

Opec governments, having taken over the majors' field of operations upstream, understandably took longer to accommodate to these open markets – at least, once the euphoria of 1979–80 was over. After all, their first decade of ownership upstream had begun with seizing power over, precisely, *prices*. Measured by that most obvious yardstick, the decade had seemed a great success. Having to acknowledge that they in turn had lost control of pricing must have caused the deepest chagrin throughout Opec. Not all the member governments – whose business is still mostly anchored upstream – are yet openly engaged in these open markets for oil. Some, perhaps, still wish they could escape the market influences. But all know that in practice they cannot.

The prices to which oil companies and governments now have to conform arise from much shorter-term considerations than they used to; also, in more widely perceived uncertainty. The consensus of short-term expectations reflected in open markets takes this uncertainty as unavoid-able, but entirely practicable to offset as a matter of trading routine. People in the industry, within companies as well as governments, who have to take decisions about physical investment according to medium-run expectations find the resultant uncertainties more awkward to live with. Their commitments are harder to hedge.

During the eighties, admittedly, shorter-term considerations became more important in all forms of business. Futures and options trading, certainly, became much more important throughout financial markets. Also, managers in every industry have to make decisions that take account of several different time-scales simultaneously. Oil is not unusual in that sense. But in oil the shift in time-scales from the seventies to the eighties was more profound. The relative importance of the different time-scales that operators in the different layers of the inter-national oil business have to consider altered in a bewildering way.

One possible rationalisation that could be advanced to cover this bewildering change might be that open-market trading can only reflect, instantly and accurately, short-term expectations primarily about behaviour *within* such markets – by highly informed traders concerned with limited time-spans. The prices discovered in such trading are inherently volatile, but rapidly self-adjusting. (For example, neither of Iraq's invasions of its neighbours in 1980 and 1990 affected those market prices much, beyond very short-lived price 'spikes'.) It can be argued that the basic price *levels* about which (or *bands* within which) these open markets fluctuate still depend upon general views prevailing about the industry fundamentals – expectations with a sufficiently long time-scale to influence physical investment decisions. On such an analysis, the weak price levels of the mid-eighties, reappearing at the beginning of the nineties, were not caused by open markets, which are simply accurate short-term measuring instruments. Had these lower levels around which short-term prices fluctuated more to do with a general growing awareness of the potential surplus that was once again revealed during the crisis of 1990–1?

Intellectually, such a rationalisation might be comforting to Opec governments upstream, suggesting that perhaps they or a few among them can retain market power over price levels or bands in the medium run. For the demand/supply balance of the nineties, its implications could be less comfortable. Gulf Opec governments, through their various commitments to increase capacity, seem liable to prolong and increase that surplus.

## A surplus phenomenon?

One recurrent question about the open markets in oil has nothing to do with their efficiency. It concerns the circumstances in which they gained predominance, and the durability of their influence if those circumstances change.

Spot pricing of crude came to the fore in 1979, as a measure of producers' power in a time of fancied shortage. But its establishment as a market marker came with the emergence of surplus. Futures pricing was not fully established until the surplus set in. Many Opec governments still express confidence, and some oilmen outside Opec believe, that the surplus is passing. Soon, their favourite argument runs, non-Opec supply, having already peaked, will level off, fail to make any further contribution to meeting the growth in demand, and then begin to decline. Then once more, in crude pricing, 'Opec will be back in the saddle.' What might that imply for these open markets?

In principle, perhaps it should make no difference. It should only alter

the *weighting* of the information around which markets have to crystal-
lise their expectations. The interpretation of Opec intentions might
become even more important. But they might be made clearer, with
more likelihood of being carried out. One unmistakable desire common
to all Opec governments at the beginning of the nineties was for price
stability (at a price to suit *them*) for a few years at least. If they could
achieve this for the prices they might hope to impose, then volatility
would presumably be reduced in spot and futures markets. If this were
accepted as damping down trading flexibility right across the oil
business – *and* as likely to last – then operators might reduce the
hedging of risks in which they currently engage. Equally, if these
markets absolutely *need* high volatility in prices to prosper, then their
activity and influence would no doubt be reduced.

Certainly most Opec governments would prefer that to happen. If
more of them became able to set and enforce restrictions on the resale
of oil to traders, that would be a direct attack upon the open markets –
but almost certainly ineffectual because impossible to enforce. More
probably, if they do get back to the driving seat, these governments
may simply become less ready to tie formula prices in term contracts
specifically to spot pricing in regional markets. (They might incidentally also return to FOB pricing, obliging customers to take the
price risks while oil is afloat. But the cost of price risk during transit
will always be passed on to final consumers one way or another. Who
assumes it in the meantime is a matter of detail, unless it affects taxes
downstream.) Neither course would be 'necessary' for Opec governments *if* they can regain price stability on their own terms. Linkages to
spot prices that become less volatile would affect their own contract
pricing less.

Non-Opec producers might be glad if Opec, in a new sellers' market,
were able to enforce a shift backwards from CIF to FOB pricing, even if
it were no more than technical. More importantly, they too of course
would enjoy the higher prices that would arise along with Opec influence. Refiners would not enjoy the change (also once for all) back from
CIF to FOB, but it might involve them in using the futures markets more
rather than less, to hedge price risks during transit. They may be
eventually almost indifferent to higher crude prices, except to the extent
that those might eventually reduce final demand for oil products.[22] Any
market transition away from surplus might in any case be gradual – up
to some general shock of recognition. (But the batteries of intellectual

[22] A refiner is normally trading in both crude and products markets as well as processing the one oil
into the others; also, holding significant stocks of both. The markets interact; so do processing and
trading opportunities.

sophistication now commercially deployed to sense the exact moment when a change in market trend does occur are already impressive.)

Experts from both sides of the business, in the late eighties and early nineties,[23] were suggesting more sophisticated strategies by which Opec governments might be able once more to capture these open markets for oil within their own sphere of influence. Such a recapture might even be geographical as well as commercial. Fateh, the spot-priced crude from Dubai, was emerging at the beginning of the nineties as potentially the most relevant market crude for the international oil trade, because of problems with all the others.[24] Futures contracts for it are traded in Singapore and London. *If* another futures market could be established for this quasi-Opec crude actually in the Gulf – or perhaps better, such a market for a larger-volume, more representative export crude there – then perhaps the Gulf, 'centre of the world oil industry by virtue of the reserves available', could once again become 'the centre of world pricing as well'.[25]

Whether Gulf Opec governments would ever be content to exert their influence from such a centre of world pricing through the operations of a genuinely independent open market there is more open to question. Could it be reconciled with whatever hopes they still retain of achieving price stability through a cartel?

One of these proposed reconciliations between Opec power and the market mechanisms was suggested from Algeria, long the most ingenious source of ideas for Opec techniques. In 1991 its then Minister of Energy proposed that Opec should set up its own trading house and offer for sale, steadily over a rolling period, a substantial volume of its members' crude exports, in tradeable contracts, constantly matching buyer and seller through its own clearing house system 'so as to exclude any speculative element from the system'. (The volume to be offered for sale was, say, 2 MBD, or about 10 per cent of Opec exports; the tradeable contracts, for, say, a million barrels each; the crudes to be offered, either those in the 'composite Opec barrel' or some other selection.) The prices achieved would be published daily; if they moved outside the range that its member governments desired or became

---

[23] Notably, M. S. Robinson, 'If oil is a commodity, why not manage it that way?', *MEES*, 4 January 1988; J. Roeber, 'Flexible response: the best hope for Opec', *MEES*, 25 January 1988; and N. Ait-Laoussine, Algerian Minister of Energy, 'Pricing of oil: the need for a new stabilising mechanism', Oxford Energy Seminar, September 1991 (reprinted in *MEES*, 16 September 1991).
[24] WTI is a landlocked crude strongly affected by its own circumstances in the domestic US market. ANS has almost ceased to be available in the US Gulf, where it had served as a spot price marker for sour crude imports to the US. Brent is a blend of light sweet crudes physically unlike the sour crudes mainly exported from Gulf Opec; also, it tends to vary in quality over time as further crudes are mixed in. Dubai's own problem is that Fateh production is low and declining further.
[25] J. Roeber, 'Winds of change in crude oil pricing', *MEES*, 9 July 1990.

excessively volatile, Opec could intervene to modulate supply. That would not pretend to be an entirely independent open market for Opec crude. But Opec governments do not regard the existing open markets elsewhere as entirely independent of manipulation by other vested interests.

Such a move into the open-market game might simply mean that the largest vested interest in the world oil trade – currently desiring stability quite as much as the others do – could join in the manipulation. It would however require Opec governments to entrust such a trading entity with the continuing power to contract for the supply of *their* crudes. Some member governments, including probably the largest exporter, would probably be reluctant to concede that, just as they have consistently been unwilling to allow the Opec secretariat any independent role.

*If* everyone in the oil market were to become less worried about price instability, then no doubt producers would be able to spend less on all aspects of risk management. But increased market power for Opec, however exercised, would bring back unease about instabilities of a different kind – for importers and their governments, at any rate. Such market power, once again, will depend on the course of supply and demand fundamentals, or expectations about them, in the medium run.

# CHAPTER 10

# Perspectives of supply

As long ago as October 1956, in a survey published by the American Petroleum Institute, the late Dr Marion King Hubbert forecast that crude oil production in the 'lower forty-eight' states of the United States would pass its peak by the year 1970, if not shortly before. Fourteen years later it did, almost precisely on time. Hubbert had suggested that a smoothed curve of production, ironing out year-to-year fluctuations, would peak before the end of the 1960s. It actually did so in 1968. He reckoned that the 'single-year spike' could occur any time between 1965 and 1975. The Texan geophysicist, whose forecast was to bring him fame (albeit for a time much derision), did not estimate volume in the 'spike' year of 1970 quite as precisely. It was 3.5 billion barrels (9.6 MBD) in 1970, against the 3 billion (8.8 MBD) that his growth curves, sketched fourteen years before had implied. But the 'smoothed' five-year average of production fitted Hubbert's curve rather more closely; and his timing of the peak turned out to be impeccable (Figure 10.1).

American crude oil production[1] in that year has never been matched since, even though the US total has at times since included more than 2 MBD from Alaska. His estimates derived from the historical perform-ance of the US oil industry in its first ninety years, the rates at which it had discovered oil and then brought it into production. For Alaska, at that time, there was no significant history to interpret, though small-scale production was developed there in the early sixties in the southern Kenai Peninsula and the Gulf of Alaska. In a 1966 update of his paper, Hubbert had specifically excluded Alaska as 'a large, essentially virgin region whose petroleum development is mainly in the future'. It still was, then. His 1966 paper was delivered six months before the well was

---

[1] Certain statistics now include, along with US crude production, the liquids produced with natural gas. In 1956 they did not.

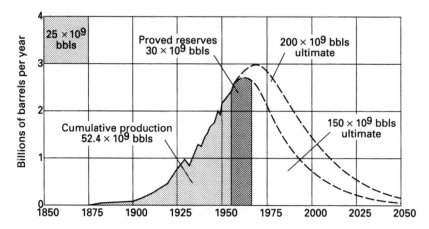

Above is an estimate by M. King Hubbert in 1956 of the crude oil production to be expected over time in the lower forty-eight states of the US if 'ultimate recoverable reserves' there were either 150 or 200 billion barrels. (Figure is reproduced from *Drilling and Production Practice* (1956) published by the American Petroleum Institute.)

Below is the actual course of US crude oil output from those states of the US – plus Alaska, where the main North Slope reserves were not discovered until 1966. Hubbert's timing of the peak in US production was precise. Actual production in the lower forty-eight since 1970 fits fairly well with his S-curve based on the higher of the two estimates of recoverable reserves that he used, 200 billion barrels, though higher prices and more intensive drilling brought somewhat higher production there. But the main supplement to US domestic production since came from Alaska, which Hubbert specifically excluded. Up to 1990 cumulative production in the lower forty-eight had in fact reached 151 billion bbl; known reserves were 26 billion bbl; and the US Geological Survey estimated in 1991 that there remain 33 to 70 billion bbl of crude oil resources still to be discovered in the nation.

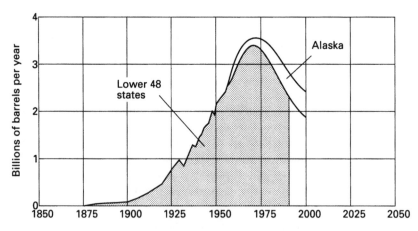

Figure 10.1. US crude oil production: as forecast in 1956 and actual.

spudded in that discovered the super-giant field Prudhoe Bay, America's largest ever, in 1968.[2]

During the following decade and a half, the rise of Alaskan supply did help to hold total US crude production fairly level. It delayed for several years the increase in oil imports that would have been expected otherwise. But the giant fields there, Prudhoe Bay and Kuparuk River, are now beginning to decline too, and US imports have been rising steadily since the mid-eighties. In the lower forty-eight states that Hubbert's forecast had covered, crude production in 1990 was about 40 per cent lower than in 1970.

Only a handful of geologists and almost no mineral resource economists agreed with that 1956 forecast at the time. (The US Geological Survey (USGS) was then suggesting that US production would not peak before the end of the century.) It was the method Hubbert used to forecast a profile of future US oil production that particularly incensed some of his colleagues. For he did *not* begin with any new or revised estimates of his own of US 'ultimate recoverable reserves' of crude oil, as other analysts of the 'life cycle' of oil production there had. He used the consensus of such estimates from the industry's leading geologists – then varying between 150 and 200 billion bbl. His own initial contribution was no more than a way of projecting the future production that those ultimate reserves, *if* the consensus estimates were right, would allow. He suggested that ultimate reserves of 150 billion bbl, taking into account the US industry's past history of discovering and producing oil, would mathematically imply that production in the conterminous states of the US (i.e., excluding Alaska, Hawaii, and the outer offshore) would peak by about 1965; and that if the ultimate reserves might be 200 billion bbl, the extra 50 billion bbl would delay the peak date by only five years, to about 1970.

Such a peak followed by decline, and so soon, appeared sharply at odds with the continued linear increase in US oil production that many oilmen had hitherto been assuming from just the same reserve estimates. So Hubbert's initial projection was highly provocative in the then climate of industry expectations. Coincidentally or not, the consensus regarding ultimate US reserves completely disappeared within a few years of Hubbert's first calculations of future production curves. The USGS and some company geologists began producing a succession of new estimates, mostly much higher, but varying wildly. Within five years, the range of estimates for ultimate US reserves varied from 145

---

[2] His forecast also excluded the outer continental shelf of the US. Offshore exploration, greatly advanced in the thirty-five years since his paper was delivered, discovered another field in 1991 under the deep waters of the Gulf of Mexico which may turn out to be a super-giant.

billion to nearly 600 billion bbl. By 1962, Hubbert abandoned any
concern at all with other people's diverse estimates of ultimate reserves
or resources – for the US, at any rate. He produced estimates of his own,
deriving solely from exploration and production history. These came
out within the range of the earlier geologists' consensus that he had
begun by interpreting.

It took until the mid-seventies for Hubbert's forecast of when US
production would peak to be accepted as having turned out right.
Production in the last years of the sixties was indeed somewhat higher
than his growth curves implied, and did not clearly depart from the
more optimistic linear projections until the early seventies. But by 1975,
significantly, the consensus of geologists' revised estimates of ultimate
recoverable reserves for the US lower forty-eight had come back much
closer to their earlier range of estimates (as Hubbert's already had).

This was not only one of the most accurate forecasts ever made about
the oil business. (Of late, unfortunately, that sounds the faintest of
praise. Any forecast about oil has come to be regarded as automatically
wrong.) In the short run, as Hubbert elaborated his reckoning during
the sixties and the press took note, it became one of the most widely
publicised professional opinions ever offered about the US oil industry.
From that time onwards, it became harder for politicians in the US and
oilmen everywhere quite to ignore the probability that the world's
largest oil market might very soon pass out of its high degree of
self-sufficiency. It was not the only suggestion that US imports would
have to increase. But it was a new and authoritative warning that
domestic oil production might soon not only become unable to keep up
with the growth of US consumption, but actually begin to decline.

Nor was this the first prediction of peak and decline for the US oil
industry. There had been as many shortly after the First World War as
shortly after the Second. But all those earlier predictions that the US
would begin to 'run out of oil' had turned out to be wrong. They had,
fairly soon, been disproved by further discoveries within the home
resource base (though helping to generate, during such periods of
uncertainty, the huge American stake in oil production abroad). Peak
predictions made in the 1950s, however, fairly soon began to look right.

In the context of international oil, these predictions, once fulfilled,
also provided the first clear demonstration that oil production, in any
major producing region of the world, *would* actually mature, level off,
and pass into decline. Only the US had then – or perhaps has even now –
a sufficiently long and well-documented oil history to offer such indications at all clearly. So inevitably, Hubbert's curve that fitted sharp-
ened the question whether, or how soon, the same passage into maturity

followed by decline might occur across the rest of world oil. In principle, since oil production extracts a finite natural resource, that might sound inevitable over time. (Geologists and most physical scientists concerned with the extractive industries take this for granted. Many economists do not.)

## The curve that fitted

Geologists' estimates of ultimate recoverable reserves conventionally involve painstaking estimates of the areas of the earth's surface – to start with, US territory – underlain by thick sedimentary strata, and technically informed estimates of the volumes of these sedimentary rocks beneath. Upon this basis, geologists offer assessments of the probabilities of finding commercially producible petroleum concentrations within these porous strata, and of the average content of oil likely to exist in such concentrations. Huge data banks of geological and geophysical evidence, inference and analysis have been accumulated by the industry's experts over the years. The probabilities assigned at many stages of these assessments, however professional, standardised, and collectively argued through in 'Delphi surveys', are necessarily to a large extent subjective.

Hubbert always claimed that his own approach, initially only to infer practicable production from such assessments by other people, was purely empirical. He considered various mathematical curves that could suggest how long any given total of recoverable reserves might take to discover and later to produce, and chose the one that he thought fitted the historical data best. He suggested that cumulative discoveries and production in this extractive industry might follow a logistic S-curve[3] over time. The industry's history would begin with the first few scattered finds, with both discoveries and production building up rapidly as exploration effort and technology progressed. But gradually, as more and more of the underlying resource was developed, there would be less to be discovered, and less reward to the exploration effort. Cumulative production would thus increase slowly in the industry's early years, and rise more and more rapidly over time until about half the ultimate recoverable reserve had been produced. From then on it would go on rising, but more and more slowly; and it would finally level off when the ultimate recoverable reserve became totally depleted and production would cease.

---

[3] Mathematically defined as a form of 'monotonically increasing curve between two horizontal asymptotes and having a point of inflection', with growth plotted against the passage of time.

If so, *annual* production would begin from zero, rise to reach one or more maxima, then commence a long secular decline, towards ultimate depletion (or at some point, abandonment as uneconomic). Also, 'as oil must be found before it can be produced, the curve of cumulative proved discoveries must closely resemble that of cumulative production,

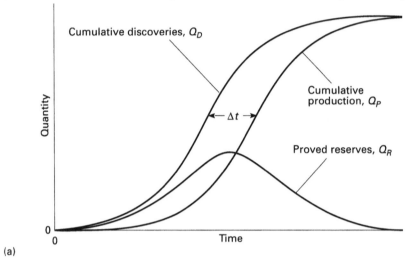

(a)

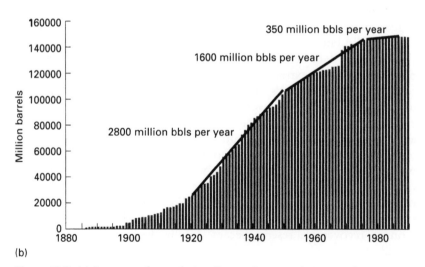

(b)

Figure 10.2. (a) S-curves of cumulative discoveries, cumulative production, and proved oil reserves. (*Source:* Hubbert, 'Advancement of petroleum exploration'.) (b) Cumulative oil discoveries in US, 1880–1989. (*Source:* BP.)

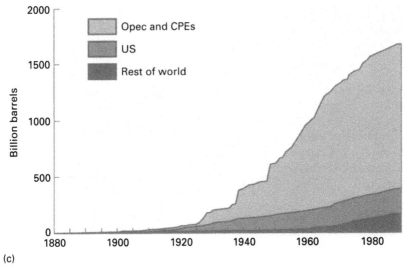

Figure 10.2c. Cumulative world oil discoveries, 1880–1989. (*Source:* BP.)

except that it must plot ahead of the production curve by some time interval *t*, which itself may vary during the cycle'.[4] Rates of oil discovery oscillate widely from year to year, because of uncertainty and the strong random element in drilling success. Rates of *annual* production, responding to demand and development, may often be short of maximum capacity. So the curves need statistical smoothing to make their trends comparable.

In such assumed logistic growth (Figure 10.2), cumulative discoveries and production would both be expected to follow an S-curve. Trends of annual discoveries and production would each follow overlapping bell-shaped trajectories, peaking at the same levels about halfway through the cycle of depletion of the ultimate reserve, but displaced by some average time-lag. Annual totals of proved reserves (which at any given date represent cumulative discoveries minus cumulative production), would follow a similar bell-shaped curve, at a much higher level, since explorers seek to keep at least several years' production in these reserve 'stocks'.

That was simply one plausible hypothesis, essentially mathematical. Its relation to reality depended on how closely one or other of that particular family of curves could be fitted. American production statistics had been established for nearly a century. Discoveries were not

[4] M. King Hubbert, *Energy Resources* (US National Academy of Sciences, National Research Council, 1962), p. 54.

directly documented nearly as well. In effect, the best evidence available over time was the simple arithmetic of adding cumulative production to 'proven reserves' at the end of each year to give *cumulative* discoveries to date. Published figures of proven reserves have their own inherent weaknesses. However, US reserve reporting had in principle been on a standard basis since 1937, and projected backwards on the basis of earlier reserve estimates to 1900. The National Petroleum Council had also begun on a refinement of the national reserve statistics, seeking to allocate later additions to reserves back to the year in which each discovery had actually been made.[5] That facilitated methods of analysis related to cumulative discoveries, or to the success rates recorded from exploration drilling (an alternative measure that Hubbert adopted in later years).

Hubbert concluded from these statistical series that historically, cumulative oil production in the US *had* indeed followed the same trajectory, after a time-lag, as its record of cumulative reserves discovered. The production S-curve followed the discovery S-curve with a lag that in 1956 he estimated at about 10–12 years; in later revisions he estimated it at about 10.5 years. Cumulative discoveries appeared to be passing their peak in the middle 1950s; hence his projections of the time when US crude production would peak, which were later vindicated.[6]

If his accurate timing of the peak indeed confirmed that US petroleum production was following a logistic S-curve, its implications would reach forward in time. Once discoveries could definitely be seen to have peaked, the method he had suggested originally to interpret other experts' probabilistic estimates of ultimate US reserves might be reversed to offer its own differently based estimate of those ultimate reserves – effectively, about twice the cumulative production up to the peak, which he felt should occur 'about halfway'.

The assumption that the successive curves were logistic, and the reserve estimate based on it, remained insecure. Certain geologists

---

[5] The initial appraisal of reserves in any oilfield is always revised upwards, usually several times. The 'new' additions to total national reserves reported each year thus always contain a proportion of 'growth in reserves' in fields discovered years before. Such annual data therefore need revision to correct this time-lagged statistical bias. American statistics regularly include such revisions, using average factors of initial reserve appreciation for later years. But the correct factor to apply continues to be a subject of some controversy.

[6] Hubbert also forecast that natural gas production in the lower forty-eight might peak before 1976. It seemed to do so in 1973, and then again in 1979. But the historical records of natural gas production, let alone reserves, were much shorter and less credible than those for crude oil. Until recent decades, gas discoveries were simply a by-product of exploration for crude. The period when production was first said to have peaked was blurred economically by particularly restrictive price controls. More recently, a 'gas bubble' of availability, surplus to effective demand, has lasted much longer than most experts forecasted. The gas data seemed then quite inadequate to support any predictions about when US gas production might peak – and indeed still appear so even now.

postulated alternative growth curves, peaking earlier and declining more slowly afterwards. Hubbert agreed that others might be plausible; he agreed that the bell-shape would not necessarily be symmetrical. But he felt the other forms of curve suggested did not fit the statistics as well.[7] Others had proposed some variable other than time to plot the curves against. Hubbert agreed that might be preferable, and did adopt an alternative method in later papers.[8] But again, he argued that this modification did not change his estimates significantly.

Questions remained, however, about the curves of actual discovery and production. There were some signs that the sharp decline in discovery rates, which Hubbert took from 1962 onwards as 'driving' the later decline of production, had tended to stabilise[9] in later years. Somewhat more crude was discovered in the US during the mid-sixties, and significantly more during the seventies, than his curves had suggested. Crude production in the lower forty-eight, though it peaked and turned down on time, did not decline as rapidly from the mid-seventies to the late eighties as Hubbert had expected. His forecast of production in the lower forty-eight states had once been nicknamed 'Hubbert's pimple'. After it actually peaked, the swelling appeared to be coming down more gradually. Some analyses carried out in the mid-1980s offered hopes that total US production (*including* Alaska and deeper offshore areas than Hubbert had allowed for) might remain level for the rest of the century. By the late eighties, however, the decline did seem to have set in, and is now generally considered inexorable.[10]

## Projections and protection

It is not difficult to suggest reasons why actual US discoveries in the 1960s and actual US production from the mid-1970s onwards diverged somewhat from the curves that Hubbert had predicted. His figuring had always assumed that 'there is as yet no evidence of an impending departure in the future from the orderly progression which has characterised the evolution of the petroleum industry during the last hundred years'. That assumption did *not* ignore the advances in

---

[7] For example, a Gompertz curve has the bell-shape skewed, descending more gradually than it rises. That would imply ultimate reserves larger than those under the symmetrical bell-shape of a logistic growth curve.

[8] Ironically, from Zapp, one of the geologists with whom he disagreed most sharply about ultimate US reserves. Zapp, in 1962, suggested plotting rates of discovery and of cumulative reserves discovered not against time but against the cumulative total footage of exploratory drilling. Hubbert accepted this method.

[9] T. J. Woods, 'Resource depletion and lower 48 oil and gas discovery rates', *OGJ*, 28 October 1985.

[10] C. J. Cleveland and R. K. Kaufman, 'Forecasting ultimate oil recovery and its rate of production'. *Energy Journal*, 12 (1991), no. 2, pp. 17–46.

technology still certain to be made in the future. Hubbert's curves, fitted to the US industry's history, had subsumed all the cumulative advances in exploration and production techniques, including increases in recovery, that had occurred in the century or so since commercial production had begun. He argued that his S-curve form indeed assumed further advances in upstream technology *proportionately* comparable in importance to all those achieved since the primitive beginnings of the industry. That would be a large order.

But in fact, even when he first put his projections forward in 1956, there was already plenty of evidence of outside circumstances affecting his 'orderly progression'. Internally, ever since the mid-thirties, oil production in the US had been adjusted to market demand – at a significantly higher price than competition might have brought about – by 'proration' in the main oil-producing states of the Union. From the war years onwards, the industry had been powerfully influenced by Federal government policies. Rates of exploration, the prime motor of Hubbert's S-curves, had long been affected by tax incentives. During the sixties, moreover, US oil production enjoyed a substantial measure of protection against foreign competition.

By the time that Hubbert reiterated his forecast in 1966, a significant proportion of the US domestic production that he was contemplating, therefore, was already, and would have remained, uncompetitive. Without the protection of import controls, applied informally from 1949 to 1959 and then formally by the US government from 1959 to 1972, the country might already have had a rather smaller, more efficient domestic industry.[11]

Proration plus protection by import controls had not only kept some uneconomic US production in being. It had also, along with remarkable US fiscal incentives, encouraged much more domestic exploration (and 'in-fill drilling' of fields known already) even in the sixties than would have been economic otherwise. That could have generated a somewhat higher rate of discoveries and additions to US reserves than would have quite fitted the droop of Hubbert's sequential S-curves. In the seventies, moreover, the upsurge of crude prices that Opec set off stimulated a surge of exploration within the US as well as elsewhere, until the mid-eighties.

Additions to US oil reserve estimates since the seventies seem to have come essentially from that more intensive drilling. (Much of it was more intensive drilling in known productive areas, which would have been hard to classify separately as exploration or development wells.) There

---

[11] L. P. Drollas, 'The search for oil in the USA', *Energy Economics*, July 1986, pp. 155–64.

may also have been another kind of addition; greater upward revision of known reserves than had occurred before. The definitions of oil and gas reserves then ruling, though established by geologists and petroleum engineers, in principle also embodied economic criteria. The reserves that the American Petroleum Institute counts as 'proved' are defined as the quantities recoverable 'with reasonable certainty ... under existing economic and operating conditions'. When existing economic conditions alter considerably, therefore, one might also expect the estimates of reserves recoverable also to change correspondingly.

Even in the US, which controlled its oil prices during much of the Opec decade, the price of newly discovered crude roughly trebled after 1973. That change in economic conditions should theoretically have justified significant upward revisions in the current assessment of proven reserves in fields already known. Some new fields earlier ruled out as uneconomic may have become worth developing too. Certainly there was significant investment from the mid-seventies onwards, particularly in California, in enhanced recovery techniques, seeking to stimulate production of heavy oil and raise average recovery factors. In its most recent assessments, the USGS is reckoning on 'ultimate resources' of 251 billion bbl of crude for the US (including Alaska, the deep offshore, and over 20 billion bbl of 'expected field growth' in reserves already proved.)[12] To date, cumulative US production has depleted about 160 billion bbl, more than 60 per cent, of those ultimate resources.

## Profiling world production

Should we logically expect the course of discovery and production for *world* oil to follow similar trajectories over time to those observed in the the US industry? Hubbert never had much doubt that we should. From his 1956 paper onwards, he had widened out his predictions to encompass world oil. There, for once, he did follow fashion. Many of the eminent American geologists with whom he engaged in controversy about US oil had already produced estimates of the world's ultimate reserves. Their peers have continued to do so up to the present. But to do so, it should be noted, moves all their calculations away from a solid foundation of imperfect but long-established historical statistics out to a wider selection of oil industries, old and new, mostly with much weaker bases of published historical data. It involved Hubbert, like the rest, in a necessarily chancier form of assessment: extrapolation by analogy, and on a heroic scale.

[12] C. D. Masters, D. H. Root and E. D. Attanasi, 'Resource constraints in petroleum production potential', *Science*, 12 July 1991, pp. 146–52.

It has been said of 'life-cycle' projections like Hubbert's that they 'can yield an accurate estimate of the ultimate recoverable resource, *provided* that the resource is far enough into its life cycle that the depletion effect begins to dominate over the other factors and depress the growth rate of cumulative discoveries'.[13] Outside the US, one can hardly be sure about that proviso. It is much more difficult to estimate with confidence how far advanced through their life-cycles other oil-producing regions may be, and to guess whether other regions not yet producing have much to contribute to oil's future. This derives partly from a lack of information, and behind that from a lack of exploration.

The limited exploration history of the Middle East *was* available when Hubbert first put forward his hypothesis. The potential import-ance of the region was already recognised, although its reserves remained deeply underestimated. The details were not generally published by then, and perhaps never have been in full. (Reserve figures are only what producing companies, and nowadays Opec governments, say they are.) But even then the reserve estimates that Hubbert sought to interpret had been put together by major international company geolo-gists with the best access to whatever was known. Until the end of the concession system in the seventies, discoveries and production in the Middle East may have been better and more consistently documented 'in-house' than reserves anywhere else.

It seems probable, indeed, that the Middle East may have passed its peak of oil *discoveries* by the time that US production peaked around 1970. Most of the huge additions to Gulf reserves announced more recently, during the late eighties, represent uprating of the main fields there, almost all discovered by the mid-sixties. If attributed to the original dates of discovery, they might indeed shift the peak of *world* discoveries backwards in time. However, the time-lags between dis-covery and production in the Middle East have never been consistent, or followed any 'orderly progression'. The delay there between discovery and production has always been much longer than anywhere else. Any life-cycle analysis that assumes production will consistently track the course of discovery has little relevance there.

*Peaks on foreign horizons?*

Only one large Middle East producing country has ever yet shown signs of advancing depletion, or more precisely of technical constraints upon

---

[13] J. D. Sterman and G. P. Richardson, 'An experiment to evaluate methods for estimating fossil fuel resources', paper presented at the Third International Symposium on Forecasting, Philadelphia, 1983.

the expansion of producing capacity. In mid-1972, in a 'Sales and Purchase Agreement' that proved to be the last which major international oil companies ever made collectively with a government of Iran, they committed the operating company there to raise production from 6 to 8 MBD by 1976. When 1976 came, it was reported that the companies had told the Shah's government that this increase had proved 'technically impracticable'. Even to maintain producing capacity would require heavy investment in secondary recovery, by gas injection from the country's enormous but undeveloped reserves of non-associated gas.

It was never quite clear, and now never will be, whether that decision to level off Iranian production in fact arose from the companies' technical judgement, the government's political decision, or perhaps both plus a realistic assessment of costs. (Later, revolution put that oil development out of court; also, the court and the companies.) Yet Iranian oil reserves, even in 1976, were estimated at over 60 billion barrels, representing nearly 30 years' production at the country's then rate. Since then, about 15 billion barrels of crude have been produced from those reserves; but by 1990, without much exploration in the meantime, they had been uprated to 93 billion barrels. At the beginning of the nineties Iran was not planning to raise its production, severely reduced during the first Gulf war, back to more than 4.5 MBD. That was decided politically, in an Islamic revolutionary state whose oil policies foreigners cannot pretend to understand. Iran has the longest-established oil industry in the Middle East, perhaps the only one there in apparent maturity. This continuing contrast between its abundant reserves and its production decisions remains something of an enigma.

The former Soviet oil industry is the only one comparable in longevity and size to the American; arguably, also, approaching it in maturity. But its historical records of exploration, production and reserves are far less complete, having been interrupted by revolution following one world war and then by a second war. Most of the time since then, its reserve figures have usually been subject to state secrecy, though often confidently guessed at from outside. In any case, Russian categories and definitions are hard to compare precisely with Western definitions of proved reserves. The country's huge areas of sedimentary rock, roughly twice those of the US, make it the only prospective area for hydrocarbons that international geologists have ever considered might be comparable with the Middle East. Given the recent enormous upward revisions of Gulf oil reserves, that no longer looks plausible. Moreover, the Soviet petroleum provinces developed of late seem to contain much more gas than oil. But the possibility of further big oil discoveries there cannot be ruled out – even at a time when current estimates of actual reserves have been revised downwards and are probably still declining.

Its postwar profile of production was utterly different from the US industry's. In 1956, when Hubbert began projecting world production profiles, Soviet output was only about a quarter of the American. By the mid-seventies it had passed US output. That rapid progress resulted mainly from the successive development of fresh oil provinces, in the Volga-Urals region, Western Siberia, and, most recently, Eastern Siberia (rather as if the US had added not one but three Alaskas). Also, much of the Soviet increase in output came from new giant fields and super-giants, more of them than the US industry has ever had.

Until recently because of state secrecy about reserves, and of late through sheer state disorganisation, much less is known in the world outside about Soviet *exploration* activity and success. The data available would be quite inadequate for any linking of discovery and production S-curves such as can be presented for the US industry. It is not clear whether discoveries there have peaked yet, even though *production* has been falling since the late eighties. Up to the beginning of the seventies there had been indications of a sharp increase in reserves and hence in cumulative discoveries (since production was rising rapidly at the same time). After the mid-seventies, there appears to have been a slow decline in Soviet reserves, implying much less success in discoveries (and probably less exploration effort), before Soviet production levelled off in the eighties. Yet at the end of that decade, further super-giant fields, admittedly mainly of gas, were still occasionally being discovered. Geologists abroad still hardly know what to make of this.

There had been as it happens one confident forecast from outside, published in 1977 by Cold War adversaries, that Soviet oil production would peak in the early eighties. That looked quite as politically loaded as the normative and exhortatory 'Plan targets' that Soviet ministries were issuing at the time. It was made by the US Central Intelligence Agency, which in 1977 reported to President Carter that Soviet oil output would peak in 1982–3 and thereafter decline rapidly, turning the USSR into a net importer of oil by the late eighties. That overreaching forecast was severely criticised by other American watchers of the Soviet economy, as well as in the USSR itself. Oilmen elsewhere were never sure how seriously to take it, any more than they might have known how far to credit a report on the American oil industry published by the KGB.

In hindsight, when Soviet production levelled off and began to fall in the late eighties, at least the parts of the CIA report that predicted rapidly rising Soviet costs began to look more plausible. Production has

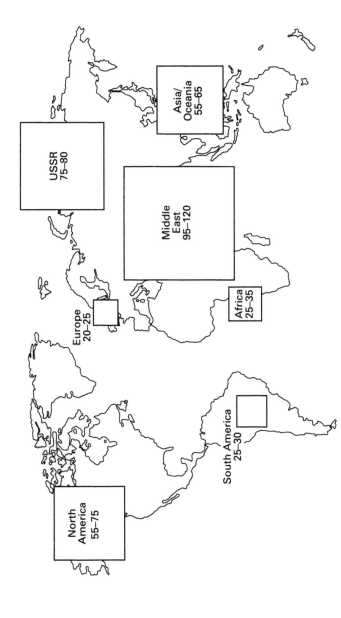

World total = 350–450 billion barrels

Figure 10.3. Potential new oil discoveries, by region. (*Source:* Shell.)

fallen since 1988–9, possibly because of the rapid depletion of reserves in some regions, but as plausibly through the utter disorganisation of petroleum management in the former USSR. The decline in production has not been as rapid as the CIA projected. (Nevertheless, its concentration of the world's largest production into relatively few very large fields *might* render the former Soviet industry's ultimate decline, as and whenever it does set in, steeper than in the US.)

Many geologists in Western oil companies still class the former Soviet Union as one of the world's best prospective remaining areas, for oil as well as gas. In their estimates of oil still to be discovered (Figure 10.3) some of them still rank the oil *potential* there second only to the Gulf. Earlier developed at the great speed that a command economy could manage in particular sectors, by 'campaigns' that seemingly almost disregarded cost, oil production declined significantly in the final convulsions of the Soviet system. But by the end of the century, with Western oil companies invited in to contribute their much more advanced technology to develop new major fields and sustain production in certain existing ones, the former USSR's eventual petroleum options may again look favourable.

That industry, however, epitomises the outstanding contrast between oil in the US and everywhere else. By American standards, it has hardly been explored. No other oil-producing region has been explored anything like as intensively as the US. Geologists disagree violently about the implications of this for their assessments of petroleum still to be discovered. But it leaves black holes in all their international guesswork, and potentially sizeable ones. (If only some of these potential surprises were to materialise, they could be pleasant ones for mankind. 'Any to come, glad of it!')

*Extrapolation by analogy*

In extrapolation from the US to the rest of the world, life-cycle analysis was not easy to use independently. Success in having forecast the timing of US peaks of discovery and production guaranteed nothing about projections of production elsewhere. Curve-fitting as a forecasting technique for world production has thus reverted to the use Hubbert had originally made of it – projecting plausible time profiles of production practicable from consensus estimates of ultimate recoverable reserves. It depends upon estimates of the world's ultimate recoverable reserves (which outside the US are liable to be even more subjective than inside).

Quite a number of such estimates had already been offered and have continued to be, postulating the world's oil believed to be recoverable but still to be discovered. Geologists employed by international major companies could draw upon better internal records of discoveries and potential in the Gulf and other former concession areas than have ever been published. Hubbert added some estimates of his own (which fitted into the consensus more than was characteristic of him). Over the years he refined these to postulate world ultimate recoverable reserves of between 1,350 and 2,100 billion barrels (1980). These gave him a basis upon which to fit production life-cycle curves, as he had originally done for the US in his 1956 paper. The S-curves that he fitted to such total reserves postulated a peak for world oil production in the mid-nineties, at about 37 billion barrels, or 100 MBD.

Many similar assessments of ultimate reserves have been made in later years by other geologists and petroleum engineers. In 1988, for example, Shell cited estimates of nearly 600 billion bbl for cumulative world oil production to end-1987; proved reserves of 887 billion bbl; and recoverable but undiscovered reserves of a further 235 billion bbl, making up a total ultimate recoverable reserve of 1722 billion bbl.[14] A BP estimate around the same date was of 2,000 billion bbl recoverable at costs up to $25/bbl (in 1985 dollars). The USGS, in 1991, estimated ultimately recoverable reserves of world oil (assuming a 34 per cent recovery factor) at 2,079 billion bbl. That was 'conventional crude oil' of 20 degrees API gravity and above (excluding extra-heavy crudes, tar sands and shales, as well as NGLs). Up to the end of 1991, cumulative world production appeared to have reached about 680 billion bbl.

Only a few experts offering those estimates of reserves nowadays add specific forecasts of any future profile for world oil production. Most of their reserve estimates, however, *do* also imply that world oil production may peak around the end of the century or shortly after.[15] Without necessarily committing themselves to the life-cycle analysis or the sequential logistic curves, geologists in the major companies have tacitly assumed trajectories of cumulative world oil production that imply much the same S-shape over time.[16]

## A collision of concepts

There was never much likelihood, from the moment that Hubbert published his first prediction of US oil output, that it would be generally accepted by economists concerned with exhaustible resources. One

---

[14] *Finding Oil and Gas* (Shell Briefing Service, London, 1988).
[15] Masters *et al.*, 'Resource constraints'.
[16] Sir Peter Baxendell, 'Enhanced oil recovery – making the most of what we've got', Institute of Mining and Metallurgy (Shell Briefing Service, London, 1984).

perhaps encounters here a fundamental conceptual difference between two disciplines of expertise (compounded, moreover, by some disunity among the resource economists). Almost all mineral economists feel that geologists and other physical scientists nearly always take too little account of the dimension of costs and prices whenever they assess reserves of extractive resources as finite and measurable at any given time, and venture to postulate timetables for the depletion of these resources. As these economists see it, whenever the progressive depletion of a mineral resource approaches physical limitations, incremental costs must of necessity rise and force its prices up. These in their turn will justify improvements in technology, allowing the extraction of poorer mineral grades (in oil, less prolific reservoirs), along with greater recovery of those already developed. Thus the operation of the price mechanism, along with advancing technology, will *extend* productive horizons and effectively enlarge the recoverable resource.

Resource economists differ between themselves, however, about how far to take this argument. Many of them, while remaining cautious about all geologists' estimates of reserves or depletion curves, accept the same underlying assumption – that finite, exhaustible resources become increasingly scarce over time. Some other resource economists, however, extend the profession's basic argument that rising costs and prices will bring fresh reserves into production beyond the technical limits of any finite reserve of a particular extractive resource. They include whatever else may be drawn in, as costs rise, to serve the same purpose. To them, the concept of a resource is dynamic; it consists essentially in the services that can be obtained from it. These are endlessly being redefined by technological progress. To the extent that petroleum fuels are replaceable by some other way of serving the same purposes, the other substituting forms of energy extend the working energy resource. In the words of Zimmerman, 'Resources are not; they become.'[17] (In that case, all quantitative assessment of any *particular* fossil fuel – or any other particular mineral resource – might seem meaningless.)

As to the historical evidence, some of these economists also doubt that in any real sense depletion of oil (or most other mineral resources) is in fact occurring at all. They would define this simply in terms of the effects that depletion *should* have had on the prices of incremental supply, which would necessarily rise. For empirical evidence of their powerfully optimistic preconception, such economists cite long-run price statistics. Over history, it is indeed hard to cite any one extractive resource of which *real* prices have demonstrably risen.

That is a conceptual disagreement going far wider than oil. Econo-

---

[17] E. S. Zimmerman, *World Resources and Industries* (Harper, 1951).

mists close to the oil industry, however, have more specific arguments on the issue. In oil, perhaps more than in some other extractive industries, estimates of the oil in place that will be recoverable tend to be constantly revised during the working lives of each oilfield. One can cite field after US field from which crude totalling several times the reserves originally estimated has already been produced, and yet the volumes of reserves now counted as proved are still the same or higher. The revisions are almost always upwards, for several years after the initial appraisal of the field for development. Hence mineral economists' optimism that *all* aggregate figures for reserves are *always* underestimated. One prediction by eminent energy economists, published shortly after Hubbert's, dismissed his and other geologists' assessments as 'fundamentally illogical'. Its own prediction, in 1960, was that crude oil production in the US by 1975, at no appreciable increase in constant dollar costs, could be of the order of 6 billion barrels, over 16.4 MBD. (In fact, US production in 1975, at prices well over three times those of 1960 in constant dollars, was about half that volume.)

Geologists and reservoir engineers, in their turn, feel this automatic optimism that proved reserve estimates always go on growing tends to become highly exaggerated. (Hubbert used to comment, 'Perhaps there is no need for exploration, or geologists. Economists can find far more oil than we ever shall without leaving their desks.' Other geologists are more conciliatory towards the mineral economists' optimism, but hold to their predictions that oil production must level off and will decline over time.) In the US at least, reserve estimates are generally uprated to take account of this growth in known fields, and to attribute reserve additions to the earlier years in which the particular fields were originally discovered. It is doubtful whether reserve estimates anywhere else are adjusted as methodically for their appreciation over time. But in several high-reserve Opec countries, reserve figures were recently being uprated directly, through new specific appraisals by the world's leading geological consultants. There are, on the other hand, a few major oil provinces where over time reserves have never come up to the initial hopes. Nigeria, Indonesia and Algeria are possible examples (for oil, though not for gas). Some suspect Alaska may turn out to be another.

Reserves cannot be proved without drilling. In a country with as long and as intensive a historical record of exploration as the US, its average results in 'proving up' reserves can perhaps be taken as fairly predictably responsive to rates of drilling.[18] There, it is convenient and may be

---

[18] Also, perhaps, because a large proportion of US reserves are nowadays in relatively small fields. Yet at times in its history, discoveries of unpredicted giant fields, such as East Texas in 1930 and perhaps Prudhoe Bay in 1968, have suddenly revealed far more 'on the shelf' than the US industry was immediately able to handle.

realistic to regard the country's proved reserves simply as a 'shelf inventory', transferred from the 'oil in place' beneath them by exploration only as and when the industry collectively chooses. (Individual producers appreciate this possibility, but seldom care to depend on it. Each appraises his reserves as comprehensively and as early in a field's producing life as is practicable. Nevertheless, fields often do go on producing at plateau level much longer than was initially foreseen.)

The US industry, however, is a special case in terms of maturity, protection and exploration incentives. What applies to its remaining 4 per cent of world reserves may not be relevant elsewhere. The concept of a shelf inventory, easily replenished, does not at present sound at all a comfortable one for former Soviet oil producers, whose reserves appear of late to have dwindled. Whatever the country's ultimate prospects, exploration there has *not* been replacing cumulative production. In the North Sea and other areas wholly offshore, there is a strong financial incentive to plan from the beginning for the highest probable reserves and production levels to which each field may eventually be uprated. (Their first facilities involved extremely heavy investment to construct and install platforms and pipelines. It was initially believed that going in again later with additional investment to increase or prolong production would be prohibitively expensive. A rapid learning curve of technology, reducing the offshore investment needed, has since somewhat allayed those fears.) Nor, above all, has this concept of proved reserves as a 'chosen' level of inventory any practical meaning in the Middle East and some other Opec regions. There, governments which took over production inherited and have later increased a huge immediate inventory of reserves that will probably take them several decades to deplete.

### Evolution plus disturbance

Whether or not petroleum development in the US ever steadily followed Hubbert's 'orderly undisturbed evolution of the industry', oil development elsewhere certainly did not. Exploration of the Middle East was orderly enough. But from their beginnings, oil development and production there were usually managed partly to suit the convenience of other oil industries abroad. (In recent years, as it happens, they have continued to be managed that way, though quite involuntarily, by their Opec governments.)

'It is possible, of course,' Hubbert admitted in 1974, 'that because of political and economic disturbances the orderly growth could be curtailed. This would have the effect of distorting the curve, making it flatter on top and extending the declining part further into the future.'

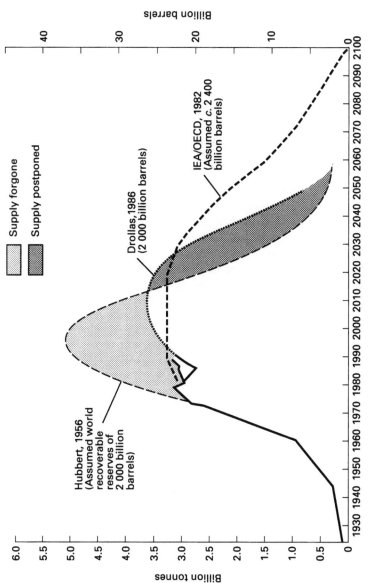

Figure 10.4. Oil production over time: hypotheses of depletion of world oil reserves. Compares estimates by Hubbert in 1956 ('Nuclear energy and the fossil fuels'), International Energy Agency in 1982 (*World Energy Outlook*) and Drollas in 1986 ('Oil supplies and the world oil market' and 'Search for oil in USA').

Undoubtedly that has occurred. Two of the few oil supply projections that have ever taken explicit account of the particular political and economic disturbances that did occur were made by a mathematical economist inside the oil business, not an earth scientist. In 1982, Dr L. P. Drollas, then of BP, modified the Hubbert forecasts of US oil production to take account of protection and of price increases in later decades, but broadly endorsed its methodology. In 1986, widening his econometric analysis to the whole world oil industry, Drollas concluded that a large-scale further growth in oil demand in the seventies had been forgone because prices were put up far too high. Hence a corresponding volume of potential oil production during the following decade and a half was never required. But the production and depletion of oil reserves that did not take place then was simply displaced in time (Figure 10.4). Drollas reckoned that the quantities of oil forgone then, if produced later, might delay the peaking of production that Hubbert had expected before the year 2000 until the first decade of next century, at a level of slightly over 70 MBD (close to the low of the range that Hubbert had postulated so long before).[19]

Other analysts, during the eighties, put forward various suggestions that world oil production might level off before the end-century peak and stretch out the depletion of reserves a few decades longer. How much longer depended on each one's opinions about ultimate reserves. A projection of plausible future supply published in 1982 by the International Energy Agency (IEA) was the first one deriving from any intergovernmental organisation to postulate a practical plateau of world oil production – indeed, one beginning about now. The IEA's supply experts then postulated a 'hypothetical world oil production profile' that might level off in 1990 at about 25 billion barrels a year, or 67 MBD, staying at that level for about three decades. For a decade already, the industry has been close to that level of production. Since then, however, other departments of IEA have gone on postulating growth in oil demand during the nineties to levels well above any such plateau of supply: lately, up to 80–85 MBD early next century. (If demand does soon draw reserves down more rapidly, as these later forecasts now suggest, then IEA's earlier reasoning about world supply might be compatible with a somewhat higher peak, but with eventual decline beginning rather earlier.)

That IEA supply projection of 1982 used somewhat higher assumptions about reserves than those used by Hubbert or Drollas – or than

[19] Drollas, 'The search for oil in the USA'; Drollas, 'Oil supplies and the world oil market in the long run', paper presented at the International Association of Energy Economists Conference, Tokyo, June 1986.

what have later become the present consensus range of estimates from the USGS, Shell and BP. Certain highly qualified geologists and economic geographers, it has to be repeated, believe there are much higher volumes still of oil to be discovered in the earth, and that improved recovery techniques will get much more of them out.[20] If they prove right, those extra reserves would prolong the levelling out of production for a few decades longer, with conventional oil 'available in the quantities demanded until well into the second quarter of the twenty-first century'. But even that would not necessarily alter the medium-term profile of world oil production very much.

If Hubbert's 'orderly progression' had proceeded undisturbed in world oil, then presumably the approach of a peak in supply by the late nineties, duly foreseen, might have begun to raise oil prices, at least gradually, by the mid-eighties. That did not happen. The evolution *was* disturbed, most noticeably by world oil prices that were lifted off a decade earlier, and by what they did to demand. Less obviously, the evolution had begun to be disturbed long before, when Middle East oil was developed more slowly than it might have been in strict accordance with comparative costs.

## Conventional oil and after

Most of the reserve estimates and all the production profiles cited above represent capacity to produce *conventional oil*. This is the crude oil readily producible today by known techniques, up to a level of cost acceptable in current and expected price ranges. (Some oil companies, in offering reserve estimates, explicitly mention a price limit, e.g. $25/bbl in 1985 dollars. Most do not, but implicitly assume one.) Beyond that definition and price, there will be a lot more oil available.

In the 1950s, conventional oil was sometimes defined as that producible by primary recovery, at natural wellhead pressure. In principle, secondary recovery (the injection of water and sometimes gas to maintain bottom-hole pressure gradients and bring the crude to the surface) was then excluded from 'ultimate reserve' estimates. In practice, it was not. It soon had to be acknowledged that the reserves reported by US producers did include a significant and rising proportion of secondary recovery. As a world average, it is estimated that primary recovery can recover 20 per cent of the oil originally in place; secondary recovery may account for another 10 per cent. So the reserve estimates advanced then – and to a lesser extent, the projections of future production drawn from

[20] P. R. Odell and K. E. Rosing, *The Future of Oil* (Kegan Paul, 1983).

them such as Hubbert's – already assumed a growing contribution from secondary recovery by water and gas.

Once secondary recovery techniques too cease to be adequate, producers begin using techniques that used to be called 'tertiary' and now are called 'enhanced recovery', to stimulate the flow of oil from existing reservoirs. The most widely used is thermal recovery, heating the oil in the reservoir by steam 'flooding' or 'soaking' to reduce its viscosity. Others include the injection of carbon dioxide or surfactant (soap-like) chemicals to reduce interface tension between oil and water underground and virtually wash more oil out of the porous rock strata. By the late eighties, about 1.5 MBD of crude was being produced by enhanced recovery in North America, the USSR, Venezuela and Indonesia. All these enhanced recovery systems involve considerable inputs of energy. So the increases in recovery that they can achieve are not all *net* additions to total energy supply.[21] In most areas, their production possibilities are very sensitive to any downward uncertainties about price.

Nevertheless, the extra yields available from enhanced recovery could be dramatic. An American study in 1984 reckoned that a crude oil price of $20/bbl could justify enhanced recovery there that would add 7 billion bbl to US reserves (then 28 billion bbl). A price of $30/bbl in 1984 dollars might effectively have doubled those US reserves. Inflation since would have pushed up those price levels; on the other hand, some earth scientists would argue that on all frontiers of the industry's practice, from the Arctic to the very deep offshore, technology continues to hold costs constant in real terms.

Current reserve estimates thus include a significant proportion of heavy oil that will require enhanced recovery, quite apart from the natural bitumens from Venezuelan, Canadian and other tar sands. Enhanced recovery is effectively the first step past any current estimates of proved oil reserves. It is a high step upward in cost (not only in production, but in the more intensive processing that the heavier hydrocarbons it can make available may require). Beyond it stretch an array of further steps towards wider availability of oil, or of effective substitutes for what oil can do.

At various levels in the array, and up the supply cost curve, will come more of the heavy oils now producible by current methods; tar sands; substitute oil products refined from coal; and, eventually, oil shales. There is no doubt that all these can be made available at some level of

---

[21] In California, where these techniques are used widely, they often require about one-third of a barrel of oil or equivalent energy to produce a barrel of crude.

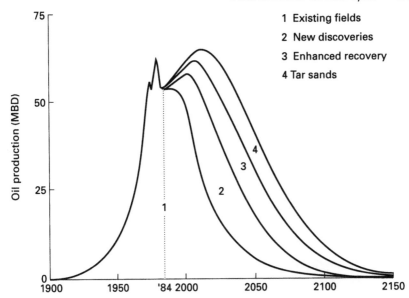

Figure 10.5. Long-term oil production scenario from existing fields, new discoveries, enhanced recovery and tar sands. (*Source:* Shell.)

cost, which is to say once conventional oil prices reach some comparable level (Figure 10.5). All that is uncertain is the levels and order of cost at which each would become competitive, and the time that each would take to develop in competitive volumes. The costs of these less conventional oils are not distinct and separate rungs up a cost ladder, at which production will begin in some neat and orderly sequence. They form a series of overlapping ranges (Figure 10.6). Some reserves of each range of heavier hydrocarbons, for example, are technically easier to develop and cheaper to produce much earlier than other reserves of similar materials. Nor, perhaps, need all of them be refined into the oil products that the industry is accustomed to process from conventional crude, as Venezuela's Orimulsion may be demonstrating. About 6 MBD of various kinds of heavy crude are already being produced within current world supplies. Significant amounts of all this array of alternatives will be there for the taking, as and when the prices of conventional oil and the products refined from it begin to mount.

But where oil is used for general energy, the next steps may in practice bypass oil as such. Gas and coal deliverable cheaply can often undercut fuel oil. Primary electricity from *existing* hydropower or nuclear stations, when no extra investment is needed, can usually be cheaper (unless or until extra capacity becomes necessary, when their capital

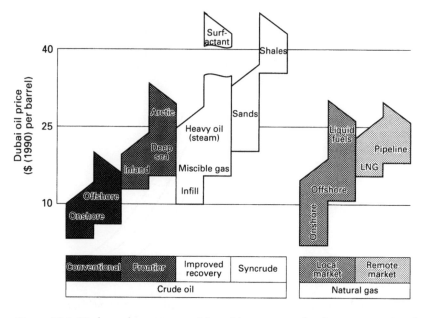

Figure 10.6. Hydrocarbon opportunities with current technology: conventional crude oil, unconventional heavy crudes, tar sands and shales that are economic to develop, and natural gas that is economic to transport to market, at various levels of crude oil price, 1990. (*Source:* Shell.)

costs may put them out of court). Even where oil is used for its specialised purpose of transport, gas can be converted into kerosene and diesel fuels for aircraft and a growing proportion of road vehicles, possibly at costs competitive with transport fuels refined from crude oil. It has often been observed that the nineties will be 'a gas decade'. Certainly gas will be the fastest-growing form of energy consumption in Europe and in many developing countries.

Hubbert's pimple of future oil production, or perhaps the shallower and longer-drawn-out dome of conventional oil supply that we can now contemplate, is thus already beginning to be supplemented and backed up by a succession of non-conventional oil and oil-substitutes that can prolong the eventual plateau of availability long into the next century. None of these supplementary fuels is an ultimate 'backstop fuel', the panacea that some Western energy economists used to hope would eventually materialise to set a price ceiling beyond which neither Opec nor anyone else could raise the price of conventional oil. But the costs at which it will become practicable to develop them even now promise considerable successive increments to supply the services that conventional oil now renders. Increasingly, it looks as if a large proportion of the world's liquid hydrocarbon resources could be produced at prices within a range of $(1991)25–30 for conversion into middle distillates. If so, that price range might set some natural ceiling for conventional crudes.

This prospect of progressively available substitutes, however, is flawed by one huge continuing anomaly, which works both ways. This is the availability, potentially much sooner but so far still postponed, of huge reserves of conventional oil producible far more cheaply than any of them. Middle East reserves *could* flood the market for years, indeed decades to come, at prices that none of these alternatives, and not much existing non-Opec energy, could match. This oil may never be put on the market at such prices; but it always could be. The developer of energy elsewhere today is not looking at a steadily and 'logically' rising ladder of costs, as some mining industries believe they are. He faces a ladder of costs from which several of the bottom rungs are temporarily missing – but might be replaced at any time. Eventually the whole ladder will come in handy. But one cannot be sure how soon it will be worth while to take the risk of mounting the upper rungs.

So even if the growth curve of this industry is levelling off, one cannot say that the medium-run supply costs of conventional oil are yet rising, so long as those unused low-cost reserves are counted in. In strictly competitive terms, it would be only when those lowest-cost oil reserves were being produced to their full potential that one could economically justify further investment in higher-cost crudes and other energies. Afterwards, those rising costs and prices would validate our recourse to the abundant succession of alternatives. Those can extend the petroleum plateau by decades. But it could be a long time before they begin to be worth while.

Looking forward into the first half of next century, prospects for the supply side of world energy remain reassuring – to the extent that fossil fuels remain environmentally acceptable or can be made so anew. The global problem is not scarcity. But the potential abundance of oil, gas and the alternatives – at one price or another – will continue to be delayed by this underlying uncertainty. Which crudes should be, and will be, produced first – or rather, the crudes from where? That has been a fundamental question for this industry for forty years. But it is one that the managers of the industry have seldom cared to discuss directly.

CHAPTER 11

# A contrast of expectations

In between the instant decisions of traders in futures markets and the long-term prognoses of geologists about ultimate oil supply, managers within the oil industry are concerned mainly with the medium run – the rest of this century, and a decade or so into the next. When looking that far forward, they are never short of learned advice.

In June 1991, an International Energy Workshop held in Vienna brought together a poll of projections regarding prospects for oil and energy in general as far as the first or second decade of next century, made by sixty governmental, business and academic organisations across the world.[1] This was the tenth time since 1981 that similar informal workshops had compiled such samplings of what the world's oil analysts were predicting. Over a decade of surprises, their sequence of results has provided a barometric record of changing climates of opinion within or close to this business. The IEW polls have often included the two intergovernmental organisations most directly concerned with the international oil trade. In 1991 Opec did take part. IEA, as it happened, had not done so since 1988, but published its own fully detailed projections in April 1991.

The Vienna workshop of 1991 did not produce any broad consensus of oil projections for the nineties. That might perhaps be taken as fortunate for everyone concerned. As Professor Edith Penrose once put it, 'Never ... has an oil industry consensus turned out to be correct.' For that matter, the ten-year record from earlier workshops had seldom produced anything that could really be called a consensus. There were always wide ranges between the highest and lowest projections polled, for example, often differing by a factor of three or more for the crude prices expected ten years ahead. In 1990 and 1991, the spread of differ-

---

[1] The International Energy Workshop was created by IIASA, the International Institute for Applied Systems Analysis, Laxenburg, Austria, and Stanford University, California, in 1981.

ent expectations polled had narrowed somewhat; the highest of the dozen price projections published in 1991 for the year 2000 was $35/bbl in 1990 dollars and the lowest $19/bbl. (A personal 'Delphi survey' of analysts attending the IEW meetings in July 1991 suggested a probable range of $19–29 for the price in 2000, with a median of $26–27/bbl.) Nevertheless, since that survey, there have been signs of polarisation into two camps of opinion, in strong disagreement about oil prospects for this decade.

One element of broad agreement throughout the first ten years of this polling had been simply the matter of direction. Throughout the period, projectors had always expected prices to go up over time. There had also been some parallelism, if not consensus, in the *changes* in most of these diverse projections. Median responses to all the questions, in each successive year of the IEW polls, have tended to shift in the same direction; and these shifts have tended to reflect the recent movements of current oil prices during the periods immediately preceding each poll. When the price of crude oil dropped from year to year, the successive median projections (though continuing to slant upwards) were also lowered (Figure 11.1). Whether based on formal econometric modelling or more simply on expert judgement, these oil projections displayed what has been called 'adaptive expectations', with medium-term views being 'heavily influenced by current prices and by trends during the recent past'.[2]

Along with these price expectations are published projections of oil consumption in the years ahead, for which the ranges of difference tend to be rather less (Figure 11.2). Those draw upon broader projections of total demand for primary energy, which show yet more agreement. Oil accounts for only 35–40 per cent of the total, but dominates energy pricing and is usually regarded as the residual supply drawn upon to meet energy demand. So differences of expert opinion about total energy are generally concentrated onto this oil component, particularly as regards prices.

In 1991, the forward views of IEA and of Opec were at opposite ends of that spectrum of expectations. Nobody, perhaps, would have expected the two organisations, standard-bearers of embattled importers on the one hand and exporters on the other, to agree. What was unexpected, however, was the way that they differed. IEA postulated much larger increases than Opec did, not only in oil prices *but also* in oil demand, through to the first decade of next century.

---

[2] A. S. Manne and L. Schrattenholzer, 'The International Energy Workshop: a progress report', *OPEC Review*, Winter 1989, pp. 415–28

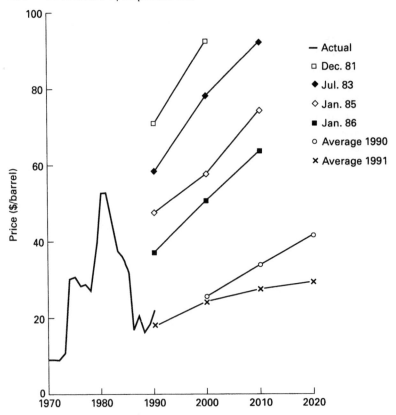

Figure 11.1. Oil price expectations, 1981–1991. Crude oil price projections polled by International Energy Workshop in successive polls, compared with actual prices to 1991. (*Source:* Manne *et al.* '1991 International Energy Workshop'.)

*By any other name ...*

Both IEA and Opec, like almost all energy projectionists in recent years, were at pains to emphasise that their figuring should *not* be considered as a forecast. The word became embarrassing and went severely out of fashion during the eighties. (The activity did not. It continued, but with somewhat less publicity.) Ironically, the word 'expectations' had done just the opposite, coming greatly into vogue during the same decade. Yet forecasts and projections are little more than expectations, extrapolated tangentially and then crystallised. Moreover, all of these analysts hedged their medium-term figuring thickly with qualifications. Everyone always needs to. Few of the hundreds of predictions published about oil demand and supply in the last thirty to forty years have turned out to be

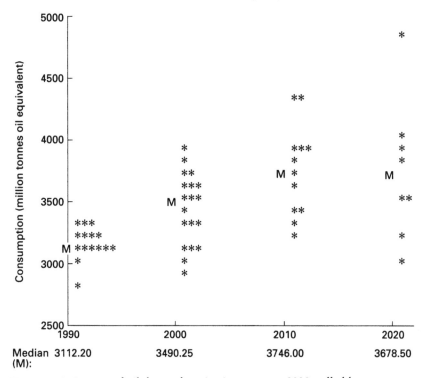

Figure 11.2. Ranges of oil demand projections to year 2020 polled by
International Energy Workshop in 1991. (*Source:* Manne *et al.*, '1991
International Energy Workshop'.)

anywhere near right. (Forecasts-cum-projections regarding total energy
demand have turned out to be rather more accurate, but not much.)

That, dependably, generates public derision, which dismays some
practitioners of this chancy art. The dismay, like the derision, misses the
main point. Both reactions over-dignify the whole game of projection-
alias-forecasting . It is, essentially, a current exercise. It only *purports* to
offer statements about the future. In reality, it offers statements of
reasoned current expectations at the time they are made, to assist
current decisions that will have medium-term consequences. The exercise is seldom satisfying, but is usually considered unavoidable in energy
industries, where capital investment often takes five to ten years to
complete and at least as long again to pay off. All such decisions have to
be made in conditions of great uncertainty.[3] The practical purpose of
forecasts, to assist the decisions, is often immediate, even fleeting. In

[3] In principle, one can compare the robustness of different investment propositions to widely
differing ranges of possible future prices and surrounding circumstances *without* assigning prob-

some cases, the investment or policy decisions that they assist may significantly alter the future circumstances that could otherwise be foreseen. (An ideal forecast, affecting enough decisions that were important, would necessarily soon render itself wrong.)

One significant element that may have caused the energy projections compiled by IEW to change roughly in parallel over time is simply that most of them use almost the same, mostly borrowed assumptions about general economic growth. Few of the analysts who are confident in constructing detailed energy models also feel as competent to make, or change, their own macroeconomic assumptions. Moreover, there are always plenty of better-qualified or more generally accepted assumptions about GDP to hand – from OECD, the World Bank and other headquarters of the world's stage army of official economists, who are constantly revising their own projections. Any model that can be devised for world energy demand depends partly on definable sets of relationships, stable or dynamic, with GDP growth in the economies consuming the energy. If most energy modellers at any one time are using much the same received, and changing, assumptions about future GDP, borrowed from the same prestigious sources, that will be one factor helping to cluster their demand projections and to shift them in the same direction at the same time.

It is true that after the two price shocks of the early and late seventies, many analysts concluded that the long-perceived linkages between GDP growth and energy demand, in the OECD industrial economies at any rate, were attenuating. National income in these economies recovered from recession in the early eighties earlier than total energy requirements, and has continued to grow somewhat faster. But after OECD energy demand began to grow again in the mid-eighties, even for oil, some of the same analysts decided that this decoupling of energy demand and GDP had been quite transient, and that long-run linkages between the two were being re-established. The question is still moot.[4] Nevertheless, even if the linkages are modified in particular models, almost every oil demand scenario put forward nowadays *does* still proceed from *some* basic assumptions about GDP in different regions of the world economy.

---

abilities to any of these futures. Deciding whether or not to go ahead with any *single* proposition, however, may inherently need an assignment of cardinal and not simply ordinal probability.

[4] Those have never been more than observed statistical relationships between economic growth, originally measured as manufacturing production in certain of the earliest industrialised economies, and energy use there (essentially of coal). Later sophistication generated, on the one hand, the still hardly precise concept of national product/income, and on the other, the measurement of total energy consumption (i.e. production plus imports less exports and stock change) in terms of some generalised 'fuel equivalent'.

No intergovernmental organisation is readier to make, update, and lend other analysts its own basic macroeconomic projections than the OECD secretariat in Paris, of which IEA is part. Opec's modellers in Vienna, too, make their own assumptions about GDP without borrowing. (Indeed, they assume, more explicitly than most other modellers, that world macroeconomic performance will be significantly affected by whatever oil price trajectory one assumes. Opec thus allows for a specific feedback between the two. Few other econometric energy models do.)

Over several postwar decades, the techniques of projection-alias-forecasting may have become technically a little more sophisticated,[5] but no more accurate. Almost all energy projections nowadays consider more than one scenario,[6] giving a spread of future values. Some earlier demonstrated mistakes and technical weaknesses in forecasting can be avoided each time the exercise is repeated.

All oil projections since the late eighties, in particular, have given more attention to prices and the elasticities of oil demand to these than before. The data they had to work upon, moreover, had accumulated during a decade of demand responses to extreme turbulence in prices, which rose sharply twice and fell sharply once. Eventually, enough should have been learned about the elasticities of demand in such volatile circumstances, even when prices fall. Few analysts, however, wholly agree about what they have learnt.

## Less investment, fewer forecasts

In the event, significantly fewer projections about oil were in fact published during the eighties by anyone but academics. This may partly have reflected the aforesaid embarrassment. After unexpected free-for-alls in prices, up in 1979 and then down in 1986, few analysts were anxious to advertise their confusion. For planners within oil companies, however, there was another quite practical reason. The primary purpose of energy projections inside companies is to assist investment decisions.

---

[5] Not as much so as many modellers assume. In 1956, in its first official forecast, often called 'the Hartley report', OECD (then OEEC) used multiple correlation analysis to calculate the elasticity of energy consumption with respect to GNP (both per head); to a 'degree of industrialisation' measure to allow for different energy–GNP income elasticities between countries); and, lastly, to the relative price of energy. *Europe's Growing Needs of Energy* (OEEC, 1956). It is not the analysis that has since become more sophisticated, simply the calculating equipment.

[6] Scenarios can be defined as descriptions of alternative future situations, embodying plausible and internally consistent assumptions about the range of factors liable to affect the outcomes of business decisions. Their use and elaboration varies from simple alternative assumptions about particular variables, e.g. the crude oil price or GDP growth rates, to comprehensive 'different worlds' designed to generate new 'strategic options'.

And during that decade, with demand jerking down and then turning more gradually upwards, the industry *as a whole* was not under its customary pressure to make decisions about physical investment. (Financial decisions to invest in acquiring other companies, or to avoid being acquired oneself, became more fashionable, and logically so. But those needed, for the most part, rather different forms of analysis and forecasting.)

During the eighties, in an ideal world economically and politically, there might indeed have been little need for any *net* additions whatever to the world's oil capacity to produce, transport, refine or distribute oil. In that decade, there was more than enough to spare of all kinds of capacity. Indeed, a great deal of tanker and basic refinery capacity *was* scrapped (though possibly not enough). In principle, producers too might simply have needed decline offset investment to maintain their production capacity in being. In the imperfect world we have, however, there were in fact considerable gross additions to production capacity, only partly offset by continuing decline in certain areas and by the mothballing or simple neglect of facilities in others.

Necessarily or not, a significant net increase in world oil production capacity *did* occur. It ended up as spare capacity in Opec, the last set of suppliers that customers chose to draw upon. Non-Opec suppliers, on the other hand, had perhaps rather less need than usual during that decade to back their investments in new production with elaborate projections of demand. Whatever total demand might be, they could be broadly confident that customers would be prepared to buy any production that *they* could develop, in preference to Opec's.

During the nineties, investment in oil can no longer be postponed as it was in the eighties. Estimates of just *how much* investment is needed to increase capacity will depend on one's assumptions regarding continued growth in demand. But in any case, even before the 1991 Gulf war devastated facilities in Kuwait and Iraq, considerable investment in production was already necessary even to maintain capacity levels. Downstream, it is still not clear whether much extra distillation capacity will be required. But the shift towards lighter products and the pressure for higher product qualities to meet environmental rules will in any case require additional investment in upgrading many refineries. Most of the investment decisions to match capacity to demand prospects in the years to 2010 and beyond have to be made during this decade. Moreover, the capital required to implement decisions already made in principle – notably, to expand Gulf production capacity – has to be assembled. Up to the time this book was completed early in 1993, firm contracts to go ahead were materialising only rather slowly.

## Conflicting views of the nineties

Oil projections for the nineties from both IEA and Opec, like those made within companies whether published or not, derived from painstaking analysis by experts of the fullest and most up-to-date information available. The intergovernmental organisations use elaborate econometric modelling, as some major oil companies do. (Not all, however: some companies discarded modelling, and even parts of their corporate planning departments, after the failures of prediction demonstrated in the eighties. Other companies, including the two largest, have always been sceptical of formal econometric modelling in assessing prospects for energy and oil.)

Opec's moderation, compared with IEA, regarding total demand for oil and world oil prices to the end of the century and beyond is illustrated in Table 11.1 and Figure 11.3 One cannot compare directly the projections that the two organisations published in 1991. These were quite differently designed, more so than some they had made in late 1989, which *were* rather more clearly comparable. But certain of the modelling assumptions underlying their demand projections were similar enough to set alongside each other fairly simply.

In its 1991 projections, the IEA took much the same line as it had since 1987, following the price collapse of 1986. Indeed, it became even more bullish about world oil demand. It used two scenarios, one assuming rising real prices for crude oil as far as the year 2000 or just after, and another assuming constant real prices. From its first and apparently favoured 'reference scenario', it then reckoned that even if average OECD import prices for crude were roughly to double between 1990 and 'early in the next decade, remaining at that level thereafter', oil demand in the market economies would rise by just on 30 per cent between 1989 and the year 2005. If crude prices were to remain constant in real terms, then IEA would expect this oil demand outside the Communist and ex-Communist countries to rise more than half by 2005.

In 1989 and early 1990, Opec's energy modellers had offered demand projections and price scenarios of a similar kind to IEA's, but with markedly dissimilar results. They did consider a price scenario rising in real terms through the nineties (though rising much less than the IEA was assuming). But they rejected that as liable to bring about stagnation in oil demand. They preferred a 'base case' price scenario similar to (although not identical with) one of IEA's, constant real *export* prices to the end of the century,[7] thereafter rising (at the same rate as economic

---

[7] IEA's constant real price scenario was for CIF *import* prices for crude delivered to OECD countries, which had a weighted average of $22.20/bbl in 1990. Opec's constant real price case was for an

Table 11.1. *Expectations for the nineties: projections from IEA and Opec compared, 1989 and 1991*

|  | 1988 | 1990 | 1995 | 2000 | 2005 | 2010 |
|---|---|---|---|---|---|---|
| **IEA** | | | | | | |
| *1989 projections* | | | | | | |
| OECD cimport price rising: | | | | | | |
| $ (1987) | 15.0 | 18.1 | 27.0 | 31.1 | 31.1 | |
| WOCA demand (MBD) | 50.7 | | 56.2 | 59.4–62.8 | 63.2 | |
| Price constant: $ (1987) | 15.0 | 18.1 | 18.1 | 18.1 | 18.1 | |
| WOCA demand (MBD) | 50.7 | | 59.7 | 64.2 | 72.4 | |
| *1991 projections* | | | | | | |
| OECD import price rising: | | | | | | |
| $ (1990) | 17.5 | 21.0[a] | | 35.5 | 35.5 | |
| WOCA demand (MBD) | | 55.5 | 62.8 | 66.8 | 70.9 | |
| Price constant: $ (1990) | | 21.0 | 21.0 | 21.0 | 21.0 | |
| WOCA demand (MBD) | | 55.5 | 63.6 | | 82.3 | |
| **Opec** | | | | | | |
| *1989 projections* | | | | | | |
| Opec export price | | | | | | |
| FOB rising: $ (1985) | 18.0 | 14.5 | 16.2 | 17.8 | | 22.0 |
| WOCA demand (MBD) | 50.5 | 51.7 | 54.0 | 54.7 | | 57.5 |
| Price constant: $ (1985) | 18.0 | 18.0 | 18.0 | 18.0 | | 18.0 |
| WOCA demand (MBD) | 50.5 | 51.7 | 55.0 | 57.1 | | 63.4 |
| *1991 projections* | | | | | | |
| Opec export price | | | | | | |
| FOB constant: $ (1990) | | 21.0[a] | 21.0 | 21.0 | 21.0 | 21.0 |
| WOCA demand (MBD) | | 51.9 | 54.8 | 57.7 | 60.4 | 63.4 |
| Higher constant: | | | | | | |
| FOB price: $ (1990) | | 25.0[a] | 25.0 | 25.0 | 25.0 | 25.0 |
| WOCA demand (MBD) | | 51.9 | 52.4 | 54.0 | 55.8 | 57.9 |

*Note:* [a] 1991.
*Sources:* IEA. Successive reports on *Energy and Oil Outlook to 2005* (Paris, 1989 and 1991).
Opec. world Energy Model, *Energy Scenarios to the Year 2010* (Vienna, 1989), and *A Long-Term Perspective* (1990).

unweighted average of FOB *export* prices for a basket of eight selected crudes shipped from its member countries, which averaged $22.25/bbl in 1990. (The close fit of the two averages was coincidental, surprising and perhaps slightly embarrassing for the Opec countries' statisticians. But the two series would always cover quite different selections of crudes.)

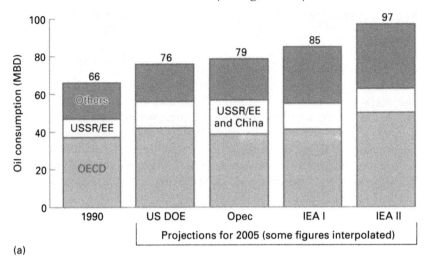

(a)

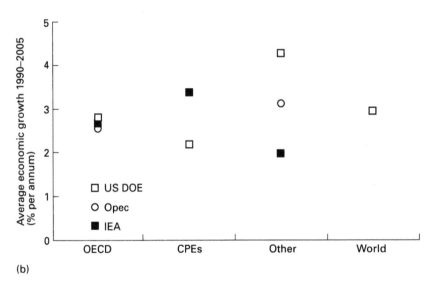

(b)

Figure 11.3. (a) Projections of world oil consumption in 2005 by IEA, Opec and US Department of Energy, 1991. (b) Economic growth assumptions underlying projections. (*Sources:* IEA, Opec, EIA.)

growth in OECD). But with such prices, they expected oil demand in the same market economies to rise by only 18 per cent between 1988 and 2005, less than half the increase that IEA was then projecting.

The next report Opec's modellers produced, at the end of December 1990, did not repeat all the kinds of projection that they had made in

1989. But it sounded (from their members' point of view) just as cautious as the previous one. Opec this second time used its model to seek pricing strategies that might 'optimise' the real value of oil revenues for Opec member countries over the next 10–20 years. Again assuming constant real prices (from 1991 onwards), Opec foresaw oil demand in the market economies rising only 17 per cent by the year 2005. That would be less than half the increase during the nineties and in the first decade of next century which IEA was projecting even if real prices nearly double, to say nothing of the even greater increase in demand it was postulating if prices remain constant in real terms. Opec also considered other constant real price scenarios for the decade, at higher levels than $21/bbl. Its modellers rejected any level above $25/bbl in real terms as liable to bring about stagnation in world demand for oil (Opec's in particular), and to reduce the oil revenues of member governments. Their 'choice' for the nineties would be to aim within the range of $21–25/bbl (in 1990 dollars), which they thought might increase oil demand by only some 8–16 per cent between 1990 and 2005, but still offer the optimal financial outcome for Opec.

Two other projections of oil demand for the nineties published in 1991 by sources close to importing and exporting governments are worth citing, not least because they did *not* disagree in the same way. The US Energy Information Administration, in its annual review,[8] projected 'US average refinery acquisition costs', alias crude prices, of $26.40 (in 1990 dollars) for the year 2000, and of $30.50 by 2010: and world oil demand of 73.2 MBD for 2000, rising to 78.7 MBD by the year 2010. Its base projections for both prices and demand were significantly lower than IEA's, and closer to Opec's. The Centre for Global Energy Studies, a 'think-tank' set up by Shaikh Yamani after he ceased to be Saudi Arabia's oil minister, sounded even more pessimistic than Opec's modellers. It calculated that even if crude prices remain constant in nominal terms, i.e. if real prices *fall* during this decade, expansion programmes already planned would leave Opec countries with excess capacity, causing further price competition.[9]

It is hard to rationalise that complete contrast of expectations between the intergovernmental modellers of importing and exporting countries at the beginning of the nineties. The 1991 IEA price projections were about in line with the highest recorded in the IEW polls later

[8] *International Energy Outlook: A Postwar Review of Energy Markets.* (US Energy Information Administration, Washington, 1991).
[9] 'The importance of the call on Opec oil', *Global Energy Report*, July–August 1991, Centre for Global Energy Studies, London.

that year, and sharply above the median of other energy analysts' price projections. The IEA projections of oil demand, again, were around the top of the range in that poll. (The other projections of comparably high demand, moreover, had assumed much lower price trajectories than IEA did.) Opec's modelling was probably not as comparable in methodology with most of the other projections polled by IEW as IEA's could have been. But for what it is worth, Opec's 'optimal price paths' and estimates of market demand in 2000-05 were in fact much closer to the medians of the IEW poll than IEA's farther-out expectations.[10]

Both these intergovernmental organisations are highly interested parties. The IEA secretariat is constantly concerned to keep its member governments interested in energy-saving and vigilant about security of supply. (It sometimes also gives an impression of being concerned, less openly, that oil prices should remain high enough to keep the development of oil and other energy outside Opec economically worth while.) The Opec secretariat has seemed of late, perhaps, to be concerned to keep its diverse member countries cautious about future oil demand, and what increases in price might do to that.

However, these two contrasting analyses of the same data by equally competent modellers need not be attributed to their clients' governmental biases. At the turn of the decade, comparable disagreements were being voiced (if not in quite such explicit detail) between international oil companies able to call on far more practical expertise. IEA's reference scenario postulated crude prices (OECD import values) rising to over \$27/bbl by 1995 and to \$35/bbl by just after 2000 (both in 1990 dollars). That price trajectory seemed broadly in line with the expectations of one of the few companies that had gone on regularly publishing its own detailed projections, Continental Oil. Similarly, British Petroleum eagerly identified signs that a new oil supply crunch could appear by the mid-nineties, because discoveries of *new* reserves were not replacing oil consumption since the late eighties. (It argued that the uprating of existing Opec reserves, primarily in the Gulf, simply tends to disguise this medium-run problem.) BP projected a crude price of \$25/bbl (in 1991 dollars) by 1995 less from an analysis of demand trends than as a *necessity* for the huge exploration and development effort – say \$250 billion over five years – it reckoned the world industry needs.

---

[10] IEA did not update its projections in 1992, and decided to carry out a complete revision of its demand model. By spring 1993 it had a new *World Energy Outlook* (to the year 2010) almost ready for its member governments. This appeared certain to revise its projections of oil demand and crude prices quite significantly downwards, closer to those of US DOE and probably of Opec.

Across the river Thames from BP, Shell's traders as well as its geologists disagreed.[11] They went on arguing that non-Opec supply could and would be stretched out further, mainly by improved technology – leaving the market soft until close to the end of the century. (Shell is not in the habit of econometric modelling, but is never short of scenarios for everything.) Up to 1991, its spokesmen steadily repeated that they expected 'volatile but directionless' prices in the range of $15–20/bbl to prevail well into the mid-nineties, perhaps even towards the end of the decade.[12]

## Demand: from where?

Most of the international projections of demand made up to the end of the eighties, even when they differed quantitatively, had one *qualitative* similarity. They postulated continued gradual growth in world demand for energy and oil as far as and beyond the year 2000. But they expected nearly all this growth to occur outside the Western industrialised economies – in the diverse array of developing countries, and in the formerly Communist economies. (By 1992, however, some analysts were writing off any further oil demand growth for the ex-CPEs this century.) Demand for oil in the industrialised economies of OECD was expected to grow only slowly, perhaps not at all.

Because of the shift in pattern of demand that they envisage, the quantities in such scenarios have a new, inherent vulnerability. Up to the late eighties, some 75 per cent or more of world energy and oil consumption had been taking place in the OECD economies. These are the world's richest economies, well able to pay for all the oil they need. Moreover, in energy statistics as well as general economic series, they are consistently and relatively well documented for demand forecasters to work upon. Their responses to changes in energy (alias oil) prices are fairly accurately measurable, and hence in principle *ought* to be predictable. Neither of those conditions holds good for many of the developing countries, or for the ex-Communist economies.

Statistics of energy demand and internal prices in developing countries have always varied widely in quality. Not many of their figures are yet adequate for analysis in relation to energy price changes deriving from the world market. Much of the energy consumption in these poorer countries remains 'vegetal', wood and farm wastes that are

---

[11] John Browne, BP Exploration, 'Meeting the oil needs of the nineties', and John Jennings, Royal Dutch/Shell, 'Oil industry perspectives in the 1990s – upstream', both papers presented at the *Oil and Money Conference*, London, November 1991.
[12] Sir Peter Holmes, 'Energy prospects for the nineties', Royal Institute of International Affairs, April 1991 (Shell Briefing Service, April 1991).

seldom bought and sold as 'commercial energy'. Their internal energy prices for the other, genuinely commercial energy are often controlled and/or subsidised. Thus these countries are partly insulated from world market forces.

Also, the ease with which loans were obtainable from the world's commercial banking system during the seventies and eighties protected many developing countries from the full impact of high oil prices. Nowadays, admittedly, there is some concentration of this group of countries' oil demand into a few newly industrialising countries that *are* able to pay commercial prices (though even in some of those countries, internal energy prices remain artificial). But during the nineties all the others are finding borrowing to finance spending on current items like their oil imports much harder. Western banks burned their fingers in pressing loans upon countries that proved hardly able to service their debts, let alone offer any realistic hope of repayment. (In recent years, the net financial flows have often been from poor borrowers back to rich creditor nations, simply to service loans.) The international banking system has been forced to retrench. Since the early eighties, there have been no Opec surpluses to 'recycle' in lavish sovereign lending elsewhere. During this decade, even the richest Opec countries themselves need to borrow.

Severe economic disorganisation in Eastern Europe, which finally became impossible to conceal in the last half of the eighties, suddenly collapsed Communist political regimes there into hopeful but disordered democracy. The economic failures, incidentally, tore holes in the statistical facade that central planners there had chosen to present to the outside world. During the mid-eighties, certain Western energy analysts had begun to feel that Soviet and some Eastern European energy consumption data were becoming more believable, and perhaps even practicable to analyse in terms of demand responses to those economies' own (also generally controlled and artificial) prices. However, the consumption data then published sound increasingly liable to have been deliberately distorted. (Nor did the various ex-Soviet oil and gas experts roaming Western energy seminars at the end of the eighties appear to take even their own *production* data for oil and gas as seriously as Western analysts had.)

Guessing how far and how fast those newly democratised countries can transform themselves economically has become a growth market for Western consultants and carpetbaggers of every kind. At the time that this book was completed, none of the myriad guesses appeared convincing. It remains possible for optimists to hope that these populations, disillusioned with central planning, well-educated and eager for change, can quite soon achieve rapid growth in new market economies comparable to the Pacific Rim successes of the eighties. At least as plausibly, one can fear that political disorganisation and the exaggerated hopes about instant capitalism among nationalist consumers in most of them may frustrate for a time the eagerness for economic change for a time, and prolong disappointments.

Narrowing one's speculations to their energy prospects, the guesswork is no easier. More realistic market pricing could in principle offer substantial savings in energy consumption in these countries even if standards of living improve, since their economies have been among the world's most wasteful users of energy of all kinds. (That was partly because during most of the postwar period Eastern Europe had received oil and gas too cheaply, receiving what amounted to subsidies of billions of dollars from Soviet energy suppliers.) On the other hand, all their populist ambitions undoubtedly include a surge in car ownership, personal travel, and the acquisition of energy-intensive consumer durables.

So long as three-quarters of world oil demand was in OECD, and could be related clearly to whichever price assumptions they chose, oil analysts had a fairly solid basis upon which to engage in the inherently uncertain exercise of forecasting. In a period in which they expect more than half the world's oil demand to shift to the developing countries and former CPEs, any forecasting of total world demand becomes much hazier. Demand in both those groups of economies is ill-measured, and responsive only to internal energy pricing that is mostly artificial. Nor has demand in either of them, so far, ever had any discernible feedback upon world oil pricing. If both sets of countries develop market economies, that should eventually change. But in the meantime they add an extra degree of uncertainty to projections of world oil demand, which were inaccurate enough even when the demand influences and responses came primarily from OECD. The extra uncertainties besetting energy in the former Soviet Union, moreover, may powerfully affect world oil supply as well as demand.

*Greener demand scenarios?*

Arguments that the 'decoupling' of the eighties was only temporary would leave macroeconomic assumptions as crucial as ever to energy projections. But they might also imply that any restraints on energy consumption could constrain general economic growth. That, in the next two to three decades, could have more awkward implications for the whole human condition. For we now have to take into account – though so far we have no clear way of measuring – possible environ-

mental limits to the energy consumption levels so far associated with
developed countries' standards of living. Such limits might be set, first,
by the known atmospheric pollution that we can already measure from
high levels of total energy consumption. That is beyond doubt, but can
technically be controlled at measurable costs. Behind tangible pollution,
however, looms the hazier but perhaps less manageable phenomenon of
global warming. *If* the most severe assessments of the greenhouse effect
upon world ambient temperatures prove well founded, then the industrialised economies will need to stabilise or even reduce their fossil fuel
consumption. If the GDP–energy linkages are re-emerging, that would
imply restraints upon OECD growth.

Less developed countries, moreover, might be asked to forgo any
hopes they have of fossil fuel consumption levels per head even
approaching those in OECD today. (Even in poverty, *if* the greenhouse
effect exists, they could be the largest contributors to it.) It is not easy to
believe that they would even countenance such self-denial. But if they do
– or can be bribed or coerced into doing so by Western pressure – then
early next century that might also begin to reduce the growth in their oil
demand which is still being assumed in most 'business-as-usual' energy
projections. What would become of current high demand assumptions
like IEA's then? And for that matter, of their assumptions about oil
prices?

A report on 'Major themes in energy' produced by the Commission of
the European Communities in 1989[13] had included a scenario aimed at
sustaining high economic growth, which nevertheless sought 'to explore
and define the conditions in which higher economic growth, a clean
environment and secure and moderately priced energy would be compatible objectives.' This assumed much wider use of the most energy-
efficient technology already available than may occur between now and
2010 given simply conventional wisdom and ordinary commercial
incentives. It also assumed a considerably greater increase in nuclear
electricity generation from 2000 onwards than is conventionally projected. Moreover, it hoped that travellers can be persuaded to use collective
transport more and individual vehicles maybe 15 per cent less.

Any of these environmentally friendly scenarios could have profound
implications for the world oil market quite soon, as Opec was not slow
to notice. The EEC scenario would imply that OECD oil demand could
be levelled off after 1995 and reduced significantly from 2000 to 2010. In
the developing countries, it assumed that oil demand would grow much
more slowly than most analysts have projected; much more slowly, too,
than populations and politicians there are undoubtedly now hoping.

[13] 'Major themes in energy', special issue of *Energy in Europe* (EEC, Brussels), September 1989.

Both the IEA and Opec projections outlined above (Table 11.1) allowed for the modest, 'business-as-usual' policies that governments are already applying to limit environmental pollution, but nothing more. Each of them also considered separately scenarios taking account of the further measures that governments have discussed and *might* take to limit global warming – in particular, carbon taxes. IEA considered the potential effects of an additional tax on all fossil fuels at $100 or $200 per tonne of carbon (equivalent to $12.30 or $24.60 per barrel on oil); Opec postulated a lower rate, $7 per barrel of oil equivalent. Both assumed rates for the other fossil fuels related to their carbon content[14] (though Opec had further qualms about 'anti-oil' taxes that it feared might possibly be applied to penalise oil alone). These carbon taxes were assumed to be applied across OECD, on top of existing excise taxes on refined products. (Thus they could have affected final prices for products and perhaps consumption in the US, where gasoline taxes are low, proportionally more than in Europe.)

IEA's analysis of the potential effects of carbon taxes was more elaborate. Its quantitative results (taking the $100 per tonne of carbon rate of tax) are exemplified in Figure 11.4. The numbers are highly debatable; but IEA's qualitative assessment of the *comparative* effects upon different primary fuels were more telling.[15] Hard coal consumption would be expected to suffer most, particularly in electricity generation, where natural gas could gain. Oil consumption would suffer more modest reductions in demand. By 2005, emissions of carbon dioxide within OECD might be reduced by about 10 per cent. That would have about the same effect in reducing carbon emissions, IEA calculated, as a radical shift towards nuclear power, aiming to generate 50 per cent of OECD electricity from it by 2005. Applied *together*, the two policies might possibly stabilise OECD carbon emissions by 2005. As IEA observed wryly:

The measures assessed are profound and perhaps even drastic when viewed from an economic, political and social context...The implications for energy producing and exporting sectors would be particularly significant. The demand for and hence production of coal in particular but also oil would be significantly lower. The same would be the case for producer or netback prices.

Even so, carbon stabilisation within OECD would be only temporary unless further action followed. Nor would it affect carbon emissions outside OECD, which have recently been increasing twice as fast.

---

[14] Taxes for the other fossil fuels were assumed to reflect their differing carbon content. For example, the $100 tax per tonne of carbon, or $12.60/bbl on oil, would equate to $69 a tonne for coal and $1.53 per MBtu of natural gas.

[15] The percentage reductions in primary energy demand through carbon taxes that IEA calculated were from its own 'reference scenario' projections of energy and oil demand to 2005 – which were higher to start with than those of Opec or most other analysts taking part in the 1991 IEW poll.

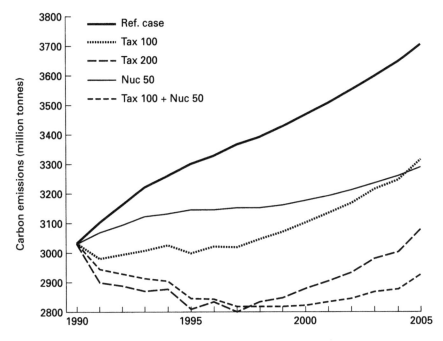

Figure 11.4. OECD carbon emissions expected to 2005 in the light of energy demand projections, 1991. (*Source:* IEA.)

According to the scientific community, stabilisation of $CO_2$ concentration levels, and hence climate, implies a 50 to 80 per cent reduction in $CO_2$ emissions and therefore, to all intents and purposes, a 50 to 80 per cent reduction in the use of coal, petroleum and natural gas. If the measures considered in this paper are viewed as unrealistic or drastic, what should one conclude about measures to reduce fossil fuel consumption by 50 to 80 per cent from current levels?[16]

What one should probably conclude, though IEA forbore to say so, is that *no* societies or their governments would as yet choose even the 'combined' scenario it had examined, let alone anything more ambitious. The extraordinary recourse to nuclear power included in one of IEA's scenarios would almost certainly be economically impracticable over the next ten to fifteen years, even in the richest economies. Politically, nuclear power is currently right out of fashion, partly because people everywhere believe it has its own ecological dangers, separate but comparably severe.

   None of these ever-greener scenarios is likely to materialise in full. The analysts polled by IEW in 1991 were also asked how much moder-

[16] International Energy Agency, *An Analysis of Energy Policy Measures and their Impact on $CO_2$ Emissions* (IEA, Paris, 1991).

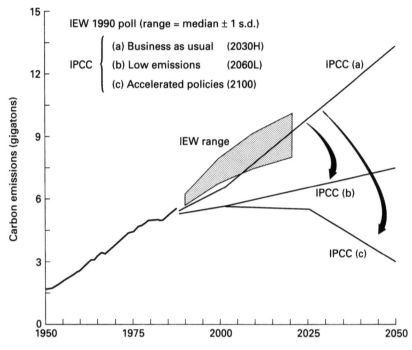

Figure 11.5. Carbon hopes versus expectations: range of predictions polled by IEW in 1991 of actual carbon emissions 1990–2020, as compared with the 'business as usual', 'low emissions' and 'accelerated policies' scenarios of the Intergovernmental Panel on Climate Change. (*Source:* Manne *et al.*, '1991 International Energy Workshop'.)

ation of future energy demand they expected *actually* to take place because of fears or policies related to global warming. In Figure 11.5 their range of practical expectations is contrasted with some of the hopes that have been expressed about responses to greener policies. Later in 1991, some governments and their energy advisers were eagerly clutching at a hope that the eruption of two volcanoes in that year might have a short-term effect of global cooling, not warming, through the discharge of dust into the atmosphere. This might give them an excuse to postpone any policy decisions even further. That particular resurgence of wistful hopes did not to last. But it helped to underline the additional uncertainties that environmental concerns have introduced into expectations and investment intentions for all the fossil fuels, including oil.

It is impossible at present to judge whether the world's latest chosen set of anxieties will turn out to have any more reality than so many others in the past have had, up to and including the *Limits to Growth* alarm in the seventies. This latest has more backing from 'the scientific community' than perhaps any before. Nor can one simply dismiss these anxieties as a Malthusian scare. (As it happens, there is one of those already in place for the twenty-first century. Global demographic projections look as ominous as ever for the time horizon around 2050.)[17] Technology has always matched such challenges before – although it has nearly always had to use more commercial energy to do so. Almost all economic scenarios reaching into the years from, say, 2020 onwards, for which energy supplies will require capital investment decisions from, say, 1995 onwards, are at present befogged by these fears and this virtuous green haze.

[17] S. P. Johnson, *World Population and the United Nations* (Cambridge University Press, 1987).

# A sustainable paradox?

If oil demand *does* grow as much in the nineties as the higher current projections suggest, where should the industry produce the extra oil? None of the items raised in the IEW polls of expert expectations about oil mentioned in the last chapter, as it happened, ever directly addressed this fundamental question about the supply side of the business. Their projections of world oil prices, usually considered the most important samplings in those polls, imply opinions about it, at least indirectly. But expectations regarding prices have no necessary relation to supply costs. The IEW polls did often include questions specifically about oil demand upon Opec, which was of critical importance in the seventies and eighties. But they never asked their experts specifically about the supply expected from the Middle East, which will remain more fundamental to world oil prices as well as supply for much longer, whatever becomes of Opec.

Chapter 10 of this book considered the medium-term world supply prospects of conventional oil and the energy forms that will succeed it, and concluded that no real threat of medium-run scarcity is visible. But notwithstanding global reassurances for the medium term, this industry has to take shorter views about one crucial question of supply. This question is not global, but localised geographically and politically. It has been exercising most oil producers since the mid-eighties. Is oil production outside Opec already passing its peak? How much can non-Opec producers maintain for how long?

This question remains as important for producers inside Opec as for those outside. All constantly scrutinise the indications that total non-Opec supply has already levelled off and may soon begin declining (Figure 12.1). Opec producers certainly hope so. Probably some of the others do too, even though they are investing heavily to maintain or increase *their* particular non-Opec production. At any rate, some of them welcome such indications. Right or wrong, these may help sustain

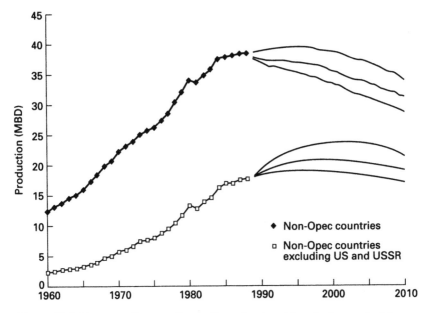

Figure 12.1. Prospects for non-Opec oil production: historical record with future projections for non-Opec countries, and for non-Opec countries excluding the US and former USSR. (*Source:* Masters *et al.*, 'Resource constraints'.)

the prices that the new production they are currently developing may fetch – and need – later in the decade.

The view that non-Opec oil supply *cannot* be expanded further can only be based on judgements about costs, not about the oil resources available. Evidence from the figures of reserves and cumulative production remains inconclusive on this issue: but non-Opec producers are not in any sense 'running out of oil'. During the years 1980 to 1990 inclusive, non-Opec countries produced just over 150 billion barrels of crude. Of that cumulative total, the non-Communist non-Opec countries produced 91 billion (fractionally more than Opec countries did in the same decade). All non-Opec producers considered together began with 205 billion barrels of proved reserves in January 1980; ten years later they had 235 billion barrels proved. During the decade, they had found and proved more oil than they had produced.

Within those fairly comfortable non-Opec totals there was one massive exception, growing steadily more important. Soviet reserves were drawn down severely during the decade, from 67 billion to 58.4 billion barrels. The world's largest producer had not nearly replaced the cumulative production that it had taken out during the decade. Also, in that one huge area there *is* direct evidence of sharply rising costs. The former Soviet republics may still offer the best possibilities of developing giant and even super-giant fields outside the Middle East. But during the next few years they face further declines in oil production that might have to be allowed to continue for macroeconomic reasons.[1] These are already affecting their total oil exports, though reducing primarily, so far, only those to Eastern Europe. Former customers there, even if they too can reduce their equally wasteful energy consumption, will have to buy more from elsewhere – *if* they can earn or borrow the hard currency required.

Almost everywhere else outside Opec, non-Communist suppliers more than replaced the decade's production in their additions to reserves. They had proved reserves of 150 billion barrels at the beginning of 1990, half as much again as a decade before. (The only notable non-Opec producer other than the former Soviet Union that was awkwardly placed according to this criterion was the UK, where the R/P ratio reported for 1991 was as low as 5.5. But Norway is much more comfortably placed. So the ratio for the whole North Sea was over 12:1, which is unremarkable but not yet disturbing.)

Even the US had achieved a net addition of about 12 per cent to its proven reserves during those ten years. Nevertheless, the world's second largest oil-producing country remains the most ambiguous area of non-Opec supply. Even with a slightly improved reserves-to-production ratio, US production may have moved into its final decline, gradual or rapid. Yet so far most of the industry's investment in new technology to eke out existing reserves, such as enhanced recovery and horizontal drilling, has been occurring in the US, without notably arresting the decline.

Western geologists prepared to look beyond the current inventory of proven reserves still argue that more of the conventional oil resources in the ground that are still to be discovered and then 'proved up' will be *outside* the Middle East. But how much meaning can be attached at any time to such estimates of 'undiscovered but recoverable reserves', and where those are likely to be, is highly debatable. They can hardly affect the industry's performance during this decade.

## Interpretations and investment choices

From analysts on the periphery of this industry, one might cite two approaches to this issue, equally sweeping but diametrically opposed.

[1] The country's energy industries, and the engineering industries that served them, were part of a 'defence-industrial complex' that took an inordinate share of national investment during most of the Cold War period. Governments of the successor republics are finding that concentration impracticable and unnecessary to continue.

One of them almost writes off *any* hopes of developing significant extra non-Opec production from now on. Earth scientists holding this view proclaim that the supplements to conventional capacity still possible in a few regions outside Opec, including the former Soviet Union, will soon be more than offset by imminent declines in the rest of non-Opec supply, even Mexico and the North Sea. They discount recourse to the heavy crudes and bitumens as distant in time: impracticably high in cost; low in recovery factor; and even when they are produced, costly to refine into the kind of oil products that consumers need. 'Good for road tar and burning in boilers, but not for making vehicle fuels because they gum up refineries', is the way one of these sceptics puts it.[2] Hence, a rapid decline soon for non-Opec oil. 'The only question is *when* global oil exports and prices will again be under Opec control.'

At the other extreme, there are economists equally prepared to dismiss as entirely spurious arguments that non-Opec oil supply will soon peak:

The Nopecs and the small Opecs are said to be running down their reserves, and sooner than we think, prices will rise and we will be back with our begging bowl at the Persian Gulf. This is, of all possible outcomes, the least likely ...

At [a price of] $15, non-cartel output will continue to creep up because in those countries oil is cheap to produce, ex-tax. Slowly the taxes adjust, as governments learn to maximise total revenues, not per-barrel take.[3]

Within the industry, practical business judgements have to be less sweeping. Not many operators currently producing oil argue that non-Opec oil supply will grow enough throughout the nineties to cover *all* of whatever growth in demand they are expecting. None doubt that it must *eventually* decline gradually. (A few stalwart economists still argue vehemently against that whole proposition; and in what have become almost scholastic disputations with earth scientists over the last two decades, have given as good as they got.) But for practical operators, as ever in this business, the argument is simply but crucially one of timing. *How long* before non-Opec supply of conventional oil begins to slide inexorably below its recent 40 MBD, and then gradually to cede the market for conventional oil to Opec?

For the international oil companies from within OECD, since the late eighties, this has suddenly opened out once again a much broader *practical* question. Unexpectedly, they are being offered a much warmer welcome in the world's second best prospective region for oil and gas development, after being shut out for several decades. Do-it-yourself

[2] L. F. Ivanhoe, 'Future crude oil supply and prices', *OGJ*, 25 July 1988.
[3] M. A. Adelman, 'Mideast governments and the oil prospect', *Energy Journal*, 10(1989), no. 2, pp. 15–24.

capitalists in the former Soviet Union are glad to draw Western companies' technical expertise – and capital – into joint ventures to develop some of the largest newly available petroleum reserves available outside the Gulf. At the same time, in one way and another, the companies may be invited back to invest in *some* of the producing countries of the Gulf, the lowest-cost oil anywhere. In terms of the volumes of *known* petroleum resources that can readily be brought towards production without further exploration, no other oil provinces compare with these two that may be reopening.

The economics of oil development in the two regions, however, still appear radically different. There are only two possible reasons why technical costs in ex-Soviet oil might turn out to be lower than in some of the other non-Opec frontier areas where international companies operate. The first is that the former Soviet Union can offer known fields appraised already, without exploration risks. The second is that some of these are super-giants, with fairly high well productivity. Most of them, however, are remote even from Soviet centres of consumption, often with high transport costs overland for internal consumption as well as to export terminals. In terms of technical cost, the Gulf can easily match or surpass both those advantages, with various giant fields known but not yet developed, which are close to seaboard or easy to link up with well-established pipeline systems.

For international companies, whatever the area, the attractions of known fields and/or low technical costs will depend on the host countries' current exploration and development terms, which determine the tax-paid costs of producing there, and their medium-run political risks. Ex-Soviet governments in Russia and its neighbouring republics may be prepared to offer exceptionally easy terms, and in particular to accept effective equity participation by the foreign companies. Compared with Gulf governments, they have no structure of existing contracts or business relationships with other oil companies that new kinds of deal might compromise. At any given price level, Gulf costs gain governments there much larger margins of economic rent, of which joint venture companies might hope for some share. But whether joint ventures there will really amount to inviting ex-concessionaires back into real equity participation is not yet clear. Oil is and may always be the Gulf countries' only real national patrimony. That is not and need never be true of the former Soviet republics.

Nor is the legitimacy of the new ex-Soviet governments in any sense dependent upon national sovereignty asserted within recent history over one foreign-owned industry. Communism's sovereignty had been asserted long ago over a huge range of Imperial Russian economic activities. It was decisively swept away in a few years by an unruly surge of democracy. Temporarily at least, that second successful Russian revolution created entirely new chances for international oil in the region. The Gulf's monocultures possess only one basic economic activity, with their ruling families' fortunes perched upon control of it. These still seem unprepared for more than gestures towards any form of democracy. They may be counting upon enough protection under US tutelage to go on avoiding much constitutional change at home.

International oil companies are relatively neutral towards all forms of government willing to do business with them. As it happens, most of these companies come from Western democracies. Most of the foreign countries where they have ever developed substantial oil production have been non-democratic. (National assemblies seldom make contract negotiations with host governments any smoother for foreign business-men. One traditional ploy of politicians seeking power is to accuse the incumbent non-democratic government of having sold the nation's birthright too cheaply.) On the other hand, the largest international companies share long experience of the Gulf and are shrewd assessors of political risks there, both in reality and as elsewhere perceived. Perhaps it is safest to assume that international companies, those that are left of the 'Seven Sisters' plus a few more, will stake some development claims for particular, readily delimitable ventures for oil in both the former Soviet Union and the Gulf; but during this decade, rather cautiously, and only where they can obtain some equity participation.

Apart from their oil prospects, new ventures in these two regions may also offer participation in gas trade, by the turn of the century, on a scale never known before. Gas, as noted already, is the favoured energy of the next two decades. It is moving in to supplement and replace other fossil energies, coal and oil, in power generation. As a highly convenient general fuel, it is becoming available in more and more regions, and able to meet whatever prices are charged for oil products. (Its pattern of costs suits long-term contracts, under which prices are indeed usually linked specifically to changes in the published prices of competing oil pro-ducts.) It seems certain to take over much of the market share that non-Opec oil will eventually relinquish. Even for transport fuels, tech-nologies deriving liquid fuels from gas have been developed towards commercial operation. Much of the additional gas consumption, too, will move through international trade. Part of it will no doubt come from Opec countries – but as it happens, not necessarily from all the main crude producers. So at the least it will diversify the sources of petroleum on which importing regions depend. And all of it will add to the competition for Opec *oil*.

*The silent anxiety*

Not many projections at the beginning of the nineties, except the modelling from Opec, EIA and CGES mentioned in the last chapter, focused on another anxiety that could bedevil oil industry expectations. This is the possibility that oil demand may *not* outrun the supply of non-Opec oil unless prices fall a good deal further.

During and after the Opec decade, some of its member governments had spent much time and thought seeking to define, and later to establish, a price level that would be at once:

   low enough, when combined with world economic growth, to keep
      oil demand growing;
   low enough also to deter further investment in additional non-Opec
      oil and other energy competitive at present prices; *but also*
   high enough to yield all Opec governments oil revenues adequate to
      keep their societies in the styles to which they have become
      accustomed.

That ambition was understandable. However, no such price was or is in prospect. *Unless* world economic growth outruns most of our current expectations, the conditions that Opec desires may remain mutually exclusive.

These countries certainly need the extra revenue. In 1986, selling 60 per cent of their former volumes at less than half the price, Opec nations' oil revenues had slumped towards 1974 levels even in nominal dollars, and were far lower in real terms. Their petrodollar surpluses have largely melted away. Several of them, along with some non-Opec oil exporters, were relegated to the multi-billion dollar debt league. Ups and downs in prices in the eighties, with world inflation quickening for a time, left their oil revenues seriously short of current budgetary requirements. The winter of 1990–1 added huge further bills for a war fought by foreigners – hardly 'hired guns', but nevertheless expecting to be, and indeed being, highly paid – and for postwar reconstruction.

*Are* Gulf oil costs still so low, given these countries' higher needs for revenue? That question had been posed even before the Gulf war. Certain economists tend to explain Opec pricing policies in terms of national revenue requirements. In spring 1989 one Western oilman chose to interpret them as a 'national budgetary overhead per barrel' which Saudi Arabia, for example, has to count in as part of its unavoidable production costs. By this reasoning, he reckoned that the Kingdom 'needed' a price of at least $15/bbl. That assessment[4] may have been

---

[4] M. S. Robinson, 'Real cost of oil isn't what you think', *PIW*, 3 April 1989, and 'Short-term influences and long-term fundamentals: stabilising and destabilising effects in the energy industries', *Energy Policy* , 20(1992), no. 10, pp. 1015–21.

with tongue in cheek, or simply cynical. It correctly expressed the real pressure of national commitments upon the Kingdom's oil revenues, but assumed that these had necessarily to be earned on production that was then running at about half the national crude capacity. If the country were able to produce and export much more crude – and by late 1990 Saudi Arabia had doubled both – it could cover any given total of budget requirements from a significantly lower 'overhead per barrel'.

Doubling national output with much the same level of prices, of course, was possible for Saudi Arabia in 1990–1 only because Iraq had devastated Kuwait's production capacity and had its own exports embargoed. That had cut Opec's readily available capacity by more than 4 MBD, at a time when non-Opec capacity was fairly fully utilised, and short-term demand reflected a military emergency. After the war, demand slackened; Kuwait capacity recovered much faster than was expected; and the exclusion of Iraqi capacity from the market remains essentially a matter of American political choice. If the expansion plans for capacity in Saudi Arabia and Iran *are* carried through by 1995 or so – which means, *if* the capital they require is invested – the market may remain oversupplied.

One way that world demand might be counted on confidently to outrun the further growth of non-Opec energy *of one kind and another* during this decade might be a further oil price collapse. Without it, the transfer of command over incremental supply back to Opec that many analysts expect may be postponed longer, or simply never happen. That is a possibility which most energy producers seem to avoid admitting: those producers inside Opec because it might immediately erode their revenues further; those outside, because it might rapidly undermine their profits, their future development and eventually their current production. Occasionally a producer breaks this silence about comparative advantage. Sir Peter Walters, in a lecture in 1989, remarked: 'If ever the oil price collapsed to levels which reflected exclusively the costs of developing oil in the Middle East, we would be faced with some very interesting choices and problems.'[5] (Sir Peter may have been relieved that henceforth, these would no longer be *his* choices and problems. He was just then retiring as chairman of BP.)

## *Will this market clear?*

Effectively, this international trade still generally prefers to meet incremental demand with high-cost rather than low-cost oil, and its

---

[5] Sir Peter Walters, Cadman Lecture, Institute of Petroleum, December 1989.

customers hardly object. This market will remain distorted so long as comparative costs are not fully reflected in crude oil prices, and are further blurred in the prices of oil products. One or two really low-cost producers in the Gulf, if they wished, *might* be able to clear this distortion of the market by cutting their crude prices to a level that not all high-cost producers could match. Arguably those few producers might eventually benefit more from such a market-clearing correction than anyone else (except perhaps oil consumers everywhere). But as yet there are few signs that they have the stomach for such a competitive move.

Any such move might puncture prices rapidly, given the instant analysis and response built into oil markets nowadays. It could reduce exploration drilling in high-cost areas fairly soon. But not much *current* production elsewhere could rapidly be put out of business unless the prices were cut to below its variable tax-paid costs[6] alone. The low-cost competitors might have to hold their prices down for years rather than months even to deter further development of new higher-cost energy production already in train. So for the one or two Gulf governments even capable of any such move, it would severely reduce their own national oil revenues for a time. That might reduce their immediate chances of finding the capital required to take full comparative advantage of their low costs. It might also temporarily jeopardise the survival of their ruling families. (And among the vulnerable higher-cost competition that they might eventually put out of business in the process would be some of the other, higher-cost members of Opec producing outside the Gulf.)

Those lowest-cost producers are probably also sceptical about engaging in price competition *à outrance,* and exploiting their full comparative advantage, because they do not believe that geopolitically it would ever be allowed to work. They doubt whether even such a transformation in pricing would exorcise importing governments' fears about security of supply or their yearnings for autarky. They suspect that in one way or another, governments of the importing countries would protect their oil consumers, let alone their high-cost domestic energy industries, from any responsive surge in demand. Avowed trade protection by tariffs or 'import fees' is not popular in principle; but during the early eighties, quite a number of non-Opec host governments were prepared to moderate their corporate taxes to keep local oil producers in business. Above all, excise taxation of transport fuels is

---

[6] In non-Opec oil, companies typically pay taxes of 80–85 per cent on their profits from production. So they would bear only 15 per cent of any cut in the crude price level that an Opec government might force. Their non-Opec host governments would suffer the rest of the price cut.

well established in most countries, and frequently advocated to save imported oil. Importing governments often used this in the past to siphon off a substantial share of Opec's monopoly rents on crude. Nowadays they might invoke the extra justification of environmental fears. Carbon taxation is an instrument already under discussion, and likely to remain popular in principle unless or until any of the currently fashionable green fears can be proved groundless.

In those few Gulf countries' own *political* circumstances, also, there is room for caution about seeking to flood the market by price-cutting. Saudi Arabia is the only country that has ever toyed with such a policy, in 1985–6. Obviously, it remains technically capable of doing so again. But as obviously, since 1990–1, it is more anxious than ever not to disturb its special relationship with the US. It still has good reason to fear its populous northern neighbours. Over time, Iraq as well as Iran will remain part of the political firmament of the Southern Gulf. Kuwait has been reduced to the political stature of the other small Gulf emirates in terms of any *independent* influence on Gulf Co-operation Council oil policy. Moreover, the limited moves towards democracy into which that close neighbour has been forced by Western opinion may give the Saudi royal family concern politically, for fear of sympathetic detonation. Iranian oil capacity appears to be the most expensive to extend of any in the Gulf; and its vast potential for exporting gas could only suffer from any lasting collapse in oil prices. Whichever government rules Iraq, albeit militarily crippled, it will remain a political wild card in the region. But open price-cutting seems hardly a strategy that could make sense for any Iraqi government in the nineties.

So even in Saudi Arabia, the motivation may not be there, if it remains optimistic about rebuilding its revenues *without* price-cutting for volume. Nevertheless, at the beginning of the nineties Saudi capacity was still underutilised. Moreover, by the mid-nineties, it and some of its neighbours are committed to increase this capacity substantially. Nothing can be more guaranteed to undermine the continuing hopes within Opec of re-establishing any firm price support.

If the Opec crude price cannot rise clear of its \$18–21/bbl price band (in nominal dollars) by the mid-nineties, then even Gulf conservatives may reconsider price-cutting to levels that non-Opec competition cannot sustain. That would at least test how low a return on investment in new production developers of equity crude and their non-Opec host governments *can* accept; and how much fiscal disadvantage importing governments are prepared to accept in order to go on giving preference to energy supply that they consider politically safer. If prices do move up slowly, but by no more than the inflation in prices of the manufactures that Opec imports, leaving oil revenues flat in real terms, then Gulf Opec's policy choices about price competition may become even more finely balanced.

It has to be noted that hardly any Opec member government outside the Gulf would share such a choice. Most other member countries have production costs closer to those of the more efficient non-Opec producers, and little spare capacity. They would have to participate in price competition, perforce. But they have no incentive to precipitate it.

### The Gulf beneath

Even if Gulf producers never in practice reduce their prices to clear the world energy market, they remain capable of doing so. Fundamentally, beneath the world's economically paradoxical oil market, there still hangs the current spare capacity of one or two Gulf producers, temporarily limited for the early nineties but once Iraqi oil returns instantly available. Next may come the extra capacity that several Opec member countries are now committed to repair or develop by about the mid-1990s. Below both yawn the huge reserves that no one in control of Middle East oil has ever yet been prepared to develop. Those may eventually cost more to develop than any investment ever previously made in the region. But they will also, undoubtedly, remain cheaper than developing additional energy production capacity anywhere else.

Oversimplifying and exaggerating sharply, one may perhaps sketch the implications of this potential competition graphically (Figure 12.2). In the early nineties, if it had been practicable to draw down Middle East reserves by say 4 per cent per year – i.e., applying R/P ratios roughly comparable with those that producers choose in developing oil elsewhere – then that one region could have supplied the whole 65–70 MBD of world oil demand. Such capacity would take years to develop, and at present nobody has the will or the capital resources required. But it is the prospect of this low-cost potential competition – constantly practicable, even if unlikely – that may sap the confidence of investors in oil and other energy development elsewhere.

A few analysts remain confident that suppliers outside the Gulf *can* develop enough oil and gas production to keep the world petroleum balance relatively undisturbed at present levels of price. Some of them are nevertheless highly conscious of the economic sacrifice that this would involve in efficiency forgone:

In so far as much of the use of this low-cost production is being replaced by the use of higher-cost energy production from other parts of the world, the inevitable consequence will be a reduction in the overall potential for economic

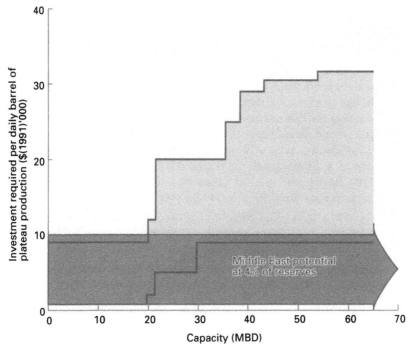

Figure 12.2. A sketch of world oil supply curves, actual and potential: reported ranges of oil development costs in early 1990s, as shown in Figure 3.1, compared with *potential* supply available from Gulf if Middle East reserves were produced with reserves/production ratio of 25:1.

growth in the western world's economic system. This means that fewer of the world's population will achieve an adequate standard of living, given that the ultimate penalty for not producing and using the world's lowest-cost energy resources is a lesser degree of economic development measured at the global level.[7]

If the world's lowest-cost energy were to be made available at its long-run supply cost, much of that ultimate penalty might initially be paid by oil producers outside Opec – but shared by their host governments, which currently tax away most of the fairly comfortable profits still being made on high-cost production. Others would have to pay this competitive penalty too: all the producers of other energy who benefit from the price umbrella that Opec, much of the time, still manages to hold above them.

[7] P. R. Odell, 'Continuing long-term hydrocarbons' dominance of world energy markets', World Renewable Energy Congress, Reading, UK, September 1990.

*Dreams of agreement*

Only a few academics can airily dismiss the possibility that the world will *eventually* need to rely more and more upon that lower-cost production (and not necessarily at lower prices). Inevitably many people will look beyond the 'clumsy cartel' pattern for some wondrous formula, fair to everyone, that ought to be able to gain Gulf producers a legitimate rent for their natural comparative advantage and, at the same time, gain world consumers relatively cheap access to this lowest-cost energy. No doubt, calls will be heard for some kind of commodity agreement as a panacea for this shared dilemma. Was this not said, in the most frequently quoted academic conclusion in petroleum economics, to have been the solution before?

Since World War II, in effect if not in form or intent, there has been and still exists an informal but effective commodity agreement in crude oil. The governments in the consuming countries restrained competition at home, and the international oil companies refrained from competing on price. Many would say that the commodity agreement worked very well. Large amounts of oil were forthcoming at a cost far below that of other sources of energy. The high price provided an incentive to establish reserves for a long period ahead. Be that as it may, we live with the consequences.[8]

Those consequences have become yet larger, and more ambiguous in terms of costs and benefits, in the twenty years since that was published.

Yet again, for some politicians and bureaucrats on both sides, hopes spring eternal of solutions via government-to-government dialogue between exporting and importing countries. But no practical prospect of any commodity agreement, formal or informal, seems on the cards at present. For the nineties, the interest seems to be rather more in scenarios aimed towards regional self-sufficiency in energy as well as other necessities. Mexico has been invited into a free trade area that has begun with North America, but may be extended to include Venezuela and other South American oil producers. A 'European Energy Charter' has been proposed to combine finance from Western Europe with ex-Soviet petroleum resources to develop greater self-sufficiency for an extended 'greater Europe'.[9] If the Russian and other ex-Soviet republics gain Japanese support to finance further development of East Siberian oil and gas resources, that could afford a stronger energy base for the North Pacific region. Whether or not any of those trading scenarios material-

---

[8] M. A. Adelman, *The World Petroleum Market* (Resources for the Future and Johns Hopkins University Press, 1972), p. 198.
[9] Communication [to the EEC at a Dublin conference] on A European Energy Charter, Dutch Government, Dublin, June 1990.

ise, they all represent further aspirations, from the world's largest oil-importing regions, to reduce dependence upon the Gulf.

All energy producers, except perhaps one, may feel that their present circumstances could hardly be improved by any downward slide in price levels. Many of the most influential governments involved, from the superpower level on down, probably prefer the current price level, perhaps gradually increasing in real terms, to any other.

In the late eighties Opec was wont to complain that it was supporting the world oil price without any help whatever from other oil suppliers. Within its limits, it was indeed doing so. Non-Opec energy suppliers continue to gain more than Opec from this lopsided supply balance. Their unit profits are far more modest, but earned on larger volumes of high-cost energy than they would probably have found worth while to have developed in fully competitive circumstances.

Even if one is prepared to gamble that this huge potentially cheap supply will in fact continue to be held off the market – which is what everyone developing energy elsewhere nowadays *is* gambling, consciously or not – this ever-present 'Gulf beneath' cannot but keep prices precarious, and increase the risks inherent in the development of all other higher-cost energy.

Cui bono?

Ideally, it can be argued that energy consumers across the rest of the world would have been better off if Gulf oil had been cheaper to *buy*, as well as to produce, than any other form of energy. Some analysts would qualify this argument: 'unmitigated benefits to consumers where excise taxes were not raised, and to some small oil-importing developing countries'.[10] The few key producers in Gulf Opec might have benefited too. In that event, world demand for oil might have been rising more closely towards its former trajectory. But as the same writer added, 'the forces that oppose a low oil price state of the world are very powerful indeed'.

If Middle East oil were dependably available at any price closer to its medium-run incremental supply cost delivered to markets, then a good deal of non-Opec oil and other energies would be hard put to compete. But at such lower ruling prices, more energy of all kinds might in fact be used. Gulf oil might gain its 'due' lion's share of an expanding energy consumption. That *might* give its lowest-cost producers more chance of regaining the levels of oil revenues that they had in the seventies than the

[10] R. Mabro, *Oxford Energy Forum* ( Oxford Institute for Energy Studies, 1991).

present alternative course – restricting output in order to maintain prices at which all sorts of non-Gulf energy can be developed, and will be.

Any such 'competitive' trajectory of energy demand, if adopted earlier, might however have collided with the new environmental anxieties that have been recognised since the seventies even sooner than the higher-priced, lower-volume energy trajectory that we are still riding. Without the two price shocks, oil consumption would almost certainly have been higher by now. So, probably, would total energy consumption have been. (Both however might have gone along with a somewhat steadier growth in income for OECD, Opec as a whole, and perhaps the whole non-Communist world.)

It is harder to guess how the balance of *environmental* effects might have differed between these alternative growth scenarios for energy demand and supply. The high oil-price path followed since 1973 certainly reduced oil consumption, and probably total fossil fuel consumption, during the eighties. Within that reduced total, more gas has been used than might have been otherwise (generating less carbon dioxide and pollutants); by the same token more coal (the worst contributor to pollution and greenhouse effects) has been used; and perhaps a little more nuclear electricity has been brought in (which remains unfathomable in its diverse environmental implications, but at least does not help warm the greenhouse).

So much – which remains ambiguous – for the recent past. Looking forward, this book has discussed the possibility of slower growth in world oil demand and a shallow dome or plateau in oil supply, which could begin to level off early next century. Oil is of course only one component of world energy, and there is no sign at all of any levelling off in total demand for energy. However sceptical one may be of our recurrent Malthusian anxieties, demographic vistas for the coming century remain daunting. Current projections imply an increase of 40–60 per cent in world population by the year 2020, and of perhaps 100 per cent by 2050. (Such extrapolations may look extreme; but world population has already doubled in the past forty years.) However population growth does turn out, most of it is certain to occur in developing countries. Their ambitions, global warming or not, include better lives for their peoples. Historically, such social improvements have never occurred without the enjoyment by everyone concerned of services that demand higher energy use. So in the countries among those that achieve economic take-off, energy demand would be expected to grow even faster than their populations. The others may simply get poorer.

Price-cutting by Gulf Opec might possibly be argued to be *economically* optimal for oil – in the medium run and in some 'global' sense. During this decade, moreover, it has become meaningful for the first time to talk about a 'global economy' as more than simply an assemblage of statistical aggregates. But if that reduction in prices were to increase total energy consumption, it would probably not be *environmentally* optimal. Also, such a reversal of pricing policy would be at the expense of most other energy production. It would certainly make all higher-cost energy production outside the Gulf, including perhaps the least environmentally harmful, less profitable to develop.

Desirable or not, and economically logical as it might seem in a world that would be ideal for some, that course of policy seems on balance unlikely to be adopted. If the price of oil can be held as high during the nineties as most people interested in this industry seem to desire, then development of some of the remaining reserves that would be cheapest to produce will probably continue to be postponed. Much of this oil – so far as we know, the world's cheapest energy – may not be produced for decades, even if world energy demand does go on growing. The paradox may indeed remain sustainable.

APPENDIX 1

# What are oil reserves?

In Chapter 2, present estimates of proved reserves, and their relevance to current production, were briefly discussed. Looking farther ahead, the whole concept of oil resources and reserves needs widening out. The US Geological Survey, since 1980, has defined:

*Resources* as concentrations of naturally occurring liquid or gaseous material in or on the Earth's crust in such form and amount that economic extraction from the concentration is currently or potentially feasible. These may be *measured, demonstrated,* or only *inferred* or *undiscovered.*

*Reserves* as that part of the resources demonstrated *in place* which could be economically extracted or produced at the time of determination (though not necessarily being extracted yet). Nowadays, reserves include only recoverable material, and no *sub-economic resources* that are not yet economic to produce. *Original reserves* are current reserves plus cumulative production to date.

The nomenclature is constantly being amended by the *cognoscenti* to refine its precision (although not always its clarity to laymen).

There is no scarcity of fossil fuels in the earth. Oil is not the most abundant of them: accumulations of coal are three to four times as large in energy content, and reserves of gas are probably comparable with those of oil. The oil produced today has simply been for half a century, and remains, the most readily accessible of these fossil fuels.

Earth scientists can reach professionally informed conjectures as to the amounts of oil, gas and coal that may exist 'in place' within certain geological strata under the earth's surface. More practically, they can guess at the proportions of these fossil fuel accumulations that may become recoverable, given current technology and economic conditions (and in some cases, such improvements as they expect by the time that exploration can discover all these accumulations). The proportions of the fuel accumulations actually discovered so far are what the industry usually describes as 'proved' reserves. (In some countries reserve figures published include part of those considered 'probable' and 'possible'.)

288

A consensus of earth scientists in the late eighties was that perhaps 70–75 per cent of the 'conventional oil' in place (defined as oil of the API gravities now generally being produced, 20 degrees API and above) had already been discovered. Of this perhaps 30–35 per cent was considered recoverable. About 10 per cent of the oil in place discovered so far, and thus close on 40 per cent of the amount expected to be recoverable, has already been produced. The discovered *and* recoverable amount remaining makes up the industry's current proved reserves of around a trillion barrels (see Table App.1).

By the same consensus reckoning, there may be about half as much again of conventional oil in place undiscovered, still to be found. If one assumes the same 'recovery factor' for undiscovered as for discovered oil, then the total reserves of conventional oil expected to be proved and ultimately recoverable work out to something over 2,000 billion barrels, of which about 30 per cent had been produced up to 1990 (and perhaps another 20 per cent, at end-1987, remained to be discovered).

As noted in Chapter 2, most of the oil in place so far discovered is in 313 giant fields; the rest in some 40,000 smaller fields. More than 60 per cent of the total resource is conventional oil, of the gravities defined above. These gravities make up nearly 90 per cent of today's oil production. Behind them rank further resources of 'unconventional oil', extra heavy crudes (below 10 degrees API) and natural bitumens that usually need special treatment to bring to the surface and transport. Present production of these heavier forms of petroleum now amounts to only about 11 per cent of world oil production. The giant fields mentioned above may include around fifty giant accumulations of these heavier grades (though two experts may classify the same field differently). These include the world's largest single accumulations of oil in place, Venezuela's Orinoco 'tarbelt' and Canada's Athabasca tar sands. The proportions of these forms of oil that will eventually become recoverable are unknown. But their recovery factor is certain to be much lower than that of conventional oil. If one assumes a recovery factor of 15 per cent for these heavier crudes, they might add about 30 per cent to the ultimately recoverable (now called 'original') reserves of conventional oil so far considered.

Table App.1 draws upon various expert assessments to hazard an extraordinarily approximate stocktaking of these successive layers of oil, in place in the earth, and potentially recoverable to varying degrees now and in the future. It is only a guesstimate of comparative orders of magnitude. Its most notable implication is that the average recovery factors experts are so far assuming are low: less than 30 per cent for conventional oil, and perhaps only 15 per cent for the heavier forms of

290 What are oil reserves?

Table App. 1. *Possible world petroleum occurrences as at end-1987*
*(billion barrels)*

| Oil in place | | Recoverable | |
|---|---|---|---|
| *Conventional oil* | | | |
| In 265 giant fields | 2,775 | Current reserves | 1,050 |
| In *c.* 40,000 | | (Proved 900) | |
|   smaller fields | 2,119 | (Probable 150) | |
| | —— | Produced to 1987 | 560 |
| | | | |
| Discovered | 4,894 | Discovered | 1,610 |
| Inferred/undiscovered | 2,267 | Undiscovered | 369 |
| | —— | | |
| | | Original reserves | |
| Total | 7,161 |   (at 29% average recovery) | 2,000 |
| *Heavy oil and natural bitumen* | | | |
| In *c.* 48 giant fields | | | |
|   and deposits | 882 | Current reserves | 606 |
| In smaller accumulations | 2,024 |   (Demonstrated 636) | |
| | —— | Produced to 1987 | 30 |
| | | | |
| Discovered/demonstrated | 2,906 | Discovered | 636 |
| Inferred/undiscovered | 1,171 | Undiscovered | 436 |
| | —— | | |
| | | Original reserves | |
| Total | 4,077 |   (at 15% average recovery) | 612 |

| | | |
|---|---|---|
| *Giant fields and deposits* | | |
| Conventional oil | 2,775 | |
| Heavy oil and natural bitumen | 882 | |
| | —— | |
| Total giant accumulations | 3,657 | |
| *Smaller fields and deposits* | 4,143 | |
| | —— | |
| Known resources | | 7,800 |
| Inferred/undiscovered | | 3,438 |
| | | —— |
| 'Ultimate' oil and natural bitumen *resource* | | 11,238 |
| 'Ultimate' reserve (at 23% average recovery) | | 2,612 |
| Produced to end-1987 | | 560 |

*Sources:* Roadifer (Mobil), 'Size distribution'; Meyer (USGS) and Duford (BP), 'Resources of heavy oil and natural bitumen'; Masters *et al.* (USGS), 'Resource constraints'.

oil; and that only about 20 per cent of the original reserve has been produced so far.

(Yet further behind the heavy crudes and bitumens there are huge resources of oil shales available. Those are solid fuels, not so different from coal, which usually need some form of mining before they can be processed to extract liquid hydrocarbons. Their costs are of a different order for significant volumes than those of conventional oil, and they are not included in this table.)

It has to be repeated that some geologists and other analysts disagree sharply with any such consensus, and argue that the oil resources originally in place, and potentially recoverable even though still to be discovered, are far larger than those considered in the table. Even if the resources are not underestimated, improvements in recovery factors through technological progress could still greatly increase the reserves practicable to obtain from them.

Ordinary people have no way of judging between these conflicting expert assessments, and fortunately have no need to. If there were a comparably expert – and articulate – minority at the other extreme, arguing that oil reserve depletion is already further advanced than we think, we might need to worry. There is not.

# A note on energy and oil statistics

Three main statistical sources are used for the many measures of oil and other forms of energy cited in this book. These were British Petroleum's annual *Statistical Review*, published since 1959, with some oil data reaching back to 1938; the United Nations *Yearbook of World Energy*, with data for all forms of energy back to 1950; and the OECD/IEA publications on *Energy Balances*, published since 1976, with data for OECD countries back to 1960. A few other sources are used for certain long-run historical series.[1]

Since the book frequently uses parallel data series from these sources for historical reference, it has to be noted that they are not precisely comparable. Statistics from them differ considerably in details of coverage and definitions, notably as regards energy trade; and have until recently followed different conventions for the 'energy equivalents' that they apply to express the main commercial primary fuels and forms of electricity in common units of measurement. (Solid fuels, oil and other liquid fuels, natural gases, and electricity from hydropower, geothermal, tidal or wind resources are primary energy. Electricity generated from fossil or nuclear fuels in power stations is secondary energy. Fuelwood and a wide range of other 'vegetal fuels' are generally considered 'non-commercial' and left out of national and world energy statistics.)

Energy equivalent values for the fossil fuels are fairly standardised, though BP uses averaged international values – i.e. one tonne of oil equals 1.5 tonnes of coal, 3 tonnes of lignite, and 1.111 cubic metres of natural gas – while the UN and IEA apply separate national averages for the fuels in each country. But BP and IEA now use different conventions from those used by the UN to value primary electricity from hydropower and other natural sources, *and* secondary electricity from nuclear stations, in common units with the recorded amounts of fossil fuels burned in thermal power stations.

[1] Notably, Gilbert Jenkins, *Oil Economists' Handbook*, 5th edn (Elsevier, 1989).

BP until 1991, and IEA until 1990, valued such primary electricity according to the 'oil equivalent' amounts of primary fuels that would need to be burned in a modern power station of 38.5 per cent thermal efficiency to produce the same number of kilowatt-hours. However, the kilowatt-hour is a precise measure of both heat and work. So UN statistics valued the various primary forms of electricity according to its full 'true' heat equivalent. That would imply electricity generation under ideal conditions, with 100 per cent efficiency, i.e. using no more primary fuel than the kWh heat value of the electricity output.

The 'partial substitution' method used by BP and IEA thus valued primary and nuclear electricity with about two-and-a-half times as much oil equivalent as the 'true heat value' method used by the UN, and tended to magnify the proportions of these kinds of electricity generation in total energy statistics. IEA since 1991, and BP since 1992, have changed the method they use. They still value hydropower and other non-thermal generation with the full heat value of electricity. But they now apply the actual thermal efficiencies achieved in geothermal stations (10 per cent) and in nuclear stations (33 per cent) to express the electricity generated in such stations in primary fuel oil equivalent. The effect is to reduce the oil equivalent value and shares of total energy represented by hydropower, tidal power and wind; but to increase the oil equivalent values and shares in total energy of nuclear electricity slightly and of geothermal electricity sharply. (The net effect of these changes in method, however, for the year 1988, was not very substantial except in particular countries. For OECD as a whole, it altered the total share of all these forms of non-thermal electricity in total primary energy supply only from 15 per cent to 13 per cent.) Up to mid-1992, when this book was completed, the UN had not published any statistics suggesting changes in its own method, to which the other two are now more closely assimilated.

The statistics in this book, which are strictly illustrative, draw eclectically upon all three sources as published up to 1991, i.e. *before* IEA's and BP's changes.

# Bibliography

*BP Statistical Review of World Energy* (BP, London, 1991 and earlier editions).
*Energy Balances of OECD Countries* (OECD/IEA, Paris, 1990 and earlier editions).
*Middle East Economic Survey* (*MEES*), Nicosia.
*Oil & Gas Journal* (*OGJ*), Tulsa, Oklahoma.
*Opec Annual Statistical Bulletin* (Opec, Vienna, 1990 and earlier editions).
*Petroleum Economist*, London.
*Petroleum Intelligence Weekly* (*PIW*), New York
*Yearbook of World Energy Statistics* (United Nations, New York, 1989 and earlier editions).

Adelman, Morris A., 'Oil production costs in four areas', *Proceedings of the Council of Economics, American Institute of Mining, Metallurgical and Petroleum Engineers*, 1966 (reprinted, *MIT Publications in Economics*, series 4, no. 30, Cambridge, Mass., 1966).
    *The World Petroleum Market* (Johns Hopkins University Press for Resources for the Future, 1972).
    'Oil producing countries' discount rates', *Resources and Energy*, 8(1986), pp. 309–29.
    'Mideast governments and the oil prospect', *Energy Journal*, 10(1989), no. 2, pp. 15–24.
    'Mineral depletion, with special reference to petroleum', *Review of Economics and Statistics*, 72(1990), no. 1, pp. 1–10.
    'Modelling world oil supply', *Energy Journal*, 14(1993), no. 1 (special issue *in memoriam* David Wood).
Ait-Laoussine, Nordine (Algerian Minister of Energy), 'Pricing of oil: the need for a new stabilising mechanism', Oxford Energy Seminar, September 1991; reprinted in *MEES*, 16 September 1991.
Barnes, Philip, *The OIES Review of Energy Costs* (Oxford Institute for Energy Studies, 1990).
Baxendell, Sir Peter, 'Enhanced oil recovery – making the most of what we've got', Institute of Mining and Metallurgy (Shell Briefing Service, London, 1984).
Begg, David, Stanley Fischer and Rudiger Dornbusch, *Economics* (McGraw Hill, 1984).

Bird, Peter J. W. N, 'Continuity and reversal in oil spot price movements', *Energy Economics*, April 1987, pp. 73–81.

Bradley, Paul G., *The Economics of Crude Petroleum Production* (North-Holland, 1967).

'Production of depleting resources: a cost-curve approach' (MIT Center for Energy Policy Research, Cambridge, Mass., 1979).

Browne, John, 'Meeting the oil needs of the nineties', paper presented at the *Oil and Money Conference*, London, November 1991.

Centre for Global Energy Studies [London], 'The cost of additional oil production capacity in the Gulf', *Global Energy Report*, January–February 1991.

'The importance of the call on Opec oil', *Global Energy Report*, July–August 1991.

'The costs of future North Sea oil production', *Global Energy Report*, January–February 1992.

Chalabi, Fadhil al-, and Adnan al-Janabi, 'Optimum production and pricing policies', in *OPEC: 20 Years and Beyond* (Westview Croom Helm, 1982), pp. 229–58.

de Chazeau, Melvin G., and Alfred E. Kahn, *Integration and Competition in the Petroleum Industry* (Yale University Press, 1959).

Cleveland, Cutter J., and Robert K. Kaufman, 'Forecasting ultimate oil recovery and its rate of production', Energy Journal 12 (1991), no. 2, pp. 17–46.

Dasgupta, Partha, and Geoffrey M. Heal, *Economic Theory and Exhaustible Resources* (Nisbet and Cambridge University Press, 1979).

Drollas, Leo, 'Oil supplies and the world oil market in the long run', paper presented at the International Association of Energy Economists Conference, Tokyo, June 1986.

'The search for oil in the USA', *Energy Economics*, July 1986, pp. 155–64.

Drollas, Leo, and Jon Greenman, *Oil: The Devil's Gold* (Duckworth, 1989).

Eden, Richard, Michael Posner, Richard Bending, Edmund Crouch and Joe Stanislaw, *Energy Economics: Growth, Resources and Policies* (Cambridge University Press, 1981).

Fathi, Saadalla al-, 'The prospects for oil prices, supply and demand', *Opec Review*, Winter 1991.

Frank, Helmut J., *Crude Oil Prices in the Middle East* (Praeger, 1966).

Frankel, Paul H., *Essentials of Petroleum* (Chapman & Hall, 1946).

Gault, John, 'Short and long term impacts of the Gulf crisis on oil markets', paper presented at the Electric Power Research Institute *Fuel Supply Seminar*, Albuquerque, New Mexico, October 1991.

(ed.) 'The petroleum industry: entering the 21st century', *Energy Policy* 20 (1992), no. 10.

Gochenour, D. Thomas, 'The coming capacity shortfall', *Energy Policy*, 20 (1992), no. 10, pp. 973–82.

Griffin, James M., and Henry B. Steele, *Energy Economics and Policy* (Academic Press, 1980).

Griffin, James M., and David J. Teece (eds.), *OPEC Behaviour and World Oil Prices* (Allen & Unwin, 1982).

Hartshorn, Jack, *Oil Companies and Governments* (Faber & Faber, 1962).

*Objectives of the Petroleum Exporting Countries* (Middle East Petroleum and Economic Publications, Nicosia, 1978).

Heal, David, 'Efficiency or self-sufficiency: choices for energy consumers', *Energy Policy*, 20 (1992), no. 10, pp. 942–9.

Heal, Geoffrey M., and Graciela Chichilnisky, *Oil and the International Economy* (Clarendon Press, 1991).

Holmes, Sir Peter, 'Energy prospects for the nineties', Royal Institute of International Affairs, April 1991 (Shell Briefing Service, London, 1991).

Hotelling, Harold, 'The economics of exhaustible resources', *Journal of Political Economy*, 31(1939), pp. 137–75.

Hubbert, M. King, 'Nuclear energy and the fossil fuels: drilling and production practice', American Petroleum Institute, Dallas, Texas, 1956, pp. 7–25.

*Energy Resources*, US National Academy of Sciences, National Research Council (US Department of Commerce, 1962).

'Degree of advancement of petroleum exploration in United States', *American Association of Petroleum Geologists' Bulletin*, 51(1967), pp. 2207–27.

'Techniques of prediction as applied to the production of oil and gas', in proceedings of a symposium held at the US Department of Commerce, Washington, D.C., June 1980 (US Department of Commerce, May 1982).

International Energy Agency, *World Energy Outlook* (OECD/IEA, Paris, 1982).

*Energy Policies of IEA Countries, 1990 Review* (OECD/IEA, Paris, 1991).

*An Analysis of Energy Policy Measures and their Impact on $CO_2$ Emissions* (OECD/IEA, Paris, 1991).

Ivanhoe, L. F., 'Future crude oil supply and prices', *OGJ*, 25 July 1988, pp. 111–12.

Jacoby, Neil H., *Multinational Oil: A Study in Industrial Dynamics* (Macmillan, 1974).

Jennings, John, 'Oil industry perspectives in the 1990s – upstream', paper presented at the *Oil and Money Conference*, London, November 1991.

Johany, Ali M., 'OPEC is not a cartel: a property rights explanation of the rise in crude oil prices' (Ph.D. dissertation, University of California, Santa Barbara, 1978).

Johnson, S. P., *World Population and the United Nations* (Cambridge University Press, 1987).

Kelly, Michael, 'Restructuring of the world oil market', Annual Meeting, National Petroleum Refiners' Association, San Francisco, 1989.

Khadr, Ali M., *Fiscal Regime Uncertainty, Risk Aversion, and Exhaustible Resource Depletion* (Oxford Institute for Energy Studies, 1987).

Mabro, Robert, 'OPEC after the oil revolution', in *OPEC and the World Oil Market*, ed. Mabro (Oxford University Press, 1986).

'OPEC and the price of oil', *Energy Journal*, 13(1992), no. 2, pp. 1–20.

Mabro, Robert, Robert Bacon, Margaret Chadwick, Mark Halliwell and David Long, *The Market for North Sea Crude Oil* (Oxford Institute for Energy Studies and Oxford University Press, 1986).

MacAvoy, Paul W., *Crude Oil Prices: as Determined by OPEC and Market Fundamentals* (Ballinger, 1983).

Macrae, Elizabeth C., and J. Erich Evered, *Exploring for Oil and Gas* (US Energy Administration, 1984).

Manne, Alan S., and Leo Schrattenholzer, 'The International Energy Workshop: a progress report', *OPEC Review*, Winter 1989, pp. 415–28.

Manne, Alan S., Leo Schrattenholzer and Keith Marchant, 'The 1991 International Energy Workshop: the poll results and a review of papers', *OPEC Review*, Winter 1991, pp. 389–411.

Masters, Charles D., Emil D. Attanasi, William D. Dietzman, Richard F. Meyer, Robert W. Mitchell and David H. Root, 'World resources of crude oil, natural gas, natural bitumen, and shale oil', in *Proceedings of the 12th World Petroleum Congress* (Wiley, 1987), pp. 3–27.

Masters, Charles D., David H. Root and Emil D. Attanasi (United States Geological Survey), 'Resource constraints in petroleum production potential', *Science*, July 1991, pp. 146–52.

Mead, Walter J., 'An economic analysis of crude oil price behaviour in the 1970s', *Journal of Energy and Development* (University of Colorado), Spring 1979, pp. 212–28.

Meyer, Richard F., and J. Richard Duford, 'Resources of heavy oil and natural bitumen worldwide', 4th Unitar/UNDP International Conference on Heavy Crude and Tar Sands, Edmonton, Canada, August 1988, paper no. 147, pp. 277–307.

Moran, Theodore, 'Managing an oligopoly of would-be sovereigns', *International Organisation*, Autumn 1987, pp. 575–607.

Odell, Peter R., *An Economic Geography of Oil* (Bell, 1963).

*Oil and World Power* (Penguin, 1986).

'Continuing long-term hydrocarbons' dominance of world energy markets', World Renewable Energy Congress, Reading, UK, September 1990.

Odell, Peter R., and K. E. Rosing, *The Future of Oil* (Kegan Paul, 1983).

Penrose, Edith F., *The Large International Firm in Developing Countries: The International Petroleum Industry* (Allen & Unwin, 1968).

Roadifer, R. E., 'Size distribution of the world's largest known oil and tar accumulations', in *Exploration for Heavy Crude Oil and Natural Bitumen*, ed. R. F. Meyer (American Association of Petroleum Geologists Studies in Geology, no. 25, 1984), pp. 3–23.

Robinson, Colin, 'The changing energy market: what can we learn from the last ten years?' (University of Surrey, Guildford, 1983).

Robinson, M. Silvan, 'Oil trading: yesterday, today, and tomorrow', in *The Oil Market in the 1990s*, ed. R. G. Reed and F. Fesharaki (Westview Press, 1989), pp. 162–71.

'If oil is a commodity, why not manage it that way?', *MEES*, 4 January 1988.

'Short-term influences and long-term fundamentals: stabilising and destabilising effects in the energy industries', *Energy Policy*, 20 (1992), no. 10, pp. 1015–21.

Roeber, Joe, 'Flexible response: the best hope for Opec', *MEES*, 25 January 1988.

*Rue Management and Oil Crisis* (Royal Institute of International Affairs, London, 1993).

Sampson, Anthony, *The Seven Sisters: The Great Oil Companies and the World They Shaped* (Viking Press, 1975).

Seymour, Ian, *OPEC, Instrument of Change* (Macmillan, 1980).

Skeet, Ian, *OPEC: Twenty-five Years of Prices and Politics* (Cambridge University Press, 1988).

Solow, Robert, 'The economics of resources and the resources of economics', *American Economic Review*, 64(1974), pp. 1–14.

Stauffer, Thomas, 'Crude oil production costs in the Middle East', *MEES*, 25 January 1993.

Stiglitz, Joseph, 'Monopoly and the rate of extraction of exhaustible resources', *American Economic Review*, 66(1976), pp. 655–61.

Treat, John Elting (ed.), *Energy Futures: Trading Opportunities for the 1990s* (Pennwell, Tulsa, Oklahoma, 1990).

United States Energy Information Administration, *International Energy Outlook: A Postwar Review of Energy Markets* (US Government Printing Office, 1991).

Walters, Sir Peter, Cadman Lecture, Institute of Petroleum, December 1989.

Woods, Thomas J., 'Resource depletion and lower 48 oil and gas discovery rates', *OGJ*, 28 October 1985.

Yergin, Daniel, *The Prize* (Simon and Schuster, 1991).

Zimmerman, E. S., *World Resources and Industries* (Harper, 1951).

# Index

Abqaiq, 60, 62
Abu Dhabi
  attitudes to Opec quota, 181, 189
  concessions not fully nationalised, 127–8
  development costs and production decline
    rates, 64
Adelman, M. A.
  'Hotelling theorem' of mineral depletion,
    185n
  MIT 'surrogate costings' of Opec
    production, 70–1, 72
  on oil production costs, 54, 64n, 67n
  Opec as a 'clumsy but successful' cartel,
    179n
  Opec governments' discount rates,
    149–51, 156–8
  pre-Opec 'informal but effective
    commodity agreement in crude oil',
    284n
  prospects for non-Opec production, 275n
Agha Jari, 61
Ait-Laoussine, N., 223n
al-Chalabi, F., 145n
al-Chalabi, Isam, 191
al-Janabi, A., 145n
al-Mazeedi, W., 140n
al-Sabah, Shaikh Ali Khalifah, 169, 189,
  192n
Alaska, 7, 15, 21, 82–4, 227
alcohol additives to gasoline, 109
Alfonzo, P., 174, 174–5, 177, 180, 186
Algeria
  more important as exporter of gas than
    oil, 172, 223
  nationalisation law revised, 128
  renewed co-operation with foreign
    companies for LNG exports, 128
allowables as annual limits to production,
  efficacy, 182–3
American Petroleum Institute (API)

gravity of crude oils, definition, 49n
'proved reserves', definition, 235
Aramco (pre-nationalisation)
  estimates of historical costs to mid-1970s
    and predictions for 1980s, 65
  plans for Saudi Arabian plateau
    production, 61, 155–6
  shareholder companies (Exxon, Mobil,
    Texaco and Socal) as four of 'Seven
    Sisters', 114; co-operation after
    nationalisation, 131–2
Attanasi, E. D., 235n
Australia, 17, 87, 109

Bank of Credit and Commerce International
  (BCCI), 128, 141
Baxendell, Sir P., 241n
Belgium, 127
Benelux countries, influence of spot products
  markets, 212
Bird, P. J. W. N., 218n
Bradley, P. G., 54, 56n, 158n
Bridgeman, Sir Maurice, 144
British National Oil Corporation (BNOC),
  199n
British Petroleum (BP)
  in development North Sea, 76–7
  disagreements with Shell over crude prices
    in mid-1990s, 263–4
  estimates of ultimate crude reserves, 241,
    247
  in Kuwait concession, 153–4
  Kuwaiti shareholding reduced, 161
  'Seven Sisters', 114
  Statistical Reviews of World Energy,
    292–3
Browne, J., 264n
Burgan, 60, 153, 186
Bush, G.
  as US President: defeat and reversal Iraqi

299

invasion of Kuwait, 22; indirect US
control of Opec production through
embargo on Iraq, 170; national energy
policy, 22, 110
as US Vice-President, 1986 mission to
Riyadh, 22

California
clean fuels, 110
enhanced recovery, 235, 248n
Canada, 19, 68, 162, 248
Athabasca tar sands, 108, 289
capital investment in oil industry
apparent reductions in Gulf investment
advantages, 65–7
in integrated operations, 120
as main purpose of industry forecasting,
255–8
MIT 'surrogate costings', 70–3
in non-Opec countires, 57, 59, 63, 64, 67,
69
in Opec countries, neglect during 1980s,
62–3
Opec plans and budgets for 1990s, 66, 67
per daily barrel of plateau production
from additional capacity, net and gross,
57, 63, 64
to develop production, 52, 54, 55
to offset decline, 64–5
capital markets, international
North Sea financing, 78
Opec governments, as investors in 1970s,
161–2, and as borrowers in 1990s, 66,
131
carbon
content in fossil fuels, 111
emissions, 110–11, 266–71
carbon taxes, 268, 281
Caribbean refineries, 100, 127, 134, 206
cartels, 10, 167–8, 169–70
catalytic crackers, 103, 106
centrally planned economies (CPEs),
self-sufficiency in energy and oil, 80, 82,
91
Centre for Global Energy Studies (CGES),
64n, 65n, 262–3
Chase Manhattan, 68–73
Chevron (Socal), 114–15, 136
Chichilnisky, G., 162n, 185n
China, 17n, 20, 34, 38, 39, 68, 80, 91, 106,
113, 138
Cleveland, C. J., 233n
coal, 17, 34–5, 85, 90, 92, 100, 110, 248, 249
Colombia, 17, 87
Commission of the European Communities,
267

commodity agreement, 284
Compagnie Française des Pétroles, 114, 139
comparative advantage, principle, 2, 279
comparative production costs, 9, 65–9, 72
MIT 'surrogate cost' estimates, 70–2
compensatory financing, 193
Continental Oil, 263
costs, *see* production costs; transport costs
crude oil
chemical composition, 93–4
qualities, 49, 99
spot market, 196–206
*see also* market markers

decline rates in field production, 58
Abu Dhabi estimates, 64
decline offset investment, 63–5
effect on costs of net and gross additions
to production capacity, 63–5
Gulf, 61–4
US, 59
Venezuela, 63
deintegration, 197
demand for oil
compared with total energy and economic
growth, 4–5, 256–7
and costs, 279–80
geographical distribution, 37–41
growth outside OECD, 106–8
historical, 2–3
and prices, 285–6
projections, 253, 259, 262–6, 278–9
depletion rates, 59–60
OECD exporters' policies, 162
Opec policies, 160–2
depreciation, 156
developing countries, energy demand, 107–8,
264–5
diesel fuel, 94, 101, 113, 250
discount rates, 58
of concessionaires and Opec governments,
149–52, 156–60
public and private, 148–9, 157–9
*see also* reserve depletion rate
discounted cash flow analysis, 54
distillate fuel (gasoil), 98, 99
Dornbusch, R., 217n
Drollas, L. P., 185n, 234n, 246 and n
Dubai, 127, 201, 203, 206, 223
Duford, J. R., 290

economic growth
and energy demand, 4, 256–7
environmental effects, 266–7
and oil production costs, 282–3
sustainable, 145

economists' versus geologists' concepts of mineral resources, 242–3, 275
Ecuador, 128, 172
Eden, R., 25n
efficient markets hypothesis, 216–17
electricity, 13, 16–17, 102, 249
Elf, 129, 139
energy
  changes in demand, 13, 107–8, 264–5
  consumption trends, 4–5, 13–14, 38–41, 107–8, 264–5
  diversifying sources of, 90
  geographical pattern, 41, 43
  self-sufficiency, 85–7, 90–2
  statistics, 292–3
  *see also* coal; electricity; gas; nuclear power; oil; transport fuels
energy co-efficients, 13
energy efficiency, 90–1
energy ratios, 13
enhanced oil recovery (EOR), 62, 248
environmental factors, 7, 28, 109, 266–71, 286
equity oil, 123
ethanol, 109–10
ethers, 109
Evered, J. E., 44
expectations, 219, 254
  short-term, 220–1
exploration
  costs, 52
  success ratios, 53
  technology, 119
exports
  co-operation within Opec 'inner core', 190
  Middle East, 75
Exxon, 114, 187

Fahd, King, 154, 178
Faisal, King, 155
Fesheraki, F., 120n
Fischer, S., 217n
forecasts
  assumptions, 256
  attitudes towards, 254–7
  needed for investment decisions, 257–8
  range for the 1990s, 259–64, 278
  *see also* reserve estimates
forward markets
  Brent, 208–9, 218
France, 18, 20, 90, 101, 114, 139, 212
Frankel, P. H., 93n
futures markets, crude oil, 206–11
  efficiency, 216–20
  International Petroleum Exchange (IPE), 209, 214

New York Mercantile Exchange (Nymex), 206, 213–14, 218
  products, 213–14

Gabon, 128, 172
gasoline, 94, 98, 99, 101
  unleaded, 109
GATT, 168
geologists, versus resource economists, 242–3, 275
Germany, 18, 20, 90, 92, 112, 127, 138, 212
Ghawar, 51, 60, 62, 105
global warming, 7, 267, 268
Greaves, W., 211n
Greenman, J., 185n
Griffin, J. M., 119n, 162n
Groningen gasfield, 79, 101
Gulf, Persian/Arabian, 114–15, 136, 153, 154
Gulf Co-operation Council, 281
Gulf of Suez, 190
Gulf war
  first (1980–8), 27, 65, 124, 190, 197
  second (1990–1), 2, 6, 23, 27, 65, 124, 125–7, 190, 258, 279

Hartshorn, J. E., 119n
Hassi Messaoud, 128
Heal, D., 85n, 86
Heal, G. M., 162n, 185n
Holmes, Sir P., 264n
horizontal integration, 117–18
Horton, R., 23
host governments, 143–4
  nationalist leverage, 180–2
Hotelling, H., 184–5
Hubbert, M. King, 225–6, 229–36, 238, 240, 243–8
Hussein, Saddam, 151, 170, 190
hydropower, 249

Ibn Saud, King, 187
IMF, 167
India, 113
Indonesia, 66, 128, 151, 171, 172, 181, 243, 248
information, market, 120–1, 217, 218–19
integration, 6
  deintegration, 197
  downstream, 167
  horizontal, 117–18
  Opec impulse to reintegrate, 133–7
  vertical, 114–15, 118–21, 214–16;
    theoretical advantages and practical experience, 119–20; in gas exports, 128–30

International Energy Agency (IEA), 21, 171, 246, 292–3
    projections, 253–4, 257, 259–64, 268–70
International Energy Workshop (IEW), 252–4, 256, 262–3, 272
International Petroleum Exchange (IPE), 209, 214
Iran, 21, 25, 51, 62, 154, 159, 161, 174, 177, 184, 187, 189, 203, 237, 279, 281
    invaded, 176, 191
    investment, 66, 125, 132–3
    nationalisation, 140, 149
    nationalism, 143, 151, 180
    revolution, 143, 181
    *see also* Gulf war
Iraq, 37, 51, 138, 143, 151, 161, 170, 174, 184, 194, 203, 221, 281
    aggression, 23, 176, 191, 279
    disregard of Opec, 190–1
    investment, 66, 124–6, 132–3
    nationalisation, 140, 181
    reserves, 60, 189
    *see also* Gulf war
Iraq National Oil Company (INOC), 125
Islam, 143, 157–8, 191
Ismail, I. A. H., 62n, 65n
Israel, 22, 190
Italy, 101, 139, 161, 212
Ivanhoe, L. F., 275n

Japan, 85, 90, 99, 104, 109, 120, 200, 215, 284
    MITI, 103, 213
    natural gas, 18, 102
    oil demand, 101, 104
    oil imports, 20, 36, 75, 100, 106, 117
Jenkins, G., 292n
Johany, A. M., 148–9, 151, 156, 161
Johnson, S. P., 271
joint ventures, 119, 276–7
    in natural gas, 129–30
    new, 123–8
    in oilfield development, 130–3

Kaufman, R. K., 233n
Kelly, M., 116, 122
Kenai Peninsula, 225
kerosene, 94, 97, 98, 101, 250
Khadr, A. M., 159n
Kirkuk field, 190
Kissinger, H., 21
Kuparuk River, 227
Kuwait, 1, 24, 37, 51, 100, 106, 132, 134, 137, 138, 151, 155, 159, 161, 169, 177, 181, 184, 189, 191, 192, 194, 203, 281
    Burgan, 60, 153, 186

production limits, 153–4
    *see also* Gulf war

Libya, 24, 51, 143, 151, 161, 180–1, 187, 189, 212
logistic programming, 119–20
lubricating oils, 94

Mabro, R., 24n, 79n, 179n, 185n, 285n
MacAvoy, P. W., 24n, 179n
Macrae, E. C., 44
Manne, A. S., 253n, 254, 255, 270
marker prices, Arabian Light, 105, 195, 202–3, 205
market markers, 195
    Alaskan North Slope (ANS), 201–3
    Brent blend, 202–3, 205, 208–9, 218
    Fateh, 203, 223
    spot market in, 201–6
    West Texas Intermediate (WTI), 201–2, 205–6, 218
markets
    efficiency, 216–20
    immaturity, 218
    informal, 208
    information, 120–1, 217, 218–19
    'open outcry', 206–7
    structural changes, 23–4
    *see also* forward markets; spot markets
Marun, 61
Masters, C. D., 15, 26–7, 44, 235n, 273, 290
methanol, 110
Mexico, 15, 32, 51, 138, 149, 177, 199, 275, 284
    Chicontapec, 50
    Reforma and Campeche, 84
Meyer, R. F., 290
Miller, M. H., 185n
Mobil, 114, 136, 187
Mongolia, 91
Moran, T. H., 193n
Mossadegh, Dr, 180

naphthas, 103
National Iranian Oil Company (NIOC), 125
National Petroleum Council, US, 232
nationalisation, 125, 128, 132, 138–68, 181, 197
    extent of, 138
    fear of, 148
    reasons for, 140
natural gas, 17, 85, 89–90, 100–1, 109, 249–50, 277
    liquefied, 102, 128–30, 133
    reserves, 34–5, 288
Nazer, H., 134 and n, 171n

Netherlands, 19, 90
  Groningen, 79, 101
New York Mercantile Exchange (Nymex),
  206, 213, 214, 218
newly democratised countries, 106–7, 265–6
Nigeria, 51, 128–9, 151, 171, 172, 243
Nigerian National Petroleum Company,
  128–9
North Sea, 15, 35, 51, 64, 71, 75, 105, 199,
  201–2, 244
  development of, 82–4
  exploration success ratio, 53
  Forties, 76–7
  gas, 90, 101
  initial viability, 76–80
  R/P ratio, 48, 59
  reserves, 274–5
Norway, 19, 48, 79, 80, 87, 90, 162, 177,
  199, 274
nuclear power, 17, 18–19, 90, 249, 269

Odell, P. R., 31n, 247n
OECD, 38–9, 41, 57, 87, 102, 104–8, 134,
  215, 256–7, 263–4, 266–8, 292–3
  energy consumption, 40, 85, 95
oil, *see* crude oil; demand for oil; market
  markers; production; reserves; supply of
  oil
oil companies
  performance and ownership, 141
  state ownership, 138–68
  *see also* integration; nationalisation
oil importers, 20–2, 35–7
oil industry
  growth levelling off? 5–8
  historical output trends, 2–4
  maturity plus instability, 9
  risk management, 29
  supply capacity, 9–10
oil prices
  administration, 175, 182–3, 192, 195, 199
  changes, 8–9, 170–1
  and demand, 285–6
  'discovered' in open markets, 206
  impact on world economy, 12
  official government selling prices
    (OGSPs), 177
  'posted', 203, 206
  price-cutting, 281, 287
  and production costs, 280–2, 285
  projected, 253, 259, 262–6
  relationship between product and crude,
    216
  and reserve depletion rates, 159–60
  short and medium fluctuations, 220–1
  and short-term expectations, 220–1

sovereignty over, 182–3
spot, 211–18
stabilisation, 174, 191–4
supporters of, 19–23; *see also* Opec
  and surplus supply, 221–4
  two-tier, 188
oil pricing
  netback, 178, 195–6, 199–200, 214
  types of, 198
oil pricing policies, 78–9, 189–91, 278–9
  integrated companies, 214–16
  lack of, 183–6
oil proration, 153, 186, 187, 234
oil shales, 248
oil tankers, 73–4, 119
oil trade
  between nations, 31–3
  between regions, 31–3
  exports, 75, 190
  imports, 20–2, 35–7
  protection, 233–5
oilfield development, joint ventures, 130–3
Oman, 64, 201, 203
Opec
  cartel, 168
  core, 174
  economic interests, 145–7
  foreign exploration, 164
  founder members, 127
  General Agreement on Participation, 181
  impact of, 10–12, 16, 24–6, 28
  joint ventures, 130–1, 133
  Long-Term Strategy, 184
  Ministerial Executive Council, 177–8
  national oil companies, 164–7
  performance, 169–94
  price hike, 78–9, 83–4, 87, 104, 123, 176,
    179, 197
  pricing influence, 222–4
  pricing policy, 178–9, 197–201, 203, 205,
    278–9
  priorities, 166
  production programming, 174–5, 177
  projections, 253–4, 257, 259–64, 268–70
  quota system, 176–7, 179, 182–3; failures
    in, 169–71
  role in restructuring world industry,
    114–37
  a series of conferences, 182
  structural change, 141–2
  well drilling, 53
Orimulsion, 108–9, 249

Pemex, 84, 199
Penrose, E., 252
Petroleos de Venezuela SA, 64, 108–9

pipelines, 51, 99, 190
Piper Alpha, 130
Platt's oil price services, 212
political risks, 5–6, 54, 148–51, 160–1, 276–7
pollution, 110–12, 267
privatisation, 139–43
production
  accounting profile, 54, 55
  current, 41
  decline rate, 58–9, 62–4, 65
  excess capacity, 262, 282
  non-Opec, 80–5
  plateau, 54, 59–68
  public and private levels, 153–7
  US peak, 14, 225–8
  world, 14, 235–6
  *see also* supply of oil
production costs
  alternative energy sources, 248–51
  and demand, 279–80
  development, 52, 54, 77–8
  and economic growth, 282–3
  exploration, 52–3
  factors underlying, 50–1
  in the Gulf, 50–1, 68–73, 276
  international comparisons, 54, 56–9,
    68–73
  minimised by 'Seven Sisters' integration?
    120
  of operating aboard, 71–2
  and prices, 280–2, 285
  Soviet Union, 276
  time profiles, 55, 56
  transport, 73

productivity per well, 51, 70
products
  futures markets, 213–14
  spot markets and prices, 211–18
profits, upstream, 123
Prudhoe Bay, 227

Qatar, 129, 132, 172, 181

Ras Tanura, 188, 202
Red Sea, 190
Reed, R. G., 120n
refining, capacity, 103–6, 119, 215
reintegration, 133–6
reserve depletion rate
  and political policies, 163
  and prices, 159–60
  public and private, 151–3
  *see also* decline rate
reserve estimates, 26–7
  and enhanced recovery, 248

geologists' versus economists', 242–3, 275
  Iran, 237
  methodology, 229–33
  Middle East, 282
  and secondary recovery, 247–8
  US, 225–9, 233–5, 274; as shelf inventory,
    244
  USSR, 237–40, 273–4
  world, 235–6, 240–1
reserves, 172, 174
  defined, 235, 288
  extent of, 289
  geographical conditions for, 44
  geographical distribution, 45–9
reserves to production ratio (R/P), 45–9, 59,
  60, 152, 172, 282
resources, *see* reserves
Richardson, G. P., 236n
risk, 201
  management, 29, 206–11
  political, 5–6, 54, 148–51, 160–1, 276–7
  technical, 130
  trading, 218
Roadifer, R. E., 290
Robinson, C., 149 and n
Robinson, M. S., 120n, 121n, 223n
Roeber, J., 223n
Roosevelt, F. D., 187
Root, D. H., 235n
Rosing, K. E., 247n
Rotterdam market, 201, 206, 211, 212, 218
Royal Dutch/Shell, 114, 128, 129, 136, 187,
  247, 264

Safaniya, 62
Samuelson, P. A., 149 and n, 185n
Saudi Arabia, 25, 27, 49, 87, 135, 140, 159,
  181, 184, 190, 191, 194
  costs, 136–7
  integration, 131–2, 133–4
  joint ventures, 126–7
  oil production, 51, 60–1, 65–6, 100,
    105–6, 154–5
  pricing policy, 22, 278–9, 281
  pricing system, 199–203, 214
  quotas, 174–8
  swing supplier, 186–9, 195–6
Schrattenholzer, L., 253n
Scotland, 192
secondary recovery, 247–8
self-sufficiency
  energy, 85–7, 90–2
  oil, 80–2
Seymour, I., 182n
Shah of Iran, 183–4, 186, 188, 237
shelf inventory, 244

Shetland Isles, 208
Siberia, 15, 68, 73, 82–3
Singapore, 206, 213, 214, 223
Solow, R., 184n
Souk el-Manakh, 141
South Africa, 17
Soviet Union, 17, 18, 34, 53, 112, 138, 141,
    154, 244, 265–6, 284
  energy consumption, 17–18, 39
  energy exports, 37–8, 87, 91, 107
  joint ventures, 276–7
  oil and gas production, 14–15, 20, 51, 80,
    237–40, 248
  output expansion, 158
  reserves, 273–4
  Tenghiz, 50
Spain, 139, 212
spot markets
  efficiency, 216–20
  in market crudes, 196–206
spot prices
  localised, 212–13
  products, 211–18
Standard Oil Trust, 136
Starrett, D. A., 185n
statistics, 292–3
Statoil, 199
Stauffer, T., 63n, 67n
Steele, H. B., 119n
Sterman, J. D., 236n
Stiglitz, J., 185n
Straits of Hormuz, 51, 190
Subroto, Dr, 66
Sullum Voe, 208
sulphur, 99
supertanker, 73–5
supply of oil
  capacity, 41
  and costs, 69, 248–51, 273
  geographical distribution, 37–8
  marginal, 202
  new non-Opec, 199
  projected, 225–51
  short-term, 272
  surplus, 221–4, 248
  *see also* production
Sweden, 127
swing supplier, 177, 186–9
  inner Opec, 189–91
Switzerland, 212
Syria, 190

tar sands, 248
Tariki, A., 175, 186
taxation
  by Opec governments, 143–5

  by governments of non-Opec
    oil-producing countries, 79, 123, 234
  by governments of oil-importing
    countries, 142, 144, 145 and n, 163n,
    234
  carbon taxes, 268, 281
Teece, D. J., 162n
Texaco, 114, 132, 136
Texas Railroad Commission, 153, 186
Total (Compagnie Française des Pétroles),
    114, 128
traffic congestion, 112–13
transport costs, oil and other energy, 73–5
transport fuel, 94–5, 98, 101–2, 250, 277
  alternatives, 109–11
  aviation, 113
  diesel, 101, 113, 250
  gas oil, 98, 99
  *see also* kerosene
Turkey, 190

uncertainty in investment decisions, 255
United Arab Emirates, 65, 127, 140, 151,
    170, 174, 188, 190, 191, 203
United Kingdom, 19, 64, 79, 87, 90, 101,
    161, 162, 199, 212
  Department of Energy, 177
  North Sea R/P ratio, 48, 59
  reserves, 274
United Nations (UN) energy satatistics, 32,
    37, 85, 167, 170, 174, 194, 292–3
United States, 20, 39, 64, 103, 106, 109,
    111–12, 117, 127, 154, 158, 161, 170,
    190, 200, 212, 281
  accounting, 54
  anti-trust laws, 118
  blockade of Iraq, 174
  exploration, 44, 52–3, 243–4
  freeze on certain Opec assets in banks,
    124
  influence on oil price, 21–2, 206
  Marshall and MacArthur aid, 100, 102
  non-oil energy, 17–19, 34, 99, 102
  oil imports, 37–8
  oil production, 14–16, 225–8, 233–5, 248
  oil 'proration system', 153, 186, 187,
    234
  Pennsylvania, 97–8
  production costs, 68, 70, 72
  R/P ratio, 47–8
  refining, 132, 134
  reserves, 274
  sanctions against Iran, Iraq, Libya, 161
  Texas Railroad Commission, 15, 186
upstream profits, 123
Upton, C. W., 185n

US Central Intelligence Agency (CIA), 238, 240
US Energy Information Administration
    (EIA), 262
US Geological Survey (USGS), 227, 235, 241,
    247, 288

Venezuela, 49, 71, 73, 100, 132, 152, 174,
    175, 177, 180–1, 184, 186, 284
  joint ventures, 127, 134–5
  oil production, 63–6, 189, 248–9
  Orinoco 'tarbelt', 108–9, 289
Verleger, P. K., 216n
vertical integration, 114–15, 118–21
  internal transfer pricing, 214–16
volcanoes and climate change, 270

Wall Street refiners, 210
Walters, Sir P., 279 and n
WOCA (world outside Communist areas),
    80, 82
WOCANA (world outside Communist areas
    and North America), 80, 114
Woods, T. J., 233n
World Bank, 167, 256

Yamani, Shaikh Ahmed Zaki, 154, 178, 187,
    188–9, 195n, 262

Zapp, A. D., 233n
Zimmerman, E. S., 242 and n

For EU product safety concerns, contact us at Calle de José Abascal, 56–1°,
28003 Madrid, Spain or eugpsr@cambridge.org.

www.ingramcontent.com/pod-product-compliance
Ingram Content Group UK Ltd.
Pitfield, Milton Keynes, MK11 3LW, UK
UKHW042211180425
457623UK00011B/163